# Purifying the Earthly Body of God

SUNY Series in
Religious Studies

Harold Coward, editor

*Kōlam* sanctifying threshold, Chennai (Madras), 1997.
Photo by Lance E. Nelson

# Purifying the Earthly Body of God

## Religion and Ecology in Hindu India

Edited by
Lance E. Nelson

*State University of New York Press*

Cover art by Padmavasan

Production by Ruth Fisher
Marketing by Nancy Farrell

Published by
State University of New York Press, Albany


Printed in the United States of America



For information, address the State University of New York Press, State University Plaza, Albany, NY 12246

**Library of Congress Cataloging-in-Publication Data**

Purifying the earthly body of God: religion and ecology in Hindu India; edited by Lance E. Nelson.
p. cm.
ISBN 0-7914-3923-2 (alk. paper). — ISBN 0-7914-3924-0 (pbk. : alk. paper)
1. Human ecology—Religious aspects—Hinduism. 2. Hinduism--Doctrines. 3. Human ecology—India.
BL 1215.N34P86 1998
294.5'178362—dc21 97-50608
CIP

10 9 8 7 6 5 4 3 2 1

To J. G. Arapura

who taught me the value of thought,
especially thought about Brahman

# Contents

# Acknowledgments

I wish to thank the scholars who contributed to this volume for their cheerful endurance during the long process of bringing it to press. Ann Grodzins Gold, especially, deserves praise for her patience, as her fine chapter was the first completed and among the most meticulously executed. As indicated in the introduction, several of the contributors were able to participate in a conference at the University of San Diego. It was sponsored by the Southern California Consortium on International Studies, as well as the Internationalization of the Curriculum Committee, the Graduate Program in Pastoral Theology, and the Department of Theological and Religious Studies at the University of San Diego, to all of which we are grateful for their support. I would also like to thank those who contributed thoughts and ideas that found expression in this volume, but because of time or other constraints were not able to contribute formally. Among these I would like to mention expressly Professor P. S. Jaini and most especially Professor J. G. Arapura, both of whom offered important suggestions. My colleagues in the Department of Theological and Religious Studies at the University of San Diego deserve grateful mention here also, for their encouragement and support, and for listening to and helping me test my ideas during departmental colloquia. Finally, I would like to thank my wife, Gabo Chong, for her encouragement and her patience during the hours that I was preoccupied with this project.

**Lance E. Nelson**

# Introduction

> Verily, this whole [world] is the body of God.
>
> —*Viṣṇu Purāṇa* 1.12.38.[1]

## Preliminary Reflections

In a perceptive essay, Yuichi Inoue writes, "Our belief in economic growth and material affluence is almost 'religious,' and obviously hard to depart from" (Inoue 1995, 283). Taking the same line of thought to its logical conclusion, A. Rodney Dobell has identified the "religion of the market" as the "dominant religion of our time" (1995, 232). He describes some of the consequences of this faith:

> The economic religion . . . seems to push inexorably toward high incomes, highly material-intensive and environmentally stressful modes of production—toward the adoption of technologies that are unselective and wasteful of economic resources and ecological integrity. At the same time, it leaves behind absolute poverty on a large scale, from which environmental degradation also flows inevitably. (1995, 235–36)

Anyone who would doubt that religion can and does have a significant impact on human behavior toward the environment would do well, then, to consider the idea that our present economic behavior is anchored in beliefs and values that function religiously. The tenets of this religion include the belief that the Market is the primary force governing human life, so that to interfere with it is tantamount to meddling with the foundations of the universe. Nature, in this faith, has no autonomy or value in itself but is merely a storehouse of resources for the mechanisms of production. High incomes and correspondingly generous and ever-increasing levels of consumption are the natural goal, the right, and—unless some economic "sin" or malefic fate intervenes—the innate destiny of all human beings. Economic growth and development are the solution to all problems (see Dobell 1995; Inoue 1995). When acted upon, these and other foundational tenets of this dubious but widely (if less than consciously) held system of belief have had, and continue to have, serious consequences for both human and nonhuman life. The environmental implications will be all too sadly familiar to those reading this volume; they need not be detailed here.

In India the religion of the market may also be fast becoming the dominant faith. However, in its individualist, Euro-American form, this economic creed has only relatively recently caught hold of the imagination of the subcontinent, and that perhaps only superficially. India, of course, has had its own religious traditions from time immemorial, and these religions too enshrine values that motivate human beings in their relations with nature. While other traditions have made and continue to make important contributions, that tradition known as Hinduism is the dominant carrier and former of the religious and cultural ethos of India. It is the Hindu tradition, and the attitudes toward the environment that it fosters, that will be the subject of this volume. The pages that follow contain the work of twelve scholars who have given considerable thought and study to issues surrounding the intersection of religion and the environment in Hindu India. No claim is made to have covered the topic comprehensively, let alone to have exhausted it. But these chapters raise new issues and focus on areas that have not yet been considered, or have so far been considered only in ways that lack critical depth.

**The Issues Before Us**

As indicated in the quotation from the *Viṣṇu Purāṇa* that heads this introduction, this volume takes its title from a striking metaphor adumbrated in the foundational scriptures of the Hindu tradition: the Vedas, the Upaniṣads, and the *purāṇas* (see Klostermaier 1987). While the image is not central for all Hindus, it was developed extensively by the Śrīvaiṣṇava theologians—especially Rāmānuja, as Mumme (chap. 6) will amply testify. The universe, we are told, is the body of God. From another vantage point, Hindu thought envisions the earth—and India itself—as goddesses (Bhū Devī, Bhārat Mā). India has from ancient times been perceived as a holy land (*puṇya-bhūmi*), crisscrossed with pilgrimage routes connecting sacred places, the latter themselves being praised as the bodies, or otherwise manifestations, of gods and goddesses. Such images will be evoked and their implications explored in several of the chapters that follow (Chapple, Sherma, Kinsley, Sullivan, Nagarajan, Alley). This book, however, will be more than a simple celebration of imagery that at first glance appears "eco-friendly." Given the gravity of the ecological crisis, even Hindu readers, I trust, will forgive my beginning on a sober note. I recount two anecdotes that are suggestive of important *negative* implications of religion for the environment in the Hindu context:

> In the streets of Banaras, by most accounts India's holiest city, a Brahmin serenely negotiates a path through piles of rotting garbage, almost unaware of their odor and ugliness. He remarks simply, "Those people (*ve log*) are not doing their job these days."[2]
>
> Reaching the crest of a mountain range overlooking the beautiful vale of Kashmir, a bus stops and a passenger in dire need asks the driver the direction of the nearest toilet. The driver expands his arms in a gesture of universal inclusivity and proclaims, "The whole world is a latrine!"[3]

If the religious background and environmental significance of these incidents are not immediately apparent, they will become so as the reader proceeds through the chapters that follow.

Of course, these examples are not at all or by any means the whole story. India, after all, has the world's largest environmental movement, one that has strong roots in indigenous practices and Gandhian ideals (Peritore 1993). Noting its rapid growth over the past twenty years, Gadgil and Guha have characterized India's environmental movement as "vibrant" (1995, 2). Numerous non-governmental organizations, not a few religiously inspired, are actively engaged in ecological issues (see Chapple 1993). Winding through the Himalayan foothills, the Western Ghats, the Nilgiris, and other mountain regions—and trekking along both seacoasts"ïf India to meet at Kanyakumari, the southern tip of the subcontinent—impressive *pada-yātrās,* or foot pilgrimages, represent perhaps the "most innovative technique of the environmental movement" in India. These Gandhian-inspired marches, traversing up to 4,000 km and stopping for rallies at numerous villages on route, have sought to promote activism at the local level and to raise general public consciousness concerning threatened ecosystems (Gadgil and Guha 1995, 101–02). As I write, Hindu religious leaders and organizations are joining S. Bahuguna, a leader of the well-known Chipko (Tree-hugging) movement, in mobilizing against the construction of a huge hydroelectric project, centering on the Tehri dam, in a seismically active area of the Himalaya foothills. Hindu temples, including the famed Sri Venkatesvara Devasthanam at Tirupati, are actively sponsoring tree-planting (*vanābhivṛddhi,* "afforestation") campaigns, promising on flyers, "He that planteth a tree is a servant of God."[4] Hindu and Jain organizations are actively opposing the construction of modern, export-oriented slaughterhouses. Organizations as diverse as the Bharatiya Vidya Bhavan ("Indian Wisdom Foundation," a prominent Hindu educational organization) and the Madras Bar Association are sponsoring lectures on environmental topics. By an order of the Supreme Court in Delhi, the Madras High Court has a "Green Bench" to deal with environmental issues; it has already issued orders closing down polluting industries and directives prodding negligent government agencies. Words like "sustainability" and "deforestation" have become common in the editorial pages of India's great newspapers, which regularly feature summaries of environmental news. Many more examples of encouraging environmental developments in India could be cited. After interviewing a broad spectrum of Indian leaders in science, government, business, and environmental NGOs, Peritore found that "the value of life and its right to exist in its full diversity, which is essential to Hindu philosophy, is strongly affirmed by all subjects" (1993, 808).

Consider, however, how much analysis has already been done of the negative environmental impact of the religions of the West and the secular ideologies that they are said, with some justification, to have spawned. Consider also that by far the bulk of what has been written on the ecological significance of the religions of India has been written by authors—both Indian and Western—whose purpose has been limited to seeking out the positive ecological potential of these traditions, and who have thus failed to take seriously enough any ecological downside. In the belief that the ecological crisis, in India as elsewhere, has reached a stage at which a more critical approach is necessary and indeed long overdue, I have encouraged the contributors to this volume to pay attention, where appropriate, to the problematics surrounding the intersection of religion and environment in the Hindu context. I have not asked them to seek out the negative, but simply to be alert for and not hesitate to analyze openly any potentially deleterious environmental implications of their material. Some of the contributors, in fact, raise serious questions about the ecological potential of aspects of the Hindu tradition. Others, because of the nature of the subject matter they are working with, accentuate the positive. Both approaches are necessary; both are valid. But the reader should not expect to find here praises of idealized forms of "Eastern" nature mysticism or the like.

Several of the contributors to this volume (Chapple, Coward, Nelson, Sullivan, Gold, Kinsley) participated in a panel on the "Religious Dimensions of Ecological Concern in South Asia" at the 1994 Annual Meeting of the American Academy of Religion. Others (Sharma and Nagarajan, and again Chapple and Nelson) presented papers at a conference on "Religion and the Environment in South Asia" at the University of San Diego in March 1996.[5] These conferences were instrumental in mobilizing the thought that appears in this volume. One conclusion of both groups was that, human nature being as it is, the *negative* outcomes of religious teachings that can be used to rationalize environmental neglect are probably greater than the *positive* influence of those that encourage conservation and protection. So again, with this in mind, contributors have been asked to take seriously any ecological drawbacks of the traditions they are considering, and to report them fairly, along with the positives.

Despite the promising developments mentioned above, the environmental situation in India is serious. "Patients from outside Delhi have pink lungs," reports an eminent heart surgeon in India's capital, "those who reside here have lungs that are charcoal-black" (Sidhva and Bailay 1997, 45). Deforestation, soil erosion, overgrazing, desertification, air pollution, pollution of rivers and coastal waters, and other problems are reaching or have surpassed crisis points. Large hydroelectric and other development projects are causing massive displacement of indigenous peoples. Toxic waste from Europe, the United States, and Australia is being dumped in India for "recycling" in plants without adequate safeguards. Government corruption and bureaucratic inertia impede progress in implementing effective environmental controls. Meanwhile, population pressure continues to increase at a disturbing rate. But I need not repeat here all the alarming statistics or depressing predictions that are readily available in the literature.[6] I will assume that readers are aware that the ecological situation in India is at least as critical as it is in other parts of Asia and the rest of the world. Our task in this volume is a more reflective one: to examine the symbol systems that underlie attitudes and behaviors toward nature in Hindu India.

To be sure, parts of India and parts of the mindset of many individual Indians are modernized and even becoming postmodern. But as Dharampal, a sensitive student of the psyche of modern India, has observed, the values that shape the mind of vast numbers of the Indian people are "etched very deep." He writes:

> The people of India, in fact, may not be living even in the eighteenth century of the West. They may still be reckoning time in terms of their Pauranic [mythic] conceptions. They may be living in one of the Pauranic Yugas [mythic world-ages], and looking at the present from the perspective of that Yuga. (1993, 17, 19)

How true this is will be borne out by the observations of a number of our contributors (see especially Gold and Alley, chaps. 7 and 12).

The Hindu universe, though under siege, is still very much alive. The contributors to this volume attempt to further our understanding of the underlying ecological assumptions and ongoing ecological implications—positive and negative—of this universe.

Before letting the contributors speak for themselves, let me outline what I believe are some of the key questions that they raise. The most general question, of course, is the extent to which indigenous religious ideas have the potential truly to support ecological awareness and behavior in India, and the extent to which some may complexify or even undermine ecological consciousness. However, I would also call the reader's attention to the following more specific issues, arranged roughly in the order of their appearance in the volume:

- Can the ascetic outlook common to many Indic religious traditions be harnessed in the direction of an ecologically positive ethic, for example, of environmental non-violence or minimal consumption? Or is the ascetic vision inextricably linked with world-denial and world-neglect? This question is addressed, from different perspectives, by Chapple, Coward, Sharma, Nelson, and Sherma (chaps. 1–6), as well as several others among the contributors.
- Can the theory of *karma*, classically formulated to explain an experience of bondage to the world, be reformulated to support a positive sense of connection to, and moral responsibility for, the natural universe? Coward (chap. 2) explores this problem.
- Does the Hindu tradition, in its conceptions of creation, cosmic time, and moral responsibility, provide the kind of teleology that would support a positive environmental ethic or inspire eco-activism? What are the implications for environmental ethics of the Hindu ideas of *līlā*, the world as God's frivolous play, or the *yugas*, the cosmic ages that are declining toward destruction and recreation? What connections do Hindus see between human morality and environmental decline, and how might these perceived connections influence environmental activism? Mumme (chap. 6), Gold (chap. 7), and Alley (chap. 12) raise issues that bear on these questions.

- Does orthodox Vedānta theology—and in particular its identification of the world with Brahman (the absolute) or the body of the Divine—lead to a reverential attitude toward nature? Or does Vedānta, in its various schools, so emphasize transcendence that the value of the world tends to be negated? Do the tantric traditions of Hinduism offer more potential in this area? On such questions, see especially Sharma, Nelson, Sherma, and Mumme (chaps. 3–6).
- Does the mythic-ritual sacralization, and even divinization, of earth and geography that is common in India translate into ecologically supportive behavior? Can it be used effectively to rationalize contemporary environmental activism? Mumme (chap. 6) and especially Sherma, Kinsley, Sullivan, Nagarajan, and Alley address this issue (chaps. 5, 9–12).
- How do Hindu concepts of purity and impurity, and the ideology of caste, problematize the environmental situation in India? Look to Sherma (chap. 5), Korom (chap. 8), and Alley (chap. 12) for insight into this issue.
- To what extent do Hindu ways of construing nature—embedded as they are in the particularities of mythic vision and ritual praxis—come into conflict with the discourse and expectations of scientifically oriented government conservation officials and environmental activists? This important question is raised by Nagarajan and Alley (chaps. 11–12).

I would note that there are, of course, other questions that will need to be asked, and indeed are now being asked, by other researchers working in this field. Moreover, I cannot promise that the contributors to the present volume have given definitive answers to all or any of the questions that they do raise. But the issues broached here are important, and the chapters that follow address them in provocative ways.

## Notes

1. tat sarvaṃ vai hareḥ tanuḥ.

2. I am indebted to Philip Lutgendorf (University of Iowa) for this anecdote.

3. sarvā duniyā laṭrīn hai. I am indebted to Douglas R. Brooks (University of Rochester) for this story.

4. T. T. Devasthanams, "Sri Venkatesvara Vanabhivriddhi Schemes" (Tirupati: T. T. Press, n.d.). I am indebted to Vasudha Narayanan (University of Florida) for a copy of this flyer. For an important recent study of ecological attitudes in the Hindu world, see Narayanan 1997.

5. Other participants in the University of San Diego conference included J. G. Arapura (McMaster University), Robert L. Brown (UCLA), Kathleen Dugan (University of San Diego), and P. S. Jaini (University of California, Berkeley). The editor is grateful to all these scholars for their participation and input, as also to the Southern California Consortium on International Studies for its generous support.

6. In addition to the well-known works of Vandana Shiva (e.g., Shiva 1989), see the works listed in the references below, especially Agarwal 1985 and Gadgil and Guha 1995.

## References

Agarwal, Anil, and Sunita Narain. 1985. *The State of India's Environment, 1984–85: The Second Citizens' Report*. New Delhi: Centre for Science and Environment.

Chapple, Christopher Key. 1993. *Nonviolence to Animals, Earth, and Self in Asian Traditions*. Albany, N.Y.: State University of New York Press.

Dharampal. 1993. *Bhāratīya Chitta Mānas and Kāla*. Translated by Jitendra Bajaj. Madras: Center for Policy Studies.

Dobell, A. Rodney. 1995. "Environmental Degradation and the Religion of the Market." In *Population, Consumption, and the Environment*, ed. Harold Coward, 229–250. Albany, N.Y.: State University of New York Press.

Gadgil, Madhav, and Ramachandra Guha. 1993. *This Fissured Land: An Ecological History of India*. Berkeley: University of California Press.

———. 1995. *Ecology and Equity: The Use and Abuse of Nature in Contemporary India*. New Delhi: Penguin.

Guha, Ramachandra. 1990. *The Unquiet Woods: Ecological Change and Peasant Resistance in the Himalaya*. Berkeley: University of California Press.

Inoue, Yuichi. 1995. "The Northern Consumption Issue after Rio and the Role of Religion and Environmentalism." In *Population, Consumption, and the Environment*, ed. Harold Coward, 279–291. Albany, N.Y.: State University of New York Press.

Klostermaier, Klaus. 1987. "The Body of God: Cosmos, Avatara, Image." In *The Charles Strong Lectures, 1972–1984*, ed. Robert B. Crotty, 103–119. Leiden: E. J. Brill.

Narayanan, Vasudha. 1997. " 'One Tree is Equal to Ten Sons': Some Hindu Responses to the Problems of Ecology, Population and Consumption." *Journal of the American Academy of Religion* 65 (June): 291–332.

Peritore, N. Patrick. 1993. "Environmental Attitudes of Indian Elites: Challenging Western Postmodernist Models." *Asian Survey* 33 (August): 804–818.

Shiva, Vandana. 1989. *The Violence of the Green Revolution*. Dehra Dun: Research Foundation for Science and the Environment.

Sidhva, Shiraz, and Rasul Bailay. 1997. "Unhealthy Air: Noxious Automobile Fumes Choke India's Capital." *Far Eastern Economic Review*, May 8, 45–46.

# Part I

# Theological and Textual Perspectives

**Christopher Key Chapple**

# 1

# Toward an Indigenous Indian Environmentalism

The rhetoric of environmentalism has a long history of development in the American milieu, which has led to the emergence of various branches and subidentifications within this movement as found in the United States. As we reflect upon environmentalism in the context of India, it is important to acknowledge that many of the categories developed in the northern hemisphere of the western world do not necessarily apply within the South Asian context. It is important to define terms and identify presuppositions when discussing environmental issues in each context before attempting a cross cultural analysis.

In the chapter that follows, I will present an overview of American environmentalism, from the early nature writers to the present. I will then examine the emergence of environmental rhetoric in India. This movement owes a debt to the Union Carbide disaster in Bhopal in 1984, an event that focused world attention on the Dickensian reality of industrial India, and prompted a new form of grassroots urban activism. In more rural contexts, such as in the Chipko movement and the debate surrounding the Narmada Dam project, the agricultural working classes have developed their own responses to ecological ravage. From both urban and rural activism, several themes or threads of environmental rhetoric have emerged within India. By surveying some of the literature on Indian environmentalism, and by reflecting on my own experiences in South Asia, I would suggest that India's environmentalism, both in philosophy and practice, will remain distinct from similar movements in different areas of the world.

## Some General Considerations

Environmental issues, because they deal with interrelating pieces, require a systems approach. The ecological sciences require an examination of life habitats such as swamps, forests, deserts, mountains, oceans, and so forth. This includes an analysis of the human impact on each of these systems, as well as a consideration of the quality of and acceptable standards for human life. Naive utilitarians deem all aspects of nature to be at the beck and call of humans. More pragmatic thinkers have seen the consequences of untrammeled human interference with the natural order of things, and have come to the conclusion that human health and well-being cannot be divorced from the health of our surrounding ecosystem. However, what might be considered environmentally appropriate by one group or subgroup in a given society might be appalling to another. Hence, anthropology, sociology, and religious studies become important pieces of the debate, both in terms of understanding varieties of environmentalism within one cultural context, and the more general features that characterize national attitudes and approaches.

## American Environmentalism

The Nature Movement in America traces its origins to a complex array of historical, religious, quasi-religious, and aesthetic factors. European colonists saw America as the New World, a place to escape the confines of European society, to establish new communities of faith without government intervention, to accumulate new capital in a land imagined to be without history, a land into which the European fleeing the past might move freely. The allure of the American wilderness frontier took on Biblical overtones when understood in reference to the Exodus of the Jews from Egypt. Depending upon which account of the return to the promised land one reads, the returning Jews found a paradise of abundant water and fruit trees, or a land long occupied and cultivated by the Canaanites, who resisted Jewish occupancy for many years. Likewise, early accounts of American settlement downplayed the displacement of native peoples and celebrated, rather than critiqued, the pioneer practice of clearcutting the great forests of the eastern seaboard to establish farms and villages.

With the rise of industrialization, urban centers grew in importance. In nineteenth century America, this resulted in huge population increases, westward expansion, the near genocide of the indigenous population, the growth of cities, all assisted by the advent of an intercontinental railroad system. Nature and the wild became more of a memory than a living presence to most Americans, and nostalgia for a simpler life laid the foundation for later environmentalism. Thoreau's essay "Walden" (1854), inspired in part by translations of the Asian literature and philosophy favored by the Transcendentalists, invited a reconsideration of values that privileged progress and industrialization over quietude and reflection. John Muir (1838–1914), the great explorer and nature afficionado and contemporary of Emerson and Thoreau, reveled in America's western landscape and lobbied successfully to set aside vast tracts of wilderness, thus initiating America's remarkable network of preserves, parks, and monuments. The National Park Service began in 1872 with the establishment of Yellowstone National Park in Wyoming.

Gifford Pinchot (1865–1946), creator and first head of the U.S. Forest Service (1905), and President Theodore Roosevelt (1858–1919) helped institutionalize the preservation and conservation movements, ensuring the continued establishment of vast parks and reserves, particularly in the West. Franklin Delano Roosevelt (1882–1945) supported the National Parks Service and established the Civilian Conservation Corps as part of the New Deal. Stephen Fox notes that "At the dedication of Shenandoah National Park in Virginia in 1936, he lovingly invoked a vision of how vacationers would come to the park to find an open fire, the smell of the woods, the wind in the trees" (1985, 199).

Despite the National Parks Service and various other local programs to ensure open space, bird sanctuaries, and the like, science and technology have burgeoned from the nineteenth century well into the present, encroaching on America's wilderness. The rise of the automobile and the advent of a middle class consumer economy led to a virtual explosion of new manufacturing techniques involving steel, rubber, innumerable chemical compounds, and eventually plastic. Not only were raw materials being consumed at an unprecedented rate to fuel first two world wars and then the post-Second World War economic boom in America, Western Europe, and Japan, but by-products in the form of new toxic pollutants were being spewed forth as never before. Furthermore, not only were the cities of the "developed" world affected by this significant shift, but the countryside became laced with chemical fertilizers, insecticides, and herbicides, many of which proved to be very harmful to the ecosystem.

By the late 1950s and early 1960s, a new type of environmentalism began to emerge. Although Aldo Leopold had spoken of land use policies and the changing landscape in *Sand County Almanac* (1949), it was not until the publication of Rachel Carson's *Silent Spring* in 1962 that the nascent environmental movement found its first voice. Perhaps the most poignant symbol of environmental ravage lay in the decimation of the Bald Eagle population by DDT, which provided a rallying point that made the cleanup of pollution a patriotic cause. With the extensive publicity generated by Earth Day in 1970, the formation of the Environmental Protection Agency in the same year, and the ratification of the Endangered Species Act in 1973 (all during the Nixon Administration), environmental activism and consciousness became an important thread in the American fabric.

The literary world and academia began to find new interest in nature and the environment starting in the 1970s. Annie Dillard's *Teaching a Stone to Talk* (1975) inspired people to pay closer attention to the gifts of the wild. Barry Lopez's *Arctic Dreams* (1986), though dealing with a more exotic locale, similarly invited its readers to observe the stark beauty of the landscape and the living beings that inhabit the earth.

Meanwhile, the early eco-philosophy that had been built on a rhetoric of individual rights by Peter Singer, Christopher Stone, and others, found its voice augmented with new approaches. Thomas Berry advocated the remythologization of cosmology and suggested that the scientific story of the flaring forth of the universe and the gradual emergence of diverse life forms, eventually forming our current "community of subjects," be retold as the New Story, a myth to nurture our consciousness in what he calls the new Ecozoic Era. Biologists, physicists, and ecologists, including Lynn Margulis and James Lovelock, proclaimed the fundamental and essential relationship between life forms and the atmosphere of our planet.

Radical environmentalism, also known as Deep Ecology, first surfaced in the writings of Murray Bookchin, most notably in his 1963 book *Our Synthetic Environment.* Later prominent nature liberation advocates include Edward A. Abbey and Dave Foreman, and today the range of activism spans local single-issue groups to worldwide organizations such as Greenpeace. On the extreme end of the spectrum we find groups such as Earthfirst! and the Animal Liberation Front.

American ecological thinking, shaped by science and an emphasis on the principles of inherent worth, natural law, and rights theory, has now been taken up by theologians and biblical scholars, who seek to find threads of environmentalism in the earlier traditions of Judaism and Christianity. This theological trend stems in part from the critique of religion found in Lynn White's watershed article, "The Historical Roots of our Ecological Crisis" (1967), an indictment of the dominion attitudes toward nature found in early Western religious texts. Rosemary Ruether and other feminist theologians have stressed the centrality of interconnectedness and cooperation in developing the ecofeminist perspective. Theologian John Cobb advocates a more earth-sensitive economy, while Jay B. McDaniel urges adoption of a more inclusive, panentheistic theology to uphold the integrity of living systems on the planet.

The American mainstream has come to embrace select environmental practices. Recycling programs in the 1990s proved profitable for cities and municipalities. Clothing manufacturers, cosmetic retailers, and fast-food restaurants found that environmental themes helped sell products, particularly following the 1990 twenty-year anniversary celebration of Earth Day.

In summary, American environmentalism took shape in the nineteenth century, when the Transcendentalists in the East and John Muir in the West rejoiced in the beauties of nature and advocated greater intimacy with one's surroundings. It resulted in the establishment of nature preserves and a sentiment that values experiences of pristine wilderness. Approximately one century after the love of nature emerged as a value and a virtue in America, environmentalism took a new, but not unrelated, course with the lobby against harmful chemical intrusions into the ecosystem. While not losing touch with pastoralism and romanticism, environmentalism took on an urgency not previously known.

Aesthetically and emotionally, the nature movement of the nineteenth century, inspired in part by the vast landscapes of the American West, stimulated interest in preservation of the wild. Philosophically, environmentalism in the twentieth century called upon the American traditions of rights, liberty, individual pursuit of happiness, individualism, and justice to support not only the preservation of land but also to promote safeguards against pollution. Many Americans now think they have a basic right to live free from fear of harm due to pollutants. Furthermore, the Endangered Species Act extends the concept of inherent worth beyond the human realm to the animal realm, and advocates safety and protection for beings that in years past had no protection under the European or American systems of justice. A typology of American environmentalism would include a romantic, reverential awe for the natural order; concern for species and land preservation; and emphasis on the potential hazards caused by industrial toxicity.

## Indian Environmentalism

This brings us to our discussion of India. The Indian experience of land differs greatly from that of the North American continent as settled by European invaders. Vast segments of the American West have never been densely populated, even by indigenous peoples. In contrast, the Indian subcontinent has been continously occupied for thousands of years. Mountains and rivers not only have long been considered sacred within India (Feldhaus 1995; chapters by Kinsley, Sullivan, and Alley in this volume), but have been seen as an integral part of the human experience, a source of both spiritual and economic strength (Spanel 1988).

Consequently, the issues of land preservation and environmentalism differ greatly in the South Asian context. Ramachandra Guha suggests that American environmental approaches may be inappropriate for India. He contrasts the "vast, beautiful, and sparsely populated [North American] continent" (Guha 1989, 79) with the densely settled subsistence, village-based economies of India. Whereas it might be possible, even today, to designate as forest or desert preserves vast tracts of North American land, it is far more difficult for India to establish more than small nature preserves. Furthermore, Guha suggests that for a nation living at barely above subsistence level, a full-blown program of preservation might be inappropriate, particularly if suggested by outsiders. It also should be noted that, in general, the Third World, of which India is part, requires far less of the environment than First World consumers, who seize the bulk of the world's resources, often at the expense of the poor who live elsewhere.

Given this social and geographic context, the terms of the debate in India differ greatly from that of North America. The land of India, its ecosystems, its climate, its agricultural uses, its cities, its economy, and its unique social and religious history require a different environmental strategy. Modern environmentalism in India, as mentioned above, began with the disaster in Bhopal in 1984. This event, which killed thousands and permanently injured millions of people, signaled that India's Green Revolution had come full circle. The magic chemicals that increased agricultural production and filled India's granaries beyond capacity, staving off the possibility of famine even during an extended drought, exploded into weapons of unimaginable destruction. India, which prior to this time had only a vague awareness of the environmental movement in the United States, suddenly became a lightning rod for grassroots environmental activity. Although M. K. Gandhi had set forth clear warnings regarding industrialization and modernity, government policies supported the chemical industry as vital to increased food production. However, while Americans bemoaned the loss of the symbolism of the Wild in the decimation of the Bald Eagle population, India faced in 1984 the more direct threat to human life that results from environmental irresponsibility.

In an earlier study, I surveyed several environmental organizations and movements that have arisen in India since the Bhopal crisis. The Centre for Science and Environment in New Delhi serves as a clearinghouse for issues of environmental concern. The Centre for Environment Education in Ahmedabad conducts an array of programs for both urban and rural peoples to help reduce smoke pollution and forest degradation throughout India. In cooperation with the Gandhi Peace Foundation, the Centre for Rural Development and Appropriate Technology of the Indian Institute of Technology in New Delhi has been experimenting with organic farming techniques. Baba Amte, winner of the 1990 Templeton Prize for Progess in Religion, has directed his activism toward environmental issues since the Bhopal disaster, with particular focus on the Narmada River dam project. Also on a grassroots level, but dating from the early part of this century, the Chipko movement, in which rural women have played leadership roles, struggles to preserve the forest lands of Northern India (Chapple 1993).

In recent years, several new studies have appeared that demonstrate the complexity of the environmental rhetoric now emerging from within India. This discourse interweaves an upholding of traditional Indian culture and civilization with a resounding critique of the negative influences of modernization. Beginning with the premise set forth by Ramachandra Guha above, I would like to explore some of the contours of this new debate. Whereas in the American context, the early rallying cry for environmental action came from scientists and social activists with theologians only taking interest in this issue of late, in India, from the outset, there has been an appeal to traditional religious sensibilities in support of environmental issues.

## Brahminical Models

This group of thinkers, activists, and writers seeks to reexamine the texts and traditions of earlier phases in Indian religious history to see if they contain insights regarding nature and land use that might be usefully translated into an environmental rhetoric. One of the early works of this genre, O. P. Dwivedi and B. N. Tiwari's *Environmental Crisis and Hindu Religion* (1987) painstakingly quotes numerous texts from the vedic, *dharmaśāstra,* and epic traditions that uphold nature as central to life processes in India. *Ecological*

*Readings in the Veda* (1994), written by Marta Vanucci, a biological oceanographer who lives in India, takes a similar approach, citing passages from the *Ṛg Veda* and *Atharva Veda* that evoke environmental themes. The abundance of nature-based deities makes this task relatively easy; Vanucci particularly emphasizes the power of Agni as key to environmental understanding: "Agni the undeceivable, who spread out all the worlds, keeper is he and guard of immortality" (*Ṛg Veda* 6.7.7; Vannucci, 43).

Numerous Vedic hymns celebrate the earth and water, asking for protection and glorifying the root consitituents of the natural world. The *Puruṣa Sūkta*, one of the best known hymns of the *Ṛg Veda*, proclaims a continuity between humans and the cosmos, stating that the gods, the heavens, and the earth itself arose from the primal person (*puruṣa*). This assertion of relationship carries an innate message of interconnectedness that could be used to advocate respect for nature and the elements. Many of the later legal books of the Brahminical tradition stipulate that trees are to be protected and that water must not be defiled.

In the past few years, several articles and books have been published that advance this naturalist, religion-based indigenous approach as a way for addressing India's ecological problems. These include "Ecology and Indian Myth" by Kapila Vatsyayan and "Nature as Feminine: Ancient Vision of Geopiety and Goddess Ecology" by Mandhu Khanna in a five volume set titled *Prakṛti: The Integral Vision* edited by Kapila Vatsyayan (1995) and published by the Indira Gandhi National Centre for the Arts. Ranchor Prime, an English devotee of the Hare Krishna movement, who is also mentioned in Bruce Sullivan's chapter in this volume, worked with the World Wildlife Fund to publish *Hinduism and Ecology: Seeds of Truth* in 1992. In this book he examines largely Vaiṣṇavite resources for environmental protection. He reintepretes the ten incarnations of Viṣṇu in an ecological vein, and suggests that Kṛṣṇa provides several examples of environmental wisdom through his care for the Vrindavan forest and purification of the Yamuna River. He cites modern and contemporary figures who have worked to reestablish the pre-British lifestyle in India, including Mahatma Gandhi; Sri Sewak Saran, a Kṛṣṇa devotee living in Vrindavan; Satish Kumar, an expatriate Indian who directs Schumacher College in Britain, which specializes in teaching a spiritual approach to the environment; Balbir Mathur, who left India to seek his fortune in America, but then returned to develop and promote Trees For Life, which has planted thousands of trees throughout India; and Sunderlal Bahuguna, a driving force "behind Chipko Andolan, the now world-famous tree-hugging movement which started among the Himalayan villages of Uttarkhand in 1973" (Prime 1992, 90).

Perhaps the most comprehensive work of this genre to date is *Pañcavaṭī: Indian Approach to Environment* (1992), written in Hindi by Banwari, editor of *Jansata,* a Hindi newspaper published in Delhi. In this book, which has been translated into English by Asha Vohra, Banwari examines the forest culture of India as providing the appropriate ecological model for life in the subcontinent. He opens with a chapter entitled "Prakṛti: Approach to Nature," a summary overview of the significance of nature in India's philosophical and religious traditions, especially the Sāṃkhya school. He then shows how key indigenous values and concepts support an ecological worldview. Banwari suggests that worship of Ganesha, the god of auspiciousness (*māṅgalya*), can lead people to emphasize the spiritual over the material, and hence help reduce the overconsumption that is beginning to plague life in India. He writes of mythical trees (*kalpavṛkṣa*) and magical forests (*vanaśrī*) and groves (*pañcavaṭī*), to which he attributes India's abundance and traditional economic strength. He writes of the care for forests and trees in India's ancient cities and towns, and celebrates the remote forests as "the land of no war," the abode of renouncers and meditators. He explains Hindu holy days in relationship to the cycles of nature and concludes the book with a discussion of the healing and medicinal powers of trees, as well as advocacy for the planting of trees (Banwari 1992). The remarkable contribution of this book lies in its careful research of the importance of the tree in Indian history, and the implied sense of continuity between antiquity and the contemporary world.

## Tribal Models

In addition to citing classical Hindu materials in support of a South Asian environmental ethic, Geeti Sen's *Indigenous Vision: Peoples of India, Attitudes to the Environment* includes several essays that bring forth tribal traditions within India as potent ecological resources. Citing the *ādivāsīs* of Gujarat as true peoples of the earth, Maurice

F. Strong suggests that the modern world can learn much from indigenous wisdom and ways. Similarly, Sitakant Mahapatra quotes from Santal and Kondh literature in celebration of the earth, albeit with an additional theme seeking human welfare:

> Let the earth be green with our crops.
> Let there be no hindrance to our movements.
> Let there prevail among us
> The spirit of mutual love and goodwill.
>
> (Sen 1992, 71)

K. S. Singh examines the Munda creation epic, the Sosobonga. In this story, the Munda tribe develops iron technology to the detriment of their environment, and then corrects this excess, restoring their land to its natural beauty and bounty. Other essays within this fascinating collection examine the traditional ways of the Oraons, the Bhils, the Gonds, the Warlis, and others, through the prism of environmentalism. The book concludes with a three-party interview, in which Dunu Roy and Geeti Sen discuss with Medha Patkar her work with tribal activists seeking to resist such projects as the huge Narmada dam and other projects. This discussion, and many of the essays, highlight the trenchant tension between the drive toward modernization in India and the desire of traditionalists to preserve ancient ways of life.

### Post-Gandhian Models

Vandana Shiva, whose *Staying Alive: Women, Ecology, and Development* (1988) opened a new chapter in world environmental theory, acknowledges the indigenous environmentalist resources available deep within the Indian psyche, but prefers a more political and pragmatic approach to the many problems that India faces. She criticizes the Western model of "maldevelopment," and in the process conjoins a modern feminist perspective with traditional Indian views regarding feminine power (*śakti*) (Braidotti et al. 1994, 92–96). She states that the modern consumerist model, enhanced by technology, disrupts traditional agricultural practices and "ruptures the co-operative unity of masculine and feminine. . . . Nature and women are turned into passive objects, to be used and exploited for the uncontrolled and uncontrollable desires of alienated man" (Shiva

1988, 6). She also criticizes the manipulation of seed technology and the widespread use of inorganic fertilizers as disruptive to India's ecosystem. She further develops this argument in her essay "The Seed and the Earth," where she states, "The crisis of health and ecology suggests that the assumption of man's ability to totally engineer the world, including seeds and women's bodies, is in question. . . . The main contribution of the ecology movement has been the awareness that there is no separation between mind and body, human and nature" (Shiva 1994, 141–142). Drawing from traditional Indian cultural values and a post-modern critique of the prevailing development model, Shiva advocates the adoption of an integrated, holistic view of both humans and their environment.

Similarly, D. L. Sheth of the Centre for the Study of Developing Societies in New Delhi states that the grassroots ecology movements of India "do not view ecology as merely a cost factor in development . . . but view ecology as a basic principle of human existence" (Sheth 1993, 284). This interpretation of environmentalism in India values the human person in the context of—rather than in opposition to—the surrounding environs.

The various authors and activists cited above seek to find models from earlier times that hold forth the possibility of an environment-friendly economy and culture. Dwivedi, Tiwari, Vanucci, Prime, and Banwari hearken back to sacred Hindu texts and stories. Geeti Sen holds forth tribal models for consideration. Shiva and Sheth advance a holistic, post-Gandhian approach to environmentalism. All these authors state their cases positively, advocating the study of early traditions, the planting of trees, and development of technology and agriculture that enhances life within India. With the exception of Vandana Shiva, who provides a critique of contemporary "development" schemes, these authors as a whole do not reject the underlying life-affirming premises of the Vedic tradition, which celebrate and support the pursuit of human pleasure and happiness.

## Renouncer Models

From the earliest phases of Indian civilization, an alternate ascetic religious philosophy has existed in parallel to the Vedic, deity-affirming, Brahminical tradition. Traces of yogic practice can be found in the ruins of Mohenjodaro and Harappa, with documentation of organized Yoga appearing in the early Upaniṣads, the Buddhist Sūtras (Suttas), and the early texts of Jainism. By probably the second century of the common era, Patañjali summarized and systematized various styles of yogic renunciation in his *Yoga Sūtra*. This brief text builds on the Sāṃkhya philosophy to advance modes for gaining control over one's compulsive behavior (*saṃskāra*) through mastery of the body, mind, and spirit continuum.

By the time of Alexander, the renouncer communities and meditative schools of India were collectively referred to as the *śramaṇa* traditions. This vector within the continuum of India's religions emphasized renunciation of worldly involvement and the adoption of a strict ethical and ascetic code. At the heart of this code for all three forms of Śramaṇism (Jainism, Buddhism, and Yoga) lay the practice and discipline of nonviolence (*ahiṃsā*). Stemming from a concern to avoid injury to all creatures, this vow of nonviolence became normative for all three Śramaṇical traditions. Its advocates also lobbied for the cessation of animal sacrifices within Brahminical Hinduism, and most likely pressured high-caste Hindus to adopt vegetarianism (Chapple 1993). Related to the vow of nonviolence, both Jainism and Yoga espouse four additional restraints: abstention from falsehood, positively stated as truthfulness (*satya*); abstention from theft (*asteya*); abstention from inappropriate sexual activity (*brahmacarya*); and abstention from the accumulation of possessions (*aparigraha*).

The Buddhist tradition adapted a code of ethics nearly identical to that followed by the Jainas and Yogins. Both Jainism and the Buddhist monastic code (*vinaya*) developed scores of additional vows, while Patañjali's Yoga system added a list of five positive ethical practices to be observed: purity (*śauca*), contentment (*saṃtoṣa*), austerity (*tapas*), study (*svadhyāya*), and devotion (*īśvarapraṇidhāna*). These vows and observances have been at the core of India's ethical fabric for over two millennia, and have helped shape both monastic and lay life within the subcontinent.

Within this ethical landscape, India has responded to historical circumstances in its own unique fashion. Perhaps the most notable application of the nonviolent ethic in Indian history can be found in the life and work of Mahatma Gandhi, whose peaceful revolution ousted colonial rule from the subcontinent. Furthermore, his initiative served as a catalyst for the decolonization of the rest of Asia and Africa. Combining techniques of passive resistance learned from Quakers and New England Transcendentalists with traditional Indian applications of austerity (*tapas*, one of the yogic observances) such as fasting and weekly silence, he contributed through his personal discipline to a new, post-colonial world order. Gandhian ideals continue to fuel a quest for social justice within India, particularly through the uplift of the lower castes and tribes.

Environmental degradation in India raises interesting new challenges for the renouncer ethical traditions. On the one hand, the respect for life emphasized in Jainism, Buddhism, and Yoga accords well with the discourse of environmental ethics. Jainism in particular, with its doctrine of countless life forms (*jīva*) taking form even as particles of earth, water, fire, and air, presents an operative cosmology that is perhaps the most sympathetic to an ecological worldview (see Tobias 1991, 1994a, 1994b). However, the underlying teleology of the Śramaṇical traditions lies not in the realm of worldly affirmation but in self-transcendence.

The goal of Yoga is to achieve *kaivalya*, a state described as disinterested spectatorship. The goal of Buddhism is to escape the suffering snares of *saṃsāra* and enter into a state of desirelessness or *nirvāṇa*. The ultimate goal of Jainism is to ascend through the fourteen stages of spirituality (*guṇa-sthāna*) and enter into a state of eternal, blessed solitude (*kevala*). Without exception, each of these traditions focuses primarily on interior processes and advocates detachment from worldly concerns. Just as Christianity has been criticized as too other-worldly and hence detrimental to the environmentalists' project, so also it might be argued that the Śramaṇical religions of India have little to offer, due to their inwardness. However, just as Christianity and Judaism are rediscovering nature metaphors in the Bible as resources for the development of an ecological ethic, and just as Brahminical texts are being mined as rich resources in celebration of the earth, so also Jainism and Yoga and Buddhism are being explored anew.

## Buddhist Environmentalism

There has been a proliferation of literature written on environmentalism by Buddhist authors in America. In 1990, Allan Hunt Badiner published a collection of 32 essays by Buddhist authors entitled *Dharma Gaia*, including a foreword by the Dalai Lama. The poet Gary Snyder has long been identified with Buddhism and the tradition of nature writing. Stephanie Kaza, a Buddhist theologian and botanical ecologist, in her *Conversations with Trees*, interweaves Buddhist philosophy and the botanical sciences.

American Buddhist environmentalism provides an interesting bridge into the next phase of our discussion. Many Americans became interested in Asian religions during the late 1960s, a period of great cultural turmoil. Zen Buddhism, in particular, provided a voluntarist alternative to traditional American religion, and the budding communities of Buddhists from New York to California allowed a sense of participation and creativity not possible within mainstream churches. Furthermore, Buddhism offered a language and ethics that supported such countercultural activities as vegetarianism and, seemingly, environmental activism. Various instances can be cited in the Buddhist canon that support kindness to animals, respect for plant life, and preservation of habitat, values that accord well with contemporary environmentalism. However, aside from notable exceptions such as Chatsumarn Kabilsingh and Phra Prachak in Thailand, most Buddhist environmentalists do not live in Buddhism's Asian homelands. Throughout Southeast Asia, ostensibly Buddhist countries pursue economic programs that degrade the environment. In Japan, noted Buddhist scholars have been wary of the appropriation of Buddhism in service of environmental ideals. N. Hakamaya, for instance, claims that "Buddhism does not accept but negates nature" (Schmithausen 1991, 38–41). This resistance to environmentalist activism in the name of Buddhism underscores the complexity of this issue and suggests that one must exert caution when attempting to engage in cross-cultural social thought, as mentioned in the reference earlier in this chapter to the critique of Ramachandra Guha.

## Jaina Environmentalism

From the perspective of traditional religious precepts in Buddhism, Jainism, and Yoga, environmental values such as minimal consumption of material resources can be upheld. Additionally, the

Jaina teaching that life forms pervade even seemingly inanimate realms bears remarkable similarity to the Gaia hypothesis advanced by James Lovelock and Lynn Margulis, which states that our unique atmosphere and even many of our rocks owe their origin to life processes. Bacteria and simple forms of life breathed forth oxygen; their decaying bodies formed limestone and continue to constantly reconstitute our soil. In their own ways, both worldviews emphasize the interconnectedness of life forms, a cardinal ecological principle.

Both ecology and the renouncer traditions of India implicitly raise issues of an ethical nature. If all life is interconnected, as indicated in both Jainism and Buddhism, it stands to reason that destruction of habitat or introduction of a new predator will affect an entire ecosystem, often with disastrous results. To preserve the integrity of nature, care must be exerted. In Jainism, the destruction of life forms through violence (*hiṃsā*) results in direct injury to one's own soul, increasing the accretion of deleterious *karma*. To avoid harm to oneself, the Jainas developed a comprehensive way of life rooted in the observance of nonviolence (*ahiṃsā*). This includes vegetarianism for all members of the Jaina community, occupational restrictions for lay Jainas, and stringent nonviolent behavior for members of monastic communities, such as sweeping one's path to avoid harm to insects, and total abandonment of all material goods, even, in the case of the most Digambara monks, renunciation of all clothing.

All of these practices, stemming from the vow of nonviolence, can be seen as enhancements for an environmentally friendly lifestyle. Jeremy Rifkin and others have written about the great environmental benefits that arise from vegetarianism (Rifkin 1992). Traditionally, Jainas have entered career paths that could, in most instances, be seen as environmentally friendly, such as trade, accounting, and publishing. The vow of nonpossession (*aparigraha*), originally conceived as a method for reducing one's karmic baggage (in both literal and metaphorical senses of the word), can today be seen as a call for modern persons to minimize their consumption, a key issue in the environmental movement.

Within the Jaina community of India, a small book entitled *Declaration on Nature* was published by L. M. Singhvi, High Commissioner for India in Great Britain. This 1990 document explicitly supports an environmental agenda from a Jaina perspective. It quotes Mahāvīra's warning that observant Jainas must be respectful of the elements and vegetation: "One who neglects or disregards the existence of earth, air, fire, water, and vegetation disregards his own existence which is entwined with them" (Singhvi 1990, 7). Singhvi himself writes that "Life is viewed as a gift of togetherness, accommodation and assistance in a universe teeming with interdependent constituents" ( Singhvi 1990, 7). Stating that there are countless souls constantly changing and interchanging life forms, he goes on to note that "Even metals and stones might have life in them and should not be dealt with recklessly" (Singhvi 1990, 11). This small book, which summarizes Jaina cosmology and ethics, has been distributed widely in an effort to extend environmental awareness throughout the Jaina community.

Several Jaina organizations have taken up the cause of environmentalism, regarding it to be a logical extension of their personal observance of nonviolence (*ahiṃsā*). The Shrimad Rajchandra Kendra near Ahmedabad announced in 1990 plans to operate a news service to "supply information on the different Jain environmental projects and on ecology issues generally to the 450 Jain newsletters and magazines in India as well as those abroad" (*Ahimsa Quarterly Magazine* 1991, 5). A reforestation project has been underway at various Jaina religious pilgrimage sites, such as Palitana in Gujarat, Ellora in Maharashtra, and Sametshirkhar and Pavapuri in Bihar. At Jain Vishva Bharati in Rajasthan, a fully accredited university, the Ahimsa Department offers a specialization in ecology. In December, 1995, the department co-sponsored a conference entitled "Living in Harmony with Nature: Survival into the Third Millenium." Topics included the environmental crisis, ecological degradation, and unrestrained consumerism. These activities at various Jaina organizations reflect some ways in which the traditional Jaina observance of *ahiṃsā* has been reinterpreted to accommodate environmental concerns.

## Yogic Environmentalism

The Yoga tradition, a pan-Indian system of spirituality utilized by nearly all the religious traditions of India, includes within its disciplines several resources that can, at minimum, increase environmental awareness. It affirms the reality of the natural world (see *Yoga Sūtra* 4.16), whereas Advaita Vedānta and other schools of Indian thought assert that the world is mere illusion. It lists several forms of concentration (*saṃyama*) that enhance one's awareness of the body and orientation within the cosmos:

> From concentration on the sun arises knowledge of the world.
> On the moon, knowledge of the ordering of the stars.
> On the polar star, knowledge of their movement.
> On the central energy wheel (*cakra*), knowledge of the ordering of the body. (*Yoga Sūtra* 3.26–29)

These abilities arise from mastery of physical postures (*āsana*) and the breath (*prāṇa*) as explained briefly in the *Yoga Sūtra* and in greater detail in later Yoga texts such as the *Haṭha Yoga Pradīpikā*. Through mastery of the physical body comes enhanced awareness of its relationship with the natural world. The senses become rarefied and receptive to experiences of how the body relates to the elements (earth, water, fire, and air) and to the movement of heavenly bodies mentioned above. Additionally, Yoga sets forth ethical principles that accord well with environmental precepts: through nonviolence (*ahiṃsā*) harm is minimized to animals; through nonpossession (*aparigraha*) one consumes only bare necessities; through purity (*śauca*) one becomes mindful of pollution and will seek to avoid it in any form. The ultimate goal of Yoga, as mentioned above, involves the cultivation of higher awareness, which, from an environmental perspective, might be seen as an ability to rise above the sorts of consumptive material concerns that can be harmful to the ecosystem.

Yoga is perhaps India's largest cultural export, in part because it does not require adherence to the many constraints of caste system or to a specific theological position. Its techniques have been employed by Hindus, Jainas, Buddhists, Sufis, and Sikhs, both in India and elsewhere; it has also become common at YMCAs and health clubs worldwide. To the extent that the development of environmental consciousness and conscience requires awareness of one's body in relation to the physical world, Yoga provides a potent, non-ideological tool.

From within the Śramaṇical or renouncer traditions, resources are emerging for the enhancement of environmental theory and action. Though Buddhism does not have a significant presence in contemporary India, Buddhists, primarily in America and Thailand, have used Buddhist principles to develop a new *dharma* for the earth. The Jainas within India and abroad have thoughtfully applied the *ahiṃsā* doctrine to environmental issues, through publication and dissemination of materials as well as hands-on projects such as tree plantings. Yoga, perhaps the most amorphous yet most widely known of the Śramaṇical traditions, does not have a central theological spokesperson or organization through which to interpret environmental issues. However, the basic precepts of a yogic lifestyle involve an emphasis on health, exercise, vegetarianism, and nonviolence that accord well with core environmental principles.

## Religion and the Environment in India

In the materials discussed above, the Vedas, the *dharmaśāstras,* the Upaniṣads, and even the *Bhagavad Gītā* have been invoked in the name of heightening environmental consciousness. Likewise, nostalgia for a pre-Hindu tribal relationship with nature has been put forth in current literature as a possible model for environmentalism. I have also suggested that the renouncer values that advocate minimal consumption of resources might also be newly interpreted for an environmentally friendly ethic.

Although the integrated reality of village economy, which served as the economic context for the Brahminical and renouncer traditions of India, certainly sustained agrarian India for millennia, and although many tribal people today continue to eke out a subsistence existence, neither model bears direct relevance for the burgeoning urban life that hundreds of millions of people in India have embraced in the past few decades. Although the classical traditions, both Brahminical and renouncer, contain nature imagery and promote abstemiousness and tribal societies generally operate in harmony with and in reliance on a tribe's immediate ecosystem, these are not likely to capture the imagination of precisely the sorts of people who stand to commit the greatest infractions against the ecological order, the people throughout South Asia who are feverishly buying cars, building condominiums, and filling their flats with prepared foods and plastics.

India's emerging middle class, rather than critiquing its movement toward Western-style development, in fact finds consumerism and its attendant human comforts quite attractive. There is little incentive for the upwardly mobile urban Indian to heed the nascent environmentalist's plea to follow and respect traditional ways. Environmentalism monitored and promoted in the form of legislation and non-governmental agency activitism is a construct originated in the developed world. As Guha and others have protested, why should India buy into a movement that stems from the First World, the greatest polluters and exporters of technology? From another angle, why should peoples of the South deny themselves the sorts of luxuries that have characterized the developed North?

To answer these questions, it is crucial that the peoples of South Asia continue to develop their Gandhian suspicion of the benefits of technological consumerism. If, as Vandana Shiva suggests, Indians can reflect on the interconnectedness of the human being with its environment, then some process of questioning the onslaught of modernization and its consequent pollution can begin.

The Brahminical models, stemming from the Upaniṣads and *dharmaśāstras,* present both beautiful and bucolic images in support of environmentalism, as indicated in much of the literature cited above. However, these texts and traditions are also problematic. As Lance Nelson argues elsewhere in this volume, if the world is seen to be unreal, then perhaps it is not important to respect or maintain it. Or perhaps the attitude will prevail that such dirty tasks should be left to persons of lower caste status, so one's purity will not be violated, as suggested by Frank Korom (this volume). The extolling of wealth, as evidenced in the *Arthaśāstra* and in the popular worldwide worship of the goddess Lakṣmī among Hindus, does not bode well for a minimalist economic theory. According to the *Ṛg Veda,* human nature is fraught with desire; through desire the many worlds of human endeavor take shape, assisted and abetted by ritual sacrifice and purposeful activity. The mainstream culture of India, not unlike the consumerist culture emerging worldwide, places great value on human comfort. Pragmatically speaking, the effectiveness of the environmental movement in India, as elsewhere, will depend upon the extent to which ecological ravage impinges on human pleasure, as demonstrated in the years following the Bhopal disaster.

**Conclusion**

In my earlier statements regarding the typology of American environmentalism, I identified three areas: awe for the natural order, concern for species and land preservation, and avoidance of harm due to industrial toxicity. India has long revered the natural order, as indicated in the sampling of tribal, Vedic, and post-Vedic materials that were cited earlier. Additional literary materials celebrating nature can be found in the writings of Bāṇa, Daṇḍin, Kālidāsa, Bhavabhūti, Tagore, and many others. Of particular note, however, is that these materials are specific to India, and if nature writing finds resurgence in light of India's environmental issues, then these and other authors might gain popularity.

The second area that I identified involved species and land preservation. India certainly contains an abundance of biological diversity, from tigers and monkeys to colorful tropical flora. Various game preserves have been set aside for land and animal protection, most notably the Bharatpur bird sanctuary near Delhi and the Periyar nature reserve in Kerala. There are a total of 19 national parks and 205 sanctuaries within India (Krishnan 1982), though none are as large as those found in the United States. India's identity has long been intertwined with its peoples' relationship with the land and its nonhuman denizens, as indicated in the many animal stories of Hinduism, Jainism, and Buddhism (see Jaini 1987, McDermott 1989, Chapple 1993). However, unlike the North American continent, where the decimation of a relatively small indigenous population paved the way for both massive immigration and preservation of huge tracts of land, India does not have the luxury of defining and setting aside vast wilderness areas as nature preserves. Even in remote areas that have been designated as development zones and perhaps will soon be flooded as damming projects proceed, thousands of people suffer possible displacement, sparking great protest and social activism (Fisher 1995). It is unthinkable that a National Parks program or National Monument program of the scope found in the United States could work in a country so densely populated. It must be noted, however, that the many pilgrimage places within India, from the Himalayas in the north to Kanya Kumari at the very southern tip of the subcontinent, form a patchwork of sacralized spaces that could be newly interpreted through the prism of environmentalism.

The third area I identified as characteristic of American environmentalism is concern about toxic substances. The hierarchical structures of Indian society present obstacles to marshalling a pan-Indian environmental movement to counter the harmful presence of toxins in India. A high rate of illiteracy makes it difficult to communicate even the most basic environmental message to the masses. Environmental clean-up requires getting dirty. People in power in India have traditionally avoided filth, leaving it to be handled by less educated members of the lower castes. Perhaps as a result, sanitation projects do not seem to receive high priority. Air pollution initiatives are virtually nonexistent, despite the proliferation of highways and overpasses that encourage the growth of largely unregulated and highly polluting vehicle traffic in New Delhi, which now rivals Mexico City in its level of airborne particle pollutants.

Indian environmentalism has traditionally emphasized general education through the news media, direct action such as in the Chipko movement, and on each individual's choice of lifestyle (Chapple 1993, 62). Until very recently, India has not promoted legislation or punitive measures in an effort to cleanse its air and waters to the extent found in the United States. So, many aspects of the American environmental program, from vast forest preserves to the Endangered Species Act to the Environmental Protection Agency, do not readily transfer to the South Asian context. However, India has pressing environmental needs that demand attention. In order for India to avoid mistakes of the past and avoid any future Bhopals, it needs to continue to build its environmental program. Even beyond the literacy-based programs mentioned above, it needs to lift up indigenous sensibilities, Brahminical rationale, Śramaṇical orthopraxy, as well as a modern program of education. Through these emerging indigenous resources and resourcefulness, India will devise its own methods and rationalities in defense of the ecosystem.

## References

*Ahimsa Quarterly Magazine*. 1991. 1 (no. 1).

Arnold, David, and Ramachandra Guha, eds. 1995. *Nature, Culture, Imperialism: Essays on the Environmental History of South Asia*. Delhi: Oxford University Press.

Badiner, Allan Hunt, ed. 1990. *Dharma Gaia: A Harvest of Essays in Buddhism and Ecology*. Berkeley: Parallax Press.

Banwari. 1992. *Pañcavaṭī: Indian Approach to Environment*. Translated by Asha Vohra. Delhi: Shri Vinayaka Publications.

Berry, Thomas. 1988. *The Dream of the Earth*. San Francisco: Sierra Club Books.

Braidotti, Rosa, Ewa Charkiewicz, Sabine Hausler, and Sakia Wiernga. 1994. *Women, the Environment and Sustainable Development: Towards a Theoretical Synthesis*. London: Zed Books.

Bunyard, Peter, and Edward Goldsmith, eds. 1988. *Gaia: The Thesis, the Mechanisms, and the Implications*. Cornwall: Wadebridge Ecological Centre.

Callicott, J. Baird. 1994. *Earth's Insights: A Survey of Ecological Ethics from the Mediterranean Basin to the Australian Outback*. Berkeley: University of California Press.

Carson, Rachel. 1962. *Silent Spring*. New York: Fawcett Publications.

Chapple, Christopher Key. 1993. *Nonviolence to Animals, Earth, and Self in Asian Traditions*. Albany, N.Y.: State University of New York Press.

———. ed. 1994. *Ecological Prospects: Scientific, Religious, and Aesthetic Perspectives*. Albany, N.Y.: State University of New York Press.

———. 1996. "India's Earth Consciousness." In *The Soul of Nature: Celebrating the Spirit of the Earth,* ed. Michael Tobias and Georgianne Cowan, New York: Plume. 145–151.

Cobb, John B., Jr. 1992. *Sustainability: Economics, Ecology, and Justice*. Maryknoll, N.Y.: Orbis Books.

Dwivedi, O. P., and B. N. Tiwari. 1987. *Environmental Crisis and Hindu Religion*. New Delhi: Gitanjali Publishing House.

Feldhaus, Anne. 1995. *Water and Womanhood: Religious Meanings of Rivers in Maharashtra*. New York: Oxford University Press.

Fisher, William F. ed. 1995. *Toward Sustainable Development: Struggling Over India's Narmada River*. Arninke, N.Y.: M. E. Sharpe.

Fox, Stephen. 1985. *The American Conservation Movement: John Muir and His Legacy*. Madison: The University of Wisconsin Press.

Guha, Ramachanda. 1989. "Radical American Environmentalism: A Third World Critique." *Environmental Ethics* 11(1): 71–83.

Jaini, Padmanabh S. 1987. "Indian Perspectives on the Spirituality of Animals." In *Buddhist Philosophy and Culture: Essays in Honour of N. A. Jayawickrema,* eds. David J. Kalupahana and W. G. Weeraratne, 169–178. Colombo: N. A. Jayawickrema Felicitation Volume Committee.

Kaza, Stephanie. 1993. *The Attentive Heart: Conversations with Trees*. New York: Fawcett Columbine.

Kipling, John Lockwood. 1904. *Beast and Man in India: A Popular Sketch of Indian Animals in their Relations with the People.* London: MacMillan.

Krishnan, M. 1982. *The Handbook of India's Wildlife.* Madras: Travelaid.

Leopold, Aldo. 1949. *A Sand County Almanac*. London: Oxford University Press.

McDaniel. Jay B. 1989. *Of God and Pelicans: A Theology of Reverence for Life*. Louisville: Westminster/John Knox Press.

———. 1995. *With Roots and Wings: Christianity in an Age of Ecology and Dialogue*. Maryknoll, N.Y.: Orbis Books.

McDermott, James P. 1989. "Animals and Humans in Early Buddhism." *Indo-Iranian Journal* 32 (no. 2): 269–80.

Nash, Roderick Frazier. 1989. *The Rights of Nature: A History of Environmental Ethics*. Madison: The University of Wisconsin Press.

Prime, Ranchor. 1992. *Hinduism and Ecology: Seeds of Truth*. London: Cassell.

Rifkin, Jeremy. 1992. *Beyond Beef: The Rise and Fall of Cattle Culture*. New York: Dutton.

Ruether, Rosemary Radford. 1992. *Gaia & God: An Ecofeminist Theology of Earth Healing*. San Francisco: Harper San Francisco.

Runte, Alfred. 1979. *National Parks: The American Experience*. Lincoln: University of Nebraska Press.

Schmithausen, Lambert. 1991. *Buddhism and Nature*. Tokyo: The International Institute for Buddhist Studies.

Sen, Geeti ed. 1992 *Indigenous Vision: Peoples of India, Attitudes to the Environment*. New Delhi: Sage Publications.

Seshadri, B. 1986. *India's Wildlife and Wildlife Reserves*. New Delhi: Sterling.

Sheth, D. L. 1993. "Politics of Social Transformation: Grassroots Movements in India." In *The Constitutional Foundations of World Peace*, ed. Richard A. Falk, Robert C. Johansen, and Samuel S. Kim, 275–87. Albany: State University of New York Press.

Shiva, Vandana. 1988. *Staying Alive: Women, Ecology, and Development*. London: Zed Books.

———, ed. 1994. *Close to Home: Women Reconnect Ecology, Health and Development Worldwide*. Philadelphia: New Society Publishers.

Singer, Peter. 1975. *Animal Liberation: A New Ethics for Our Treatment of Animals*. New York: Avon Books.

Singhvi, L. M. 1990. *Declaration on Nature*. Office of Jaina High Commissioner for India. N.p.

Spanel, Ann. 1988. "Interview with Vandana Shiva." *Woman of Power* 9: 27–31.

Swimme, Brian, and Thomas Berry. 1992. *The Universe Story: From the Primordial Flaring Forth to the Ecozoic Era*. San Francisco: Harper San Francisco.

Tobias, Michael. 1991. *Life Force: The World of Jainism*. Berkeley: Asian Humanities Press.

———. 1994a. "Jainism and Ecology." In *Worldviews and Ecology: Religion, Philosophy, and the Environment*, ed. Mary Evelyn Tucker and John A. Grim, 138–149. Maryknoll: Orbis Books.

———. 1994b. *World War III: Population and the Biosphere at the End of the Millennium*. Santa Fe: Bear & Company.

Tobias, Michael, and Georgianne Cowan, eds. 1994. *The Soul of Nature: Visions of a Living Earth*. New York: Continuum.

Tucker, Mary Evelyn, and John A. Grim, eds. *Worldviews and Ecology: Religion, Philosophy, and the Environment*. Maryknoll: Orbis Books.

Vannucci, Marta. 1994. *Ecological Readings in the Veda*. New Delhi: D.K. Print World.

Vatsyayan, Kapila, ed. 1995. *Prakṛti: The Integral Vision*. 5 vols. New Delhi: Indira Gandhi National Centre for the Arts.

**Harold Coward**

# 2

# The Ecological Implications of Karma Theory

## Introduction

The current environmental crisis is posing new ethical questions to each philosophical and religious tradition. How are we as humans to respond to the natural environment of which we are a part: to the air, water, and earth which our modern industrial activity is rapidly polluting, to the diversity of plants and animals which large-scale agriculture is threatening? This question is as real and urgent for South Asia as it is for Europe or North America. Smog suffocates Bombay, the Ganges is polluted, and fertilizer use is degrading India's soil. In some areas, large-scale monoculture farming practices have been introduced threatening natural diversity. What wisdom do the Indian traditions offer in response to this new challenge?

In contrast to the Western traditions where humans are frequently described as being separate from nature over which they have dominion, Indian thought has seen humans (in their embodied lives) as an intimately interconnected part of nature.[1] To harm any aspect of nature—be it air, water, plants, or animals—is tantamount to harming oneself. Thus there is a clear and unambiguous environmental ethic within Indian thought. The fact that such an ethic has not protected South Asia from the environmental problems of modern industry and agriculture suggests that it has not been sufficiently understood and applied. While ecological reflection has been vigorously pursued in the West for the past two decades, it has been slow to appear in India, perhaps because it was assumed that this was a Western and not a South Asian problem. But the catastrophe of Bhopal, the Bombay smog, the pollution of the Ganges, and the acid rain deterioration of the Taj Mahal make it clear that the environmental crisis has reached full flower in India.

Responses from within Indian thought have begun to appear. Highlighting scriptural sources in the Vedas, Upaniṣads and *Bhagavad Gītā,* Hindus speak of the cosmos (including the stars, the atmosphere, the earth, plants, animals, and humans) as God's body. Since everything is divine, an ethic of reverence and respect is demanded from humans toward all other manifestations of God's body. This line of thought has been emphasized in recent publications on environmental ethics by S. Cromwell Crawford, Eliot Deutsch, Gerald Larson, Klaus Klostermaier, Geeti Sen, O. P. Dwivedi, Muktananda, Chidvilasananda, and others.[2] Vandana Shiva has championed the indigenous knowledge of women and the important role it has played in the conservation of biodiversity in traditional Indian agriculture (see Shiva 1992).

Eliot Deutsch (1989, 263–64) and Cromwell Crawford (1989, 7) also mention the "law of *karma*" as binding individuals to the environment, but neither writer gives the idea development. *Karma* theory is a basic presupposition for Jaina and Buddhist as well as Hindu thought. Yet none of the good book-length studies of *karma* by Wendy Doniger, Ronald Neufeldt, Herman Tull, or Bruce Reichenbach examine the implications of *karma* theory for environmental ethics.[3] This chapter will undertake a beginning to that task and briefly apply the analysis to environmental problems. Since the theory of *karma* is pan-Indian, this analysis could provide a basis for an ethical response to environmental problems that is authentically Indian.

The method followed in this chapter is not historical. It most closely approximates Tillich's "correlational method" (Tillich 1951, 59–66) in which one starts with the questions of the day and then searches the sources of a tradition for answers. The assumption is that the revelation or wisdom of a tradition is elucidated generation after generation by the questions each has faced. The richness of a tradition's wisdom is demonstrated by its ability to offer helpful answers to new questions—answers that will not have been noted by previous generations who may not have been seized by the question. The environmental question did not occur to previous generations the way it has to ours with the overcrowding of the planet and the excessive use of natural resources. And when the environmental question is put, I suggest that a helpful and ethically responsible answer as to how humans ought to interact with the environment can be generated from *karma* theory. Because it is a new answer to a new question, it is not surprising that one does not find it in previous texts or that people did not use it to guide their behavior in past ages.

## Karma Theory and Environmental Ethics

Unlike modern Western views that separate nature from humans and subject it to human domination, *karma* theory rejects such dualism and maintains, especially from a Jaina perspective, that there is no radical separation between humans and other forms of beings (animals, plants, air, water, atoms of matter). Instead, a radical continuity is proposed. All are souls (*jīvas*) entrapped in different states of karmic bondage (Jaini 1979, 107–133). Humans, animals, plants, and molecules of air, water, or earth are all composed of souls (*jīvas*) entrapped in varying kinds and quantities of *karma. Karma,* for the Jainas, is composed of material traces of past actions that "float free" in every part of space and adhere to the soul because of the "stickiness" of the passions (*kaṣāyas*), desires (*rāga*), and hatred (*dveṣa*) with which it is covered (Jaini 1979, 112). For our purposes it is not necessary to delineate the Jaina view of the various kinds and colors of *karma* that stick to and weigh down the soul causing it to appear as earth, water, air, plant, animal or human. Suffice it to say that all are in varying levels of karmic bondage, in which they will be continually reborn until a complete release from *karma* is achieved.

For the Jaina, the most powerful force to move one toward the goal of release is the practice of nonviolence (*ahiṃsā*) in everything one thinks or does (Jaini 1979, 167). Thus, the Jaina ethic of nonviolence requires not just reverence toward other humans but also reverence toward souls which, because of their particular karmic covering, appear as animals, plants, rocks, earth, water, or air. One cannot imagine a more comprehensive and exhaustive application of a nonviolence ethic than that which the Jaina theory of *karma* produces. Certainly there is no room for human domination and exploitation of other states of nature which, for the Jaina, are simply souls (*jīvas*) in other karmic states. While few may be willing to accept the Jaina prescription, namely, the practice of nonviolence (*ahiṃsā*) toward all forms of life (human, animal, organic, and inorganic) leading ultimately to the freely chosen act of self-starvation (*sallekhanā*), the strong emphasis upon the need to reverence life in all its forms, including even the inorganic, has been influential in India. Reverencing plant and animal life offers important correctives to modern agriculture and its use of monoculture and chemicals. Similarly, seeing earth, air, and water as beings in different forms, as Jaina *karma* theory does, provides an ethic that rejects the ruthless exploitation of natural resources that modern industrial development practices and the environmental pollution (including disasters like Bhopal) that result.

While the Jaina conceptualization of *karma* theory may be too radical, in spite of its logical consistency, to be taken seriously by modern India, the Yoga analysis of *karma* entails an environmental moral responsibility that cannot be sidestepped. There are many definitions of *karma* in Indian thought, some making *karma* appear quite deterministic or fatalistic. Fatalistic strands are indeed present in Indian thought on *karma* (see Bhattacharji 1995, 76) and would lead to a view of environmental degradation as being the responsibility of God rather than of humans. But an equally strong viewpoint emphasizes the role of free will in *karma* theory, giving humans a strong moral responsibility in environmental matters. The latter is especially true if we examine the conception of *karma* found in Patañjali's *Yoga Sūtras*.[4] *Karma* is described by Patañjali as a memory trace (*saṃskāra*) recorded in the unconscious by any action a person has done or thought a person has had.[5] We should note here that for Yoga a thought is as real and important as an action. We think first and then act, so thought is, therefore, of primary significance. The karmic memory trace (*saṃskāra*) remains in the unconscious as a predisposition toward doing the same action or having the same thought again in the future. All that is required is that the appropriate set of circumstances present themselves, and the karmic memory trace, like a seed that has been watered and given warmth, bursts forth as an impulsion toward the same kind of action or thought from which it originated. If one, through the exercise of free choice, chooses to act on the impulse and do the same action or entertain the same thought again, then that karmic seed is allowed to flower, resulting in a reinforcing of the memory trace within the unconscious. Sufficient repetitions of the same action or thought produce a strengthening of the predisposition (*saṃskāra*), and the establishing of a habit pattern. Such a karmic habit pattern, or *vāsanā,* is the Yoga equivalent for the modern psychological notion of motivation. The unconscious, in Yoga terminology, is nothing more than the sum of all the stored-up karmic traces of freely chosen actions and thoughts of the past.

Notice that, in the above analysis, the karmic impulse from the unconscious does not *cause* anything, it is not mechanistic in nature. Rather, it simply *predisposes* you toward an action or thought. It is all up to your own free choice, which means that the moral responsibility for your choices rests squarely upon your own shoulders. Even the initial impulse arising from the *saṃskāra* or memory trace in the unconscious got there in the first place by a freely chosen action on your part in the past, and therefore, it is an impulse for which you are morally responsible. Therefore, in the Yoga view of *karma,* there is no escaping the moral responsibility for the actions one chooses or even the impulses toward action arising from one's unconscious. Thus through the use of your own free choice, you decide either to go along with the karmic impulse, in which case it is reinforced and strengthened, or to say "no" and negate it, in which case its strength diminishes until it is finally removed from the unconscious. *Karmas* can be either good or bad. Good actions and thoughts lay down good karmic traces in the unconscious for the predisposing of future good karmic impulses. Evil actions and thoughts do the reverse. Scripture and tradition taken together distinguish between good and evil. And with regard to the environment, Jaina, Hindu, and Buddhist traditions all agree that the environment is to be reverenced and not harmed. We have detailed the Jaina view in this regard above.

There is one more aspect to the way in which *karma* functions that must not be forgotten. We have seen how, according to the theory of *karma,* we are each morally responsible for the good or evil thoughts or actions toward the environment that we freely choose during this life. But according to Yoga and Indian thought generally, that moral responsibility extends backward to include all the actions and thoughts of our previous lives, which created the dispositions toward the environment we are currently experiencing. This is the notion of *saṃsāra* or rebirth. According to this concept, one's unconscious contains not only all the karmic traces of the actions and thoughts of this life but also of those from the life before this, and so on backwards infinitely since, in Indian thought, there is no absolute beginning. In reality, then, one's unconscious is like a huge granary full of karmic seeds or memory traces that are constantly sprouting up, as conducive situations arise, impelling one toward good or evil actions or thoughts. From the point of view of environmental ethics, this means that the impulses I am now feeling in the way I behave toward animals, plants, earth, air, and water are a direct result of the way I have freely chosen to behave in past lives. If my arising karmic impulses are suggesting irresponsible behavior toward the environment, it is because I have acted in immoral ways toward the environment in this and previous lives. And since I chose to behave in those ways, I created for myself the impulses now arising from my own unconscious. If I find myself wanting to cut down the forest, foul the water, pollute the air, and selfishly over consume the earth's resources, I cannot blame these impulses on God, the devil, my parents, or society. They are coming into my mind at this time because I laid them down as seeds or memory traces in my unconscious in the past (in this or previous lives). So I, alone, am responsible for the environmental impulses, good or bad, that I am now experiencing.

But I am not fatally trapped by my past environmental *karma.* In spite of my impulses toward action, I still have the free choice to go with or to negate such impulses. While I may have habitually fouled the air or water in past actions (in this and previous lives), I can still use my free choice now, when the situation arises, not to accept such an impulse again. According to *karma* theory, it would be as if a seed has sprouted and not been given moisture or warmth, causing it to whither and die without flowering. By using my free choice to negate irresponsible environmental impulses when they arise, it is as if they receive no water or warmth and thus die without flowering into a repeated action. In this way, through repeated good choices, environmentally destructive karmic patterns can be removed from my unconscious and replaced by good environmental impulses. From the perspective of *karma* theory, I am totally responsible for both my impulses toward the environment and the way I choose to act or not act on those impulses. And the way I choose to act today creates the karmic impulses I will experience tomorrow and in future lives in my interaction with the environment. I alone, therefore, am responsible for the condition I will create for the future.

But it is not just my own present and future I am creating through my acts of free choice. Remember that for *karma* theory, my existence as a being is not independent but in a continuum with all other beings, with all of nature (*prakṛti*). Therefore, what I choose to think and do affects not only my present and future life but also the rest of the environment of which I am an interconnected part. In this regard, my karmic responsibility is both individual and cosmic. The way I make my choices conditions not only my future lives but also the future of all other beings, which—in the *karma* perspective—includes all of nature.

## Conclusion

Karma theory provides a strong and clear environmental ethic from within South Asian thought. Its twin thrusts of human continuity with all forms of life (including the inorganic) and moral responsibility for one's impulses and actions provide a sound basis for what Eliot Deutsch had called an ethic of "natural reverence" (1989, 259–60). As we have seen, *karma* theory binds humans into continuity with natural processes. While human freedom is emphasized, it is a freedom circumscribed with moral responsibility to the environment with which each of us is intimately interconnected. *Karma,* as Deutsch puts it, "ties together everything that one does in patterns of action informed by habits acquired in past experience, and shows the subtle ramifications or consequences of one's makings [actions] throughout one's environment" (1989, 263). Whereas Western ideas of the separation of humans from nature lead to actions of exploitation and irresponsible consumption, the *karma* conception of humans and nature belonging together in moral freedom results in a natural reverencing of the environment. Awareness that the excessive burning of carbon fuels is changing the earth's climate and threatening the continued existence of some forms of life is sufficient cause, given *karma* theory, for us to be required to change our thinking and our behavior. In a world seriously challenged by overpopulation and overconsumption, the requirement for nonviolence toward all of nature's forms (*ahiṃsā*) and the need to give up avaricious action and thought (*aparigraha*), together with Yoga's emphasis upon the moral responsibility and freedom to actualize such goals, is indeed a positive prescription. The fact that the Yoga view of *karma* does not allow one even the smallest opening to wriggle out of personal responsibility to the environment is very important in contemporary South Asian cultures, where a sense of social ethic often seems absent.

Gerald Larson has recently warned against the comparativist tendency to look for "Conceptual Resources" in South Asia as a way to construct prescriptions for the world's environmental problems (1989, 267–77). He correctly warns against the mistake of disembedding ideas from the South Asian culture or comprehensive way of life and applying them to environmental problems in the West. Larson's counsel can also be reversed. It is probably not helpful to import Western concepts such as the deep ecology theory of Arne Naess (with its reliance on contemporary ecology and quantum theory) as a philosophical basis for environmental ethics in South Asia (Callicott 1989, 58–61). Rather one should look to the environmental ideas embedded within the Indian worldview. Here, as we have argued, traditional *karma* theory has much to offer.

## Notes

1. By "embodied lives" I refer to the *prakṛti* aspect of the human person in the Sāṃkhya-Yoga formulation and Rāmānuja's *saguṇa* conception of the human person as a part of God's body. In both cases humans are understood to be in continuity with and a part of nature. The radical break between humans and nature in Sāṁkhya-Yoga, for example, comes only with *kaivalya* or release when the ontological separation of *prakṛti* and *puruṣa* is realized and one is released from life in *karma-saṃsāra*. But up

until that moment, one lives in an evolved state of *prakṛti* (with *buddhi, ahaṃkāra, manas,* sense organs, and body) in interaction with the rest of nature (animals, plants, and inorganic matter) produced by *prakṛti*'s continued evolution. Thus, embodied (and "enminded") humans are intimately interconnected with all other manifestations of *prakṛti* with which they must morally interact according to the teaching of *ahiṃsā* (see *Yoga Sūtras* 2.30). While the *Yoga Sūtras* define *ahiṃsā* in relation to "living creatures," the Jains extend this principle of moral responsibility to its logical conclusion, thus including all plants and inorganic matter (rocks, earth, air, water). From Rāmānuja's perspective, all of this is simply God's body, *saguṇa* Brahman, from which there is no radical separation even in release. Śaṅkara, of course, disagrees and sees release as requiring a *nirguṇa* state of complete separation from *saguṇa* or karmic life. In Vedic thought the *karma* (good and bad actions) of the individual are seen to directly affect the rest of nature or the cosmos, of which the human is but a part (see Tull 1989, chap. 2). Throughout this essay, my analysis is focused on *karma* in *saguṇa* life, and the ecological responsibility which that entails. While I focus on Patañjali's conception of *karma,* I contend that Patañjali's view is largely assumed by Rāmānuja (see Lipner 1986, 71–72) and by Śaṅkara at the *saguṇa* level.

2. See S. Cromwell Crawford, *The Evolution of Hindu Ethical Ideals* (Delhi: Arnold-Heinemann, 1984); S. Cromwell Crawford, "Hindu Ethics for Modern Life," in *World Religions and Global Ethics* (New York: Paragon, 1989), 5–35; Eliot Deutsch, "A Metaphysical Grounding for Natural Reverence: East-West," and Gerald Larson, "'Conceptual Resources' in South Asia for Environmental Ethics," in *Nature in Asian Traditions of Thought: Essays in Environmental Philosophy,* ed. J. Baird Callicott and Roger T. Ames (Albany: State University of New York Press, 1989), 259–65 and 267–77; Klaus Klostermaier, "The Body of God," in Robert B. Crothy, ed., *The Charles Strong Lectures 1972–84* (Leiden: Brill, 1987), 103–20; Geeti Sen, *Indigenous Vision: Peoples of India Attitudes to the Environment* (Delhi: Sage, 1992); O. P. Dwivedi and B. N. Tiwari, *Environmental Crisis and Hindu Religion* (Delhi: Gitanjali Publications, 1987); *Darshan: Nature the Face of God,* vol. 36, 1990 (N.Y.: SYDA Foundation); M. Vannucci, *Ecological Readings in the Veda* (Delhi: D. K. Printworld, 1993).

3. See *Karma and Rebirth in Classical Indian Traditions,* ed. Wendy Doniger O'Flaherty (Berkeley: University of California Press, 1980); *Karma and Rebirth: Post Classical Developments,* ed. Ronald W. Neufeldt (Albany: State University of New York Press, 1986); Herman W. Tull, *The Vedic Origins of Karma* (Albany: State University of New York Press, 1989); Bruce R. Reichenbach, *The Law of Karma: A Philosophical Study* (Honolulu: University of Hawaii Press, 1990).

4. *Patañjaliyogadarśanam* (Varanasi: Bhāratīya Vidyā Prakāśana, 1963). A helpful English translation is by Rama Prasada (Allahabad: Bhubaneswari Asrama, 1924). Readily available, but more literal, is the translation by J. H. Woods (Harvard Oriental Series, vol. 17; Varanasi: Motilal Banarsidass, 1966). The key passages for the *Yoga Sūtras'* conception of *karma* are 2.12–14 and 4.7–9. In 4.9, it is made clear that the memory traces (*saṃskāras*) continue to exist uninterruptedly between births. While the Yoga system is ultimately a duality between pure consciousness (*puruṣa*) and nature, including mind, ego, senses, body, and all of organic and inorganic matter (*prakṛti*), for the purpose of our present study we follow Patañjali's analysis only up to the *samprajñāta* or seeded stage of *samādhi.* At this and all lower levels, there is no dualism between humans and the environment as all are formed of and within the structures of *prakṛti.* My analysis shows that at this level, before reaching the highest level of ultimate release, while one is still in bondage to *prakṛti, karma* theory can develop a strong moral responsibility from humans for all other levels of *prakṛti* (the environment). Such behavior is indeed enjoined in the *Yoga Sūtras* as building good *karma,* which moves one slowly to that final condition (*asamprajñāta-samādhi*) from which final release from *prakṛti* is realized. Thus there is no inconsistency between the two goals.

5. See *Yoga Sūtra* 4.9. For my translation and exposition of the Sanskrit texts from the *Yoga Sūtras,* see Coward 1983.

## References

Bhattacharji, Sukumari. 1995. *Fatalism in Ancient India.* Calcutta: Baulmon Prakashan.

Callicott, J. Baird. 1989. "The Metaphysical Implications of Ecology." In *Nature in Asian Traditions: Essays in Environmental Philosophy,* ed. J. Baird Callicott and Roger T. Ames, 51–66. Albany: State University of New York Press.

Coward, Harold. 1983. "Psychology and Karma." *Philosophy East and West* 33 (January): 367–75.

Crawford, S. Cromwell. 1989. "Hindu Ethics for Modern Life." In *World Religions and Global Ethics,* ed. S. Cromwell Crawford, 5–35. New York: Paragon House.

Deutsch, Eliot. 1989. "A Metaphysical Grounding for Natural Reverence: East-West." In *Nature in Asian Traditions of Thought: Essays in Environmental Philosophy,* ed. J. Baird Callicott and Roger T. Ames, 259–66. Albany: State University of New York Press.

Jaini, Padmanabh S. 1979. *The Jaina Path of Purification.* Berkeley: University of California Press.

Larson, Gerald J. 1989. " 'Conceptual Resources' in South Asia for 'Environmental Ethics.'" In *Nature in Asian Traditions of Thought: Essays in Environmental Philosophy,* ed. J. Baird Callicott and Roger T. Ames, 267–78. Albany: State University of New York Press.

Lipner, Julius. 1986. *The Face of Truth.* London: Macmillan Press.

Shiva, Vandana. 1992. "Women's Indigenous Knowledge and Biodiversity Convention." In *Indigenous Vision,* ed. Geeti Sen, 205–14. Delhi: Sage.

Tillich, Paul. 1951. *Systematic Theology.* Vol. 1. Chicago: University of Chicago Press.

Tull, Herman W. 1989. *The Vedic Origins of Karma.* Albany: State University of New York Press.

**Arvind Sharma**

# 3

# Attitudes to Nature in the Early Upaniṣads

## Introduction

The *Bṛhadāraṇyaka* and the *Chāndogya* are reckoned among the earliest Upaniṣads (Radhakrishnan 1953, 22), and I would like to begin these reflections by a consideration of the attitudes to nature in these texts. In view especially of the more negative attitude toward the world found in the later Vedānta tradition (see below, and Nelson and Sherma, this volume), it is worthwhile examining the view of nature in the scriptures which the later theologians regarded as foundational.

## Nature in the *Bṛhadāraṇyaka*

Consider the following extraordinary passage from the *Bṛhadāraṇyaka Upaniṣad*:

> Now this self, verily, is the world of all beings. In so far as he makes offerings and sacrifices, he becomes the world of the gods In so far as he learns (the Vedas), he becomes the world of the seers. In so far as he offers libations to the fathers and desires offspring, he becomes the world of the fathers. In so

> far as he gives shelter and food to men, he becomes the world of men. In so far as he gives grass and water to the animals, he becomes the world of animals. In so far as beasts and birds, even to the ants find a living in his houses he becomes their world. Verily, as one wishes non-injury for his own world, so all beings wish non-injury for him who has this knowledge. This, indeed, is known and well investigated. (*BU* 1.4.16)[1]

This passage contains perhaps the earliest allusion to what were to become known in *smṛti* literature as the *pañca-mahāyajñas,* or the Five Great Sacrifices, involving offerings to the gods, the seers, the manes, human beings, and animals. You will notice that so far as attitude to nature is concerned, in this passage "the interdependence of man and the world [of nature] including deities, seers, fathers, animals is brought out" in a profoundly metaphysical way (Radhakrishnan 1953, 172).

Such a metaphysics at this stage did not entail a denial of the world and nature, at least in the same way, as later came to be associated with the school of Advaita Vedānta, for which, as I have said, this *Upaniṣad* constitutes a major text. This point is borne out by the following statement of the *Upaniṣad*:

> As a spider moves along the thread, as small sparks come forth from the fire, even so from this Self come forth all breaths, all worlds, all divinities, all beings. Its secret meaning is the truth of truth. Vital breaths are the truth and their truth is It (Self). (*BU* 2.1.20)

I would particularly want to focus on the expression: *satyasya satyam*: the Truth of Truth. As Radhakrishnan is quick to note: "The world is not to be repudiated as false. It is true, but it is true, only derivatively" (Radhakrishnan 1953, 190).

This positive attitude to nature is also confirmed by the following passage:

> This earth is (like) honey for all creatures, and all creatures are (like) honey for this earth. This shining, immortal person who is in this earth and with reference to oneself, this shining, immortal person who is in the body, he, indeed, is just this self. This is immortal, this is *Brahman*, this is all. (*BU* 2.5.1)

Radhakrishnan's comment on the passage runs as follows: "The earth and all living beings are mutually dependent, even as bees and honey are. The bees make the honey and the honey supports the bees: *parasparam upakāryopakāraka-bhāve phalitam aha*" (Radhakrishnan, 202). The Sanskrit is from Ānandagiri: "This results in a relationship of helping, and being helped by, each other." Note also that this verse suggests an intimate connection between earth and the Self.

At this point I would like to suggest that the true import of this passage has perhaps been missed here. The comments of Radhakrishnan and Ānandagiri are helpful, but I am afraid that the lens used to interpret them is a narrow one of formal classical Advaita. Now what right do I have to call the advaitic lens narrow, when the great utterances of Advaita proclaim, "All this is verily Brahman" (*sarvaṃ khalv idam brahma, ChU* 3.14.1), and also, "You are that Brahman" (*tat tvam asi, ChU* 6.8.7)? What I have in mind has been stated well by M. Hiriyanna, when he writes:

> The ultimate teaching of Advaita is the sole reality of *Brahman. The unity taught here, no doubt, includes both man and nature*; but as the first and foremost interest of man is man himself and not nature, the truth as embodied in "That thou art," or the fundamental identity of the individual and the absolute, is given prominence in the teaching. The disciple has accordingly to concentrate his attention on this aspect of the doctrine, and look upon the other, relating to nature, as more or less secondary. (Hiriyanna 1949, 171–172; emphasis added)

It may well be the case, however, that the idea of nature "being more or less secondary" does not belong to the *Bṛhadāraṇyaka Upaniṣad* itself so much as to the later interpretations of Advaita Vedānta. In other words, the attitude to nature reflected in the text is much more positive than it was destined to become in classical Advaita.

This fact is borne out by other passages in the same section of the *Upaniṣad*. For example, consider the following:

> Then he sips it (saying) "*On that adorable light*: The winds blow sweetly for the righteous, the rivers pour forth honey.

> May the herbs be sweet unto us. To earth, hail. *Let us meditate on the divine glory*: May the night and the day be sweet. May the dust of the earth be sweet. May heaven, our father, be sweet to us. To the atmosphere, hail. *May he inspire (illumine) our understanding*: May the tree be sweet unto us. May the sun be sweet, may the cows be filled with sweetness for us. To the heaven, hail.["] He repeats the whole Sāvitrī hymn and all the verses about the honey (saying), ["]May I indeed be all this, hail to the earth, atmosphere and heaven.["] Having thus sipped all, having washed his hands, he lies down behind the fire with his head towards the east. In the morning he worships the sun (saying) of the quarters (of heaven), "You are the one lotus flower. May I become the one lotus flower among men." Then he goes back the same way [by which he came], sits behind the fire (on the altar) and recites the (genealogical) line (of teachers). (*BU* 6.3.6)

Please note that here the famous Gāyatrī *mantra* (or Sāvitrī hymn) has been woven into the passage (as indicated by my italics) and provided with a naturalistic orientation. Until I read this text I was under the impression that it was Rabindranath Tagore (1861–1941) who had done so, that is, provided the Gāyatrī with a nature-oriented interpretation. I had even proposed that he had done this as a result of his Neo-Hindu appropriation of Kālidāsa—the famous Sanskrit poet known for his love of nature. Now I have to consider the possibility that Rabindranath Tagore was a much more careful student of the Upaniṣads than I gave him credit for—and can give myself credit for!

### Nature as in a Meditative State in the *Chāndogya*

Like the *Bṛhadāraṇyaka Upaniṣad*, the *Chāndogya* also is distinguished by a particularly alluring attitude towards nature. Two passages in that *Upaniṣad* I find particularly poetic and evocative. At one point the *Chāndogya* says: "As here hungry children sit (expectantly) around their mother, even so do all beings sit around the fire sacrifice, yea they sit around the fire sacrifice" (*ChU* 5.24.5). Those familiar with Sanskrit will not fail to feel the evocative power in the line and its symbolism: *yathaiha kṣudhitā bālā mātaram paryupāsate* (just as hungry children sit expectantly around their mother).

What strikes me as significant in this verse is the interpenetrative evocation of ritual and nature, and a subterranean sense of the affinity of human beings, nature, and ritual offering—a triple convergence expressed earlier in the same section as follows:

> If, without knowing this, one offers the fire sacrifice, that would be just as if he were to remove the live coals and pour the offering on (dead) ashes.
>
> But if, knowing it thus, one offers the fire sacrifice he offers it in all worlds, in all beings, in all selves, he will perform sacrifices with a full knowledge of their meaning and purpose.[2]

From this, it appears that Arne Naess may not be off the mark in looking to the Hindu *ātman* idea for suggestions of a deeper sense of identification with all of nature (Naess 1988).

Having introduced certain lines which caught my fancy in relation to the attitude towards nature in this early Upaniṣad, I would now like to share a phrase which makes some ecologists ecstatic. It says: *dhyāyatīva pṛthivī*, "The earth, as it were, is in a state of meditation" (*ChU* 7.6.1, my translation). And the same verse asks us also to envision the atmosphere, the heavens, the waters, and the mountains as being similarly engaged. Radhakrishnan remarks: "Even as men who contemplate acquire repose, become firm and established, the earth, etc., are said to be firm and established, as a result of their meditation" (Radhakrishnan, 474).

"The earth, as it were, is in a state of meditation." I first read this as a statement made by Ramana Maharshi, found it strikingly beautiful, and in my ignorance for a considerable time attributed it to him until I located it in this *Upaniṣad*. Ramana Maharshi apparently had flawless taste—so far as statements indicating attitudes to nature in early Upaniṣads are concerned. It is difficult to recall this statement without the Apollo shot of the blue earth coming to mind: when humanity saw this world as one world for the first time.

## Extensions of These Ideas in the Later Tradition

This glorification of the earth was destined to receive unexpected extension in Śrīvaiṣṇavism, wherein the goddess Earth becomes the spouse of Viṣṇu (see Mumme, this volume). Pious Śrīvaiṣṇavas recite the following verse on alighting from the bed in the morning:

> O Goddess, who has the ocean as her girdle and the mountains as the bosom and who is the wife of Viṣṇu—obedience to thee. Please forgive the touch of my feet.[3]

Here is the Gaia hypothesis in a Vaiṣṇava guise for you!

This makes clear that the attitudes toward nature in the early Upaniṣads did influence later developments or, to say the same thing in Hindu idiom, what the *śruti* said did influence *smṛti*. Thus, to take another example, *Bṛhadāraṇyaka* 1.5.14 admonishes against killing any living being, even a lizard, on the new moon night. The *Manu Smṛti* does not perhaps come that close to inculcating a "deep ecology," but it does stipulate:

> According to the usefulness of the several (kinds of) trees a fine must be inflicted for injuring them; that is the settled rule.
>
> If a blow is struck against men or *animals* in order to (give them) pain, (the judge) shall inflict a fine in proportion to the amount of pain (caused). (*M* 8.285-286, emphasis added)

The upaniṣadic anticipation of the *pañca-mahāyajñas* has already been alluded to. The same positive attitude to nature again finds festive expression in later literature in the ceremony of Vṛkṣotsavavidhi (the tree festival). P. V. Kane describes the purāṇic conception:

> Great importance was attached to the planting of trees. [*Matsya Purāṇa*] 59 (verses 1–20 same as [*Padma Purāṇa*] V.24.192–211) contains the procedure of tree festival. It is briefly as follows:—trees in a garden should be sprinkled with *sarvauṣadhi* water, decked with fragrant powder and flowers and cloth should be wound round them; the trees should be pierced with a golden needle (imitating karṇavedha [ear-piercing]) and

collyrium applied to them with a golden pencil; on the platforms of trees seven or eight golden fruits should be placed, jars containing pieces of gold should be established under the trees: *homa* to be offered to Indra, Lokapālas and Vanaspati; a milch cow covered with white cloth, decked with gold ornaments and having horns tipped with gold should be let loose from the midst of trees; the performer (owner of the trees) should honour all priests with gifts of cows, golden chains, rings, clothes &c. and feed brāhmaṇas with a dinner full of milk for four days; *homa* with yavas, black sesame and mustard and *palāśa* fuel sticks and festival on 4th day; performer reaps all desires. [*Matsya Purāṇa*] 154.512 states that a son is equal to ten deep reservoirs of water and a tree planted is equal to ten sons. It is said by [*Varāha Purāṇa*] (172. 36–37) that just as a good son saves his family, so a tree laden with flowers and fruits saves its owner from falling into hell, and that one who plants five mango trees does not go to Hell; [*Viṣṇudharmottara Purāṇa*] (III.297.13) remarks about trees "a single tree nurtured by a man performs what a son would do, in that it gratifies gods with its flowers, travelers with its shade, men with its fruits; there is no fall in hell for the planter of a tree." (Kane 1974, 415–416).

## Problematizing the Issue

The extension of the approach represented by the early Upaniṣads in the later tradition, however, presents some problems. It also has its shadow side. It could, for instance, be pointed out that in the later tradition Advaita Vedānta, for which the *Bṛhadāraṇyaka* and the *Chāndogya* are major texts, became primarily associated with its formulation by Śaṅkara. Several aspects of this formulation, and by implication the early Upaniṣads themselves, are open to criticism from an ecological perspective. For example, it could be argued (1) that Śaṅkara's system does not reintegrate the absolute with the universe, at least not in a way which could be considered eco-friendly; (2) that reverence for nature therefore remains an Advaitic non sequitur; (3) that ultimate value in the system does not attach to things of the world, as per *Bṛhadāraṇyaka* 2.4.5 ("Verily, not for the sake of all is all dear but all is dear for the sake of the Self"); (4) that Advaita's description of the universe as a world of appearance or *māyā* and the description of *māyā* as *anirvacanīya* (inexplicable) and *tuccha* (insignificant) are far from helpful; (5) that the Advaitic doctrine of the incompatibility of action and knowledge militates against eco-activism; and (6) that Advaita's tradition of ascetic denial of the world does the same. Lance Nelson, in his chapter in this volume, raises many of these concerns.

These are complex issues and it would be difficult to do anything like justice to them here. Perhaps the best one can do is offer some counter-perspectives. Modern Advaitins such as Ramana Maharshi consider point (1) as a misrepresentation of Śaṅkara's view (Osborne 1971, 11), and the fact that Ramana's own reverence for nature is consistent with the tenor of the early Upaniṣads must be taken into account in reference to point (2). Similarly, while according to *Bṛhadāraṇyaka* 2.4.5 all value is located in the Self alone, where pray is the Self located? Again, when *māyā* is described as *anirvacanīya* or inexplicable, it only means that it cannot be explained independently of Brahman (Hiriyanna 1949, 161). Its description as insignificant as an end in itself could, in fact, deter consumerism! Similarly, the doctrine of the incompatibility of knowledge and action really deconstructs the "actor" rather than action, while ascetic denial involves not so much the renunciation of the world as renunciation of one's attachment to it (Marcaurelle 1993). More generally, what the Advaitins denounce is not so much the world—*jagat* as such—but *saṃsāra* or involvement with the world. The fact that the early Upaniṣads describe the bliss of Brahman in terms of the joys of the earth exponentially and progressively multiplied (*BU* 4.3.33), or the joys of the other world as extensions of the joys of this world (*ChU* 8.2), is also not without its own significance.

## Some Comparative Reflections

The attitude to nature in the Upaniṣads is capable of being related not only to later Hinduism but also to other religious traditions in a comparative spirit. *Bṛhadāraṇyaka* 2.1.8 mentions meditation on one's likeness as Brahman, reminiscent of the idea of human beings having been created in the image of God in Christian texts. God's attitude toward nature then, however identified, becomes paradigmatic for human beings. Similarly, ecological thinking in Buddhism has been loosely connected with the doctrine of *pratītyasamutpāda* (dependent co-origination), a doctrine anticipated, according to Radhakrishnan, in *Chāndogya* 7.24.2: "One thing is established in another" (*anyo hy anyasmin pratiṣthita iti*). Thus the seeds of ideas which become representative of attitudes to nature in Christianity and Buddhism, it might be claimed, are also hinted at in the early Upaniṣads.

## Concluding Cautions

I would like to conclude these brief reflections with a caveat. I may be justly accused of having presented a rosy picture of attitudes to nature in the early Upaniṣads. I would like to correct this romantic image by pointing out that at the time these Upaniṣads were composed ecological problems of the kind we find today did not exist. If anything, the problem—from a practical point of view—would have been exploitation of the abundant resources of nature. In the Vedas fire is called *pathikṛt* or pioneer—one who makes a path, presumably by burning a hole in the forest. By the time of the Upaniṣads it is more or less confined to the sacrificial pit. The point I am trying to make is that the issue has become problematical only recently, at a very different historical moment, and therefore even the upaniṣadic attitude needs to be problematized. Still, while we would search the Upaniṣads for solutions for our ecological crisis perhaps in vain, the attitude to nature found there might provide us with the right frame of mind for doing so.

## Notes

1. All translations from the Upaniṣads, unless otherwise indicated, are from Radhakrishnan (1953).

2. sa ya idam avidvān agni-hotraṃ juhoti, yathāṅgārān apohya bhasmani juhuyāt, tādṛk tat syāt. atha ya etad evaṃ vidvān agni-hotraṃ juhoti,

tasya sarveṣu lokeṣu sarveṣu bhuteṣu sarveṣv ātmasu hutam bhavati (*ChU* 5.24.1-2).

3. samudra-raśane devi parvata-stana-maṇḍale I viṣṇu-patni! namas tubhyam pāda-sparśaṃ kṣamasva me.

## References

### Primary Sources, with Abbreviations


*BU* — *Bṛhadāraṇyaka Upaniṣad*. Translated by Radhakrishnan (1953).

*ChU* — *Chāndogya Upaniṣad*. Translated by Radhakrishnan (1953).

*M* — *The Laws of Manu*. Translated by G. Bülher. Oxford: Clarendon Press, 1886.


### Secondary Sources


Kane, P. V. 1974. *History of Dharmasastra*. Vol. 5, pt. 1. Poona: Bhandarkar Oriental Research Institute.

Hiriyanna, M. 1949. *The Essentials of Indian Philosophy*. London: Allen & Unwin.

Marcaurelle, Roger. 1993. "Śaṅkara and Renunciation: A Reinterpretation." Ph.D. diss., McGill University.

Naess, Arne. 1988. "*Self* Realization: An Ecological Approach to Being in the World." In *Thinking like a Mountain: Towards a Council of All Beings*, ed. John Seed, 19–30. Philadelphia: New Society Publishers.

Osborne, Arthur, ed. 1971. *The Teachings of Bhagavan Sri Ramana Maharshi in His Own Words*. Tiruvannamalai: Sri Ramanasramam.

Radhakrishnan, S., ed. and trans. 1953. *The Principal Upanisads*. London: Allen & Unwin.

**Lance E. Nelson**

# 4

# The Dualism of Nondualism: Advaita Vedānta and the Irrelevance of Nature

## Introduction

Ecofeminists and others who have given thought to the relationship between worldviews and environmental attitudes see certain elements of the dominant Western mindset as especially detrimental to ecological concern. The majority of these factors are symptoms of what Rosemary Radford Ruether and others have identified as a "transcendental dualism" that elevates spirit above matter. First and foremost is the opposition between self and other. Typically, the authentic self is understood as spiritual, and consciousness is granted a "supernatural apriority" to the world (Ruether 1975, 195). This leads to the all too familiar hierarchical placement of spirit, usually co-opted as the special province of a male elite, over a nature identified with birth, death, and the feminine. The essential spiritual task is then defined as a quest for autonomy from the restrictions of nature. Emphasizing transcendence, this kind of spirituality generates alienation from, and disdain for, the natural world.[1]

Scholars lamenting the ill effects of such dualistic modes of thought frequently characterize them as Western patterns. Often there are wistful glancings eastward and intimations that there are ways of thinking in Asia based on interconnection rather than dichotomy. In this regard, Hindu and Buddhist systems that make nondualism (*advaita, advaya*) their central doctrine have received some attention, though less painstakingly than they deserve. For purposes of this paper, I would single out Anne Klein as one scholar who has avoided superficiality in this pursuit. Noting "the extreme difficulty of constructing a religious model that *undermines* dualistic tendencies," she has examined Mahāyāna Buddhist nondualism with a view to its implications for feminist thought (1985, 73–98). Her evaluation is careful, and her conclusions are largely positive.

The *Chāndogya Upaniṣad,* one of the foundational scriptures of the Hindu Vedānta, proclaims: "All this [world], verily, is Brahman (the Absolute)" (3.14.1). One might hope, from this, to find in Hindu nondualist thought some positive implications for environmental awareness in India. Indeed, there are several theological traditions within Hinduism that articulate different visions of nondualism. Prominent examples include the Śuddhādvaita ("Pure Nondualism") of Vallabhācārya, several schools of Kashmir Śaivism, and the unsystematic but nevertheless compelling nondualist visions found in various Śākta *tantras* and *purāṇas* (see Sherma, this volume). In this chapter, I wish to focus on the tradition of Hindu nondualism most well known in the West, the Advaita (nondualist) Vedānta founded by Śaṅkara (eighth century C.E.). I will consider its implications for ecological ethics, a matter not unrelated to the feminist issues that occupied Klein in her study of Buddhist nondualism.

Unlike Klein's conclusions, however, mine will not be positive. Against much that has been written in the literature on religion and ecology, I have come to the conclusion that this school's potential contribution to ecological awareness has been vastly overestimated. No doubt, Advaita represents a profound spirituality. In positive relation to the interests of ecology, it fosters values such as simplicity of life, frugality, and—for the ascetic at least—nonviolence. But Advaita also encourages attitudes of devaluation and neglect of the natural universe. While not, of course, directly responsible for environmental degradation, such attitudes, as they filter out into the general culture, carry the potential to seriously undermine environmental concern.

As Lanoy and others have pointed out, it is the *saṃnyāsins,* the Brahmanical renouncers, who have had the highest social status in India and "who have been the main culture bearers . . . since very ancient times" (Lanoy 1974, 210). It is the renouncers who have been, especially, the creators of Hindu spirituality and the teachers of the Hindu masses. Among these *saṃnyāsins,* the Śaṅkara tradition—which preserves and propagates Advaita—has been dominant, both in numbers and prestige, for more than 1,000 years. Indeed, over the past hundred years or so the authority of Advaita has increased because it was claimed as the central theology of the modern Hindu renaissance. It goes without saying, therefore, that its influence on the Hindu outlook and Hindu culture has been profound and pervasive. What it has to say about nature has been and continues to be important. To be sure, Advaita has long been known for its ascetic denial of the world in favor of spirit. Nevertheless, there is a need to look again at this aspect of the tradition in light of a certain naivete about it in the current literature on religion and ecology.

## Advaita's Supposed Natural Reverence

S. Cromwell Crawford, in his *The Evolution of Hindu Ethical Ideals,* argues that the "unitive view" of Hindu philosophy "can provide the basis for an environmental ethic." The philosophy of Brahman, he states, supplies the one essential ingredient of an environmentally sound ethic, namely, "reverence for nature." He points to the belief that Ātman (the true Self) is one with Brahman, the idea that all beings are separate only apparently, actually being emanations of the one Brahman. This gives Hinduism a "cosmic" outlook on life: "The nature of the self in Hinduism includes all lesser forms of existence." Indeed, the universe, though it appears to be merely material, is actually the universal consciousness itself. This doctrine, Crawford believes, "provides the philosophic basis for the Hindu's veneration of the natural world." In short, the Hindu tradition has an "ecological conscience" (Crawford 1982, 149–150).

Crawford, though he mentions Śaṅkara, does not seem to base his discussion directly on the views of Advaita as such. He seems rather to be relying on a study of primary scriptures, especially the Upaniṣads and the *Bhagavad Gītā,* interpreted from a more general Neo-Vedāntic stance. Eliot Deutsch, known for his work on Advaita, has also written on Hindu resources for environmental ethics. While he focuses more specifically on the nondualist Vedānta tradition, Deutsch's conclusions are nevertheless similar to Crawford's.

In a 1970 paper entitled "Vedānta and Ecology," Deutsch tries to show how Advaita contributes three ideas critical to any adequate environmental ethic. The theory of *karma* he sees as the South Asian statement of the first idea, that humanity is interconnected with everything in the natural world (see Coward's chapter in the present volume). The second notion, that humanity shares an essential identity with all other living things, takes the concept of interconnection further. Deutsch finds support for it in the specifically Vedāntic notion of the unity of all things in Brahman. This implies "that fundamentally all life is one, that in essence everything is reality." Deutsch argues that this way of thinking "finds its natural expression in a reverence for all living things." His final point is related to this notion of reverence. A logical corollary of the Vedāntic "emanationist" theory of creation, it is the idea that everything in nature has "intrinsic spiritual worth." In this connection, Deutsch offers Vedānta as an antidote to the Western dualism that alienates us from our bodies and from nature: "This means that for Vedānta there is no sharp duality between the body and spirit of man; each, rather, contributes to the whole and may express the full integrity of the whole" (Deutsch 1970, 81–83).

A common theme in both Crawford and Deutsch is the reverence for nature that the Brahman doctrine is supposed to encourage. Other writers have come to similar conclusions. In an article entitled "The Value of the World as the Mystery of God in Advaita Vedānta," Anantanand Rambachan writes: "The Advaita proposition about the essential unity of all existence in and through God . . . requires the development of a sense of identity and empathy with the natural world" (1989, 296). Lina Gupta likewise claims that the Brahman doctrine leads to the perception: "All parts of this Nature have intrinsic value; as such, all of Nature should be treated with dignity, kindness, and righteousness" (1994, 113).

Such portrayals of Hindu nondualism are all too common in the modern literature on religion and ecology (see Chapple 1993, 52; Kinsley 1995, 63, 65; Naess 1988, 24–27). In what follows, however, I will demonstrate that they are seriously misleading, at least to the extent that they claim to represent the classical Advaita of Śaṅkara and his followers.[2] First, I will show the falsity of the suggestion that Advaita Vedānta finds spiritual value inherent in nature. I will then proceed to explain precisely how Śaṅkara and his tradition devalue the natural world and how, in the Advaitic liberation experience, the world is not revered but rather tolerated until it passes completely away. My conclusion will be that Advaita Vedānta is not the kind of nondualism that those searching for ecologically supportive modes of thought might wish it to be.

## The Denial of Intrinsic Worth

Reverence implies value in the object being revered, indeed extraordinary value. Does Advaita lead its adherents to experience nature in this way? Does it teach that there is, in Deutsch's words, an "intrinsic spiritual worth" in everything in the natural world, such that nature should be cherished and protected?

*Bṛhadāraṇyaka Upaniṣad* (BU) 2.4 records a well-known dialogue between the sage Yājñavalkya and his wife Maitreyī. As Yājñavalkya is married, indeed to two wives, and shows considerable affection toward Maitreyī, we might hope for some sense of relatedness to things of the earth and nature. The sage, however, is about to leave the worldly life, and his wives, for a higher state, that of the ascetic renouncer. Asked by his wife for a final word of wisdom before he departs, Yājñavalkya is genuinely touched: "You have truly been dear to me; now you have increased your dearness." But his heart is truly elsewhere, and in a well-known passage he proceeds to undercut this tender valuation:

> Lo, verily, not for the sake of the husband is the husband dear, but for the sake of the Self (Ātman) is the husband dear. Lo, verily, not for the sake of the wife is the wife dear, but for the sake of the Self is the wife dear.

He continues with the same formula, including sons, cattle, wealth, caste status, and even the Vedas. His analysis broadens to include the most general: the gods, the beings, the worlds. "Lo, verily," he finally declares, "not for the sake of all is all dear, but for the sake of the Self is all dear."

Now, we might read this as a statement that the husband, wife, and so on have value as expressions of the Self.[3] But this is not what Yājñavalkya is saying. He is expressing the renouncer's devaluation of phenomena in favor of the supreme value of the Absolute. "With the intention of teaching non-attachment, the means to immortality," Śaṅkara explains, "Yājñavalkya creates a distaste for the wife, husband, sons, and so on, so they may be renounced" (*BUŚ* 2.4.5). Reverence for the things of life and nature, according to this view, is misdirected. It should be redirected toward its proper object: the Self. Yājñavalkya advises Maitreyī, "It is the Self [not the husband] that should be seen, heard, reflected upon, meditated upon." *BU* 1.4.8 declares, "One should meditate on the Self alone as dear." Expanding this notion, Vidyāraṇya tells us that, since the Self is the highest object of love, one should become indifferent to all objects of experience and transfer one's love to the Self. Objects of experience exist only for the sake of the experiencer, the Self (*PD* 12.32; 7.202, 206). In this way of thinking, value is located in the Self alone. Far from being worthy of reverence, all that is other than the Ātman, including nature, is without value. Thus Sureśvara: "That supreme [Brahman-Ātman] is declared to be the savor (*rasa*) of this effected [world], which is itself without savor."[4]

## Fear of Nature, Change, and Multiplicity

Advaita Vedānta embraces the negative evaluation of life in the natural world that is common among India's spiritual traditions. Speaking of the worldview of South Asian asceticism, Eliade points out that "when the sense of the religiousness of the cosmos has become lost . . . cyclic time becomes terrifying" (1959, 107). Advaita is a prominent example of this outlook. Far from encouraging reverence for nature, it inculcates fear of it. It is no accident that the practicing Advaitin is required by Śaṅkara and his tradition to be a celibate world-renouncer (see Nelson, 1993). Śaṅkara and his disciples see the universe of birth and rebirth (*saṃsāra*) as a "terrible ocean" infested with sea-monsters. In it we are drowning, and from it we need rescue (*MāUKŚ* 4, colophon). Individual selves trapped in *saṃsāra* go from birth to birth without attaining peace. They are like worms, caught in a river, being swept along from one whirlpool to another (*PD* 1.30). The sole purpose of the Advaitic *guru* is to overcome the monster of ignorance, together with its manifestation, the world (*PD* 1.1). What should our attitude to participation in life be? Śaṅkara answers that we should regard *saṃsāra* as a terrible (*ghora*) and vast ocean, existence in which should be feared, even despised.[5] He stipulates that, before beginning study of the Vedānta, a student must have intense yearning for liberation from this world (*mumukṣutva, BSŚ* 1.1.1). In this state, the student cries, "When and how, O Lord, shall I be released from the bondage of *saṃsāra*?"[6]

When we find mention of nonhuman species in Advaita literature, they are not—as Crawford and others have suggested—valued as fellow embodiments of spirit. Instead, they are held before us as symbols of the sufferings experienced in *saṃsāra*. The universe is not a community, but a hierarchy, in which gods enjoy great happiness, human beings experience moderate happiness and pain, and animals suffer "extreme misery" (*atyanta-duḥkha, BSŚ* 2.1.34). As the result of evil *karma,* souls are born as plants, which endure suffering when they are harvested, cooked, and eaten (*BSŚ* 3.1.24). Trees and other plants, we are told, serve as bodies in which the results of sins may be experienced through reincarnation (*VP* 7). *Chāndogya Upaniṣad* (*ChU*) 5.10.7–8 promises birth as a dog or a pig to those whose conduct has been evil. Those who neglect both spiritual knowledge and ritual works will be, the text tells us, reborn again and again in despicable births as "small creatures." Śaṅkara comments:

> They take birth as these small creatures—gadflies, mosquitoes, and other insects—which are reborn again and again. . . . " Be born and die," thus [their] mode of life is said to be caused by the Lord. They spend their time in mere birth and death, having opportunity for neither ritual nor enjoyment.

Such tiny creatures pass their lives in misery. They are "driven into terrible darkness from which it is difficult to escape, as if into a bottomless sea without any raft, without hope of crossing it."[7] For this and other reasons, the best possible birth is that of a human being. Better still, a human male. Better still, a male Brahmin, for such can become renouncers and escape the entire process (see *VC* 2 and Nelson 1993).

Distilled philosophically, the Advaitin's fear of the world leads to a radical antipathy to change and multiplicity. The Advaitin yearns for the unchanging, the radically unitary. He[8] defines the real as that which is absolutely without variation (*kūṭastha-nitya, nityaḥ avikriyaḥ, BSŚ* 1.1.4, 2.1.14; *BhGŚ* 2.16–18). It is pure, immutable consciousness, transcendent to the notoriously mutable world of nature. In precise contradistinction to the rich diversity of the natural universe, it is absolutely one, devoid of all multiplicity. The Upaniṣad (*BU* 4.4.19) declares of Brahman:

> Here there is no plurality (*nānātva*) whatsoever. One goes from death to death who sees here plurality, as it were.

Śaṅkara tells us, "Oneness (*ekatva*) alone is the single highest truth." Multiplicity arises as a product of false perception (*mithyā-jñāna*).[9]

## The Objectification and Devaluation of Nature

In Advaita metaphysics, the world of nature—the suspect world of change and multiplicity—undergoes a wholesale objectification and radical ontological devaluation. This process includes, of course, the human body and mind. Advaita, betraying its legacy from the archaic Sāṃkhya dualism, bases itself on a noetic discrimination (*viveka*) between Self and non-Self (*anātman*), a sorting-out process that is at least provisionally dualistic. Śaṅkara posits the capacity of "discrimination between the Eternal and the non-eternal" (*nityānitya-vastu-viveka, BSŚ* 1.1.1) as an essential preliminary to the study of Vedānta. The idea is restated in the title of a work attributed to Śaṅkara, the *Dṛgdṛśyaviveka,* "The Discrimination Between the Seer (*dṛk*) and the Seen (*dṛśya*)." This is not, to be sure, the familiar Western dualism of mind and body. We must discriminate instead between spirit and matter, the pure subject and its objects. Mind—along with emotion, memory, and all that constitutes personality—is regarded as a subtle form of matter. It must be rejected, together with body and nature, in favor of the pure awareness of the Self.

It is pointless, therefore, and utterly misleading to say that Advaita overcomes the Western duality of mind and body. If anything, the Advaitin is less comfortable in his body than the Westerner. The body, taken as a symbol of change, decay, and the bondage of spirit, is objectified as an object of mistrust. The *Aparokṣānubhūti* repeats, in no less than five successive verses, the refrain: "I am not the body, whose nature is unreal (*asad-rūpa*). The wise call this true knowledge."[10] The goal of the Advaita discipline is to realize that the Self is in fact other than matter, other than the body, and that its embodiedness is only apparent. The truth to be realized is that the Self is eternally liberated, eternally disembodied (*aśarīra*).[11]

But, we might ask, can we speak of "matter" in a system in which all is Brahman? The answer, surprising as it might seem, must be yes. For along with the idea of objectivity (*dṛśyatva*) comes the notion of insentience (*jaḍatva*). All that is other than Self is insentient, unconscious (*jaḍa, ajñāna*). Under *BS* 2.1.4–6 Śaṅkara argues against the Sāṃkhya that it is possible for Brahman, which is conscious, to be the cause of the world, which is unconscious. That the cause is conscious does not entail that the effect must also be. The world itself, as phenomenal, is in fact unconscious (*acetana*) and impure (*aśuddha*). Padmapāda, a disciple of Śaṅkara, tells us that ignorance, the source of the world-appearance, is an insentient power.[12] Since *māyā* (the creative power of Brahman) and all its products, including mind, are insentient, the universe as universe is unconscious, inert—as emphatically as in the dualistic Sāṃkhya. To say, as Crawford does, that the natural world is the supreme Consciousness itself is thus, in the context of Advaita, out of the question.

The goal of the Advaitin is in fact to attain a state of utter independence (*nirālambatā*) in which spirit is no longer reliant on, or limited by, the body, the mind, or the world of nature (see *AA* 123). Having objectified nature and reduced it to insentience, the ascetic takes the next step: he turns his attention away from it. To help him overcome his natural human identification with, and attachment to, his false phenomenal supports, the ascetic must practice "seeing the defects" in them (*doṣa-darśana*). The body, he must convince himself, is inert (*jaḍa*) and "besmeared with endless impurities."[13] Indeed, he must cultivate positive disgust for it and all other phenomena. Thus we read:

> The defects of the body, mind, and objects of experience are innumerable. The discriminating have no more liking for them than for milk-porridge vomited by a dog.[14]

This distaste should extend to include the entire creation. The Advaitin contemplates it as false (*māyika*), transient (*āgamāpāyin*), insignificant (*tuccha*), painful (*duḥkha-rūpa*), and to be abandoned (*heya*).[15] Ultimately the ascetic must aim at a total "renunciation of the universe" (*tyāgo prapañca-rūpasya, AA* 106).

All too predictably, the universe of nature from which the Advaitin seeks autonomy is constructed, both grammatically and symbolically, as feminine.[16] As *prakṛti*, "matter," and *māyā*, a mysterious projection, it is stigmatized by Śaṅkara and his followers as *mithyā*, less than real, something that ought ultimately be canceled (*bādhya*).

## Nonduality Through Denial

The truth is that Advaita Vedānta is not nondualistic in the sense of providing a vision that accepts the world as a facet of the real. A preliminary denial of the world as apprehended by egoic consciousness must, of course, be allowed for in any religious system. This accomplished, the upaniṣadic dictum "All this, verily, is Brahman" (*ChU* 3.14.1) would seem to lead to a final reclamation of the world, in the vision of the sage, as Absolute. This, in fact, is what occurs in Tantric nondualism, Mahāyāna Buddhism (especially in East Asia), and the teaching of Sri Aurobindo. The mixture of tantric elements in late Advaita, the tantric Advaita of Ramakrishna, and the Neo-Vedānta of Vivekananda and others has created the impression that a similar revalorization of the universe occurs in classical Advaita.[17] It does not. The orthodox Śaṅkara Advaita tradition never recovers the world as equivalent to the Absolute, as does Mahāyāna Buddhism with its radical equation of *saṃsāra* and Nirvāṇa. The Advaitin never reverses his flight from the terrors of time and nature, as do the *bodhisattvas* of the Mahāyāna, who commit themselves to remaining in the rounds of *saṃsāra* for eternity. We never find in Advaita a vision of the world as the moving expansion of the Divinity, as is found in Ramakrishna's nondualism. "O Mother," sings this tantric visionary, "Thou art verily Brahman and Thou art verily śakti. . . . Thou art the Absolute and Thou dost manifest Thyself as the Relative" (Ramakrishna 1974, 178). Ramakrishna compares the *jñānin* (knower) lost in the unity of the attributeless Brahman to a person who has climbed to the roof of a house and forgotten the steps altogether. This, however, is not the most complete realization:

> The vijnāni, who is more intimately acquainted with Brahman, realizes something more. He realizes that the steps are made of the same materials as the roof: bricks, lime, and brick-dust. That which is realized intuitively as Brahman . . . is then found to have become the universe and all its living beings. (Ramakrishna 1974, 155)

Ramakrishna explains that it is this realization that allows for *bhakti,* ecstatic devotion to God, even after Brahman-knowledge, a possibility that Śaṅkara denies (see *BhGŚ* 12.13; Nelson 1993).

Advaita cannot, of course, disavow the revelation that world and Brahman are identical. The Upaniṣads are emphatic on this, in more places than one.[18] But Advaita's fear of change and multiplicity prevents it from seeing the potential of these passages for sacralizing the cosmos. In Śaṅkara's interpretation of *ChU* 3.14.1, the world is Brahman only because it originates from Brahman (*brahma-kāraṇam*). This must be understood in light of Śaṅkara's *vivarta-vāda,* which states that the world is not a transformation of the ultimate, but an appearance (*vivarta*). It is an appearance in (not of) Brahman, having been falsely superimposed on Brahman, which serves as its ground (*adhiṣṭhāna, ālambana*).[19] To the extent that the world participates in the existence (*sat*) of the ground, it is real. But insofar as it appears at all—with form in any sense, in any way manifold or changing—it is false (*mithyā*). All that is made of clay is, considered as clay, identical with its cause. But only the clay is real (*mṛtikety eva satyam, ChU* 6.1.4; see *BSŚ* 2.1.14).

The ontological status of the appearance is dubious, inexplicable, as disclosed in the formula "indescribable as being either real nor unreal" (*sad-asadbhyām anirvacanīya*). Says Vidyāraṇya:

> The pot is not different from the clay, since it does not exist apart from the clay; but neither is it identical with the clay, as in the original unmolded clay it is not perceived. Therefore it is indescribable.[20]

From this we can again see how Advaita never escapes from its dualistic Sāṃkhya heritage. It cannot accept the world as identical with Brahman, for that would admit change into spirit. It therefore, like Sāmkhya, wants to keep the world outside the Absolute. But how can it do that without contradicting the upaniṣadic teaching "one only, without second" (*ChU* 6.2.1)? The world must be left hanging, neither real nor unreal, neither different from nor identical with the Absolute.

This is not Advaita's final position, to be sure. But the next step is not a re-evaluation of nature as divine. The logic of Advaita takes us rather toward denial. "The unreal portion (*anṛtāṃśa*)," Vidyāraṇya teaches, "need not be known, for knowledge of it is useless (*anupayoga*)."[21] All elements of experience other than pure knowledge (*bodha-mātra*) must be eliminated to arrive at Brahman, which is pure knowledge (*PD* 3.21). The *Aparokṣānubhūti* agrees: "One should see the cause [Brahman] in the effect [the world] and then reject the effect completely."[22]

This mode of thinking finds its logical culmination in the teaching that, from the highest (*pāramārthika*) perspective, the world simply does not exist. Indeed, the earliest recorded formulation of Advaita is Gauḍapāda's doctrine of non-origination (*ajāti*). The world of nature and all its creatures may appear before the mind of ignorance, but in truth they are not there. Despite appearances, the idea than any being ever comes into existence is false.[23] The causality of Brahman is asserted only provisionally, as a exegetical and pedagogical device. Having facilitated the interpretation of scripture and pointed our thinking toward the ultimate, it is finally cast aside. Speaking from the *pāramārthika* standpoint, Sureśvara declares that Brahman is neither cause nor effect (*akāryākaraṇa*). Not being a cause, it can, moreover, give rise to no effects (*TUBhV* 2.140–143). The result:

> [The world] does not now exist, because the Self is always [one] without second and absolutely unchanging. Therefore the final truth is that it never was, nor is [it now], nor will it [ever] come to be.[24]

Elsewhere, the same author tells us that, for those who have seen the real, the idea of the origination, persistence, and eventual dissolution of the universe is impossible (*BUBhV* 2.1.411).

## The Vision of the Knower: Does the Evaluation of Nature Change with Liberation?

In a more recent piece entitled "A Metaphysical Grounding for Natural Reverence: East–West," Deutsch (1989) presents an understanding of Advaita that is more authentic than that given in his earlier article, cited above. He allows that Advaita does present a "radical discontinuity between reality and nature" in which the latter is utterly devalued. Despite this fact, he still argues that Advaita provides the "surest foundation" for natural reverence. How is this possible? Advaita's devaluation of nature has, according to Deutsch's analysis, an unexpected result. The liberation (*mokṣa* or *mukti*) experience leads to profound detachment and hence true freedom, without which reverence is not really possible. "Paradoxically," he writes, "when nature is seen to be valueless in the most radical way, it can then be made valuable with us in creative play." Spiritual freedom enables us to approach nature with an authentic concern that is liberated from the desires of the ego and hence more truly aware of nature's real needs. If one can understand spirit, nature, and their relationship in the Advaitic way, thus attaining freedom and detachment, the world becomes "value-laden" and "a natural reverence then becomes one's basic attitude with nature" (Deutsch 1989, 265).

To evaluate this argument, we must look at what Advaita says about the experience of the liberated saint. The situation in which one realizes true freedom in this world, as described by Deutsch, Advaita calls *jīvanmukti* or "living liberation" (see Nelson 1996). If we look for indications of exactly how the liberated sage, the *mukta,* experiences the world, we find, in fact, no evidence of reverence for nature and no grounds for supposing it.

Where Śaṅkara does grant continued empirical experience for the *mukta,* it is under the analogy of a person with an eye defect. Even though they know better, he suggests, persons with double vision may continue to see two moons where, in fact, there is only one (*BSŚ* 4.1.15). The second moon does not disappear, despite knowledge of the true situation. The false appearance remains. Nevertheless they know that it is not really there; they are aware of it as a false perception. Maṇḍana uses this analogy—which shows it was current before Śaṅkara—and so does Śaṅkara's direct disciple, Padmapāda (*BSdh* 1, *PP* 9). It is common in the later literature.

The use of this "two-moon" analogy to explain the experience of the *mukta* shows that in Advaita there is no such thing as what has been called nondual perception, that is, immediate awareness of phenomena as not different from the Absolute (see Loy 1988, chap. 2). Phenomena may continue in the state of living liberation. But insofar as they do, they are experienced as false perceptions, irritating intrusions of a remote, inexplicable, empirical other into the self-luminous fullness of the Self.

Vācaspati confirms this suspicion, also using a disease model to explain the experience of the *jīvanmukta.* Knowers of Brahman may continue to engage in empirical activity, he tells us, but they do not believe in its reality.

> For example, even though knowing for certain that sugar is sweet, persons afflicted by a disorder of the bile continue to experience a bitter taste. [We know this] because having tasted [sugar], they spit it out, and then discard it.[25]

Again, the Advaitin compares the liberated sage's empirical experience to a false perception unhappily engendered by an illness.

Elsewhere we find other equally instructive metaphors indicating the value that the liberated nondualist places on his experience of natural phenomena. In his *Brahmasiddhi,* Maṇḍana describes the *jīvanmukta* as experiencing his body as no more than a shadow (*chāyā-mātra, BSdh* 3). Describing his experience of living liberation, Sarvajñātman declares, "I see my body as the cast-off skin of a snake . . . and the universe as if it were a burnt rope" (*SŚ* 4.54–55; cf. *BU* 4.4.7). Other Advaitins say the world becomes like a burnt cloth; it may retain its shape, but it is ineffectual (*SLS* 4). According to Vidyāraṇya the world of duality, if it remains in liberation, is like a dead rat or a corpse, i.e., a repulsive object that we would naturally seek to avoid. It is an edgeless weapon, once dangerous but now no longer able to harm. Even *brahma-loka,* the highest heavenly world, is seen to be "like straw" (*PD* 7.279–81, 6.285).

The theme of perceiving the world as unreal is common in later texts. The *Pañcadaśī* teaches that knowledge makes one conscious of the unreal nature (*māyātva, mṛṣātmatā*) of the universe. The liberated ascetic is conscious of the world's falsity (*jagan-mithyātva-dhī*). For him, the whole appearance is insignificant, negligible (*tuccha, PD* 4.40; 6.12–14, 129–130; 7.136). The *Pañcīkaraṇavārttika* (56–59), though initially stating that the *jīvanmukta* "does not see this world" (*jagad etan na vīkṣate*), nevertheless concedes that in practical life it is sometimes experienced. Still, the liberated sage perceives the world as false (*mithyā*), like mistaken directions or a divided moon, and the body as an illusion (*pratibhāsa*). The continuity of his karma is a "mere appearance" (*ābhāsa-mātra*).[26] The *Vivekacūḍāmaṇi* describes the *jīvanmukta* as "beholding this world as one seen in dreams."[27]

These are hardly terms of reverence. If not intended to generate positive disgust, they certainly continue the ascetic devaluation of nature, even in the liberated state. At best, the world for the *jīvanmukta* is ontologically hollow, exhausted, a mere husk or shadow. The goal is ultimately to go beyond empirical experience altogether.

## The Dissolution of the World

The comparison of the world to a dream is, in fact, quite common in Advaita. It is also described as a magic show or an imaginary city in the sky (*gandharva-nagara*).[28] The intended point is that, once Brahman is known, the sleeper awakes and the dream disappears, the false appearance dissolves. The *mukta* arrives at a state in which there is no experience of the world at all. Thus Yājñavalkya:

> But when to the knower of Brahman everything has become the Self, then what should one see and through what, what should one smell and through what, what should one taste and through what, . . . what should one hear and through what, . . . what should one touch and through what? (*BU* 4.5.15)

"Knowledge," Śaṅkara tells us, "arises of itself and cancels ignorance, and on account of that, this entire world of names and forms together with its inhabitants, which had been superimposed by ignorance, vanishes away like the world of a dream."[29] Again: "All the Upaniṣads declare that, in the supreme state (*paramārtha-avasthā*), all empirical experience is absent (*sarva-vyavahāra-abhāva*)."[30] Elsewhere he asserts that the material elements are dissolved (*pravilāpita*) by knowledge of Brahman "like rivers entering the ocean," after which they disappear (*vinaśyanti*). At this point, he declares, "pure knowledge—infinite, supreme, pellucid—alone remains."[31]

Instructive in this connection is a portion of Madhusūdana Sarasvatī's commentary on *Bhagavad Gītā* 3.18. The great Advaitin scholastic describes three stages in the attainment of *jīvanmukti,* a scheme he borrows from the *Yogavāsiṣṭha.* In the first level, the *yogin* is able to enter into a state of unconditioned absorption in the Self (*nirvikalpa-samādhi*). In this state, he can return to normal consciousness at will. He is called an "excellent knower of Brahman." With practice, he may attain a deeper absorption from which he cannot stir himself but must be roused by others. Such an adept is known as the "more excellent knower of Brahman." Then comes a state in which the meditative trance is so deep that the practitioner can neither emerge by himself nor be stirred by others. Here, the *yogin* has absolutely no cognition of difference (*sarvathā bheda-darśanābhāva*), being constantly and completely identified with the Self (*sarvadā tan-maya*) and totally cut off from empirical experience. In this condition, he makes no effort for self-preservation. God himself maintains his life and breath, and others take care of his physical needs. Abiding in supreme bliss, he is known as a "most excellent knower of Brahman."[32]

In her discussion of the implications of Mahāyāna nondualism, Klein (1985, 85) insists that a genuine nondualist model should be compatible with activity, otherwise it "would only perpetuate the patriarchal conviction that dichotomy—and thus hierarchy, opposition, and disharmony—is essential to purposeful accomplishment." The combination of activity and full awareness is no problem for the Mahayanist who has attained Buddhahood (Klein 1985, 84). How does the liberated Advaitin fare on this score? We find a striking account in Prakāśātman of the unsteadiness of the liberated sage's experience. In his influential *Pañcapādikavivaraṇa,* Prakāśātman teaches that the liberated sage cannot simultaneously be aware of the world and of his identity with Brahman. Oneness with the Self can be enjoyed only when he is lost in meditative enstasis (*samādhi*). At other times, because the continued activity of his bodily *karma* remains as a defect (*doṣa*) to cloud his vision, the knower will fall into consciousness of duality (*dvaita-darśana, PPV,* p. 786).

Bhāratītīrtha continues this theme. Like Prakāśātman, the author of the *Vivaraṇaprameyaṃsamgraha* believes that awareness of unity cannot coexist with the perception of multiplicity:

> One should not think it possible for the liberated sage (*jīvanmukta*) to have the experience of the oneness of the Self (*ātmaikyānubhava*) and the cognition of duality (*dvaita-darśana*), which are mutually contradictory, at the same time. For we do not assert their simultaneity, but rather that they arise and are overpowered in succession.[33]

Since the experience of nonduality is unstable, any activity that the liberated sage might engage in becomes an indicator that he has slipped into dualistic awareness. Even the *saṃnyāsin*'s minimal daily undertakings, sanctioned by scripture, signify shortcoming: "The activity of going about for alms," we are told, "is caused by karmic defects."[34] For this reason, it seems, Bhāratītīrtha formulates an intriguing argument for the well-known rule that the renouncer ought to abstain from Vedic rites. He tells us that such rituals must follow fixed schedules, and that, once begun, serious consequences follow if they are not seen through to their proper conclusion. The sage's participation in activity, however, is dependent upon the activation of karmic impulses, the operation of which is both unpredictable and unreliable: "For the knower of Reality, the emergence (*udbhava*) of the defect caused by commenced *karma* is not fixed as to place and time, and it is not possible for it to continue long enough for him to complete any [ritual] performance that he has undertaken."[35] For the sage to begin any ceremonial undertaking would be dangerous, for any moment he might slip back into *samādhi*!

The implication of such discussions, of course, is that the Brahman-knower somehow is more fully liberated when in *samādhi* than when engaged in activity. Despite their differences, all of these writers assume that any experience of the world is somehow based on a remnant of ignorance or karmic residuum. The ideal state must then be one in which there is no empirical experience, of nature or anything else. Hence the common use, even in Śaṅkara, of the term "isolation" (*kaivalya*)—borrowed from the dualistic Sāṃkhya-Yoga—to describe the final goal. In *kaivalya,* the *mukta* attains complete disjunction from the world. Mind, body, and nature are left behind. This is the Advaitin's true aim. The Śaṅkara *saṃnyāsin* yearns to be disembodied (*videha*). Living liberation is an exalted achievement, but literal disembodiment at death—termed *videhamukti*—is the preferred state.[36] The liberated sage whose *karma* requires him to bear temporal existence yet longer suffers, Vidyāraṇya tells us, like someone enduring forced labor (*viṣṭi-gṛhīta-vat, PD* 7.143).

## Conclusion

The logic of Advaita—and its longing for liberation from all form—move it inexorably in the direction of an acosmic monism. Consider the following declarations of Sri Nisargadatta Maharaj, a modern Hindu preceptor highly regarded in contemporary Advaita circles for his uncompromising nondualist vision:

> My consciousness, because of which I experience the world, is prior to everything. . . . When the dissolution of the universes took place [at the end of the previous world-age], I was unaffected.

> The fact is that nothing is born. There is no world. The world appears but it is not there. . . . There is no birth at all; even now there is no birth. (Powell 1994, 41, 200)

We find echoes here of Gauḍapāda's doctrine of non-origination (*ajāti*) and Śaṅkara's teaching of the disappearance of the empirical universe with the dawn of knowledge, both of which have been discussed above.

It is difficult to see in such modes of thought anything less than an extreme version of the world-negating, transcendental *dualism* that supports environmental neglect. Advaita achieves its brand of "nonduality"[37] not inclusively but exclusively, at great cost: the world of nature is finally cast out of the Absolute, out of existence. Finding here the same alienation from the natural universe that is manifest in the Jaina, Sāṃkhya-Yoga, and early Buddhist traditions, we might well ask whether Ludwig Feuerbach's epitome of Christian world-denial applies equally to the Advaitin ascetic:

> In the inmost depths of thy soul, thou wouldest rather there be no world, for where the world is, there is matter, and where there is matter there is weight and resistance, space and time, limitation and necessity. (Feuerbach 1957, 110)

No doubt the Advaitin would resist such a characterization. Nevertheless, I would argue that it is useful to reflect on the extent to which it is applicable. We have seen that Advaita's nonduality aims at utter transcendence. From the absolute (*pāramārthika*) perspective, the world is simply not there. From the empirical (*vyāvahārika*) perspective, the world is admitted as an inexplicable appearance, neither real nor unreal, neither different from nor identical with Brahman. To be sure, the ontological "indescribability" (*anirvacanīyatva*) that Śaṅkara's followers ascribe to the world is different from the assertion that the latter is a complete illusion. Advaita's critics often miss this point. But, that having been said, Advaita is still far from being a world-affirming doctrine. Again, Feuerbach's words are relevant:

> Nevertheless, there is a world and there is matter. How dost thou escape from the dilemma of this contradiction? How dost

> thou expel the world from thy consciousness, that it may not disturb thee in the beatitude of thy unlimited soul? Only . . . by giving it an arbitrary existence, always hovering between existence and non-existence, always awaiting its annihilation. (Feuerbach 1957, 110)

Ultimately, of course, this arbitrary existence must be transcended, and we have finally—to repeat—an acosmic monism. Whether or not these quotations from Feuerbach are truly representative of the spirit of Advaita (or, for that matter, Christianity) is debatable. Certainly, at least some strands of the tradition reflect this kind of world-loathing, and even at its best, classical Advaita fosters devaluation and disregard of the world. One might argue that Advaita was in some respects an esoteric *gnosis,* reserved for an elite, Brahmin circle of monks and scholars (see Nelson 1993). As such, it could be said, it represented a final, *mokṣa*-oriented critique of prior, more widely held Hindu visions, a small island of world-negation surrounded by a large sea of world sacralization. Still, that it came to carry—and still carries—such prestige in Hindu India cannot but entail important consequences for the ecological situation in the sub-continent.[38]

Into the waters of India's sacred Mother Ganges (*Gaṅgā Mātā*) millions of gallons of raw sewage, hundreds of incompletely cremated corpses, and huge amounts of chemical waste are dumped daily. As Alley points out in her chapter in this volume, an ecological disaster is fermenting: the situation is approaching critical (see also Conrad 1983 and Broder 1985). Yet a Benares taxi driver can still say, "The Ganges is God and [God] can't be polluted" (Conrad 1983). To be sure, the taxi driver is not formally an Advaitin. He nevertheless echoes, whether consciously or unconsciously, the thought of the Advaita tradition. He restates the argument of the *Kaṭha Upaniṣad* and the *Bhagavad Gītā* that the destruction of the natural, material component of life does not affect spirit:

> It is never born, nor does it ever die. . . . It is unborn, eternal, everlasting, ancient. It is not killed when the body is killed. . . . Weapons cannot cut it; fire cannot burn it; water cannot wet it; wind cannot dry it. (*BhG* 2.20, 23; see *Kaṭha* 1.2.19)

He reaffirms what he has learned through his culture from the preceptors of Advaita, namely, that only God (or Brahman) is fully real, that the divine is untouched by the pollution of the world, and that the natural universe is ultimately unimportant (*tuccha*).

The *Aparokṣānubhūti,* from which I have taken several passages in this paper, is a popular manual of Advaita attributed to Śaṅkara.[39] It is sold in flimsy paperback for three rupees. It is not difficult to imagine what attitudes toward nature our taxi driver might learn if he chanced to read, or hear a sermon based on, verse four of this text:

> Pure non-attachment is disregard for all objects—from the god Brahmā down to plants and minerals—like the indifference one has toward the excrement of a crow (*kāka-viṣṭhā*).[40]

Would this inspire him to revere nature as spiritual life, or would it rather teach him the irrelevance of nature to spiritual life?

## Notes

This chapter is a substantially revised version of an article that originally appeared in the *Journal of Dharma* (Nelson 1991). The author is grateful to the editors of that publication for permission to include it in this volume.

1. See Ruether 1975, 186–96; also chapters by Greta Gaard, Janis Birkeland, and Marti Kheel in Gaard 1993.

2. By "classical" or "orthodox" Advaita, I mean that represented in works of Śaṅkara, his disciples Sureśvara and Padmapāda, and the elite, conservative, scholastic *saṃnyāsin/paṇḍit* tradition that follows them. This chapter focuses almost entirely on this tradition, from Śaṅkara through Madhusūdana Sarasvatī and his disciples. I therefore exclude from detailed consideration other schools of nondualist thought, the tantric *advaita* of Sri Ramakrishna and his followers, the Śaivite influenced nondualism of Ramana Maharshi, and the views of modern academic interpreters of Advaita.

3. This is how my students in Southern California prefer to read it: "He sees his wife as an expression of God."

4. nīrasasyāsya kāryasya raso 'sau paramaḥ smṛtaḥ (*TUBhV* 2.421, p. 132).

5. tasmāc caivaṃ vidhāṃ saṃsāra-gatiṃ jugupseta bībhatseta ghṛṇī bhaven mā bhūd evaṃ-vidhe saṃsāra-mahodadhau ghore pāta iti (*ChUŚ* 5.10.8).

6. saṃsāra-bandha-nirmuktiḥ kataṃ me syāt kadā vidhe (*AA* 9). Mahāyāna Buddhism begins with this awareness of the painfulness and profound insufficiency of time and nature. In the end, however, it reverses this evaluation with a radical reclamation of and commitment to the world, as expressed in the ideal of the *bodhisattva*. See below.

7. tānīmāni bhūtāni kṣudrāṇi daṃśa-maśaka-kīṭādīny asakṛd āvartīni bhavanti . . . I jāyasva mriyasvetīśvara-nimitta-ceṣṭocyate I janana-maraṇa-lakṣaṇenaiva kālayāpanā bhavati I na tu kriyāsu bhogeṣu vā kālo 'stīty arthaḥ I . . . dhvānte ca ghore dustare praveśitāḥ, sāgara ivāgādhe 'plave nirāśāś cottaraṇaṃ prati (*ChUŚ* 5.10.8).

8. Since Śaṅkara requires that the practicing Advaitin be a male Brahmin *saṃnyāsin,* I deliberately avoid using gender-inclusive language when speaking of him. See Nelson 1993.

9. ekatvam evaikaṃ pāramārthikaṃ darśayati mithyājñāna-vijṛmbhitaṃ ca nānātvam (*BSŚ* 2.1.14).

10. nāhaṃ deho hy asad-rūpo jñānam ity ucyate budhaiḥ (*AA* 24–28).

11. *Maitrī Upaniṣad* 4.6, for example, speaks of "the supreme, the immortal, the bodiless (*aśarīra*) Brahman" (brahmaṇaḥ . . . parasyāmṛta-syāśarīrasya). See also *Kaṭha* 1.2.22, *BhG* 13.31, and *BSŚ* 1.1.4.

12. *jaḍātmikā avidyā-śakti* (Dasgupta 1975, 2:105; Satchidanandendra 1989, 388).

13. *ananta-mala-saṃśliṣṭa* (AA 36–37).

14. deha-doṣāṃs citta-doṣān bogya-doṣān anekaśaḥ / śunā vānte pāyase no kāmas tad-vad vivekinaḥ (*PD* 14.25).

15. Madhusūdana Sarasvatī's *Tīkā* on his *Śrībhagavadbhaktirasāyana* 1.32 (edited by Janārdana Śāstrī Pāṇḍeya [Varanasi: Motilal Banarsidass, 1961]).

16. Vandana Shiva, an important voice of the ecology movement in India, focuses almost entirely on the West, and the Third World's experience of colonialism, modernization, modernist developmentalism, and so on, as the root of her country's environmental devastation. She thus tends to ignore the pre-colonial aspects of the problem. Not trained as a scholar of religion, she also tends to give idealized readings of the environmental

implications of certain aspects of Hindu thought (see Vandana Shiva, *Staying Alive* [London: Zen Books, 1988], 40, 42). For more on this, see Sherma's chapter in this volume.

17. Neo-Vedānta adds to the mix, juxtaposed (paradoxically?) with the tantric element, ethical concerns derived from the West.

18. In addition to *ChU* 3.14.1, see, e.g., *BU* 2.4.6, "These worlds, these gods, these beings, and this all are this Self"; *MuU* 2.2.12, "This universe is but Brahman alone"; *ChU* 7.25.2, "All this is but the Self alone."

19. "[Brahman's] being the material cause consists in its being the substratum of the superimposition of the universe—or the substratum of the *māyā* that transforms itself with the form of the world" (upādānatvaṃ ca jagad-adhyāsādhiṣṭhānatvam, jagad-ākāreṇa pariṇamamāna-māyādhiṣṭhānatvam vā [*VP* 7, p. 155]).

20. sa ghaṭo na mṛdo bhinno viyoge sati anīkṣaṇāt / nāpy abhinnaḥ purā piṇḍa-daśāyām anavekṣaṇāt // ato 'nirvacanīyo 'yam (*PD* 13.35–36).

21. anṛtāṃśo na boddhavyas tad-bodhānupayogataḥ (*PD* 13.56).

22. kārye hi kāraṇam paśyet paścāt kāryaṃ visarjayet (*AA* 139).

23. *MāK* 4.4–5, 19, 31, 71; see also 2.32.

24. nedānīm advitīyatvāt kauṭasthyād ātmanaḥ sadā | bhaviṣyaty asty abhūn nāto vastu-vṛttam apekṣya tu (*TUBhV* 2.144, p. 75).

25. yathā guḍasya mādhurya-viniścaye 'pi pittopahatendriyāṇām tiktatāvabhāsānuvṛttiḥ, āsvādya thūtkṛtya tyāgāt (*Bhā* on 1.1.1, p. 80).

26. *Pañcīkaraṇavārtikam* of Sureśvarācārya, edited by T. H. Viswanatha Sastri (Srirangam: Sri Vani Vilas Press, 1970).

27. svapnālokita-loka-vaj jagad idaṃ paśyan (*VC* 425).

28. *PD* 2.68; *MāK* 2.31. See also *MāK* 2.15; *PD* 6.210–11, 18; 7.172, 175; 13.86, 95, 98; *AA* 56, 62.

29. vidyā svayam evotpadyate tayā cāvidyā bādhyate / tataś cāvidyādhyastaḥ saloko 'yaṃ nāma-rūpa-prapañcaḥ svapna-prapañca-vat pravilīyate (*BSŚ* 3.2.21).

30. evaṃ paramārthāvasthāyāṃ sarva-vyavahārābhāvaṃ vadanti vedāntāḥ sarve (*BSŚ* 2.1.14).

31. tadvat prajñānam anantam apāraṃ svacchaṃ vyavatiṣṭhate (*BUŚ* 2.4.12).

32. brahma-vid-variṣṭha (*GAD* on *BhG* 3.18). This scheme is also given in *JMV* 4.

33. na caivaṃ jīvanmuktasyātmaikyānubhava-dvaita-darśanayoḥ viruddhayoḥ sāhityaṃ prasajyeta iti mantavyam / na hi vayaṃ tayor yaugapadyaṃ brūmaḥ, kiṃ tu paryāyeṇodbhavābhibhavau (*VPS* 9.32).

34. bhikṣāṭanādi-pravṛttis tu ārabdha-karma-doṣa-mūlā (*VPS* 9.32).

35. tattva-darśinas tu ārabdha-karma-nimitta-doṣodbhavasya deśa-kāla-niyamābhāvena prārabdhānuṣṭhāna-samāpti-paryantam avasthānāyogāt (*VPS* 9.32).

36. Free in life, the *jīvanmukta* still looks toward the final freedom that occurs at death: "being liberated, he is [further] liberated" (*vimuktaś ca vimucyate* [*Kaṭha* 2.2.1]); "I shall remain only so long as I have not been released; then I shall attain" (*CU* 6.14.2). According to *JMV* 3 (quoting *Laghuyogavāsiṣṭha* 28.27), disembodied liberation (*videhamukti*) is "the state most pure, free from corruption." In it "even the luminous, creative aspect of matter (*sattva*), the support of the highest virtues, is dissolved" (samagrāgrya-guṇādhāram api sattvaṃ pravilīyate / videha-muktav amale pade parama-pāvane [*JMV* 3, p. 129]).

37. It could be argued that Advaita does not present a true nonduality, at least as the term is understood in contemporary philosophy of religion (see Loy 1988). But I do not wish to take up this issue here.

38. Again, I do not attempt to present here the interpretations of academic proponents of Advaita, Neo-Vedānta, nondualism, or perennialism, in India or the West. They have their own varied reasons for reading cosmic inclusivity, even natural reverence, into Advaita (reasons that the *saṃnyāsin*/*paṇḍit* exponents of traditional Advaita do not share). They especially will accuse me of misunderstanding the subtleties of the Advaita position. For example, it could be argued that Śaṅkara's denial of empirical experience in *mukti,* his assertion that the world vanishes "like a dream," could be explained as his way of saying that nondual perception is so radically different from ordinary perception as to be a kind of non-perception (see Loy 1988, chap. 2). Whether or not this is true, and I think I have shown it is not, such hermeneutical subtlety is beside the point when we are talking of the cultural and ecological influence of Advaita. I am concerned here with the effect that the Advaita tradition *as a whole* has had on the collective mind of South Asia. Also irrelevant, therefore, are any distinctions between the teachings of Śaṅkara and that of his later followers, important as such differences no doubt are in other contexts.

39. This attribution has been shown by scholars to be mistaken, but we are concerned here with the popular understanding.

40. brahmādi-sthāvarānteṣu vairāyaṃ viṣayeṣu anu / yathaiva kāka-viṣṭhāyāṃ vairāgyaṃ tad hi nirmalam (*AA* 4).

## References

### Primary Sources, with Abbreviations


*AA* *Aparokṣānubhūti or Self-Realization of [?] Śrī Śaṅkarācārya.* Edited and translated by Swami Vimuktananda. Calcutta: Advaita Ashrama, 1977. (All translations cited are my own.)

*Bhā* *The Bhāmatī of Vācaspati on Śaṅkara's Brahmasūtrabhāṣya.* Edited and translated by S. S. Suryanarayana Sastri and C. Kunhan Raja. Madras: Theosophical Publishing House, 1933. (All translations cited are my own.)

*BhG* *Bhagavad Gītā.* See *BhGŚ.*

*BhGŚ* *Śrīmadbhagavadgītā with the Commentaries Śrīmat-Śāṅkara-bhāṣya with Ānandagiri, Nīlakaṇṭhī, Bhāṣyotkarṣadīpikā of Dhanapati, Śridharī, Gītārthasaṃgraha of Abhinavaguptācārya, and Gūḍhārthadīpikā of Madhusūdana.* Edited by Wasudev Laxman Sāstrī Panśīkar. 2d ed. Delhi: Munshiram Manoharlal Publishers, 1978.

*BS* *Brahma Sūtras of Bādarāyaṇa.* See *BSŚ.*

*BSdh* *Brahmasiddhi by Acharya Maṇḍanamiśra.* Edited by S. Kuppuswami Sastri. Sri Garib Das Oriental Series, no. 16. Delhi: Sri Satguru Publications, 1984; reprint, Madras Government Oriental Series 4. Madras: Government Oriental Manuscripts Library, 1937.

*BSŚ* *Brahmasūtra with Śāṅkarabhāṣya. Works of Śaṅkara in Original Sanskrit,* vol. 3. Delhi: Motilal Banarsidass, 1985.

*BU* *Bṛhadāraṇyaka Upaniṣad.* See *BUŚ.*

*BUBhV* *Shri Sureshvarāchārya's Bṛhadāraṇyakopaniṣadbhāṣyavārtikam.* Edited by Shri S. Subrahmanya Shastri. Advaita Ratna Manjusha 23 and 30. Mt. Abu: Mahesh Research Institute, 1982, 1990.

*BUŚ* *Bṛhadāraṇyakopaniṣad with Śāṅkarabhāṣya.* Edited by Kāśīnātha Śāstrī Āgāśe. Ānandāśrama Sanskrit Series 15. Poona: Ānandāśrama, 1953.

| | |
|---|---|
| *ChU* | *Chāndogya Upaniṣad.* See *TPUŚ.* |
| *ChUŚ* | *Chāndogya Upaniṣad* with Śaṅkara's *Bhāṣya.* See *TPUŚ.* |
| *GAD* | *Gūḍhārthadīpikā* of Madhusūdana Sarasvatī. See *BhGŚ.* |
| *JMV* | *Jīvanmuktiviveka of Vidyāraṇya.* Edited and translated by S. Subrahmanya Sastri and T. R. Srinivasa Ayyangar. Madras: The Adyar Library and Research Center, 1978. (All translations cited are my own.) |
| *Kaṭha* | *Kaṭha Upaniṣad.* See *TPUŚ.* |
| *MāK* | *Māṇḍūkya Kārikā* of Gauḍapāda. See *TPUŚ.* |
| *MāU* | *Māṇḍūkya Upaniṣad.* See *TPUŚ.* |
| *MāUKŚ* | *Māṇḍūkya Upaniṣad* with Gauḍapāda's *Kārikā* and Śaṅkara's *Bhāṣya.* See *TPUŚ.* |
| *MuU* | *Muṇḍaka Upaniṣad.* See *TPUŚ.* |
| *PD* | *Pañcadaśī of Śrī Vidyāraṇya Swāmī.* Edited and translated by Swami Swahananda. Madras: Sri Ramakrishna Math, 1975. (All translations cited are my own.) |
| *PP* | *Pañcapādikā* of Padmapāda. See *PPV.* |
| *PPV* | *The Pañcapādikā of Śrī Padmapādācārya with the Pañcapādikāvivaraṇa of Śrī Prakāśātman.* Edited by S. Śrīrāma Śāstrī and S. R. Krishnamurthi Śāstrī. Madras Government Oriental Series 155. Madras: Government Oriental Manuscripts Library, 1958. |
| *SLS* | *Siddhāntaleśasaṃgraha of Appayya Dīkṣita.* Edited by S. S. Suryanarayana Sastri. Vol. 2. Madras: University of Madras, 1937. |
| *SŚ* | *Saṃkṣepaśārīrika of Sarvajñātman.* Edited and translated by N. Veezhinathan. Madras: University of Madras, 1985. (All translations cited are my own.) |
| *TPUŚ* | *Ten Principal Upanishads with Śāṅkarabhāṣya. Works of Śaṅkara in the Original Sanskrit.* Vol. 1. Delhi: Motilal Banarsidass, 1964. |
| *TU* | *Taittirīya Upaniṣad.* See *TPUŚ.* |
| *TUBhV* | *Taittirīyopaniṣadbhāṣyavārttika of Sureśvara.* Ānandāśramasaṃkṛtagrathāvaliḥ 13. Puṇyapattane: Ānandāśramasaṃsthā, 1977. |

*VC* *Vivekacūḍāmaṇi of* [?] *Śrī Śaṅkarācārya.* Edited and translated by Swāmī Mādhavānanda. Calcutta: Advaita Ashrama, 1982. (All translations cited are my own.)

*VP* *Vedāntaparibhāṣā of Dharmarāja Adhvarīndra.* Edited and translated by Swami Madhavananda. Calcutta: Advaita Ashrama, 1983. (All translations cited are my own.)

*VPS* *The Vivaraṇaprameyasaṅgraha of Bhāratītīrtha.* Edited by S. S. Suryanarayana Sastri and Saileswar Sen. Andhra University Series, no. 25. Waltair: Āndhraviśvakalāpariṣad, 1941.

## Secondary Sources

Broder, Jonathan. 1985. "Pollution Threatens the Ancient Purity of the Ganges." *San Francisco Examiner,* 31 March, 8–9 (Travel).

Callicott, J. Baird, and Roger T. Ames. 1989. *Nature in Asian Traditions of Thought: Essays in Environmental Philosophy.* Albany, N.Y.: State University of New York Press.

Chapple, Christopher Key. 1993. *Nonviolence to Animals, Earth, and Self in Asian Traditions.* Albany, N.Y.: State University of New York Press.

Conrad III, Barnaby. 1983. "A Daring Plan to Clean Up the Ganges." *San Francisco Examiner,* 3 July, 7 (P).

Crawford, S. Cromwell. 1982. *The Evolution of Hindu Ethical Ideals.* 2d ed. Honolulu: The University Press of Hawaii.

Dasgupta, Surendranath. 1975. *A History of Indian Philosophy.* Vol. 2. Delhi: Motilal Banarsidass.

Deutsch, Eliot. 1970. "Vedānta and Ecology." *Indian Philosophical Annual* 7. Madras: The Center for Advanced Study in Philosophy, 79–88.

———. 1989. "A Metaphysical Grounding for Natural Reverence: East-West." In *Nature in Asian Traditions of Thought,* ed. J. Baird Callicott and Roger T. Ames, 259–65. Albany, N.Y.: State University of New York Press.

Eliade, Mircea. 1959. *The Sacred and the Profane.* New York: Harcourt Brace Jovanovich.

Feuerbach, Ludwig. 1957. *The Essence of Christianity.* New York: Harper & Row.

Gaard, Greta, ed. 1993. *Ecofeminism: Women, Animals, Nature.* Philadelphia: Temple University Press.

Gupta, Lina. 1994. "Ganga: Purity, Pollution, and Hinduism." In *Ecofeminism and the Sacred,* ed. Carol J. Adams, 99–116. New York: Continuum.

Kinsley, David. 1995. *Ecology and Religion: Ecological Spirituality in Cross-Cultural Perspective.* Englewood Cliffs, N.J.: Prentice-Hall.

Klein, Anne. 1985. "Nondualism and the Great Bliss Queen: A Study in Tibetan Buddhist Ontology and Symbolism." *Journal of Feminist Studies in Religion* 1 (Spring): 73–98.

Lanoy, Richard. 1974. *The Speaking Tree: A Study of Indian Culture and Society.* London: Oxford University Press.

Loy, David. 1988. *Nonduality: A Study in Comparative Philosophy.* New Haven: Yale University Press.

Naess, Arne. 1988. "Self Realization: An Ecological Approach to Being in the World." In *Thinking like a Mountain: Towards a Council of All Beings,* ed. John Seed, 19-30. Philadelphia: New Society Publishers.

Nelson, Lance. 1991. "Reverence for Nature or the Irrelevance of Nature? Advaita Vedanta and Ecological Concern." *Journal of Dharma* 16 (July–Sept): 282–301.

———. 1993. "Theism for the Masses, Non-dualism for the Monastic Elite: A Fresh Look at Śaṅkara's Trans-theistic Spirituality." In *The Struggle Over the Past: Fundamentalism in the Modern World,* ed. William Shea, 61–77. Latham, Md.: University Press of America.

———. 1996. "Living Liberation in Śaṅkara and Classical Advaita: Sharing the Holy Waiting of God." In *Living Liberation in Hindu Thought,* ed. Andrew O. Fort and Patricia Y. Mumme, 17–62. Albany, N.Y.: State University of New York Press.

Powell, Robert, ed. 1994. *The Ultimate Medicine: As Prescribed by Sri Nisargadatta Maharaj.* San Diego: Blue Dove Press.

Ramakrishna. 1974. *The Gospel of Sri Ramakrishna.* Translated by Swami Nikhilananda. Abridged ed. New York: Ramakrishna-Vivekanada Center.

Rambachan, Anantanand. 1989. "The Value of the World as the Mystery of God in Advaita Vedānta." *Journal of Dharma 14* (July–September): 287–97.

Ruether, Rosemary Radford. 1975. *New Woman, New Earth: Sexist Ideologies and Human Liberation.* New York: Seabury.

Satchidanandendra, Swami. 1989. *The Method of the Vedanta.* London: Kegan Paul International.

**Rita DasGupta Sherma**

# 5

# Sacred Immanence: Reflections of Ecofeminism in Hindu Tantra

## Introduction

Religion has always had a far-reaching impact on our understanding of the nature and meaning of existence and has conditioned our response to the world around us. Thus, religion can be a source of inspiration for action that honors and sustains the earth and its myriad forms of life. Alternately, it can serve as an impediment to such action. Much depends on how religious doctrines are interpreted, and also, which doctrinal worldviews attain prominence.

In the case of Hinduism, resources exist for the development of a vision that could promote ecological action. The Vedas contain hymns praising the wonders of nature; vedic rites and rituals were most often concerned with creating more abundance and fruitfulness in the realm of daily life. Upaniṣadic philosophy seeks to discover the eternal present beneath the mask of fleeting moments and can enhance and enrich our experience of life if it inspires an awareness of the everpresent power of the universe that underlies everyday existence. Certain texts of the purāṇic period also expound doctrines that confer sanctity on the earth and give a positive valence to the phenomenal world.

The vision of the earth as a sacred hierophany and material form of the divine is perhaps most dramatically displayed in Goddess theology, first crystallized in the sixth century text—a part of the *Mārkaṇḍeya Purāṇa*—called the *Devī Māhātmya,* or "Glorification of the Goddess" (Brown 1990). This vision finds further expression in various purāṇic stories and culminates in the sophisticated systematization of the nature and functions of *śakti* (the highest feminine principle) in the tantric tradition. Hindu Tantra, especially in its Śākta (Goddess-worshipping) strains offers a rich and nuanced resource for the construction of an eco-conscious spirituality.

This chapter will explore the ontology of Hindu Tantra as a viable source of inspiration for the development of a Hindu ecofeminist theological vision. In order to clarify the position of ecofeminism in the ecology movement and the relevance of Śākta-based tantric philosophy to evolving ecofeminist spiritual conceptions, I begin the discussion with a brief review of the principles of ecofeminism. Certain Hindu concepts and beliefs such as *māyā, prakṛti,* purity/impurity categories, and the perception of female nature—which have traditionally been interpreted in a way that devalues material life, women, and the natural world—will then be examined through an ecofeminist lens and re-envisioned from the tantric perspective. Finally, I will address the question of the viability of the tantric worldview—which is based on the notion of the radical immanence of the divine—as a theological basis for a broader ecological perspective.

## Ecofeminism: A Paradigm Shift

The pollution that is ubiquitous in India today can, as we shall see, be partly explained by attitudes engendered by indigenous religious-cultural constructs of the world and nature. But the more immediate cause of the problem is, of course, the triumphant, rapid, and ill-planned growth of an imported phenomenon: the Western industrial and technological complex. It is as a protest against this phenomenon and its cultural, philosophical, and theological underpinnings that ecofeminism arose. Ecofeminism calls to our attention the fact that the commodification and objectification of all things has had a devastating effect on the fragile balance of nature, and in developing countries in particular has led to the exploitation of, and traffic in, women and children. Within the arena of global ecological movements, the contribution of ecofeminism lies in the recognition of the fact that the degradation and exploitation of women (and other marginalized peoples), and the destruction of nature, are rationalized by the same theoretical structure and often supported by the same religious constructs.

In order to understand the ideological basis of the ecological crisis, and ecofeminism's role in attempts to shift global perspectives on the environment, this essay begins with an analysis of the paradigm that justifies the destruction of the ecosystem and contrasts it with the new paradigm that is articulated by ecofeminism. We shall later see how this new paradigm can, in the Hindu context, find support in tantric philosophy.

The present mercantile paradigm is one of expansion and exploitation, one that denies the interdependence of all life. It draws boundaries between self-interest and that which is in the interests of the community at large, between the needs of humans on one hand and the needs of the planet as a whole on the other. Its epistemology relies solely on rational and empirical methods of knowledge, the marketplace is its temple, the fiscal "bottom line" is its God. This perspective—championed by major trans-national corporations and financial establishments—advocates the proliferation of a consumer monoculture and global technological industrialization and urbanization, which is to the detriment of the environment and rural economies. Based on a mercantile paradigm founded on a false principle of perpetual growth and projected on a macroeconomic scale, this worldview, in its entirety, is manifestly unsustainable materially, ecologically, psychologically and spiritually.

Over the last two decades, the ecofeminist movement has emerged to challenge the existing mercantile paradigm and has attempted to shift the values that underlie the current exploitation of the earth. Ecofeminist theory rests on the axioms of deep ecology and the structure of feminist thought. Feminism, in this context connotes that "which offers women liberation, whether that be in terms of freedom from oppressive thought, or oppressive social structures."[1] The ecofeminist ethic rests on the premise that the ultimate goal of feminism is the eradication of all systems of exploitation, whether against women, marginalized peoples, animals, or the earth. It holds that when nature and femaleness are linked, the honoring of one raises the position of the other in human thought and culture. Alternately, the denigration of either devalues the other. I will later explore the ramifications of this linkage in Hindu thought.

Ecofeminism seeks to recognize the interconnectedness of all life and to manifest this understanding in action.The ecofeminist assertion of the fundamental interdependence of all phenomena precludes the sanctioning of any action arising from a dichotomous worldview based on a radical self/other disjunction. Greta Gaard asserts that, although ecofeminists may agree with social ecologists that the primary cause of all oppression is hierarchy, ecofeminism adds that hierarchy occurs as a result of this self/other opposition (Gaard 1993, 2–3).

Since the publication of Rosemary Radford Ruether's *New Woman/New Earth* in the 1970s, the hermeneutics of feminist theologies have revealed the androcentric biases of certain patriarchal religions that identify nature with the feminine. Patriarchal religions are often religions of transcendence which tend to emphasize the ascetic, penitential, or renunciative form of the spiritual quest. Their theologies usually associate impurity with the body, equate temptation with women, and encourage world–negating visions, all of which support the diminution of women's status and the ravaging of nature. Once the superiority of a gender or a class of people has been established by religious tenets, service and servitude follow for that which has been deemed inferior. Such doctrines are strengthened by apocalyptic visions of impending doom and beliefs about the illusory or delusory nature of embodied existence, all of which devalue nature and creation.

When the soteriology of such traditions assimilates women to nature and embodiment, and then requires the transcending of sexuality, of worldly life, and of embodiment—all of which are associated symbolically with women—it sacralizes subjugation. Rationalization of oppression is achieved by the axiom that "superiority justifies subordination" (Warren 1990). The hierarchical dualisms of androcentric theologies (heaven/earth, spiritual/material, male/female) often supply the rationale for the superiority of the human male over women and nature.

For ecofeminism, "mind or consciousness is not something that originates in some transcendent world outside of nature, but in the place where nature itself becomes conscious."[2] A perspective which reflects an integration of mind/consciousness with nature/embodiment would give rise to a genuine theology of immanence. Ecofeminist spirituality tends to envision the divine not as ruler or heavenly monarch, nor as a removed and distant higher reality, but as "the immanent source of life that sustains the whole planetary community."[3]

As a theology of radical divine immanence, Hindu Śākta tantra offers a philosophical structure that can form the foundation for a Hindu ecofeminist spirituality. This paper attempts to explore certain life-affirming tenets of Hindu Tantra, juxtaposing them against aspects of traditional Hindu thought that tend to devalue materiality and, hence, nature.

I would like to make it clear at the outset that I am not suggesting that Śākta tantra provides the only spiritual answer, from a Hindu perspective, to the environmental crisis. What I am suggesting is that Śākta tantra contains an ontology, a theological emphasis on divine immanence, and certain doctrinal perspectives (on the initiation of women and their right to be lineage masters, purity, caste-consciousness, and so forth) that should be taken into consideration for inclusion in any serious eco-oriented reconstruction of Hindu theology.

## Hindu Ideological Constructs that Discourage Ecological Consciousness

The pervasive pollution that exists in India today has been blamed by some on the Indian appropriation of the Western industrial complex. It has been argued that the restructuring of societal and religious values as a consequence of industrialization has led to the resulting displacement of traditional pre-technological economic and ecological principles. To a certain extent, this is true. But that is not the whole picture. It does not account for the significant pollution stemming from non-industrial sources and caused by individuals and rural communities.

Moreover, if it is the ill-planned indigenous appropriation of Western industrial models that has had the most damaging impact, it is necessary, in the interests of realism, to examine the indigenous religio-cultural ideologies that allow or support the proliferation of native mercantile interests to the detriment of the environment, women, and marginalized peoples. It is not only the Western religious and philosophical tradition that has legitimized environmental destruction and human subjugation; non-Western traditions can also be held responsible. The quest for a Hindu ethic which could support and inspire ecological consciousness requires an analysis of the religious basis of commonly-held values which are not in harmony with the ecofeminist vision. An attempt to ameliorate the ecological situation in India must simultaneously involve an analysis of the implications of indigenous notions of nature and materiality for the environment.

Too often, those concerned with India's environmental devastation focus narrowly on the legacy of colonialism, modernization, Westernization, and so forth, ignoring pre-colonial aspects of the problem and issues which have entirely indigenous roots, such as the population problem. For example, the work of Vandana Shiva, an important voice of the ecology movement in India, is undergirded by a critique of the ideology of the Western techno-industrial paradigm. This oppositional stance vis-à-vis the West does not seem to allow sufficient room in Shiva's writings for a proper analysis of the indigenous Hindu cultural constructs that are also responsible for undermining present ecological efforts and have likewise provided a religious rationale for a lack of concern about nature. According to Shiva, "the modern creation myth that male Western minds propagate is based on the sacrifice of nature, women and the Third World" (Shiva 1988, 221). But, we must ask, are such attitudes found only in the West?

To be sure, Hindu culture as a whole has inscribed sanctity on much of nature. Holy pilgrimage sites form a network across India of sacred hierophanies wherein the divine is powerfully evinced. However, this has traditionally not led to a sense of stewardship.

Certain threads in the tapestry of Hindu beliefs weave a network of suspicion and denial over those aspects of life that most clearly manifest physical, material, embodied existence and reflect the precarious, uncontrollable, ephemeral nature of life. It seems that the creators of Hindu culture (largely male) were very much aware of the limited control that they had over the deterioration of their own bodies, the unpredictability of the cycles of nature, and the inevitable vicissitudes of worldly life. Women—due to their biological functioning—could more easily be identified with embodiedness and nature's unpredictable rhythms, viewed as more material than spiritual, and consequently perceived as more worldly, less pure than men. Hence, in India as elsewhere, nature, the human body and its functions, worldly life, and women were associated and enmeshed in a net of devaluation.

The devalued world reflected Hindu notions of femaleness, and women came to symbolize the worldly inasmuch as they represented embodiment and sexuality, family life, dependence on and embeddedness in societal structures, all of which came to be identified as *saṃsāra* and regarded as impediments to success on the spiritual path. The identification between family life and *saṃsāra* is so complete that certain Indian languages use the word *saṃsāra* to denote "household."[4]

Of the philosophical systems of classical Hinduism, Sāṃkhya, Vedānta, and Patañjali's Yoga are especially germane to our discussion. Sāṃkhya, though no longer a living philosophical tradition, has had great impact on classical Hindu thought and informs a wide spectrum of cosmological and soteriological perspectives. These three systems have often prescribed difficult ascetic disciplines or complex contemplative practices, in order to extricate the individual from the grip of the feminine principle, variously termed *prakṛti* or *māyā*.

The following three sub-sections identify features of Hindu doctrine or philosophy which can and do work against the development of an ecological consciousness in the Hindu psyche. These three aspects are (a) the identification of the feminine maternal with materiality, (b) the purity/impurity dichotomy, and (c) the devaluation of the feminine principle (*māyā*, *prakṛti*) and of the phenomenal world that it represents, by philosophies of transcendence. We will later see how the Hindu tantric perspective views these issues in a very different way.

## Feminization of Nature

Hindus sacralize various natural sites and invest them with a transcendent value. Such places thereby become pilgrimage sites and elicit great veneration (as Kinsley observes in his chapter in this volume). However, when natural phenomena are sacralized, they are also often feminized. This, as I shall show, undermines the potential for ecological benefit inherent in the process of sacralization.

Many Hindu sacred sites, natural phenomena such as rivers, certain types of plants and trees, the earth itself, and nature as a whole, are perceived as feminine. Even the landmass of India itself is seen as a goddess, Bhārat Mātā (Mother India). Bhūmi Devī (the goddess Earth), Gaṅgā Mātā (Mother Ganges), Bhārat Mātā, *prakṛti* (the feminine principle as "nature"), and all *śakti pīṭha*s (pilgrimage sites that are the mythic locations of various parts of the body of the Goddess Satī) reflect Hinduism's ubiquitous feminization of the natural world. In classical Hinduism, the symbolic feminization of nature is accompanied by the symbolic materialization of femaleness. The nature/material/feminine axis is then juxtaposed against the transcendent/spiritual/masculine axis, and relegated to a supporting role.

When natural sites and phenomena are feminized, they are also frequently maternalized and become thereby symbolically associated with the complex of expectations surrounding human motherhood in India. The construct of maternal nature in Hinduism is quite different than that of paternal nature. Biological reproduction is perceived as the germination of the male seed in the female field. The male seed contains all the individuating characteristics and thus bequeaths identity; the female field is the nurturing ground, providing succor. This concept is of great antiquity and is found in Vedic texts, the *Mahābhārata*, and the *dharmaśāstras*, especially the *Manu Smṛiti,* on which much of Hindu cultural codes of conduct are based. This flawed concept of reproductive biology thus has significant implications for kinship ties and the status of women.

Traditionally, the metaphor of seed and field has been used to rationalize the man's rights over the woman's body and her children, and his ownership of the fruits of her productive work. Her religiosity is also used, to benefit the male, as a currency to acquire spiritual favors from familial deities for his welfare. In the *smṛiti* literature, the female characters evince a great concern for the welfare of their male relatives and most importantly, devote their lives to the well-being of their husbands. The texts exhibit a conflation of divinity and domesticity, in which the woman's religious life revolves around the nucleus of her devotion to her husband, who undergoes an apotheosis through the institution of marriage.

All of a woman's activities—from cooking the family meal, to bearing children (sons), to the maintenance of a harmonious and well-ordered household—are perceived to be the worship of her personal deity, her *pati* (lord/husband). Her self-sacrifice on his behalf is analogous to the vedic sacrificial offering to the gods. Her daily domestic chores take on the role of ritual activity. Another outcome of this conflation of domesticity and divinity is the appropriation, by women, of certain yogic austerities (e.g., fasting) and religious vows (*vratas*) used as offerings to the deities in order to secure a specific spiritual or material benefit for the husband/god.[5]

Thus, though motherhood is highly honored in Hindu kinship systems, it seems that this honor is based on her self-negation, the ability to endure privations for the family, and the willingness to nurture and give sustenance, no matter what the sacrifice, with no thought of her own needs. When the natural world is feminized, the above conception of maternal nature is projected onto the earth or any natural phenomenon that is considered sacred. Consequently, whether it is Bhūmi Devī or Bhārat Mātā or a sacred grove, the expectation is that the sacred site will bless, nurture, purify or perform any other supportive maternal act without any requirement for sustenance in return. Due to such expectations, the potential for ecological benefit to the sacred place is not fulfilled.

The Gaṅgā is an example of this vision of the quintessential nurturing, purifying, sustaining mother; she is a goddess whose material manifestation is the water of the river that bears her name. Viewed through the lens of the homologized feminine/maternal/earth perspective, the Gaṅgā is not in need of our support and nurturance; she is loved and revered precisely because she can bear the burden of our demands, allow us to use her for our sustenance, and cleanse us materially and spiritually. According to the *Agni Purāṇa* (6.61) the Gaṅgā is "the healer of the sickness called *saṃsāra*." Kelly Alley elaborates on this understanding of the Gaṅgā in her chapter in this volume.

## Purity and Pollution

Concepts of ritual purity and impurity are found in religious traditions all over the world. Some religions delineate differences between subtle gradations of purity while others only endorse general guidelines. Hinduism contains complex social and religious structures for the containment and purging of ritual impurity.

In general, there is an wide range of human activity that is associated with religious impurity. In Hinduism, three areas of concern appear to be most important in reference to this category. These are bodily emissions, inauspicious aspects of life-cycle events, and elements that problematize the creation and maintenance of sacred space.

Since bodily emissions are natural to biological functioning, the focus lies not on preventing their occurrence but on their containment, control, and purification. In this category, menstruation is perceived as a carrier and harbinger of impurity. The impurity bestowed by it marks all Hindu women as belonging to a permanently impure gender.

The life-cycle event that causes the highest degree of impurity is death. The impurity bestowed by death affects the entire family, but especially the wife, whose widowhood renders her permanently inauspicious. Death is so defiling for Hindus that no religious ceremony for the deceased can take place within the confines of a sacred place. Cremation grounds are far removed from habitations, and the corpse must be offered to the purifying grace of fire and the ashes to water. The latter leads directly to the contamination of bodies of water. Again, Alley's chapter in this volume offers a detailed examination of the effects of the notions of purity and impurity on the river Gaṅgā.

The establishment of a space as sacred requires boundaries to exclude elements of impurity and the performance of ritual purification to enhance and maintain purity. Rites of purification usually employ a variety of elements or actions which are often understood to contain intrinsic purifying potency. Fire and water are commonly used elements in purificatory rites. The constant preoccupation with the erection of boundaries between sacred and profane space spills over into the categories of secular life and forms a pervasive, boundary-consciousness informed by dichotomies such as pure/impure, acceptable/untouchable, and self/other. Clearly, such notions are not compatible with the ecological vision which supports a perception of space and self as interconnected and continuous.

Another method of purging ritual impurity in purity-conscious religions is to transfer it onto human or animal scapegoats. In the

Hindu context, the transference of impurity occurs on a large social scale and creates an entire social class of scapegoats. The institution of "untouchability" was created, in fact, to bear a huge share of the burden of impurity so that the higher castes would be free of the defilement created by the performance of the "untouchable jobs." And, as Frank Korom points out in his chapter in this volume, they are free as well of any culturally induced sense of responsibility for cleaning up their environment, whether it be trash in the streets or toxic waste.

Purity has far-reaching moral, psychological, and spiritual connotations in Hinduism which are reflected in the dual spheres of Hindu religious life—that of the religiously observant householder and the salvation-seeking renouncer/ascetic. For the householder, the propitiation of the gods, initially through vedic sacrificial offerings and later through worship rituals, was seen as foundational to the proper execution of dharmic obligations. Ritual specialists, the Brahmin priests, occupied a central position in the psyche of the Hindu male householder, since they enabled him to obtain the celestial blessings deemed necessary to the discharging of his duties and insuring the well-being of his family. Ritual specialists placed a premium on purity as a function of the sacrificial ritual. Purity was considered tantamount to the noumenal, and by default, the phenomenal became, symbolically, the realm of the impure. I have already shown how, as materiality came to be more closely associated with femininity, women began to be identified with impurity.

Just as *dharma,* or religious duty, was the spiritual center of the householder's life, *mokṣa* was pivotal to the aspirations of the ascetic, who had renounced worldly life. *Mokṣa* is liberation from the vicissitudes of life and from the cycle of rebirth through the realization of the self as divine. Purity-consciousness as an component of ascetic practice is seen as early as the *Maitrī Upaniṣad,* which outlines five of the eight parts of the later, fully developed Yoga system. These five parts deal with control of breathing, control of the senses, meditation, focusing the mind, and mystic absorption (the state of identification of the self as pure spirit). All of these emphasize the normal state of the body as something needing purification and strict control. The body is depicted in the *Maitrī Upaniṣad* as a polluted and revolting object:

> This body arises from sexual intercourse. It passes through development in hell [the womb]. Then it comes forth through the urinary opening. (3.4)

Purification of the body is attainable through the practice of austerities. Another verse advises, "One should be in a pure place, himself pure, abiding in pureness (*sattva*), studying the Real (*sat*). . . ." (6.30).

As the ascetic tradition developed, desire—in the broadest sense—came to be perceived as the nemesis of purity. "Woman" came to be seen as the symbol for desire. To give in to desire (*kāma*) is to enmesh oneself in *prakṛti.* Thus the aim of liberation became the realization of the self or *puruṣa* in its purity, a state that could only be achieved by complete ascetic purification of the body and mind. According to Sāṃkhya doctrine, the purification required for such a realization was radical: it involved a complete disjunction from material nature (seen as the feminine adjunct of the self) in order to enable the latent spiritual nature (perceived to be the masculine aspect) to fully manifest itself. Yoga was seen as the technology of transformation that transmuted the impure nature of the body and mind through processes of control, and thus made the goal of *mokṣa* attainable.

Although purity is not disconnected from notions of hygiene, it has a deeper meaning in the Hindu context than physical cleanliness (*śauca*) alone. The purity referred to in Hindu texts often has spiritual-ritual significance, whether in the realm of the householder or the ascetic. Thus things pure and impure are conceived in a representational way; association with certain objects, phenomena, or individuals represents a danger of pollution to one's entire spiritual-psycho-physical being which would require extensive rituals of purification to remove. If the purificatory rites are not performed in an appropriate manner, the danger to one's outer and inner self remain.

Ecological action involves active participation in cleaning up the environment. This is especially true in the Indian context, where a great deal of pollution is caused by non-industrial sources and where financial resources are scarce, impeding the processing of waste at the local and national level. Taking responsibility for environmental work at the grassroots level often requires the willingness to take responsibility for the proper disposal of personal waste and to be physically involved in cleaning up the surrounding environment. This would be problematic for many Hindus operating under a purity-conscious mentality, because the process of cleaning the environment of a given community would bring the individual in contact with numerous persons, objects, and substances deemed defiling in a religious sense. This would violate, in the process, the individual's personal spiritual-ritual purity (see Korom, this volume).

Thus, the notion of purity as a ritual category variously informs the functions of the whole spectrum of Hindu religious life in general and the religious and secular lives of women in particular. It also promotes the conception of the phenomenal world as steeped in impurity. This purity/impurity dualism is, of course, an example of the kind of dichotomous perspective that is inconsistent with the insight of interconnectedness that is integral to the ecofeminist vision.

## Philosophies of Transcendence and the Devaluation of the Feminine Principle

Religious traditions often emphasize either a metaphysic of transcendence or a metaphysic of immanence. Philosophies of transcendence valorize a supreme being, a higher realm, or a state of realization that transcends embodiment, the emotions, and connectedness to material life, and discourages a passionate engagement with the world, seeing full participation therein as a hindrance to spiritual growth. It follows that if the phenomenal world and embodiment are perceived as obstacles, no deep commitment can be expected to this earth or its living forms. At best, a disengaged attitude of "non-harming" (*ahiṃsā*) can be hoped for. A religious tradition emphasizing transcendence would also be expected to give a high valence to spiritual individualism, discouraging a sense of community and the communal responsibility that this partnership with others would entail.

As we have seen, the Sāṃkhya system espouses a stark spirit/matter dichotomy, identifying pure spirit, *puruṣa*, as the masculine principle and materiality/phenomenality as the feminine principle, *prakṛti*. Patañjali's Yoga system adopts Sāṃkhya philosophy and uses various techniques to cleanse the self of its material nature as much as possible, considering its embodied state, to enable the pure spirit within to shine through with radiance or *tejas*.

*Prakṛti* (also referred to as *pradhāna*, primal matter) exists solely for the purpose of catering to the emancipation of the *puruṣa*. Vyāsa in his commentary on *Yoga Sūtra* 1.18, explains that *pradhāna* is transformed into the world, the sense organs, and the intellect, all of which are distinct from the *puruṣa*. For the seer, the whole world of objects serves only one function, that of catalyzing liberation. Liberation is the recognition that the true nature of the seer is distinct from the object seen. When this knowledge is attained, the objective world of nature—the realm of the feminine principle—serves no further purpose for the liberated seer.

Patañjali's *Yoga Sūtras* betray a highly negative attitude toward embodiment. *Yoga Sūtra* 2.5 states that regarding the transient as the permanent, the impure as the pure, and the corporeal as the self is the root of *avidyā* (spiritual ignorance). By way of explanation, Vyāsa uses the female body as a metaphor for impure corporeality:

> The body has been declared by the sages as something impure. Such a loathesome and unclean body is, however, regarded as pure; for example, in the description "This maiden, charming and tender as a new moon, with her body appearing to be formed of honey or nectar, has emanated, as it were from the moon. . . ." This also illustrates the false cognition of the sacred in what is profane, and of the beneficial in what is really not so.

In *Yoga Sūtra* 2.40, Patañjali states: "From the practice of purification, aversion towards one's own body is developed and thus aversion extends to contact with other bodies." In his commentary, Vyāsa writes that when revulsion arises for one's own body, a distaste develops for the company of others, for one finds it distasteful to come into contact with the unclean body of another person. Swami Hariharananda, a commentator on the *Yoga Sūtras*, adds that by performing the prescribed yogic practices, the desire for contact with women and children totally disapppears.[6] Clearly, such a perception of the self as separate and aloof from the world and other beings is precisely the antithesis of the ecofeminist view of the self as relational and interconnected with the whole planetary community.

The Sāṃkhya-Yoga philosophy of dichotomies thus engendered a dualistic conception of reality (*puruṣa* and *prakṛti*), with the material, feminine principle—increasingly identified with "woman"—as the devalued component. Sāṃkhya is not the only philosophical system to devalue the feminine, creative principle. Another feminized principle, *māyā*, is important in Hindu cosmology and soteriology. The term *māyā* appears early in Vedic literature where it is associated with the female divinity Virāj who is described in terms of a universal creative force that animates all life. Even in these early references, the imagery connected with *māyā* is ambivalent, as shown in the *Atharva-Veda* (8.10.22):

> She rose; she came to the *asuras*. The *asuras* called to her, "O Māyā, come here.". . . Dvimurdha Artvya milked her; he milked that very Māyā. The *asuras* subsist on that Māyā.[7]

Although she is identified with Virāj, a feminine, immanent, cosmic creative force, *māyā* is described in this passage as nurturing the *asuras,* demonic beings who are clearly deluded and ignorant. Teun Goudriaan identifies three ways in which *māyā* can be conceived: (1) it is the power of creating (or projecting) an appearance (later understood as illusory); (2) it is the actualization of that creation; and (3) it is the manifest, material form that has been created (or projected) (Goudriaan 1978, 2–3). Hence, *prakṛti*, the feminine principle of materiality, can be apprehended as a form of *māyā*. This connection between *māyā* and *prakṛti* is developed more fully in later literature. In the *Śvetāśvatara Upaniṣad* (4.10), *māyā* is clearly identified with *prakṛti*: "Know then that *prakṛti* is *māyā* and the wielder of *māyā* is the Great Lord. This whole world is pervaded by beings that are part of Him." In another passage, *māyā* is again seen as analogous to mutable materiality and is conceived as an obstacle to be overcome. *Pradhāna* here expresses the same meaning as *prakṛti*—phenomenal, perishable materiality.

> What is perishable is *pradhāna* (primary matter). What is immortal and imperishable is Hara (the Lord). Over both the

> perishable and the self (*ātman*) one God rules. By meditating on Him, by uniting with Him, by reflecting on His being more and more, there is finally cessation from all the illusion of the world (*māyā*). (1.10)

The negative perception of *māyā* is also suggested in the *Praśna Upaniṣad* 1.15–16, where it is associated with crookedness (*jihma*), falsehood (*anṛta*), and trickery; the passage proclaims that only those free of *māyā* will attain knowledge of the supreme Brahman. The notion of Brahman as a transcendent reality, removed from the natural world, is reflected in *Bṛhadāraṇyaka Upaniṣad* 2.3.6, where Brahman is described as not this, not that (*neti, neti*), that is, not of this phenomenal world.

As the Advaita Vedānta tradition developed and the principle of *māyā* became increasingly important, a clearly unfavorable connotation surrounded the concept of *māyā*, and the world which was created by it came to be correspondingly devalued. *Mokṣa* required the renunciation of the world, a lower reality in the clutches of *māyā*, which became associated with *avidyā*, or metaphysical ignorance. The knowledge of Brahman was *vidyā* and led to *mokṣa*: liberation from the karmic cycle, and from embodied existence. *Māyā* thus became the power of false perception that veiled the highest reality, condemned beings to *saṃsāra*, and was responsible for the ignorance that led to suffering. It was through the delusory power of *māyā* that the formless, attributeless, undifferentiated Brahman appeared as the universe of multiplicity—the conditioned, relative, morphogenic field. Lance Nelson discusses the repercussions of the negative Advaitin attitude towards the multiplicity and mutability of the natural world in his chapter in this volume.

It is clear, then, that the feminine principle (*māyā, prakṛti*), representing mutable materiality, is not revered or honored in Sāṃkhya, Yoga, or Advaita Vedānta—three major schools of classical Hindu philosophy. Hence, any interpretation of the inspirational value of the "feminine principle as nature" for ecological purposes must be re-evaluated. Vandana Shiva, for example, sees positive implications for ecology in the *puruṣa/prakṛti* construct. She writes that Western views of nature are informed by man/woman, person/nature dichotomies and claims that "in Indian cosmology, by contrast, person and nature (Purusha-Prakriti) are a dialectical unity which forms the basis for a harmony between man and woman and between humans and nature" and thus "becomes the basis for ecological thought and action in India" (Shiva 1988, 40). According to Shiva's reading of the *puruṣa/prakṛti* construct, there is no ontological dualism between self and nature. Shiva's understanding of the interplay between the masculine and feminine principles is inaccurate from the classical Hindu Yoga-Vedānta perspective. Her interpretation is only viable from the standpoint of Tantra, where the Goddess as *prakṛti/śakti* is, as we shall see, identified with the highest spiritual principle, and there is, ultimately, no dualism. Without this qualification, however, Shiva's praise of the *puruṣa/prakṛti* doctrine is somewhat misleading.

Ecological work is only possible in cooperation, and depends not only on self-interest, but also on one's inner convictions and ethics. Our ethical perspectives are often unconsciously formed by our religious traditions and their attitudes toward the relations between oneself and the world. These attitudes shape our perceptions of individual responsibility to the environment. When a respected, deeply-rooted tradition devalues the world, sees phenomenal existence as a lower reality, and maintains that our highest goal should be to realize the transcendent nature of our true, inner selves as opposed to, higher than, and disconnected from this material world, it has an impact on our psyches. It can profoundly affect the way we think, feel, and act toward the environment around us—whether or not we are actually engaged in the recommended spiritual practices of transcendence.

## Sacred Immanence: The World According to Tantra

Fortunately, there is much in the Hindu worldview that *is* supportive of worldly life and reverential toward nature and the feminine. Non-ascetic, life-affirming perspectives are as old as the Vedas and remain a vital force to this day. Perhaps the clearest expression of the Hindu valorization of the phenomenal world is Śākta philosophy, which views the universe as the material manifestation of Śākti (in this context, the Universal Goddess). Śākta theology perceives the supreme being/highest reality as the Great Goddess. She is not only the conscious matrix of the universe and the power of becoming, she is also the primordial material substance of the universe. Śaivism, particularly nondual Kashmir Śaivism, also includes the manifest world as a fully real aspect of the divine and incorporates the concept of *śakti* as divine immanence in its ontology and soteriology. The feminine principle, and hence the material world, is given a higher value in the Śaiva/Śākta ethos than it is in the philosophies of transcendence previously discussed. Indeed, as we shall see, it is given absolute value.

The idea of sacred immanence, the affirmation of the force and presence of the supreme reality in every dimension of the manifest universe, is powerfully expressed in Śākta theology and is the hallmark of tantric Śāktism. Models of the Goddess represented by Śākta strains in Hindu theology expand the roles of the divine feminine and associate the feminine with transcendence as well as immanence. It is, however, an emphasis on the sacred nature of "this world" and the valorization of earthly life that especially distinguishes Goddess theology.

The term *śakti* appears early in Vedic literature, where it tends to denote some sort of potency, capability, or service (Pintchman 1994, 97–98). The *Śvetāśvatara Upaniṣad* (4.1) describes a Supreme Being who, by the manifold application of his creative power (*śakti*), manifests the polymorphous universe. The conceptualization of *śakti* as a creative force inherent in all things began its development in the philosophical literature of the classical period but did not represent a fully systematized principle representing a Universal Goddess with cosmogonic, soteriological, and theistic significance until the sixth or seventh century C.E. (Coburn 1991).

The first elaboration of the theology of the Great Goddess occurs in the *Devī Māhātmya*, which melds together various philosophical constructs—such as *śakti, māyā, prakṛti,* and the notion of ultimate reality—to create a portrait of the Great Goddess. The text portrays her as the causal agent of creation and implicitly identifies her with the ground of Being—thus endowing her with transcendence. As Śakti, she is the creative and sustaining, as well as the destructive (or reabsorptive) power, underlying the manifest cosmos. She is the matrix of the universe and as *mūla prakṛti*, its material substance. Hence, she is fully immanent in the world. Indeed, according to the *Devī Māhātmya*, the Goddess does not employ a specific power or force to create the world—ultimately, she *is* the world, and all its diverse forms are aspects of her Being. This is of paramount importance for an ecofeminist spirituality that seeks a metaphysical perspective in which the earth fully expresses the divine.

## Tantric Concepts of the Nature of the Feminine

Hindu Tantra offers a profound and detailed system for goddess worship and enfolds within its canon the glorification of women, not only as nurturing aspects of the Goddess, but as embodiments of her manifold energies: creative, destructive, delusory and enlightening. Tantra draws on various ancient, indigenous village and tribal practices, and on the legacy of vedic rites. In doing so, it articulates methods of connecting with the pervasive but diffuse powers of the Goddess in order to channel these energies for spiritual or material benefit. Material life is not devalued or perceived as an obstacle to liberation. Neither are women, though they are still consistently identified with the material principle.

Tantrism transforms the Sāṃkhya dualism into a bipolar view of reality, which in its final resolution becomes a consummate nondualism, unlike the Sāṃkhya–based "dualistic nondualism" of Advaita Vedānta (see Nelson, this volume). Tantra accepts the Sāṃkhya correlation of materiality with the feminine principle, but the latter is elevated in stature to accommodate tantric reverence for the Great Goddess as the genetrix of the universe. Despite the fact that she is the principle of change and materiality, which other schools devalue, she is perceived as the ultimate reality—transcendent as well as immanent, approachable, and all-pervasive.

The *Mahānirvāṇa Tantra* 4.34–35 presents Śakti as matrix of the universe of forms, the source into which the universe dissolves at the end of cosmic cycles, and in the vision of *sādhana* (spiritual practice), identical with Brahman. In the text the Devī explicitly states, "As union with the Brahman is attainable through worship of Him, so it may be attained by sādhana of me" (4.4). In *Kulacūḍāmaṇi Nigama* 1.16–17, the Goddess, in the form of Bhairavī, describes the first stage of her being as the quiescent, primordial, transcendent state where she is in blissful union with

Śiva (*śiva–śakti–samarasa*). This state is identified with ultimate reality, the *niṣkala* Brahman.

Some texts endow Śakti with an ontological primacy. S. B. Dasgupta maintains that there are tantric as well as puranic texts which perceive Śakti as the ultimate truth and Śiva, the *śaktimat* (the "holder of Śakti"), as her male aspect:

> [This] view makes Shakti the highest truth, and Shiva is conceived of as the best support of Shakti. Shakti is the more important as the contained, while Shiva is the container. . . . It is from this point of view that the Mother worshippers would give a subsidiary place to Shiva, whereas Shakti as the Mother is taken to be the highest. (Dasgupta 1982, 72–3)

Dasgupta (1982, 73) identifies Tripurasundarī in the *tantras,* and Lalitā Devī in the *Brahmāṇḍa Purāṇa* with this aspect of the Goddess. The *Vāmakeśvara Tantra* expresses the primacy of Śakti (Tripurasundarī) in a way that clearly emphasizes her autonomy and dynamic, causative self-agency.

> Tripura [the Goddess] is the ultimate primordial Śakti, the light of manifestation. At dissolution She is the abode of all things, still remaining Herself [not merged into Śiva]. . . . After she emanates there is no more need for the Lord. Devoid of Śakti, Śākta [Paramasiva] cannot act. . . . She becomes Śiva, with no qualities, no characteristics, devoid of the form of Time . . . She becomes oneness, pure being . . . She is pure spirit and also the process of manifestation. (4.4–16)

The *Lalitā Sahasranāma* describes her as *ātma* (the Self in all beings, v. 617), *paramā* (Supreme Being, v. 618), and *ekākinī* (the One, v. 665).

Because the omnipresent power of Śakti is felt to be expressed most fully in the feminine, worship of women is enjoined. There are many references in tantric literature to the proper procedure for the worship of woman as Śakti incarnate. *Kulacūḍāmaṇi Nigama* 2.30 describes for the *sādhaka* (male tantric aspirant) details of the ritual worship of his wife—including the process of initiation if she is not yet an aspirant. The woman is not expected to remain a silent object of devotion during the worship (*pūjā*); she is a dynamic partner in the process and must feel the awakening of Śakti within to bless the worshipper and experience spiritual ascent herself.[8]

The Śākta *tantras* forbid the horrors of *satī*, child marriage, and other abuses. The tantric texts encourage education for women before marriage and advise the *sādhaka* to honor all women (see for example, *Kulacūḍāmaṇi Nigama* 3.46–57). *Mahānirvāṇa Tantra* 11.49, for example, prescribes fasting for two days as a punishment for a man who has spoken rudely to a woman, and 11.45 recommends execution for the rape of a woman "even if she is the wife of a *caṇḍāla* (outcaste)." *Yoni Tantra* 7.9 proclaims, "Women are divine, women are life, women are truly jewels." The *Kulārṇava Tantra* advises:

> Pay respect to womankind, as they are all born of the family of the Divine Mother. Punish them not in however mild a manner, whatever the transgression. Their excellences, not failings, are to be stressed. (chap. 7, p. 75)

The catholicity of Tantra extends beyond recognizing the divine presence in all women to the recognition of the divinity of all persons regardless of gender, class, or caste. The *Kulārṇava Tantra*, for example, proclaims that upon initiation into the tantric path, all status-based distinctions of caste and class dissolve.[9] And *Mahānirvāṇa Tantra* 4.42 asserts that even a *caṇḍāla* (a member of a highly "polluted" caste responsible for the disposal of corpses) who has knowledge of Brahman is superior to a Brahmin who does not possess this knowledge.

The *tantras* encourage women's spirituality and confer on them the right to be a *guru* to male or female disciples. Indeed, in some texts initiation by a female *guru* is considered the highest form of induction into tantric *yoga*.[10] Even now, there exist families in Mithila who follow the tradition that the initiation must be given by a woman.[11] To the enlightened Śākta tantric, the whole universe is Śakti, but she is most powerfully manifest in the feminine way of being. Although the feminine principle has ontological equivalence to the masculine principle, it enjoys primacy in the spheres of ritual, devotion, and iconography.

Sanjukta Gupta has argued that divine role models have a significant impact on the way women perceive their own spiritual potential and the way in which men react to women's religious autonomy. She maintains that tantric perceptions about the nature of the divine feminine—foundational to the Śākta and Śaiva ethos—are particularly conducive to women's religious autonomy, and stand in sharp contrast to the distinctly different conception of the feminine principle in Vaiṣṇava sects. She maintains that Śaiva reverence for the independence and self-agency of Śakti has translated into respect for women's right to spiritual self-determination, as evidenced by the lives of important Śaiva poetess saints (Gupta 1991, 195). By contrast, in Vaiṣṇava theology, Śakti, though present, has no autonomous power. Always under Viṣṇu's active control, she is the divine model for the ideal Hindu wife—in perfect submission to a life of service and dedication to her husband. Unlike the Śaiva *yoginīs* described by Gupta, who were able to identify with an image of the divine feminine that was dynamic and independent, the only role models traditionally available to Vaiṣṇava women saints were "ideals of conjugal fidelity and meek docility." This led, for example, to frustration at their femaleness—as in the case of the saint Bahina Bai—or compromise with the difficult circumstances—as in the case of Mīra (Gupta 1991, 209).

According to tantric doctrine, Śakti contains all aspects of life: creation and dissolution, bliss and agony, the sensual and the sublime. Since the supreme power of Śakti is personified as feminine, these different facets are worshipped, or rather meditated upon, as female deities, often referred to as the Mahāvidyās. Tantric ritual worship is primarily directed to these goddesses, who are seen as manifestations of the energy of Śakti. Each Mahāvidyā represents a specific energy, composed of certain frequencies that have a pattern of their own and a vibrational field that creates different intonations. These frequencies are most often represented by visual patterns called *yantra* and auditory patterns called *mantra*.

The powerful female deities of tantric *sādhana* (psycho-spiritual discipline) are strong, autonomous, often fierce, and invariably possess self-agency and self-determination. In Śākta Tantra, it is the male principle that is reduced to a *śava* (corpse) when deprived of the animating force of the Goddess.

In the tantric texts, it is often the gentle goddess Pārvatī who asks Śiva to reveal the knowledge necessary for liberation. Various other gentle goddesses such as Kāmeśvarī and Mātaṅgī (a form of Sarasvatī) are also revered. Nevertheless, it is the fierce goddesses that dominate tantric ritual and iconography. Deities such as Tārā, Kālī, Dhūmāvatī, Chinnamastā, and other similar awe-inspiring female deities pervade tantric lore.

Kālī, perhaps the most complex and awesome manifestation of the Great Goddess, has a special position of honor in many *tantras*. She is affirmed as the supreme Mahāvidyā in the *Yoginī, Kāmākhyā,* and *Niruttara*, and the *Nigamakalpataru* and *Picchilā* assert that the greatest *mantra* is that of Kālī.[12] In the *Mahānirvāṇa Tantra*, Śakti is most frequently referred to as Kālī.

The ubiquitous presence of Kālī and other volatile, independent goddesses reflect tantric conceptions of the nature of the divine feminine and its affirmation of those aspects of the creative feminine that are unpredictable, dynamic, imperious, and transformative. Tantra goes beyond the maternal and nurturing aspects of the nature of the feminine—both human and divine. This perspective encourages a more reverential attitude toward nature and natural phenomena that are identified with goddesses and discourages the notion that sacred locations will nurture and sustain without adequate care and reverence. The *Tantrarāja Tantra* directly identifies different cosmic geographical locations with various aspects (*vidyās*) of Śakti.[13] This outlook can be extended to honor the needs of the earth as a whole when conceived as a living embodiment of the Divine Feminine.

Through a process of devolution, Śakti first manifests as (a) *cit-śakti*, the power of consciousness, then as (b) *māyā-śakti*, the power which veils the unity underlying the multiplicity of phenomena and creates the appearance of manifold realities, and finally as (c) embodied life in her form as *prakṛti-śakti*, the primordial substance of the universe. She is the energy that moves in the cosmic cycles of creation, preservation, destruction (or reabsorption into herself) and recreation. Because she is the force of consciousness inherent in all things, and indeed because all things are actually modes of her being, the natural universe is imbued with sanctity.

Through increasingly sophisticated rituals and meditations, tantric disciplines seek to create an awareness of the sacred presence of Śakti in all things. Through the sacralization of the mundane actions of daily life, and of the sensate functions of the human body, the aspirant is led from a dualistic mentality to the experiential realization of the ground of ultimate reality, a timeless, ineffable unity. The tantric perspective encompasses an ultimate reality that, in the vision of enlightenment, is an absolute nonduality. Yet, it is nevertheless dynamic, including and allowing for multiplicities and even dichotomies. Through tantric *sādhana*, a dualistic apprehension of reality is transformed into this state of unity-consciousness—one that includes, not obliterates, the ever-changing world of manifold forms and phenomena. In his chapter, Lance Nelson outlines the contrasting Advaita view, which betrays a deep antipathy to the mutability and multiplicity of the natural world.

## The Tantric Perception of Embodiment

From an ecofeminist perspective, the perception of the body is of prime importance. A negative view of the body results in the devaluation of nature which, for each individual, is first and foremost experienced in his/her physical being. Philosophy and knowledge may point the way to enlightenment, but sights, sounds, smells, color, texture, taste and touch all evoke far deeper echoes of feeling and resonate with our sense of being. Tantrics have been cognizant of this and have endowed the body with a positive valence. They have emphasized sensate experience in their rituals, honoring the order and functioning of nature in an immediate and intimate way.

The human body is regarded very differently in Tantra than in the orthodox ascetic traditions. Of primary importance is the fact that the tantric practitioner does not have to renounce ordinary life, since Tantra affirms the divine presence in all activity. Consequently, a practitioner can lead the life of a householder and simultaneously practice her/his *sādhana* without fear of contamination from the impurities of everyday activities.

In the tantric paradigm, there is no stark matter/spirit dichotomy splitting body and soul, in which the body is the devalued pole of the axis. In tantric doctrine the body is not only the means of spiritual realization, it also contains the truth which is to be realized. Tantra recognizes that the ultimate reality underlying the universe is the same as that which forms the foundation of the embodied state. The microcosm reflects the macrocosm. Harsh ascetic practices mortifying the "impure" flesh are not needed here;

essential instead is the conscious, emotional, cognitive, and physical realization of the inherently pure nature of the body. The *Kulārṇava Tantra* (chap. 6, p. 65) declares that "the body itself is the temple . . . enclosed in *karma*, it is *jīva* [the individual self], freed from *karma*, it is Sadashiva [the Supreme Self]." Tantric texts often include an implicit critique of Brahminical asceticism:

> They hope to realize the highest by austerities emaciating the body! If the ignorant could achieve freedom only by punishing the body, the serpent should lie dead when the anthill is struck. . . . Truly, such privations and self-denials are only for deceiving the world. The only means for liberation is the knowledge of the Truth, the Divine.[14]

The cycle of life, seen as the stage on which the play of the divine feminine is enacted, is sacred to Tantra. Sanctity is inscribed on the female body, which is the symbol and vessel of Śakti's own creative energies. The biological functioning of a woman's body no longer does her dishonor in the eyes of Tantra; it is what marks her as the Goddess incarnate (see, for example, *Yoni Tantra*). Her sexuality, on which Sāṃkhya projects the imprisoning, polluting power of the *guṇas*, becomes in Tantra a means for the realization of the sublime.[15]

As we have seen, Sāṃkhya-influenced soteriologies see the individual as consisting of both *prakṛti* and *puruṣa*, but maintain that the two belong to completely separate realms, one purely spiritual, the other purely material. The realization of the self as *puruṣa* involves a complete rejection of materiality, devaluing the body and the natural world in the process. Tantric doctrine is life and world-affirming and maintains that realization (experiential knowledge of the immanence of the divine in all things) can only take place on this earth and in this body. The *Kulārṇava Tantra* states:

> It is only on this earth—that too in this human body—that one can choose one's line of development and take the means to progress accordingly. . . . For truth is to be realized here in this life. . . . It is vain to expect that things will change and improve after death in worlds which are happier than ours. As here, so there. (chap. 1, p. 21)

To be sure, Śāṃkhya does believe in *jīvanmukti* (liberation while living), and Advaita Vedānta affirms that *mukti* must first be realized—though it cannot be completed—in the body. However, these systems approach embodiment, and embeddedness in nature, as the obstacles which must be transcended in order to know the ultimate freedom.[16] In Tantra, the body-mind complex is not to be transcended; it is to be divinized. Tantra's method is not rejection but inclusion and transmutation.

Whereas the ascetic working within the Sāṃkhya-Yoga perspective begins with the assumption of impurity as inherent in the embodied state,[17] the tantric practitioner starts with the belief that his/her body is the phenomenal manifestation of the noumenal. This is evidenced in the tantric notion of a series of vital currents flowing in the subtle body through inner, etheric channels and seven focal points of energy called the *cakras*. Each *cakra* level represents a progressive state of realization. The life force, or power of Śakti, called the *kuṇḍalinī* resides in a dormant state at the lowest *cakra* in the average person, resulting in the individual remaining unaware of the power and presence of Śakti within. The objective of much of tantric *sādhana* is the catalyzation and dynamic rechanneling of the force of Śakti upward through the *cakras*.

The sacramentally sensuous nature of tantric rites is designed to arouse the dormant *kuṇḍalinī*. The passionate, emotional intensity of tantric *sādhana,* turned to the goal of realizing the immanence of the divine within, aims at directing the *kuṇḍalinī* through the *cakras*, vivifying each center and raising it to the conclusion of its journey in the final *cakra*, wherein lies unity-consciousness. The key to the attainment of this goal is meditation on the *cakras* as the abodes of different manifestations of Śakti and Śiva, which enhances the aspirant's perception of the body as the site of celestial forces.

This penchant for sacralizing the body finds further expression in the tantric practices of *bhūta-śuddhi* and *nyāsa*. In *bhūta-śuddhi*, the aspirant engages in the Yoga practice of *prāṇāyāma* (breathing techniques) and chants Devī-*mantras* (sacred sounds that embody the Goddess) in order to clear all negative thoughts, emotions, and sensations and to heighten the perception that his/her body is divine. In the *nyāsa* ritual, the practitioner makes affirmations such as, "The vital forces of the blessed Goddess are here (in the body) . . . may the speech, mind, sight, hearing, and sense of smell of the Great Goddess which is in me ever abide here in peace and happiness."[18] Repeating various Devī-*mantras*, the aspirant touches all parts of the body with the fingertips, ritually infusing the body with the power of Śakti. In Tantra, the body is already the abode of the Goddess; the rituals of *bhūta-śuddhi* and *nyāsa* only serve to communicate this to the consciousness of the seeker, and by raising that consciousness, both rituals serve to manifest the indwelling Śakti.

## The Feminine Principle and Non-Dualism in Tantra

In Hindu thought, the Absolute is that which is not conditioned by finite relations either because it (a) *excludes* all relations, thus automatically transcending them as an aloof "Other" or (b) *includes* all relations, synthesizing while still exceeding them. The first conception is the Advaita Vedānta understanding, the second, the Śākta. This difference can have very significant implications for conceptions about the world, embodied life, and nature.

In Advaita Vedānta, for example, the world is said to be a product of *māyā*, both *māyā* and its result being ontologically dubious: neither real (for nothing is real but the *nirguṇa* Brahman) nor totally unreal (for the world does have a provisional validity as the common experience of all who are not liberated). *Māyā* in Tantra, on the other hand, is the fully real power of the Goddess to differentiate herself into the multiple forms of the fully real universe. In Tantra, reality has two aspects: the manifest world and self-existent, unmanifest potentiality. The universe is the embodiment of the Goddess and as such, not only real in an ontological sense, but a sacred hierophany.

In Tantric doctrine, the Goddess as *prakṛti-śakti* is the primordial material substance of the cosmos; all forms and phenomena are her myriad manifestations. As *cit-śakti,* she suffuses all life with intelligence/consciousness, and as *māyā-śakti,* she becomes the necessary power of differentiation by which all contrasting forms and phenomena are created and the underlying unity is veiled. *Māyā-śakti* is also the power by which the multiforms of the universe can sustain individual identities and not be immediately reabsorbed into an undifferentiated whole. Distinct phenomena neither melt into a unity in which their individual qualities are subsumed, nor do they exist in independent solitude wrapped in their distinctness. They exist in a state of interdependence, an idea much emphasized in the relational ecological perspective of ecofeminism. The Divine Mother is *śakti,* the world manifests through her, but even when acting as *māyā-śakti*—the power that veils the true unified nature of reality and as such, can be considered delusory—*śakti* is never unreal (*asat*) or unconscious (*acit*), though it may appear that way to the unenlightened.

Śiva and Śakti as *sat-cit-ānanda* (Being-Consciousness-Bliss) exist in indistinguishable union (*śiva-śakti-samarasa*) as formless, undifferentiated, infinite potentiality before the Divine Mother transforms herself, through the power of *māyā*, into the manifest universe of opposing pairs. Even when the world is manifested, it is not "other" than a form of the Absolute, which (unlike the *nirguṇa* Brahman of Advaita), is not static but dynamic. Hence the oft-proclaimed tantric dictum: "Śakti is not different from Śiva; Śiva is not different from Śakti." As the *Kulārṇava Tantra* states, all dichotomies and dualities are manifestations of Śiva-Śakti, and as such, derive from a foundational unity, and partake of the fullness of ultimate reality:

> Prakriti and Purusha, Support and the Supported, Bhoga and Moksha, Prana and Apana, Word and Meaning, Injunction and Prohibition, Happiness and Misery, all these manifestations that go in pairs, the constant Duals of the presiding and effectuating poises are forsooth Ourselves [Siva and Sakti]. All forms, male and female are but emanations of Us Two. (chap. 3, p. 45)

### Purity in Tantra: "To the Pure, All Things Are Pure"

Arising out of an established orthodox hierarchical society based on distinctions, Tantra proceeded to shatter distinctions and proclaim the innate purity of all things and the potential divinity of all beings. There are no historical records that ascertain the exact date of the emergence of Tantra. Many elements of tantric ritual and praxis reach back into the pre-Vedic period of Indian history.

The notion of a Great Goddess as the matrix of the universe seems to have had currency in the pre-Vedic period and continued to be the prime focus of those peoples of the Indian sub-continent who were geographically, or for reasons of caste, far removed from the major centers of Brahminical Sanskrit culture.[19] Unassimilated tribal people, outcastes, lower castes, and women all contributed to the tantric tradition.[20]

Tantra evinces an attitude of condescension towards orthodoxy and orthopraxy, and through the central ritual of its "left-handed" branch (as we shall see), subverts the logic of purity and pollution around which orthodox Hindu practice revolves. It presents a worldview in which the goal of the aspirant is a purity so sublime that all things, no matter how seemingly impure, are pure to his/her gaze. *Mahānirvāṇa Tantra* 4.23 states that for the individual "who knows that the Brahman is in all things and eternal, what is there that can be impure?" In the tantric worldview, purity and impurity are states of mind which we project onto objects. Tantric doctrine asserts that to the pure, all things are pure. The *Jñānārṇava Tantra* maintains that, based on this belief, and with the objective of demonstrating the same to the aspirant, the ritual use of substances ordinarily accounted impure may be appropriate for certain qualified practitioners.[21]

Tantric ritual divides itself into the left-handed and right-handed paths—*vāmācāra* and *dakṣināċāra* respectively—so named after the respective locations of the female aspirant in relation to the male in the ritual setting. In *vāmācāra*, the woman is seated on the left of the man. In *dakṣinācāra*, she is on the right and does not engage in sacramental sex, but is nonetheless seen as the embodiment of Śakti and worshipped accordingly. That two schools of Tantra would name themselves in this fashion is one indicator among many of the pivotal significance of women in the tantric tradition. Some have argued that the function of the woman in tantric ritual is to further the man's *sādhana*—that she is no more than a ritual object. However, this is not borne out by the numerous references in tantric texts regarding the initiation of women,[22] the experiences of modern tantric *yoginīs*,[23] and the tradition of *viparīta-rati,* where the woman adept (*sādhikā*) is the *vāmācāra* aspirant and the active agent.[24] It is in the texts and rituals pertinent to the *vāmācārins* that the rebellious stance against orthodox Hindu thinking is most visible.

The cardinal ritual of left-handed tantra is the *pañca-tattva* (ritual of the five elements), which includes five forbidden constituents. The ritual requires the participation of two people, a man and a woman—preferably both tantric aspirants.[25] The *pañca-tattva* is often referred to as the five M's (*pañca-makāra*) since the elements of the ritual begin with *m*: *māṃsa* (meat), *matsya* (fish), *mudrā* (parched grain), *madya* (wine), and *maithuna* (sexual intercourse). The ritual involves a complex liturgy invoking the presence of the Goddess by means of secret *mantras, devī-yantras,* and *śakti-pūjā* (worship of the woman). Participants partake of the sacraments. Aspirants are not permitted to undertake *pañca-tattva* without many years of rigorous physical and mental discipline (yoga and meditation) and an advanced visionary (mystical/experiential) understanding of the omnipresence of the divine.[26] The *pañca-tattva* ritual's conflation of the sacred and the profane is highly offensive to conventional Hindu sensibility and runs counter to all normative models of purity and impurity, sanctity and desecration in Hindu consciousness.

It seems that the element of shock inherent in the ritual becomes itself a highly potent catalyst capable of catapulting the mind out of its familiar dualistic thought patterns and into the realm of unity-consciousness.[27] By partaking of five defiling things in the setting of this meditative ritual, the aspirant affirms their underlying purity and shatters the cognitive processes of the unenlightened mind that fractionalizes all life into myriad brittle distinctions. No difference remains between the clean and unclean, the sacred and the profane, purity and impurity. All phenomena take on the glow of divine power and presence.

The iconoclasm of the *dakṣinācārins* is less concrete and more doctrinal; it is in theory rather than praxis. The *dakṣinācārins* do not perform the *pañca-tattva* ritual in a literal fashion, but use substitutes for the five forbidden elements. All sects of Tantra, however, acknowledge that the quest for self-realization involves an awareness of divine omnipresence. Asserting the doctrine of the universality of Brahman and the innate sacrality of all things, the *Mahānirvāṇa Tantra* repeatedly admonishes against traditional practices such as pilgrimage, elaborate funeral ceremonies, and other actions aimed at purifying the body and mind.[28] The text argues that since Brahman, the principle of ultimate reality which is the source of all, cannot be polluted, the aspirant who has realized this unity may consume anything as food, may take action without regard to purity, and have concourse with any individual regardless of caste or state of *śauca* (physical purity), for s/he recognizes the fundamentally pure nature intrinsic to all phenomena.

Many tantric texts contain an explicit critique of the logic of placing a negative spiritual valence on certain actions of daily living or specific substances or persons deemed impure. The *Kaulāvalīnirṇaya Tantra* portrays the tantric adept in a ritual setting in the following manner:

> On the left is the woman skilled in dalliance and on the right is the drinking cup, in front is hog's flesh cooked hot with chillies . . . Kula dharma [the sect of Tantra] which contains the teachings of the Great Guru [Śiva] is deep in meaning and difficult of attainment even by Yogis.[29]

In the above passage, several elements representing impurity are present. First, the woman is seated on the left, and the left side is considered impure; the implied sexual activity would pollute any ritual environment; liquor, an impure substance, is being imbibed; and of all meats, hog's flesh is considered particularly defiling. Certain tantric texts seem to take great pleasure in subverting and reversing traditional orthodox Hindu convictions and practices regarding impurity.

One significant source of active pollution is the graveyard; contact with the dead is deeply defiling, especially if the dead are of lower castes. The cremation ground is where the tantric must "confront and assimilate, in its most concrete form, the meaning of death together with the absolute social defilement it entails."[30] The tantric aspirant must learn to love and accept the Divine Mother of the universe in all her forms because enlightenment entails the existential realization of the presence of Śakti in all her functions, processes, and manifestations. Only when a seeker sees the vision of Śakti in all things, beautiful or hideous, pure or impure, is s/he truly liberated.

Tantra prides itself on being the spiritual vehicle for passionate, dynamic, and intense people. Tantra recognizes three basic types of human temperaments and correlates them to the three *guṇas*: The most common, the unenlightened (*paśu-bhāva*), is identified with *tamas*; the heroic (*vīra-bhāva*) with *rajas*; and the godlike (*divya-bhāva*) with *sattva*. The *paśu* is enjoined to worship the Goddess with traditional ritual (*pūjā*), and is excluded from the *pañca-tattva* rite and from using any forbidden or dangerous elements in ritual. Much is heard in the tantric texts about *vīra-bhāva*, the temperament of the heroic. The heroic temperament is considered especially suitable to the practice of *vāmācāra* Tantra. The *rajas guṇa,* which represents dynamic activity, is strongly present in the *vīra* (hero). Being heroic, the *vīra* can dive in where the less courageous fear to tread and confront, in the rituals of Tantra, the dangers of passion, fear, and impurity in order to realize that it is the Goddess herself who veils her own presence in all things through *māyā-śakti*, and that it is again she who reveals this liberating knowledge to the seeker in her form as *vidyā-śakti*, the power of knowledge.

According to Patañjali's Yoga, the passion, desire, fervor, and dynamism that *rajas* represents is a great obstacle to progress on the path to the dispassionate recognition of oneself as pure spirit. *Rajas* is also the intrinsic nature of the dangerous potency of female presence, for she is impure materiality personified as desire. The color red in Sāṃkhya signifies the impurity of woman and the imprisoning force of *rajas*. But the sacramental color of Tantra is red. It is sacred to the Goddess for it symbolizes life and the generative process.

Commentaries on Patañjali's *Yoga Sūtras* depict the womb as the foul and impure harbinger of the impurity of embodied life which it brings forth.[31] This would be anathema to tantrics for whom the cardinal iconographic symbol of Śakti is the inverted triangle or *yoni,* representing the vulva and the womb, the abstract depiction of the life-giving power of the Goddess. The *pañca-tattva* ritual begins with the drawing of the *yoni* on the altar, by the man, and concludes with his literal worship of the woman as an embodiment of Śakti.[32]

## Motivation and Morality

There is motivation in Tantra to worship and celebrate the natural world. But is there any motivation to protect the natural world with a moral purpose? Indeed, Tantra has often been criticized as being amoral because, it is said, that it makes no distinctions between right and wrong, or harmful and beneficial, for all is Śakti. From the ecological perspective, it can be argued that, if all is Śakti—including the toxic waste, the fetid pollution, the exhaust fumes—then all is sublime and needs no corrective action. However, such an argument would ignore the tantric stance regarding the motivation behind human action. The pollution and toxicity are no doubt, according to Tantra, aspects of Śakti as material substance. But what must be taken into account here is the fact that there are schools of Śākta Tantra that, as we shall see, do in fact differentiate between the motives behind actions that are detrimental to others and those that are beneficial. This strain of tantric thought holds individuals accountable for their actions, as is evidenced by texts that condemn those who cause harm to others or engage in excessive self-indulgence and "sinful" behavior—often consigning the perpetrator to hell. The *Mahānirvāṇa Tantra*, for example, warns:

> Thou hast truly spoken, O Devī, of the evil ways of men, who, knowing what is for their welfare, yet, maddened by sinful desire for things which bring immediate enjoyment, are devoid of the sense of right and wrong, and desert the True Path. (11.12–13)

> O Kula-nāyikā! know that there are two kinds of sin—that which contributes merely to the injury of one's own self, and that which causes injury to others. Those sinful men who are not purified by either punishment or expiation cannot but go to hell, and are despised both in this world and the next. (11.16–17)

Most human beings have not experienced the mystical revelation of unity-consciousness and are therefore, according to tantric thought, unenlightened. For them, many Śākta *tantras* do not advocate a lack of discrimination between good and bad. It is only at the highest level of realization that all dualities and opposing pairs merge. But even the self-realized *guru* is expected to behave in accordance with rules of good conduct. Although the enlightened adept has experienced ultimate reality, s/he lives within the realm of phenomenal reality—thus, the rules of behavior necessary for harmonious living still apply.[33] The *Kulārṇava Tantra* states that "such yogins in diverse guises, intent on the welfare of men, walk the earth . . . (with) compassion for all men."[34] Another section of the same text provides a long list of attributes which characterize the ideal tantric master. In addition to many other qualities, the self-realized *guru* must be compassionate to all creatures; merciful; devoid of egotism, anger, greed, and hatred; able to distinguish between good and bad; and possessed of a feeling of oneness with all.[35] The tantric aspirant is expected to be—among other thing—free of sin, cruelty, and hatred; s/he must be non-injurious to others, observe the rules of right conduct, and do good to all creatures.[36] Some texts also expressly forbid the killing of animals, except for the purpose of sacrifice to a *deva*.[37]

The universe is Śakti, and all phenomena, creative and destructive, are aspects of Śakti. This should not, however, be taken to mean that destructive acts committed by humans are to be condoned. Certain *tantras* recommend severe punishment or societal censure against those who cause injury to others.[38] For example, the *Mahānirvāṇa Tantra* states:

> The cruel man who wilfully kills another man should always be sentenced to death. (11.71)
>
> He who misappropriates property entrusted to him, the malicious man, the cheat, he who creates ill-feeling between men . . . should be banished from the kingdom by the King. (11.83)

It is true that Tantra recognizes the destructive and terrifying dimensions of the Goddess as aspects of the play (*līlā*) of the divine Mother. But according to Śākta mythology, whenever there is a grave danger to the world due to the proliferation of evil, the Goddess manifests herself and vanquishes the forces of evil. It can be argued that this is paradoxical because the demons are Śakti as well. Yet, as we have seen, Tantra maintains that although ultimate reality transcends all dualities, phenomenal reality, which is the realm of conventional life, requires a discrimination between the harmful and the beneficial.

Tantra contains an implicit suggestion that the unenlightened are more likely to act in ways that do not harm the world when there is a fear of divine retribution. This is evidenced in the *Mahānirvāṇa Tantra*'s admonition to protect the universe:

> The Lord protects this universe. Whoever wishes to destroy it will be themselves destroyed, and whosoever protects it, the Lord of the Universe Himself protects. Therefore should one act for the good of the world. (12.129)

While the power of Śakti can be destructive as well as creative, the tantric approach to living emphasizes the *life-giving* Śakti. This is evidenced by the tantric conflation of spiritual realization (*yoga*) with celebratory enjoyment (*bhoga*), which is actualized in sacramental rituals including flowers, food, music, and wine. The worship of the life-giving aspects of Śakti is also visible in tantric ritual iconography, which gives strong emphasis to the symbol of the *yoni*. Every *yantra* is composed of combinations of this symbol. Each time the tantric aspirant creates a representation of the *yoni*—either by drawing it or creating it out of natural materials—it is meant to heighten his or her reverence for the regenerative power of the Goddess. One of the reasons for tantric veneration of the feminine is this respect for the power to bring forth life in all its forms; even female animals are protected from slaughter.[39]

## Conclusion: Pitfalls and Possibilities

The doctrines of Hindu Tantra, though conditioned by historical and cultural factors, have certain affinities with the ecofeminist vision, inasmuch as Tantra: (1) celebrates all aspects of life, both spiritual and worldly; (2) elevates the feminine principle of materiality and mutability, to the extent of identifying it as ontologically equivalent to the ultimate; (3) liberates the feminine divine, and thereby the construction of female gender in general, from the constraints of fertility and nurturance alone; (4) affirms the underlying purity of all phenomena, objects, and individuals as expressions of the Goddess; (5) supports women's and marginalized peoples' aspirations for religious self-agency and for attaining the highest realization; (6) eschews harsh asceticism, venerating the body and its sensations as reflective of the immanence of the divine; and

(7) posits no spirit/matter dichotomy, envisioning the earth as the phenomenal manifestation of the Goddess, not as a non-ultimate lower reality.

While tantric philosophy is helpful for the cultivation of an earth-centered spirituality, Tantra's dynamic approach to individual spiritual empowerment can be an equally important source of inspiration. Hindu concepts such as *karma*, transmigration, and cyclical time have been used to justify a lack of action on the part of the individual. The disenfranchisement of the individual is reinforced by caste and gender constructions that have historically created a loss of self-agency for women and lower castes. When the belief that one can make a significant impact in the world is undermined, inertia sets in and discourages any effort at transforming the environment, whether social, economic, or ecological. The tantric approach provides personal access to divine power unmediated by intermediary priestly agents, and imbues the practitioner with the capacity not only for personal transformation but also for the amelioration of pragmatic existential conditions.

The tantric seeker works under the premise that the truth that lies hidden within the self is the same truth that pervades the universe from foundation to firmament. I would term this theological worldview a *theology of identification*, as it posits an identification between self, cosmos, and the Absolute. However, the application of this theology of identification has traditionally not been extended, in the tantric context, to include a radical empathetic connectedness with the human community or the ecosystem. It is likely that the tantric approach to the theology of identification, which seems to have consistently functioned under the credo "the world is within the self" (as evidenced, for example, by the homologization of the self with the cosmos), leads tantrics to disregard the flip side of this theological perspective—that the self also pervades the world. To regard the world as a macrocosm of the self, rather than the self as the microcosm of the world, would be to extend the interest and caring normally reserved for personal needs to the world that has now become part of oneself.

The inability to perceive the theology of identification as a two-way street has serious ethical implications. Far from destroying the personal, self-centered ego-consciousness, it can strengthen it and result in a feeling of superiority and callous disregard for others deemed inconsequential due to their spiritual inferiority. This can take on even more sinister dimensions when the tantric heritage of accessing, channeling, and utilizing suprasensory forces is taken into account.

Tantrics have traditionally been denounced by orthodox Hindus for their conjurational practices. Whereas *bhakti* and other paths acceptable to traditional Hinduism have as their sole aim a salvific connection with the Absolute, Tantra traditionally provides various resources for its adherents to access power for material as well as salvific ends. Tantra's approach to power has always been readily applicable, in certain schools, to any goal or desire. Many *tantras* contain explicit ritual instructions for the conjuring of power to remedy ills, improve personal relationships, maintain health, create harmony and prosperity, and so forth.[40] Other *tantras* provide similar instructions for the dispelling of countermanding forces, for the control and manipulation of others, for creating discord, and even for causing malady or death.[41] The tendency of some tantrics to conjure power for various, at times nefarious, uses has placed on Tantra the heavy burden of ignominy for which its ambivalent stance towards the conjuring and uses of power are partly responsible.

It behooves us, therefore, to consider the paradigm of power and its uses, as it relates to the tantric ethos, before formulating any strategy for the placement of tantric theology in a position of honor vis-à-vis the issue of Hindu ecofeminism. For one thing is certain, before any aspect of Tantra is adopted for the purpose of providing a framework for action towards universal well-being, the conjurational angle of tantric notions of theophany must be recognized and accounted for.

It is the lack of distinction in certain tantric schools between the responsible and compassionate use of power, and its irresponsible or egotistical use, that has created a cloud of suspicion around Tantra. There are advantages inherent in a system that acknowledges the ability of humans to access knowledge, power, and strength from a source beyond empirical experience. If nothing else, it empowers individuals to take life into their own hands, heal it, and shape it according to their own visions. This is no mean feat in the Hindu context, where historically, a sense of determinism has robbed many of the will to affect change and acknowledge their own responsibility. Furthermore, most tantric rituals of healing or procuring (physiological, psychological, material, or inter-relational well-being) make use of a wide variety of natural materials that create a palpable connectedness to the earth and nature, and sacralize, through religious usage, these and related natural substances. Nevertheless, it is incumbent upon those who practice the teachings of a particular faith tradition to ensure that their actions aid and not harm others. A framework that ensures the responsible and compassionate use of accessed power within the tantric system is necessary for an ecofeminist re-envisioning of tantric theology to be effective.

To summarize, if we maintain (as I do), that a theological foundation is necessary for the ultimate success of any long-term enterprise for the healing of the earth and its ecosystem, we must choose a model that takes into account what ecofeminism terms the "self/other dichotomy." In the Hindu context, such a model should contain the resources to transform our conventional dualistic mode of perception to one of identification with the world. The tantric model posits that the self is Śakti and that Śakti is the world, thereby creating a dialectic of identification between self and world. Ideally, the process by which this understanding is arrived at begins with the sacralization of the body as the site of the same cosmic forces that control the universe and ends in the eradication of the personal ego-consciousness, which is replaced by a profound realization of oneness with the Absolute. The weakness in the tantric system seems to lie in its emphasis on the perception of the self as microcosm of the world, rather than the world as macrocosm of the self. If tantric reverence for the immanent Goddess is interpreted according to the latter perception, Tantra can become more than a resource for Hindu eco-theological reconstruction. It can become a channel through which Hindu nondualism can inspire a viable philosophy on which to base a transformed vision of the earth.

No ancient system of thought, including Tantra, can be applied directly to the ecological or any other contemporary problem. However, any attempt to redirect entrenched, ecologically destructive behavior patterns without accounting for religious convictions would find resistance among the adherents of established traditions. An ecological agenda supported by faith elicits greater commitment.

A quest for philosophical or theological support for action that improves our present condition requires a creative scriptural exegesis informed by the need to re-envision traditional teachings in the light of modern concerns. For a reinterpretation of scripture to become a living force for change—rather than a strained apology—a hermeneutic of engaged transformation is necessary. Such a hermeneutical approach must simultaneously critique anachronistic aspects of the tradition and highlight important seed ideas that carry, in this case, the potential to inspire action that protects the earth.

## Notes

1. Cynthia Humes, "Is the Devī Māhātmya a Feminist Scripture?" in *Feminism and the Hindu Goddess*, ed. Alf Hiltebeitel and Kathleen Erndle, forthcoming. I would like to take this opportunity to express my warmest gratitude to Dr. Cynthia Humes, Claremont McKenna College, for her insights, guidance, encouragement, and inspiration.

2. Rosemary Radford Ruether, "Ecofeminism," in *Ecofeminism and the Sacred*, ed. Carol J. Adams (New York: Continuum, 1993), 21.

3. Ruether, "Ecofeminism," 21.

4. Bengali, Tamil, Malayalam among others.

5. For an elaboration of the effects of purity consciousness on the lives of women, see Harold G. Coward, "Purity in Hinduism: With Particular Reference to Patañjali's Yoga Sūtras," in *Hindu Ethics,* by Harold G. Coward, Julius J. Lipner, and Katherine K. Young (Albany, N.Y.: State University of New York Press, 1989), 9–39.

6. Swami Hariharananda Aranya's commentary in *Yoga Philosophy of Patañjali*, ed. and ann. Swami Hariharananda, rev. ed. (Albany, N.Y.: State University of New York Press, 1983), 223.

7. Quoted in Tracy Pintchman, *The Rise of the Goddess in the Hindu Tradition* (Albany, N.Y.: State University of New York Press, 1994), 36.

8. See Ajit Mookerjee and Madhu Khanna, *The Tantric Way* (London: Thames & Hudson, 1977), 184.

9. *Kulārṇava Tantra* 10, pp. 108–109.

10. Cf. *Praṇatosinī Tantra* 2, quoted in Sanjukta Gupta, "Women in the Śaiva/Śākta Ethos," in *Roles and Rituals for Hindu Women*, ed. Julia Leslie (Cranbury, N.J.: Associated University Presses, 1991), 193–209.

11. Gupta, "Women in the Śaiva/Śākta Ethos," 208.

12. Vimalananda Swami. In his commentary on the *Karpūrādi Stotra*, ed. and trans. Arthur Avalon, 2d ed. (Madras: Ganesh & Co., 1953), 30.

13. *Tantrarāja Tantra*, p. 85.

14. *Kulārṇava Tantra*, 1, p. 24.

15. See *Yoni Tantra*.

16. See Christopher Key Chapple, "Living Liberation in Sāṃkhya and Yoga," and Lance E. Nelson, "Living Liberation in Śaṅkara and Classical Advaita," in *Living Liberation in Hindu Thought*, ed. Andrew O. Fort and Patricia Y. Mumme (Albany, N.Y.: State University of New York Press, 1996), 115–134, 17–62.

17. See, for example, *Yoga Sūtra* 2.40 and Vyāsa's commentary thereon.

18. J. S. Woodroffe, *Shakti and Shakta* (Madras: Vedanta Press, 1951), 554; also *Mahānirvāṇa Tantra* 5.180–90.

19. Many *tantras* are written in vernacular or non-scholarly Sanskrit. In *Hinduism: A Cultural Perspective,* 2d ed. (Englewood Cliffs, N.J.: Prentice Hall, 1993), David Kinsley observes that the ungrammatical Sanskrit of many tantric texts indicate that the erudite, scholarly elite were not responsible for writing many of the *tantras*, thus confirming the belief that Tantra was a movement which involved marginalized peoples.

20. See N. N. Bhattacharyya, *History of the Śākta Religion* (New Delhi: Munshiram Manoharlal, 1974).

21. Woodroffe, *Sakti and Shakta,* 545.

22. See, for example, *Kulacūḍāmaṇi Nigama* 3.13–15.

23. For a brief description of the attitudes of contemporary tantric *yoginīs,* see Lynn Teskey Denton, "Varieties of Hindu Female Asceticism," in *Roles and Rituals for Hindu Women*, ed. Julia Leslie (Cranbury, N.J.: Associated University Presses, 1991), 211–31.

24. See, for example, *Yoni Tantra* 2.12.

25. For a concise description and meaning of the *pañca-tattva* rite, see Mookerjee and Khanna, *The Tantric Way*, 185–88.

26. The *Kulārṇava Tantra* 2, pp. 35–37, explicitly admonishes those who do not follow the path in the right spirit (i.e., who lack the perception of the Divine Mother in all things) and engage in the ritual without the guidance of a *guru* or proper *sādhana*; see also *Mahānirvāṇa Tantra* 11.104.

The *Kulacūḍāmaṇi Nigama* 3.13–15, for example, insists on both male and female participants being initiates; *Mahānirvāṇa Tantra* 6.18–20 recommends that women participants should also be tantric initiates.

27. See Kinsley, *Hinduism,* 65–66, for a discussion of the element of shock in tantric rites.

28. See also *Kulārṇava Tantra* 1, p. 28.

29. *Kaulāvalīnirṇaya Tantra*, p. 24.

30. Philip Rawson, *Art of Tantra* (London: Oxford University Press, 1978), 31.

31. See, for example, Vācaspati Miśra's explanation of *Yoga Sūtra* 2.5.

32. See *Kulacūḍāmaṇi Nigama*, 2.14–30.

33. See Aghedananda Bharati on the tantric emphasis on normative conceptions of morality in his *The Tantric Tradition* (London: Rider & Co. 1965), 21.

34. *Kulārṇava Tantra* 6, pp. 67–68.

35. *Kulārṇava Tantra* 9, pp. 90–91.

36. *Kulārṇava Tantra* 9, pp. 87–89.

37. See *Mahānirvāṇa Tantra* 11.143.

38. For guidelines on behavior and social conduct, see *Mahānirvāṇa Tantra* 11.18–152.

39. See *Mahānirvāṇa Tantra* 6.7.

40. See, for example, *Vāmakeśvara Tantra*.

41. See, for example, *Ḍāmara Tantra*.

## References

### Primary Sources with Translations

*Agni Purāṇa*. Translated by N. Gangadharan. Delhi: Motilal Banarsidass, 1985.

*Bṛhadāraṇyaka Upaniṣad*. In *The Thirteen Principal Upanishads*, translated by Robert E. Hume. 2d ed., rev. Madras: Oxford University Press, 1958.

*Ḍāmara Tantra*. Translated by P. K. Rai. Varanasi: Praghya Prakashan, 1988.

*Devī Māhātmya*. In *Encountering the Goddess: A Translation of the Devī Māhātmya and a Study of Its Interpretation*, translated by James Coburn. Albany, N.Y.: State University of New York Press, 1991.

*Kāma-Kalā Vilāsa*. Translated by Arthur Avalon. 2d ed. Madras: Ganesh & Co., 1953.

*Karpūrādi Stotra*. Edited and translated by Arthur Avalon. 2d ed. Madras: Ganesh & Co., 1953.

*Kaulāvalīnirṇaya Tantra*. Edited and translated by Arthur Avalon. Calcutta: Sanskrit Press Depository, 1928.

*Kulacūḍāmaṇi Nigama*. Translated by Arthur Avalon. Madras: Ganesh & Co., 1956.

*Kulārṇava Tantra*. Translated by M. P. Pandit. Edited by Sir John Woodroffe. 2d ed. Madras: Ganesh & Co., 1973.

*Lalitā Sahasranāma*. Translated by M. N. Namboodiri. San Ramon: Mata Amritanandamayi Center, 1996.

*Mahānirvāṇa Tantra*. Edited and translated by Arthur Avalon. 3d ed. Madras: Ganesh & Co., 1953.

*Maitrī Upaniṣad*. In *The Thirteen Principal Upanishads*, translated by Robert E. Hume. 2d ed., rev. Madras: Oxford University Press, 1958.

*Manusmṛti*. In *The Laws of Manu*, translated by G. Buhler. Sacred Books of the East, vol. 25. Delhi: Motilal Banarsidass, 1988.

*Prāṇatoṣinī Tantra*. Edited by Rama Toshana Vidya Bhusana. Calcutta: Vasumati Sahitya Mandir, n.d.

*Praśna Upaniṣad*. In *The Principal Upaniṣads*, translated by S. Radhakrishnan. New Delhi: INDUS-Harper Collins Publ. India, 1995.

*Sāṃkhya Kārikā*. Sanskrit text with translation. In *Classical Samkhya*, by Gerald J. Larson. 2d ed. Delhi: Motilal Banarsidass, 1979.

*Śvetāśvatara Upaniṣad*. In *The Principal Upaniṣads*, translated by S. Radhakrishnan. New Delhi: INDUS-Harper Collins Publ. India, 1995.

*Tantrarāja Tantra*. Translated by Sir John Woodroffe. Madras: Ganesh & Co., 1954.

*Vāmakeśvara Tantra*. Translated by Michael Magee. Calcutta: Bharatiya Marg Publ., 1987.

*Yoga Sūtras*. In *Yoga Philosophy of Patañjali*, translated with annotations by Swami Hariharananda Aranya. Rev. ed. Albany, N.Y.: State University of New York Press, 1983.

*Yoni Tantra*. Translated by Lokanath Maharaj. San Francisco: Azoth Publ., 1985.

### Secondary Sources

Brown, C. Mackenzie. 1990. *The Triumph of the Goddess*. Albany, N.Y.: State University of New York Press.

Coburn, James. 1991. *Encountering the Goddess: A Translation of the Devī Māhātmya and a Study of Its Interpretation*. Albany, N.Y.: State University of New York Press.

Dasgupta, Shashi Bushan. 1982. "Evolution of Mother Worship in India." In *Great Women of India*, ed. Swami Madhavananda and Ramesh Chandra Majumdar. Mayavati Pithoragarh, Himalayas: Advaita Ashrama.

Gaard, Greta. 1993. *Ecofeminism: Women, Animals, Nature*. Philadelphia: Temple University Press.

Goudriaan, Teun. 1978. *Māyā Human and Divine*. Delhi: Motilal Banarsidass.

Shiva, Vandana. 1988. *Staying Alive: Women, Ecology and Survival in India*. New Delhi: Kali for Women.

Warren, Karen, and Nancy Tuana, eds. *APA Newsletter on Feminism and Philosophy* 90 (Fall 1991): 179–97.

Woodroffe, J. S. 1951. *Shakti and Shakta*. 2d ed. Madras: Vedanta Press.

Woods, J. H. 1966. *The Yoga System of Patañjali*. Delhi: Motilal Banarsidass.

**Patricia Y. Mumme**

# 6

# Models and Images for a Vaiṣṇava Environmental Theology: The Potential Contribution of Śrīvaiṣṇavism

## Introduction

The environmental degradation that scientists say is now threatening the continued existence of all species is certainly everyone's responsibility. Many contemporary Christian theologians in the West have become acutely aware of the environmental threat and their own tradition's historical contribution to it. What is urgently needed, they say, is a new understanding of the relation of nature, God, and human beings in the minds of those within the Christian tradition that will inspire them to contribute to and work toward environmental healing before it is too late.

Christian eco-theologians have assigned themselves the task of retrieving or developing scriptural and theological support for environmentalism. The more tradition-minded among them, including both scholarly and popular authors, search the Bible and Christian theological history for themes, images, and models that would help support a Christian environmental ethic. In their eco-theological readings of scripture, the Genesis creation stories affirm the goodness and harmony of nature in God's eyes and the responsibility of human beings as stewards of that creation; the Deuteronomist and the Psalmists proclaim the land and nature's fertility to be gifts from God to be treasured; the Hebrew Prophets warn of ecolological disaster if human beings violate their responsibilities of stewardship; the Noah story teaches that God wants humankind to preserve species; the Logos doctrine means that Jesus Christ pervades his creation, and thus that sharing the fruits of the land is a sacramental act on par with the Eucharist; apocalyptic prophecy promising a new earth in spiritual and ecological harmony is held out as the hope of Christian environmental activists.[1]

A handful of bolder theologians, more willing to depart from scripture, suggest Christians need to adopt new models for conceiving the Divine and/or God's relation to the universe. John Cobb's Process Theology, Sallie McFague's notion of the universe as God's body, and Rosemary Ruether's image of God as mother have been suggested as potential cornerstones of a re-visioned Christian theology. Though these new models may break with mainstream theological tradition, their proponents usually try to root them in neglected strands of Christian scripture, practice, and tradition. Their proponents claim these new models are superior to their more traditional counterparts for two basic reasons. First, they are consistent with contemporary scientific theory, which has made many traditional theological models obsolete. Second, and perhaps more important, these models are potentially fruitful for giving a theological backing for urgent social agendas such as ecology, feminism, and the liberation of oppressed peoples. Thus these new models contrast sharply with older theological models, which have contributed to environmental insensitivity and racial, gender, and economic oppression in Western civilization.[2]

Awareness of impending ecological disaster and theological response to it has evolved more slowly in India, even though the rate of environmental degradation there is surely no less alarming than in the West. But in recent years the ecological movement, like the feminist movement, has been roused in India. If Indian intellectual history follows that of the West, theological support for these movements from within the various religious communities of India will be forthcoming. But it is hard to predict from what quarter this support will arise or, more seriously, whether this support will be sufficiently vigorous to marshal the massive shift in social thinking and public policy so desperately needed to keep India from a disastrous environmental meltdown in the not-so-distant future. The latter doubt, of course, can be raised about the work of ecological theologians and secular environmental ethicists in the West. Do such movements herald the development of a salutary, worldwide environmental reformation of social policy, or will all the books on environmental ethics and eco-theology prove to be merely a futile exercise in "too little, too late"?

I am painfully aware that the whole eco-theological enterprise may have no more effect than rearranging the deck chairs on the Titanic. Nevertheless, in this chapter I will explore, from the perspective of a sympathetic outsider, whether and to what extent the Vaiṣṇava tradition, and specifically the Śrīvaiṣṇava tradition of South India, might contribute to the development of a theological basis for an environmental movement that India so desperately needs. As Rosemary Ruether says, "there is no ready-made ecological spirituality and ethic in past traditions." The ecological crisis in the post-nuclear, post-industrial era is so profoundly new to human experience that no current religious tradition will be adequate, as is, to meet it. "Whatever useful elements may exist" in Western or Eastern traditions, she says, "must be reinterpreted to make them usable in the face of both new scientific knowledge and the destructive power of the technology it has made possible" (Ruether 1992, 206).

As Ruether suggests, a contemporary ecological theology must be fashioned, not found (Ruether 1992, 206); but different traditions may be more or less amenable to this effort. To my mind, Christian theologians seem to have a difficult struggle teasing images and models out of the Bible and Christian heritage that are able to provide support for ecological thinking, though they have managed to do so with considerable creative hermeneutical thinking and ingenuity. Some have looked wistfully at the religious and philosophical traditions of Asia as being more hospitable to ecological modes of thinking (e.g., Ruether 1992, 205). However, Lance Nelson (this volume) shows that Śaṅkara's Advaita (nondualist) tradition, the *darśana* with no doubt the most prestige and potential influence among contemporary Hindu intellectuals, is perhaps no better suited than Christianity to supporting environmentalism, at least in its classical formulation. Some Neo-Vedānta thinkers have tried with considerable creative re-visioning to get it to support social action programs, but only by breaking with classical Advaita in ways that they do not readily admit. In contrast, the Vaiṣṇava tradition in general, and the Śrīvaiṣṇava tradition of Rāmānuja and his followers in particular, strikes me as being much more hospitable to ecological thought. Unlike Advaita Vedānta, Rāmānuja's Viśiṣṭādvaita (qualified nondualist) tradition sees the world as both real and valuable to God. Unfortunately, like Christianity, Śrīvaiṣṇavism envisions a clearly other-worldly salvation and has traditionally emphasized monarchical and patriarchal images of God, giving it some of the same theological obstacles that Christianity must overcome in order to support environmentalism. But I submit that, at the same time, the Śrīvaiṣṇava tradition has a wealth of traditional mythic and theological elements that could be readily recast to fashion a Vaiṣṇava Hindu ecological theology. Were Christian eco-theologians more familiar with Śrīvaiṣṇavism, I think they might be veritably "green" with envy over the potential of some of its traditional models and images to support an environmentally friendly theology.

Before going further, however, I should clarify my personal qualifications for probing Śrīvaiṣṇavism's potential contribution to Hindu eco-theology. I am not a member of the Śrīvaiṣṇava community, though I have spent much of the last twenty years reading and translating the works of Śrīvaiṣṇava theologians and working closely with members of the tradition to do this. As an outsider I cannot "do" Śrīvaiṣṇava theology. But my familiarity with the tradition is more than textual and involves a wider variety of texts than the philosophical Viśiṣṭādvaita works of Rāmānuja that have been the focus of most Western scholars interested in Śrīvaiṣṇava theological models (such as Klostermaier 1987 and Lott 1976).

What approaches of such scholars often underappreciate is that the Śrīvaiṣṇava tradition, though built on the philosophical scaffolding that Rāmānuja erected, is a living, popular tradition with a vast literary heritage, both erudite and popular. My work has been largely with a more grassroots level of Śrīvaiṣṇava theology, the Tamil Maṇipravāḷa works of its founding *ācāryas* in the four centuries after Rāmānuja. This literature, written for an audience of committed devotees, is far more creative, poetic, and liberal in its use of theological images and mythic motifs than Rāmānuja's Sanskrit philosophical works. To use a Christian analogy, Rāmānuja's *Śrībhāṣya* is systematic and erudite like Aquinas' *Summa Theologica* or Barth's *Church Dogmatics*. The Maṇipravāḷa writings of Piḷḷai Lokācārya, Maṇavāḷamāmuni, and Periyavāccān Piḷḷai are popular and engaging, like the Sunday sermons of Martin Luther, Billy Graham, or Martin Luther King, Jr.—or, for that matter, the speeches of Mohandas Gandhi.

It is equally true in India and the West that to be successful in inspiring the kind of mass movement necessary to avert an ecological crisis, environmental theology must appeal to the popular level of a religious tradition, not merely to its intellectual elites. The Christian ecological theology with the most impact on Western social policy will be the one which actually gets taught in the Sunday school curriculum and covered in the popular press, not the one most admired by professors in the Academy. Similarly, the ecological Hinduism with the best chance of meeting South Asia's environmental challenges will be the one which will spring from a living community with deep roots—such as Śrīvaiṣṇavism—and will speak to the piety of the Hindu masses. In what follows, I will explore how the Śrīvaiṣṇava tradition's theological heritage of models, motifs, and mythical images—as I understand them—might be used to form a Vaiṣṇava ecological theology that could resonate with many Hindus, should some theologian within the community arise to create it.

## The Universe as God's Emanation and Body

A common criticism ecological theologians make of traditional Christian theology is that it has tended to devalue the world and nature and to give little attention to the relationship of interdependence between human beings and the natural realm. In the West, overemphasis on God's transcendence has divorced the divine and the spiritual from nature and the material realm, in order to avoid pantheism and (more recently) to free theology and religion from conflict with emerging scientific knowledge. (Some theologies, such as Bultmann's, have radically devalued nature as completely irrelevant to religion and religious experience.) The monarchical, patriarchal images of God as the architect who fashions the world out of nothing and rules over it with sovereignty fits with the view that humans, the crown of his creation, are the viceroys of nature. Christian theologies that emphasize these models, in their zeal to avoid pantheism, have left little room for divine immanence in the world, except through the incarnation of God in Jesus. Most problematically, such theologies have contributed to Western culture's desacralization and devaluation of nature and all non-human species, and wittingly or unwittingly, helped legitimate their irresponsible exploitation (McFague 1993, chap. 5).

Sallie McFague is a Christian theologian who has critiqued the prevailing models and argued that they need to be replaced. Rather than seeing God as architect who creates out of nothing, she suggests that God be seen as emanating and/or procreating the universe, much as a mother gives birth to a child out of her own womb; the resulting universe is one which God pervades and inhabits immanently, as a spirit or soul pervades and inhabits a body. Such a model—she calls it "panentheism"—avoids the extremes of both pantheism and disembodied transcendence:

> Pantheism says that God is embodied, necessarily and totally; traditional [transcendental] theism claims that God is disembodied, necessarily and totally; panentheism suggests that God is embodied but not necessarily or totally. Rather God is sacramentally embodied: God is mediated, expressed, in and through embodiment, but not necessarily or totally. (McFague 1993, 145–46)

In the panentheistic model, McFague says, "God is not exhausted by finite beings, not even all finite beings, yet God is in all finite creatures and apart from God there is nothing; nor is God apart from anything." Here, God is the spirit that is the source of all reality as well as its underlying, vivifying principle. But "God is not identical with the universe, for the universe is dependent on God in a way that God is not dependent on the universe" (McFague 1993, 145).

Śrīvaiṣṇavism already has a panentheistic theology and emanistic view of creation which fully fits McFague's description. Rāmānuja, its founding theologian, describes the world as the emanation of the divine and the body of God, and uses this conception as the cornerstone of his Viśiṣṭādvaita Vedānta philosophy.

But, as Eric Lott explains, Rāmānuja is not the originator of this panentheistic model; it has deep roots in Hindu scripture.

Rāmānuja reads Hindu scripture to affirm that Viṣṇu, the Supreme Lord, the Brahman of the Upaniṣads, is both the material and efficient cause of the created universe, emanating the world out of his own body. *Ṛg Veda* 10.90, the *Puruṣa Sūkta,* presents the universe as originating out of the sacrifice of the body of a cosmic "person," Puruṣa, whose various bodily parts are transformed into space and time, the sun and moon, earth and living creatures, and various social classes of human beings. The *Śatapaṭha Brāhmaṇa* identifies this Puruṣa with Nārāyaṇa, which became another name for Viṣṇu, and thus this hymn became particularly important to Vaiṣṇava thought.[3] Other procreative models which suggest that the Lord creates out of his own body abound in scripture. As a spider emits a thread (*Bṛhadāraṇyaka Up.* 2.1.20 and *Muṇḍaka Up.* 1.1.7) or as grass arises from the earth, or as hairs arise from the body, so too, from the the Imperishable Lord, arises all of creation (*Muṇḍaka Up.* 1.1.7). The Lord is declared to produce the many creatures as male and female create life (*Muṇḍaka Up.* 2.1.5).

Eric Lott suggests that it is the primacy of the image of the world as the body of the Lord in the *Bhagavad Gītā* which inspired Rāmānuja to use it as the center of his own theology (Lott 1976, 45). The *Bhagavad Gītā* climaxes in chapter 11, when Arjuna is given a divine eye to enable him to see the universe itself in the body of Kṛṣṇa, the supreme Brahman and Lord of all (*viśveśvara*). Kṛṣṇa tells Arjuna to "behold the whole universe . . . all unified in my body" (*BhG* 11.7). Arjuna responds by addressing him as "the Lord of All" and the "One who contains all forms" (*viśveśvara, viśvarūpa*). Throughout India there are many Vaiṣṇava temples with inspiring portrayals of Arjuna's vision of Kṛṣṇa as Viśveśvara or Viśvarūpa in iconography or painting.

This image from the *Bhagavad Gītā* also seems to have inspired the ninth century C.E. Vaiṣṇava poet saint Nammāḻvār, whose poems of praise to Viṣṇu, the *Tiruvāymoḻi*, are considered the Tamil Veda by Śrīvaiṣṇavas.[4] The first decade of his *Tiruvāymoḻi* contains a hymn which portrays this same idea, that the created world of nature—including both living and non-living beings—forms the everchanging body of God. Much of the exquisite beauty of his Tamil verse comes through in A. K. Ramanujan's translation:

We here and that man, this man,
  and that other in-between,
and that woman, this woman,
  and that other, whoever,
those people, and these,
  and these others in-between,
this thing, that thing,
  and this other in-between, whichever,
all things dying, these things
  those things, those others in-between,
good things, bad things,
  things that were, that will be
being all of them,
  he stands there.

(*Tiruvāymoḻi* 1.1.4; Ramanujan 1981, 3)

Rāmānuja quotes a passage from the *Viṣṇu Purāṇa* with a similar message that clearly expresses the continuity between the Lord and the world created by, for, and out of himself:

> The earth, the waters, fire, the air, the space, all the senses, the mind, and the individual self, and in short the world as a whole, is he. He is the soul of all beings and the universe is his form, as he is imperishable. The processes like creation that happen to entities are for his sake. He is the creature and he is the author of creation. He protects, withdraws, and is what is protected. Viṣṇu, the excellent one, the beneficient one, the adorable one, is of universal form as he assumes the states [from] Brahma [on down]. (*VP* 1.2.68–70, quoted in *VS* 160)

It is important to point out that Śrīvaiṣṇava theology is panentheistic, not pantheistic. Many scriptures testify that though Viṣṇu, the Supreme Brahman, emanates the world out of his body, he is not simply coextensive with his creation, for he transcends it. Even the aforementioned *Puruṣa Sūkta* (*Ṛg Veda* 10.90) says that all creatures below are merely a tenth of him. Theologians in Rāmānuja's tradition often quote the *Antaryāmī Brāhmaṇa* of the *Bṛhadāraṇyaka Upaniṣad,* which describes Brahman as:

> He who, dwelling in all things, *yet is other than all things* [italics mine], whom all things do not know, whose body all things are, who controls all things from within—he is your Self, the Inner Controller, the Immortal. (*Bṛhadāraṇyaka Up.* 3.7.15)

The *Bhagavad Gītā* further clarifies that the Lord, while procreating, pervading, and controlling all things from within, yet stands apart from them:

> Whatever states of being there may be . . . they are all from Me alone. I am not [contained] in them; they are [contained] in me. (*BhG* 7.12)

> By me all this universe is pervaded through my unmanifested form. All beings abide in me, but I do not abide in them. (*BhG* 9.4)

The upaniṣadic analogy of the spider and its web, often quoted by Rāmānuja,[5] is particularly illustrative of the Viśiṣṭādvaita view of the soul-body relationship between the Lord and the world. First, it suggests the simultaneous reality of the Lord and the world; if a spider can produce a real web from its body, why cannot the Lord? Furthermore, it points to their difference in nature, even though the latter arises from the former, its material and efficient cause. Here (unlike in pantheistic theologies) there is no room to claim that God is tainted with the world's evil, for defects in its web do not touch the spider, nor do defects in the body affect the soul (*BSR* 1.4.27). In the same way, the Lord's purity and freedom from all evil is maintained in spite of the existence of *karma*, sin, and evil in the world that forms his body. The analogy also shows that like the web to the spider, the body is subservient to the soul, and the world subservient to the Lord; the former is dependent on the latter for its existence and exists only for the purpose of the latter. Indeed, Rāmānuja says subservience to the Lord is the essential nature of all souls and all material things.[6]

In the Śrīvaiṣṇava tradition, the relationships between body and soul, between the web and the spider, between attributes and their substances, between the world of souls and matter and the God who created them, all boil down to the relationship of *śeṣa* and *śeṣī*. Rāmānuja's definition of these terms from sacrificial terminology, sometimes translated as "subsidiary entity" and "principal entity," is often quoted by later Śrīvaiṣṇava *ācāryas:*

> That whose nature lies solely in being valued through a desire to contribute a special excellence to another entity is the *śeṣa.* The other [that to which the subsidiary contributes excellence] is the *śeṣī.* (*VS* 182)

With this background, we can understand how Rāmānuja sums up the relationship between God and the world in his *Vedārtha Saṅgraha:*

> This is the fundamental relationship between the Supreme and the universe of individual selves and physical entities. It is the relationship of soul and body, the inseparable relationship of the supporter and the supported, that of the controller and the controlled, and that of the principal entity (*śeṣī)* and the subsidiary entity (*śeṣa*). That which takes possession of another entity entirely as the latter's support, controller, and principal, is called the soul of that latter entity. That which, in its entirety, depends upon, is controlled by and subserves another, and is therefore its inseparable mode, is called the body of the latter. Such is the relation between the individual self and its body. Even so [is the relationship] between the Supreme Self and everything that is its body. (*VS* 95, translation modified)

The Śrīvaiṣṇava panentheistic theology maintains a balance between divine transcendence and immanence which preserves the transcendent purity of the divine while firmly establishing and preserving the value of the world. The soul-body relationship between the world and the divine is an intimate one, marked by real communication between the three realms of God, souls, and matter. God is not divorced from or discontinuous with his creatures, but eternally and inseparably related to them (Lott 1976, 148–49). Both individual sentient souls and the material world of insentient matter are manifestations of and bodies for the Lord, which exist under divine control and for the divine purpose. In Śrīvaiṣṇava thought, the dependence and subservience of the world and souls upon the Lord does not devalue them, but rather establishes their value as beings whose essential purpose is to contribute excellence to their Lord and maker. The manifest world exists "for his sake," as the *Viṣṇu Purāṇa* says, and all things therein, as his *śeṣas*, are valuable in that they manifests the divine nature and contribute "special excellence" to God's glory.

McFague and other Christian theologians have called for the adoption of the model of the universe as God's body, and/or an expansion of the notion of divine incarnation to include the whole world, because they believe that a new valuation of embodiedness is necessary in order to value the well-being of the world and its creatures. A panentheistic, incarnational theological model that sees the world as the divine body, as McFague puts it,

> underscores our bodiliness, our concrete physical existence and experience that we share with all other creatures; it is a model on the side of the well-being of the planet, for it raises the issue of ethical regard toward all bodies as all are interrelated and interdependent. (McFague 1993, 150)

If McFague is right that only a theology which values and sacralizes embodiedness can provide support for an ecological theology, then Śrīvaiṣṇava theology can fill the bill. I submit that it is an incarnational theology par excellence, with no conflict between divinity and embodiedness. Śrīvaiṣṇava catechisms such as Piḷḷai Lokācārya's *Arthapañcaka* recognize five forms of God: His *para* or supreme form and the *vyūha, vibhava, antaryāmin,* and *arcāvatāra* forms (*AP* 15–19). And all five forms are embodied forms! The *vyūha* forms of Saṃkarṣaṇa, Pradyumna, and Aniruddha (from Pāñcarātra theology) are cosmological in purpose: these are the specific forms by which the Lord periodically emanates and creates the physical world, sustains it, and destroys it at the end of the eon. Thus it is through his *vyūha* forms that the Lord is embodied in the created material universe as a whole. The *vibhava* or *avatāra* form includes all the Lord's periodic incarnations into human or animal form, like Rāmā and Kṛṣṇa, in order to establish *dharma* and protect and preserve the world. The *antaryāmin* is the Lord's form as the inner controller or soul of the soul, where God takes as his body each finite soul, as explained in numerous upaniṣadic passages.

The *arcāvatāra* (incarnation for worship) form comes about when the Lord takes a temple or household image of stone, metal, or clay as his body, for the purpose of making himself accessible to his devotees that they may worship and serve him. What is perhaps most striking is that, in Śrīvaiṣṇava theology, even the Lord's highest form, his *para* or *para-Vāsudeva* form, is also an embodied form. The Lord manifests out of himself the heavenly realm of Paramapāda or Vaikuṇṭha, consisting of pure matter (*śuddha-sattva*), and dwells there in a superior body of that same matter, gloriously resplendent with his innumerable auspicious qualities, which are free from all evil. With this body he enjoys sporting with his wife Lakṣmī, in the company of his angels (*nityasuris)* and the freed souls, who are likewise endowed with bodies of pure matter, which enable them to take any form in order to serve the divine couple. When even the heavenly realm is peopled by embodied beings relating to each other, then clearly embodiment *per se* cannot be seen as necessarily antithetical to the divine, nor can it be devalued as intrinsically involved with suffering and evil. Rather, embodiment is a natural manifestation and expression of divinity. Everywhere and in every way God exists, he exists in a body. Granted, these bodies are of various kinds: the bodies which the Lord's *para* and *vibhava* forms take are seen to be of pure matter (*śuddha-sattva*); sentient souls are the bodies for the *antaryāmin* form of the Divine; the bodies of the *vyūha* and *arcāvatāra* forms are the only bodies constructed of gross matter (*prakṛti*), and hence the only ones truly subject to suffering and evil. Yet the Lord is found in all such bodies; the Lord's various bodies are valuable in that they allow his glory to be manifest and thereby contribute excellence to him.

## Viṣṇu As Preserver: The Dharmic Order and Ecological Ethics

One of the first images that would arise in the mind of any Hindu upon the mention of the name Viṣṇu would be this deity's role in the Hindu trinity as the preserver or sustainer of the universe. The purāṇic notion that Viṣṇu is the preserver, Brahmā is the creator, and Śiva is the destroyer has wide currency among contemporary Hindu intellectuals. Even though the Vaiṣṇava tradition would assert that Viṣṇu is responsible for all three functions,[7] still the image of Viṣṇu—the God of gods—as especially concerned with the sustenance of the universe and maintenance of its dharmic order looms large in the minds of Vaiṣṇavas and is supported by countless myths and scriptural texts. Viṣṇu is no deistic creator who leaves the world to the care of his creatures. Viṣṇu's name is taken to be derived from the verb *viś*, to pervade, signifying that Viṣṇu pervades his creation, enlivening and controlling it from within.[8] Viṣṇu establishes *dharma* and is in charge of maintaining and, if necessary, re-establishing this *dharma* whenever it is threatened by disorder or *adharma*. This notion comes through clearly in Kṛṣṇa's declaration to Arjuna in the *Bhagavad Gītā:*

> Though I myself am unborn, imperishable, the Lord of all creatures. . . . Whenever there is a decline of *dharma* and the rise of *adharma,* O Bhārata, I send forth myself [in an *avatāra* form]. For the protection of the good, for the destruction of the wicked, and for the establishment of *dharma*, I come into being from age to age. (*BhG* 4.6–8, my translation)

The *Lakṣmī Tantra,* a text often quoted in Śrīvaiṣṇava circles, shows that the maintenance of dharmic order in the world is Viṣṇu's primary concern and desire. Here Śrī, Viṣṇu's divine consort, says that the reason one should obey Vedic laws is:

> in order not to disrupt *dharma,* to protect the family, to maintain the world and support order, and to please me and Viṣṇu, the God of gods and wielder of the discus. (*LT* 17.96–98)

The ecological significance of Viṣṇu's role as preserver of *dharma* can be enhanced by noting that the concept of *dharma* itself is capable of an ecological reinterpretation. Like the related Vedic word *ṛta*, *dharma* in many scriptural passages means not only social order but also cosmic order. As the *Taittirīya Āraṇyaka* says (10.79):

> *Dharma* is the foundation of the whole universe. . . . Upon *dharma* everything is founded. Therefore, *dharma* is called the highest good. (DeBary 1958, 215–16)

The Nārāyaṇīya section of the *Mahābhārata,* especially important to Vaiṣṇavas, says:

> *Dharma* [from the root *dhṛ,* "to sustain"] is so called on account of its capacity for sustaining [the world]. On account of *dharma,* creatures (*prajā*) are sustained separately in their respective stations. Whatever sustains, that is proper; that indeed is *dharma.*[9]

Thus the traditional Hindu notion of *dharma* is naturally extendable to include the modern notion of ecological order and balance. For surely it is ecological order and stability which is the foundation of the whole biosphere and which sustains all species "in their respective stations." This relatively small step in theological reasoning can have important implications. The following passage from the *Manu Smṛti* (8.15) takes on new vigor if the word *dharma* is read as "ecological order": "*Dharma,* when violated, verily, destroys; *dharma,* when preserved, preserves; therefore, *dharma* should not be violated, lest the violated *dharma* destroy us."[10]

Furthermore, texts from *dharmaśāstra* and *itihāsa-purāṇa* often include dharmic injunctions for humans to act in ways that support ecological order. The *Manu Smṛti* prohibits polluting the water of rivers (*MS* 4.56). The *dharma* texts of Āpastamba and Yājñavalkya both prohibit wanton cutting of leaves, flowers, and twigs.[11] The *Viṣṇu Purāṇa* declares, "God, Keśava, is pleased with a person who does not harm or destroy other non-speaking creatures or animals" (*VP* 3.8.15). Yājñavalkya's text warns that hell awaits those who kill domesticated and protected animals.[12]

In the Vaiṣṇava tradition, commands from *dharmaśāstra* are not seen as mere social convention for those who ignorantly identify with their body and social role but as the word and command of Viṣṇu, the supreme Lord. The Śrīvaiṣṇava theologians are fond of quoting an untraced *śloka,* presumably from Pāñcarātra, where Viṣṇu says, "*Śruti* and *smṛti* are my commands; he who acts transgressing these is a lawbreaker, a traitor to me. Even if he is devoted to me, he is not a Vaiṣṇava."[13]

The notion that Viṣṇu, the supreme God, establishes and actively preserves *dharma*, loves and demands obedience to it, and condemns and fights against those who disrupt it, can go a long way toward grounding a Vaiṣṇava environmental ethic. What is right or moral, as the Śrīvaiṣṇava tradition claims, is what is pleasing to Viṣṇu and in accord with *dharma*; what is evil or immoral is what Viṣṇu finds displeasing and runs contrary to *dharma*.[14] If *dharma* includes ecological order, and *adharma* includes ecological imbalance, and if scripture supports that what Viṣṇu wants is the maintenance of *dharma* and what Viṣṇu hates is *adharma*, then a firm foundation for a Vaiṣṇava ecological ethic is laid.

The skeptic might ask: even if support for ecological order is desired by God, why should one do what the Lord wants? The Śrīvaiṣṇava tradition has two answers for this. First of all, good and bad *karma* and the necessary consequences of them are due to nothing but the Lord's pleasure and displeasure at the action of sentient souls who obey or disobey his commands. Those sentient souls in *saṃsāra* who violate *dharma* incur the Lord's displeasure and suffer for their action in this life or the next. Those who follow and support *dharma* please the Lord and incur reward in their next life.[15]

But this ethic applies only to those who are still bound in *saṃsāra* and are aiming at improving their status therein. What about those who are *mumukṣus*, souls desirous of release from *saṃsāra*? Śrīvaiṣṇavism would seem to have the same problem in grounding an environmental ethic that traditional Christian theologies face: if the ultimate goal and human destiny is salvation outside of this world—and if that should be our foremost goal—should not our efforts be directed thereto, rather than toward maintaining this world? Why should one whose goal is to get out of this world support an environmental ethic to preserve it?

Śrīvaiṣṇava soteriology says that salvation comes from *prapatti*, simple surrender to the Lord in recognition of one's soul's inherent subservience (*śeṣatva*) to and dependence on him. *Prapatti* is a momentary act, a turning of the will away from selfish egoism and greed (*ahaṃkāra* and *mamākara*) toward loving dependence on the Lord, in response to the Lord's saving grace. The arguments within the Śrīvaiṣṇava tradition about the nature of *prapatti* need not concern us here.[16] But the tradition teaches unanimously that (1) after *prapatti*, the soul's release from saṃsāric bondage at the end of this life is assured, and (2) the life of a *prapanna*—one who has submitted to the Lord—is to be occupied with service. Service to the Lord, says Rāmānuja and the Śrīvaiṣṇava tradition, is the destiny of the sentient soul, on account of its inherent nature as *śeṣa,* one whose purpose is to contribute excellence to the *śeṣī,* the Lord.[17] Service will ultimately culminate after the death of one's last body, when one crosses over *saṃsāra* to Paramapāda. There, with a new body of pure matter, one will blissfully serve the supreme body of the Lord in Vaikuṇṭha forever, and the soul's inherent nature (*svarūpa*) of servitude (*śeṣatva*) will be fully manifest (*Mumu* 170–71).

This soteriology would not seem to give much grounding for environmental activism, except for the Śrīvaiṣṇava *ācāryas'* unanimous and emphatic insistence that service to the Lord should begin here on earth, immediately after one's surrender to the Lord. Even though one's knowledge and ability to act will still be inhibited by having a material body that continues to be subject to ripening *karma*, and even though the Lord's presence here in this world is not as fully manifest as it is in Vaikuṇṭha, nevertheless service to the Lord—the soul's ultimate purpose and destiny—can and should begin to manifest in the life of the *prapanna* (*Mumu* 112, 173–84). Indeed, there is nothing else for such a Vaiṣṇava to do, for he has already "done what must be done" to assure his salvation (*Mumu* 94). Once the means (*upāya)* for salvation is accomplished, what follows is the manifestation of the goal (*upeya*) of service.

What forms should this earthly service take? Śrīvaiṣṇava theologians have emphasized several types of service beyond fulfillment of normal *varṇāśrama-dharma* obligations: first, temple service, where one serves the Lord's body in the form of his *arcāvatāra*;[18] second, service to the Lord's devotees—those whom the Lord especially loves and, according to the *Bhagavad Gītā*, regards as his very self;[19] and third, service to support the world (*loka-saṅgraha*) and the dharmic order as described in the *Bhagavad Gītā*.[20] It would be easy for a contemporary Śrīvaiṣṇava *ācārya* to argue that service to support the earth, the ecosystem, and the environment is consistent with these three forms of the *prapanna*'s service. If the soul's destiny as a *śeṣa* is to serve the Lord's body, then here on earth that service can begin as service to the earth and its creatures, for these too, according to Śrīvaiṣṇavism, are the Lord's body, no less than the *arcāvatāra*. Those whom the Lord loves include all creatures, for these are his body, which he regards as his self, and for whose salvation and protection he has often incarnated. Service to support the world *(loka-saṅgraha)* and the dharmic order could conceivably include environmental activism, which would certainly be pleasing to the Lord because of His express desire to maintain dharmic order. Thus Śrīvaiṣṇava theology, with its vision of Viṣṇu as the preserver of dharmic order and its emphasis on serving the Lord, has the capacity to support a strong environmental ethic, in spite of its other-worldly conception of salvation.

## The Universe and Divine Purpose: Nature As God's Playground

Christian ecological theologians are struggling to come up with a doctrine of nature which clarifies its divine purpose. Many traditional Christian theologies have been very anthropocentric, seeing nature merely as a servant of humankind or a backdrop for God's soteriological plan. Such theologies have not supported environmental responsibility and have lost credibility in the face of increasing scientific evidence that human beings may not be the crown of creation. The notion of a divine plan focusing on human beings, toward which all history is leading, sits ill with what modern evolutionary theory teaches us: There have been immense stretches of time since creation, in which human history is merely a blip. The process by which species emerge, evolve, and become extinct is a groping, seemingly random process of mutation and natural selection, with no single teleological line but many blind branches. Furthermore, God's love and justice, central to most interpretations of the divine plan, are difficult to square with the violence and cruelty of the nature portrayed in evolutionary theory, marked by fierce competition for survival both within and between species.

Śrīvaiṣṇava thinkers and authors have not even begun to adapt their traditional theology to current evolutionary theory; if and when they do, they will no doubt encounter as many difficulties as Christian theologians have. But there are some ways in which the Śrīvaiṣṇava theology of nature may be compatible with scientific theory and at the same time help support an environmental ethic. A future, updated Śrīvaiṣṇava "theology of nature" would do well to focus on the traditional notion of *līlā*, God's sport or play, in articulating the purpose, role, and value of nature.

We have already explained how, according to Śrīvaiṣṇavism, both sentient souls and the material realm of *prakṛti*, as the Lord's bodies, have their value as his *śeṣas*—those whose destiny and purpose is to "contribute some excellence" to their Lord and *śeṣī*. Ultimately, as we have seen, the destiny of sentient souls is to do that by serving him in Vaikuṇṭha. But if, as the *Viṣṇu Purāṇa* states, they exist in all their states for his sake,[21] what are the more immediate ways in which sentient souls and material nature contribute excellence to the Lord in their saṃsāric state? Śrīvaiṣṇava tradition does answer this question, but first some background on its view of the structure of the universe is needed.

Rāmānuja and his followers distinguish two levels of the created world. The *nitya-vibhūti* is the eternal heavenly realm of Paramapāda, constructed of pure matter (*śuddha-sattva*). The *līlā-vibhūti* is the saṃsāric realm constructed of gross matter or *prakṛti* (with its constituent three *guṇas* of *sattva, rajas,* and *tamas*), which is subject to periodic creation and destruction. As stated above, in the blissful realm of Paramapāda, the magnificent, supreme body of the Lord and his consort are served by the eternally free angels or *nityasuris* and the freed souls in their bodies of pure matter. But in the saṃsāric realm, there is suffering and death as sentient souls transmigrate according to their *karma* into the bodies of demons in the various hells; plants, animals, and humans in the earthly realm; and deities in the various heavens.

The relation between Paramapāda and *saṃsāra* is hierarchical, and even the saṃsāric realm is hierarchically ordered in accord with the ranking of the three *guṇas: sattva* or goodness dominates in the heavenly realms which are attained by sacrificial works, *tamas* or darkness dominates in the hells, and *rajas* or energy dominates in the earthly, middle region.[22] Eco-theologians, particularly ecofeminists are generally suspicious of hierarchical models of the universe. However, unlike the Great Chain of Being of medieval Christianity, this Vaiṣṇava model emphasizes the continuity between levels. Any sentient soul can and has been incarnated in all of the saṃsāric realms. Souls in all levels are equal in their essential nature; all can eventually be freed to take their place alongside the angels (*nityasuris*) in the eternal heavenly realm.[23] In the Vaiṣṇava model, the relation between the human and animal realms is particularly close. The Lord himself has descended in *avatāras* having both animal and human form, and so have some of the *nityasuris* or eternally free angels, who often accompany him.[24] Vaiṣṇavas are adamant vegetarians, and killing animals is a sin only quantitatively—not qualitatively—different from killing human beings. Freedom from *saṃsāra* can most readily be won from the human and animal realms, not the hells or the heavenly realms.[25] Consequently, Śrīvaiṣṇava tradition looks down on seeking rebirth in the saṃsāric heavens through Vedic sacrifice.

What is the ultimate purpose of this complex hierarchical universe which the Lord creates and sustains? Vaiṣṇava thought emphasizes that the Lord himself has no specific purpose or goal to fulfill in creating the world, for this would threaten Divine perfection by implying that he is somehow incomplete or lacking in himself. Rather, Vaiṣṇavas claim that the manifest world exists as a joyful outlet for his creative sport or play, *līlā*, and thereby glorifies him. Rāmānuja illustrates this with a very instructive analogy: the Lord's "purpose" in creating and maintaining the created world, he says, is no different from that of a mighty emperor who, with no more outlets for his qualities of courage and valor, might engage in some recreation such as ball games, simply for the purpose of sport or play (*līlā*) (*BSR* 2.1.33; Carman 1978, 118–19). A powerful ruler does not engage in such sports out of any need to accomplish a specific goal, but only to find some outlet and expression for his power. Such games serve only a kind of "purposeless purpose" which glorifies the king's nature in joyful self-expression of his prowess. Thus Rāmānuja describes the Lord as the one "whose sport (*līlā*) it is to create, sustain and dissolve the whole universe, completely filled with diverse, wonderful and countless objects of enjoyment and orders of beings that enjoy [them]" (*BhGR*, p. 2).

Though the purpose of both realms of creation amount to *līlā*, joyful and expressive play or sport, the later Śrīvaiṣṇava tradition brings out a distinction hinted at in Rāmānuja's *Vedārtha Saṅgraha*: that there are two different types of enjoyment which the Lord receives from the eternal realm of Paramapāda and the created and ever-changing realm of *saṃsāra* (*VS* 214–15). The eternal realm, untouched by suffering, exists to provide the Lord with *bhoga* or unmitigated, blissful delight. The saṃsāric realm exists to provide the Lord with *līlā*, sport *per se*. Sports and games involve losing and winning, agreed upon goals to be won, and penalties to be avoided, and thus the potential for joy and suffering alike. Similarly, in the saṃsāric realm which exists for the sport of the Lord, the ultimate goal of the players is *mokṣa*, and the rules are the dharmic order and the law of *karma,* by which one experiences the results of one's good and bad deeds in the form of joy or suffering. The Lord himself is the owner of both the field and the players, and he is the audience who enjoys the game (the "field-knower" or *kṣetrajña*). But the Śrīvaiṣṇava tradition also portrays the Lord in a role something like the coach and cheerleader for the players, encouraging them through his teaching and his *avatāras* to win the game. Śrīvaiṣṇava theologians delight in portraying how the Lord worries, frets, and struggles to try to free souls from *saṃsāra* within the parameters of its rules.[26]

This sports analogy has important implications, I think, for allowing Śrīvaiṣṇava theology to reconcile divine purpose and God's saving action with a realistic assessment of the cruelty and suffering found in nature. Suffering, struggle, loss, and gain are part of the natural realm, the saṃsāric realm, just as they are inherent to any sport or game. The possibility of suffering and defeat in sports enhances the pleasure of the fans; similarly, suffering, death, and loss in *saṃsāra* enhance the pleasure of the Lord, the Ultimate Fan of the *līlā-vibhūti*, the realm of sport. The eternal heavenly realm of delight or *bhoga*, much like a concert of fine music, contributes to the Lord's glory by providing unending bliss and joy for him and for all concerned. But it is only in the realm of the created world that the Lord can enjoy both "the thrill of victory and the agony of defeat." Nature and the saṃsāric realm resemble the Olympic Games, a never-ending multi-athalon that expresses, glorifies, and delights the Lord who devised it. Thus the created world—precisely because of its capacity for evil, death, struggle, and suffering—has value in enhancing the Lord's pleasure and glory in ways that the heavenly realm cannot.

Thus, in light of the concept of *līlā* and the "sports model" which elaborates it, Śrīvaiṣṇava theology is able to see the created universe and natural realm as valuable to God not only in spite of, but indeed partly because of the drama of life and death we find there, with all its cruelty and suffering. When Christian ecotheologians speak of nature glorifying God and manifesting his purposes, it seems to me that they must romanticize it to square with their profession of God's goodness, or at least overlook or downplay the "survival of the fittest" ethic which seems built into the very structure of the natural order. They cannot clearly answer why a compassionate God would design nature to be as cruel and barbarous as evolutionary theory suggests, or why such a God would find it valuable. The Śrīvaiṣṇava tradition is better able to reconcile God's beneficence and nature's cruelty through its vision of a God who delights in the sport of nature and its evolutionary "game," who seeks to maintain the dharmic ecological order which allows the game to flourish, and who nevertheless works with compassion and grace to deliver sentient souls, its "players," from their travails.

The Lord's "enjoyment" of nature's sport of birth and death need not undermine or detract from a Vaiṣṇava-inspired incentive for either the Lord or human beings to preserve the environment. For as the preserver of *dharma,* the Lord cares both about the individual players in the realm of sport and about the dharmic order as a whole, which makes the game possible. As evolutionary theory suggests, the death and birth of individuals, the extinction of old species and the evolution of new ones, are all natural processes in what for Śrīvaiṣṇavas would be the ever-changing realm of *prakṛti*. This whole process could be seen as contributing to the Lord's *līlā*. Nevertheless, there are limits to how much death and destruction of creatures can take place without constituting a threat to dharmic order itself. As the *Bhagavad Gītā* explains, whenever dharmic order is threatened by *adharma*, Viṣṇu takes direct action, coming down onto the field himself as an *avatāra*, to re-establish dharmic order by suppressing whatever demonic force of *adharma* is threatening it. The Lord's saving activity in the form of his *avatāras* is yet another manifestation of his *līlā*, but one which shows the Lord's commitment to the preservation of the game and its players! There is yet another way, I think, that the mythology of Viṣṇu's *avatāras* has an important potential in supporting environmental activism—as I shall explain in the next section.

## Viṣṇu's Varāha *Avatāra:* A Myth for the Ecological Movement

To capture the zeal and devotion of the masses, a religious movement needs to be able to call upon powerful mythic themes with deep cultural roots. Western history has seen countless Christian religious movements drawing from the messianic myth of the second coming of Christ. The popularity of Martin Luther King, Jr.'s Civil Rights movement owes much to King's ability to draw parallels between his movement and the Exodus story. In India, both Gandhi and contemporary Indian politicians have appealed to the Rāma myth to legitimate their movements. So far the ecological movement in the West has not been able to rally around a single mythological theme from the Judeo-Christian tradition to support its mission. Eco-theologians are still groping to redefine and reshape the creation and Jesus stories in ways that might support an ecological theology.

By contrast, the Vaiṣṇava tradition possesses, in its vast mythic arsenal, one very powerful myth which can easily be adapted to support the ecological movement. The story of Viṣṇu's Varāha or Boar *avatāra* has deep roots that go back to the *Śatapaṭha Brāhmaṇa* and *Taittirīya Saṃhita*[27] and are fleshed out in various later epic and purāṇic versions, notably the *Mahābhārata* and the *Viṣṇu, Matsya,* and *Bhāgavata Purāṇas.*[28] The most well-known versions of the story, however, are not the ones written in Sanskrit tomes, but those told by grandparents to children, dramatized in village theater, and portrayed in temple iconography. As the popular story goes, back in the Satya Yuga, the earth was submerged in the waters, dragged there—according to some versions of the story—by an evil demon named Hiraṇyākṣa. Viṣṇu, true to his character as sustainer of *dharma,* took the form of a boar. He battled and killed the demon in a protracted struggle, and diving to the bottom of the ocean, raised up the earth on his tusks and spread it out as it is today. The earth itself, in many versions of the story, is envisioned as a beautiful goddess. Vaiṣṇava temples all over India often portray the moment after this rescue in a statue of Viṣṇu with a boar's head, emerging victoriously from the waters with the lovely goddess Bhū Devī—the Earth—perched on his upraised tusks. Śrīvaiṣṇava tradition, on account of this myth, sees Bhū Devī, the earth goddess, as one of Viṣṇu's consorts or wives, along with Śrī or Lakṣmī, the goddess of prosperity, with which she is sometimes identified. According to traditional Śrīvaiṣṇava hagiography, Aṇḍāḷ, the only woman among the poet-saints or *Āḻvārs*, was a later incarnation of Bhū Devī; she was found as a baby under a plant in a temple, and grew up to "marry" the temple image of her Lord Viṣṇu.

I suspect this mythic image of Viṣṇu as Varāha, the husband and lover of the earth, who rescues her from her distress and affliction, would have a powerful potential to motivate a Vaiṣṇava ecological movement.[29] In fact, the details of the myth seem to have an eerily prophetic analogy to the contemporary ecological crisis. The striking parallel between the descriptions of the earth's plight in the accounts of the Varāha myth found in *itihāsa-purāṇa* and the current ecological crisis brought on by overpopulation and pollution have caught the eye of at least one contemporary Hindu intellectual—Shanti Lal Nagar, in his recent study of the Varāha myth in Indian culture (Nagar 1993, 36–39). If predictions of global warming are correct, the earth may soon find itself quite literally sunk into the oceans, and the demon of industrial and corporate greed (Hiraṇyākṣa means "golden eyes"!) may be largely to blame. An Indian ecological movement growing out of the Vaiṣṇava tradition would do well to name itself after the Varāha myth, and present itself as a movement re-enacting for the present age the mission of Varāha—doing battle with the demons of polluting industries to rescue a distressed earth from its ecological crisis and reinstate the ecological dharmic order. What better myth could one want to support an ecological movement?

Ecofeminists might not be so enthused, for some of them have criticized a similar secular mythic theme used in Western environmentalist discourse: the notion of "mother nature" as a "damsel in distress" who must be "rescued" by a knight in shining armor. Ecofeminists decry the patriarchal roots of this metaphor that sees nature and women both as helpless and in need of male authority.[30] Such criticism of the Western myth would also seem to apply to the Hindu Varāha myth, though ameliorated perhaps by the fact that here it is the Lord himself who is portrayed as the husband and lover of the Earth. However, if an effective environmental movement cannot be marshalled until all forms of patriarchy and sexism have been eradicated from both Western and Indian culture, I fear that this will be too late. Does not the urgency of the ecological crisis argue for using whatever social and religious doctrines, institutions, and mythic themes that can be found in a culture to support environmental movements? The Varāha myth may not help the cause of feminism, and may well foster a way of thinking about the earth that can cause problems later; but its powerful potential to give immediate support to a Hindu environmental movement that is facing a severe environmental crisis argues that it should be exploited now.

## Conclusion

In the preceding pages I have sketched a few outlines of a Vaiṣṇava environmental theology that could provide support for the environmental movement in India. The main problem with this theology is that it does not exist at present. I agree with Rosemary Ruether that, to be genuine, an environmental theology must come from voices inside the tradition, and not from outside scholars such as myself. "The plumbing of each tradition, and its reinterpretation for today's crises, is a profound task that needs to begin in the context of communities of accountability." This does not preclude cross-cultural theological conversations, she says, for "we must ultimately draw upon all our spiritual resources in a global community of interrelated spiritual traditions." But the members of individual communities are the ones who are "best suited to dig these roots and offer their fruits to the rest of us. Those without these roots should be cautious in claiming plants not our own, respectful of those who speak from within" (Ruether 1992, 206).

Is the Śrīvaiṣṇava community up to the task of plumbing its tradition, reinterpreting and applying it to today's ecological crisis? Are there figures within Vaiṣṇavism or Hinduism in general who can or will be able to fashion an effective environmental theology that can motivate the masses? Time alone will tell if an environmental Gandhi will arise in India to lead a mass movement to avert ecological disaster. As an outsider, I have only tried to point to the ammunition within the Vaiṣṇava tradition which such a figure might be able to use, were such a person to come forward. What Rosemary Ruether says of the Christian tradition seems equally applicable to the Hindu Vaiṣṇava tradition:

> The Christian tradition is one of those communities of accountability that has profoundly valuable themes for ecological spirituality and practice. It also has problematic defects. . . . But, for that reason, its liberating potential should not be disregarded. Those too alienated from this tradition to allow it to speak to them have every right to seek other spiritual traditions that can nurture them. But the vast majority of the more than one billion Christians of the world can be lured

> into an ecological consciousness only if they see that it grows in some ways from the soil in which they are planted. (Ruether 1992, 206–7)

The seeds of a theology that could rouse the nearly one billion Hindus in the world to a deeper ecological consciousness are yet dormant in the Śrīvaiṣṇava tradition, but—as I have tried to show—the soil is fertile.

## Notes

1. See, for instance, the essays in *Ecological Healing* (Wright and Kill 1993).

2. See, for example, McFague 1993, viii–x and 88, where both reasons are given to support her theological model of the world as the body of God.

3. See *The Sacred Books of the East*, vol. 44, 172, 403; cited in Lott 1976, 29.

4. See John Carman and Vasudha Narayanan, *The Tamil Veda: Piḷḷāṉ's Interpretation of the Tiruvāymoḻi* (Chicago: University of Chicago Press, 1989) and Nancy Ann Nayar, *Poetry as Theology: The Śrīvaiṣṇava Stotra in the Age of Rāmānuja* (Wiesbaden: Otto Harassowitz, 1992).

5. As in *BSR* 1.2.22 and 1.4.28.

6. Rāmānuja, in *VS* 99, says, "The essential nature of the individual self is such that it is wholly subservient and instrumental to God and therefore God is its inner self." See also *TT* 1.38–41.

7. In *VS* 159 Rāmānuja quotes *VP* 1.1.31 to say that all three functions ultimately belong to Viṣṇu.

8. This is an often quoted etymology of Viṣṇu's name. See *Śrī Vishnu Sahasranāma with the Bhāshya of Śrī Paraśara Bhaṭṭar*, ed. and trans. by A. Srinivasa Raghavan (Madras: Śrī Visishtadvaita Pracharini Sabha, 1983), 108.

9. dhāraṇād dharma ity āhur dharmeṇa vidhṛtāḥ prajāḥ / yat syād dhāraṇa saṃyuktaṃ sa dharma iti niścayaḥ (*Mbh* 12.110.11).

10. dharma eva hato hanti dharmo rakṣati rakṣataḥ / tasmād dharmo na hantavyo mā no dharmo hato 'vadhīt (*MS* 8.15; translation from DeBary 1958, 216).

11. *Yājñavalkyasmṛti* 3.276 and *Āpastambadharmasūtra* 1.2.7.4, as cited in Braj Kishore Swain's "Plant Ecology and the Law of the Relationship," *Journal of Dharma* 16 (July–September 1991): 224–25.

12. *Yājñavalkyasmṛti,* Ācārādhyāya 180, cited in O. P. Dwivedi, "*Satyagraha* for Conservation: Awakening the Spirit of Hinduism," *This Sacred Earth: Religion, Nature, Environment*, ed. Roger S. Gottlieb (New York: Routledge, 1996), 156.

13. śrutis smṛtir mamaivājnā yastāmullaṅghya varttate / ājnācchedi mama drohi madbhakto 'pi na vaiṣṇavaḥ (Quoted by Maṇavāḷamāmuni in *ŚVB* 15.278, and by Vedānta Deśika in *RTS* chap. 17).

14. See *VS* 124–26 and 194–97.

15. See Rāmānuja on *VS* 194–97.

16. See Mumme 1988, chaps. 3 and 4.

17. See Rāmānuja in *VS* 182 and 250, and Maṇavāḷamāmuni in *Mumu* 177.

18. See Maṇavāḷamāmuni on *ĀH* 31.

19. See Carman 1978, 190–93 and *RTS* chaps. 15 and 16.

20. See *BhG* 3.23–24, Maṇavāḷamāmuni on *ŚVB* 278, and Mumme 1988, 154.

21. *VP* 1.1.69, quoted by Rāmānuja in *VS* 160.

22. The last chapters of the *BhG*, with its analysis of existence in accord with the three *guṇas*, is the basis for much Vaiṣṇava theological speculation about the structure of the world.

23. Rāmānuja in *VS* 101 shows continuity and even equality within the hierarchical realms of *saṃsāra*: " 'The wise look upon as equal one blessed with knowledge and humility, a mere Brahmin, a cow, an elephant, a dog and an outcaste' (*BhG* 5.18). The wise are those who can distinguish the essential nature of the self even though it is associated with any of the varied kinds of bodies, such as the heavenly, human, animal and plant. They are enlightened about the nature of the self, as transcending the varied and specialized modifications of material nature. They discern the equal nature of all selves, embodied in the most unequal and dissimilar material forms. Therefore they are said to have the vision of equality."

24. However, in Śrīvaiṣṇava theology, when the Lord incarnates in his *avatāra* or *vibhava* manifestations, though the form of his body may be human or animal, the substance of his body is seen to be of pure matter or *śuddha-sattva*, not the gross matter in which the souls of humans and animals trapped in *saṃsāra* are incarnate. This docetic interpretation of the *avatāras*, which Rāmānuja (*VS* 162) attributes to the *Mahābhārata*, was apparently seen as necessary to preserve the Lord's purity. It is not clear to me whether Śrīvaiṣṇavas would insist that the incarnate forms of the *nityasuris* are also of *śuddha-sattva*, since this would include some of the Śrīvaiṣṇava *ācāryas* themselves, such as Rāmānuja, who is often claimed to be an incarnation of Anantaśeṣa.

25. The *Bhāgavata Purāṇa*'s story of the elephant Gajendra, who prayed to Viṣṇu when his leg was seized by a crocodile, and received *mokṣa*, is a good example of a popular myth showing that salvation can be received by animals. The Śrīvaiṣṇava tradition is unanimous in teaching that *mokṣa* cannot be reached, however, by souls in the saṃsāric heavens won by sacrificial good works.

26. This is a common theme in the introductions to Śrīvaiṣṇava theological works, which delight in portraying the Lord's attempts to rescue souls through creation, revelation of the Veda, *avatāras*, and so forth. See Rāmānuja's introduction to *BSR* and Maṇavāḷamāmuni's introduction to *Mumu*.

27. See Wendy Doniger O'Flaherty, *Hindu Myths* (New York: Penguin Books, 1975), 184–87.

28. See *Mahābhārata* 3.142.28ff (according to Nagar 1993, 5) and *Viṣṇu Purāṇa* 5.5.15, *Matsya Purāṇa* chaps. 47 and 247–48, and *Bhāgavata Purāṇa* 3.13.18–45, according to V. R. Ramadhandra Dikshitar, *The Purāṇa Index*, vol. 3 (Madras: University of Madras, 1955), 153–54.

29. It would not be the first time this myth has been used to legitimate a socio-political movement. According to Shanti Lal Nagar, various Hindu dynasties from the second century B.C.E. on, notably the Kushanas and Guptas, used this mythic theme to justify and popularize their expulsion of foreign invasions and/or victory over rival heterodox kings (Nagar 1993, 2–7).

30. See Chaia Heller's "For the Love of Nature: Ecology and the Cult of the Romantic," in *Ecofeminism: Women, Animals, Nature*, ed. Greta Gaard (Philadelphia, Temple University Press, 1993), 219–42, for a thought-provoking ecofeminist critique of this metaphor.

## References

### Primary Sources, with Abbreviations


*ĀH* *Ācārya Hṛdayam* of Aḻakiya Maṇavāḷa Perumāl Nāyaṉār, with Maṇavāḷamāmuni's commentary. Śrīmad Varavaramunīndra Granthamālā, 3. Edited and published by P. B. Annangaracharya. Kanchi, 1966.

*AP* *Artha Pañchaka* of Piḷḷai Lokācārya. English and Hindi translation by T. Bheemacharya and S. N. Shastri. Indore: Bharati Publications, 1972.

*BhG* See *BhGR*

*BhGR* *The Gītābhāṣya of Rāmānuja*. Translated by M. R. Sampatkumaran. Bombay: Ananthacharya Indological Research Institute, 1985.

*BSR* *The Vedānta Sūtras with the Śrī-Bhāsya of Rāmājujāchārya*. Translated by M. Rangacharya and M. B. Varadaraja Iyangar. 3 vols. Madras: Educational Publishing Co., 1965.

*LT* *Lakṣmī Tantra*. Edited by V. Krishnamacharya. Madras: Adyar Library, 1959.

*Mbh* *Mahābhārata*. Edited by Visnu S. Sukthankar, et al. 19 vols. Poona: Bhandarkar Oriental Research Institute, 1927–66.

*MS* *Manusmṛti*. Edited by Haragovinda Sastri. Varanasi: Chowkahmba Sanskrit Series, 1965.

*Mumu* *The Mumukṣuppati of Piḷḷai Lokācārya, with Maṇavāḷamāmuni's Commentary*. Edited and published by S. Krishnaswami Iyengar. Trichy, n.d. See also the translation by Patricia Y. Mumme. Bombay: Ananthacharya Indological Research Institute, 1987.

*RTS* *Śrīmad Rahasyatrayasāra* of Vedānta Deśika. Translated by M. R. Rajagopala Ayyangar. Kumbakonam: Agnihothram Rāmānuja Thathachariar, 1956.

*ŚVB* *Śrīvacana Bhūsaṇa* of Piḷḷai Lokācārya, with Maṇavāḷmāmuni's commentary. Edited by P. Raghava Rāmānuja Swami. Madras: R. Rajagopal Naidu, 1936.

*TT* *Tattvatraya* of Piḷḷai Lokāchārya. Translated by M. B. Narasimha Iyengar. Madras: M. C. Krishnan, 1960.

*Up.* *The Thirteen Principal Upanishads*. 2d ed. Translated by Robert E. Hume. Delhi: Oxford University Press, 1983.

*VP* *Śrīviṣṇupurāṇam*. Edited by P. B. Annangaracharya. Kanchipuram: Granthamala, 1972.

*VS* *Vedārtha Saṅgraha* of Rāmānuja. Edited and translated by S. S. Raghavachar. Mysore: Śrī Ramakrishna Asrama, 1978.

**Secondary Sources**

Carman, John Braisted. 1978. *The Theology of Rāmānuja: An Essay in Interreligious Understanding*. New Haven: Yale University Press.

DeBary, William Theodore, ed. 1958. *Sources of Indian Tradition*. Vol. 1. New York: Columbia University Press.

Klostermaier, Klaus. 1987. "The Body of God." In *The Charles Strong Lectures*, ed. Robert B. Crotty, 103–19. Leiden: E. J. Brill.

———. 1991. "Bhakti, Ahiṁsā, and Ecology." *Journal of Dharma* 16 (July–September 1991) 246–54.

Lott, Eric. 1976. *God and the Universe in the Vedāntic Theology of Rāmānuja*. Madras: Ramanuja Research Society.

McFague, Sallie. 1993. *The Body of God: An Ecological Theology*. Minneapolis: Fortress Press.

Nagar, Shanti Lal. 1993. *Varāha in Indian Art, Culture, and Literature*. New Delhi: Aryan Books International.

Ramanujan, A. K. 1981. *Hymns for the Drowning*. Princeton: Princeton University Press, 1981.

Ruether, Rosemary Radford. 1992. *Gaia and God: An Ecofeminist Theology of Earth Healing*. San Francisco: Harper SanFrancisco.

Wright, Nancy G., and Donald Kill. 1993. *Ecological Healing: A Christian Vision*. Maryknoll, N.Y.: Orbis Books.

# Part II

# Views from the Field

**Ann Grodzins Gold**

# 7

# Sin and Rain: Moral Ecology in Rural North India

## Introduction

In December 1992 I went to Rajasthan to study cultural constructions of the environment.[1] My specific focus was to be the intertwining of popular Hinduism with agriculture and herding practices. I returned to a place, Ghatiyali in Ajmer District, where I had lived over a decade earlier, in order to study the religious values motivating pilgrimage (Gold 1988). In imagining this new fieldwork, I conjectured that rituals surrounding production (planting, harvest, livestock health, and so forth) in the harsh, semiarid environment would reveal something about the ways popular Hinduism conditioned people's treatment of and ideas about their natural surroundings. I hoped to understand the interplay of symbolic and practical dimensions within a farming community's ecological relationships.[2] My central research question was whether and how religious values affect the ways people interact with their environment when engaged in production as well as in prayer or storytelling. I warn readers from the start that no clear answers emerged. In rural Rajasthan as in many parts of the globe, for anthropologists as for peasants, the late twentieth century is a time of multiple uncertainties.

As I struggled to find the right people to ask the right questions, I soon discovered that the ritual cycles that I had thought to study were in an accelerated transitional flux, and that this flux was intrinsic to and conditioned by some much larger patterns.[3] Thus I found myself increasingly gripped by narratives of change. I knew vaguely from casual comments people had made during my earlier residence in this area, and from the general literature on deforestation and the decline of common property resources in Rajasthan, that the landscape had undergone radical transformations within the last half-century, and thus within living memories.[4] I recalled persons telling me in 1980 of a dense, dark, and frightening forest[5] with lions and tigers, where now we saw scrubby, barren, largely open land. I had found this hard to imagine, and paid it little special attention.

Most of my earlier research was concerned with the pressing realities in human lives of invisible entities: deities, ghosts, witches. I understood that such personified imperceptible beings moved and motivated the present in discernible ways. But the vanished trees and absent wild animals did not then seem to me to be as pressing or vivid an imaginative reality; in that impression I was mistaken. Transformations in the landscape, I learned in 1993, have affected hearts and minds poignantly, even as do the changes in family composition and interpersonal relationships that lie at the heart of ghost and witch stories.[6]

Hard in search of ideas about nature, but a little baffled by where to find them, my closest collaborator in the village, Bhoju Ram Gujar, and I began to ask old people about the vanished trees.[7] Old people were in any case the easiest persons to find at home; old men, especially, were the only adults in the village with plenty of time and inclination to talk.[8] Each person spoke from a situated social position and an individual set of life experiences. Some even told conflicting stories. Nonetheless, an environmental history emerged that was remarkably consistent in tenor from one account to another. People portrayed interlocked changes in landscape, agriculture, society, religion and morality.

My focus in this chapter is on villagers' perceptions of changes in landscape, weather, and *dharma* or morality. They pose explicitly causal links among these, but the causality they describe is neither singular nor linear. I suggest that the understanding of change conveyed to me and Bhoju by Ghatiyalians is fundamentally ecological in its sensitivity to the weblike interconnectedness of concurrent transformations.

Deforestation is certainly the most dramatically visible change. Ghatiyali, whose name derives from its valley location, is surrounded by hills—once densely wooded but now largely denuded. Each hill formation has a name, and some of these evoke the vanished woodlands. For example, one is called "Wild Pig Hill" and another "Thieves Pass"—each having once afforded shelter in its dense foliage to marauders, whether animal or human. The largest range is named Kāṇṭolā (perhaps from *kāṇṭo* for thorn), which one person glossed as "where there once was deep jungle."

Deforestation is associated with numerous alterations in human relationships, both political and interpersonal. Most specifically it reflects a wanton increase in the pursuit of selfish or familial interests. Deforestation is also a result of expanding agricultural land due to population growth and subsequent reduction of grazing ground. Lack of grazing space and foliage for fodder has necessitated reduced herds of cattle and buffalo. This impinges on domestic and communal harmony, people believe, because a diet high in milk products cools tempers and strengthens health, while a diet poor in dairy causes weak minds, testy spirits, vulnerable bodies. Moreover, with less cattle there is less dung, and consequent increased dependency on chemical fertilizer. A diet of grains grown with chemical fertilizer—many people told us—also causes rudeness, and lowers resistance to disease.

The causal web spreads further, its strands ultimately including immodest women, abandoned rituals, imported fabrics, and Western medicines among other items. But I must return to the weather, my subject in this chapter. I wish to highlight those strands in the ecological web connecting less trees with perceived climate change. It was easy to elicit discussion about the reasons for the trees' disappearance, as well as this transformation's long-term consequences. I first discuss villagers' ideas about why the trees are gone. I turn then to their more complicated discussions of why there appears to be less rainfall.

A few villagers express their appraisal of today's degenerate times with reference to the Kali Yuga, an era of culminating devolution defined in Sanskritic Hindu cosmic chronology, and commonly understood as the present.[9] While most who mentioned Kali Yuga were literate Brahmins, we now and then heard it evoked by uneducated farmers as well. In any case, a strong sense of moral and geophysical decay—with or without the Kali Yuga label—was pervasive at all levels of village society.

In concluding this chapter, in order to set Ghatiyalians' ideas about morality and climate change within some broader frameworks both in anthropology of religion and in Hindu cosmology, I consider a convergence between textual descriptions of Kali Yuga and those modern, popular ideas about today's diminishing quality of life that form this chapter's main substance. In textual depictions of Kali Yuga from the Sanskrit *purāṇas*, as in the social and environmental change narratives we elicited from Ghatiyalians, ecological breakdown and moral laxness have a thoroughly interpenetrating logic. This logic claims that human behaviors are irrevocably interwoven with the natural environment's condition, that the deterioration of one implies and involves the other. I briefly note that some potent environmentalist activist rhetorics of the nineties draw inspiration from just such convergence, reinterpreted to pose a necessary moral ecology for the future.[10]

## Why the Trees Are Gone

I must begin with some background particular to the setting of my research. For while many of the experiences and images of change that unfolded in our interviews undoubtedly reflect patterns existing in many parts of Rajasthan and throughout North India, it was often hard to keep this in mind. As stories of Ghatiyali's past unfolded, they made it appear unique: the stories of a singular place, its named localities and inhabitants. A key player in this remembered past was a strong personality: the *ṭhākur* or local ruler named Vansh Pradip Singh. Vansh Pradip Singh reigned over the very little kingdom of Sawar and its twenty-seven subordinate villages—located in the Banas River basin of central Rajasthan—for more than thirty years, from his ascension to the throne in 1914, until his death in 1947.[11] Ghatiyali had, and still has, the largest population within this principality, after the capital and market town of Sawar where the kingdom's main fort is located.

Vansh Pradip Singh's figure looms larger than life in many villagers' memories even today. This ruler had a strong interest in all kinds of religious works, and was a fervent protector of the forest and of wildlife (Mathur 1977). Indeed, everyone old enough to remember him told—with varied proportions of bitterness, astonishment, and admiration—how he had scattered popcorn for the wild boars who destroyed his subjects' crops, and caused persons who harmed any forest animals, or cut reserved trees, to be ignominiously beaten and fined.

Vansh Pradip Singh's death without progeny in 1947 resulted in a succession dispute to the Sawar throne that lasted until 1951. In that year his widow's adopted "son," Vrij Raj Singh, who was of the same generation as Vansh Pradip and already ruled nearby Chausala, was enthroned. During this four-year interregnum (coinciding coincidentally but not incidentally with a tumultuous period in India's history), a rapid decimation of trees and forest animals began. Within a single decade, the densely wooded hills—where lions, deer, jackal, and great destructive herds of wild boars once found sustenance and shelter—were stripped almost bare. Shortly after Vrij Raj Singh's succession to the Sawar royal seat, a series of land reform bills radically disempowered the former princes.[12]

With the advent of what villagers call "the Rule of Congress"—that is, the modern electoral government of independent India—the forest was finished. In Ghatiyali, people strongly associate in their minds the former ruling kings, old growths of indigenous trees, and wild animals. These three came to an end together, and as the tales are told, it appears this was both a sweet and bitter transformation. Most people, when asked pointblank if they were happier twenty years ago or today, answered "today" without equivocation: cash is more plentiful, taxes are a tiny fraction of their former weight, and villagers relish freedom from the indignities of unrestricted monarchy. Yet it is generally acknowledged that the "quality of life"—indexed by factors such as community solidarity, joint family harmony, and the good taste of food—has diminished. The ecological mood is one of loss, which the barren hills reveal.[13]

Dayal Gujar, a former herder, probably in his sixties, forced by ill health to stay at home, explicitly connects the changed landscape with the changed political regime. Others with whom we spoke believed, along with Dayal Gujar, that no one charged with law enforcement in the present era possessed or could exercise an authoritative power in any way comparable to that of the "great kings," the *rājā mahārājā*.[14] This does not mean that people lament their passing, but they are aware of its consequences for local government's effectiveness. Bhoju spoke with Dayal about environmental change as he experienced it in his years as a goatherd.

> **Bhoju:** For how many years did you graze goats?
>
> **Dayal:** For forty years.
>
> **Bhoju:** Between this time and that what are the differences?
>
> **Dayal:** Four *ānās* to a rupee [that is, the present is diminished, equal only to a quarter of what used to be].[15]
>
> **Bhoju:** What are all the differences?
>
> **Dayal:** At that time there were many boars, many wild cows, many deer, living in herds of hundreds, in such large groups. There were antelopes, and the boars and the lions even came right up to the village.
>
> Just as the *rājā mahārājā* are now finished *(khatm)* the jungle too is finished. . . . the kings were finished, their time *(vakt)* was finished, then people started to cut the trees because there was no responsible authority *(zimmedārī)*.
>
> **Bhoju:** But what about the forestry department, the guard *(syāṇā)*?
>
> **Dayal:** No, . . . the Congress came and they are all government workers, so there is no responsible authority.

The term usually used for the designated "cattle guard," whose job is to protect the trees from grazing livestock and firewood cutters, is the same today as in the past: *syāṇā*. But the sanctions today's government-appointed *syāṇā* wields, and his status in the village, are very different from those attributed to past guards who were agents of the king. For while the latter were strong-arms who abused their powers and exploited the people, the authority behind them was absolute, royal. Moreover, it was "responsible authority" because it was established, rooted, in the kingdom. The contemporary guard, as "government worker," has no permanent stake in the community where he is posted and from which he may be transferred. People believe (usually rightly) that he pursues his own interests at the expense of the village's.

Violence against trees was perpetuated in the early 1950s at several levels of the social order and in varied settings. Even as villagers stripped the uncultivated commons to store up firewood, the new *ṭhākur's* family sold off the roadside trees for cash. The ruler who succeeded Vansh Pradip Singh was well aware that the privileges of princely power were doomed. It was common knowledge in Ghatiyali, or at least common gossip, that this ruler's family members themselves had destroyed the shade trees along the seven-kilometer Sawar-Ghatiyali road. In contrast to Vansh Pradip Singh who had caused trees to be planted—a meritorious act recommended for kings in ancient Sanskrit texts[16]—his heirs (who were not his descendants) had them cut and sold. Thus, as villagers tell it, the royal family seized the moment to pursue selfishness as their right, thus using their charter for power very much in the same way as does today's cattle guard. People viewed this selling of shade trees as a paradigmatic act of amorality, and one that set the tone for what was to come.

Bhoju discusses these linked events with an elderly and educated Brahmin, Suva Lal Chasta, and his somewhat younger castefellow Bhairu Lal Chasta. Here as in other interviews the process of stripping trees is described in metaphors of consumption.[17]

> **Suva Lal:** Those who were to protect the jungle ate it. And besides that, the *rājā mahārājā* thought, "The jungle is ours." So after Independence, they thought, "It is our property." So they arranged to have it cut and sell it fast.
>
> Along the Sawar-Ghatiyali road, there were so many trees, every ten minutes on both sides. When they knew that the government was taking things over, they thought, "We planted these trees and they are ours."
>
> **Bhairu Lal:** They weren't sorry. They had planted and watered them and raised them, and their rule was over, so they cut them.

Dayal Gujar also describes the selling of shade trees, giving an account similar to the Brahmin men's:

**Dayal:** He [Vansh Pradip Singh] thought, "Between the gate of the Sawar castle and Ghatiyali there should be shade for my people," and he planted trees all along the road: *nīm, pīpal* and *ber* [all religiously valued species].

**Bhoju:** Where did all those trees go?

**Dayal:** They were eaten by the hungry [that is, Vansh Pradip Singh's successors]. They cut them all and sold them and ate them.

**Bhoju:** Was this sin (*pāp*) for them?

**Dayal:** Yes.

**Bhoju:** So why did they cut them?

**Dayal:** People think it is sin, but still they do it. What else can they do?

**Bhoju:** Does God *(bhagvān)* give punishment for this sin?

**Dayal:** God gives much punishment. He will give punishment to Vansh Pradip Singh's successors, or whoever cuts trees.

A burden of sin is ascribed to the rulers who had the trees cut and sold. This lapse into amoral behavior is emblematic of similar moral decay in society at large, just as the cutting and selling of roadside shade trees is used to evoke the greater commons problem and subsequent deforestation. In both situations a similar logic is at work: "I might as well get mine, because if I do not, someone else will only take advantage of the situation." In the past, we may suppose a sense of collective good demanding individual restraint operated to control village woodcutters, while a sense of appropriate kingly virtue combined with confidence in long-term investment potential controlled the ruling family.[18] After land reform, such restraints came loose at both ends of the hierarchy, and were not effectively replaced.

Today's forestry agent is perceived not only as amoral but as ineffective. Haidar Ali, a Muslim shopkeeper, contrasts the current forestry department's work with the enforcement carried out in the kings' era:

> **Haidar Ali:** The kinds of trees that once were no longer remain. The government servants sold them all and ate them, and people think it is just a game of sin (*pāp-līlā*).[19]
>
> In the time of the *rājā mahārājā* there were twenty forestry guards, but nowadays the government sends only one man.
>
> Suppose we build a thorn wall around our field but it starts to eat the field, how will it protect what it eats? [He follows this thought with a traditional saying:] "The hedge of thorns will eat the field, so how will the field be protected" (bāṛ khet ko khāyegī to khet kī rakṣā kaise hogī)?

This well-known proverb, I am told, may apply to kings as well as forestry guards. In other words, the seeds of exploitation lie within the practice of protection. This saying expresses common and widespread feelings, and is only one among many folklore texts reflecting on the untrustworthy nature of power-holders great and small.[20]

Nonetheless, not everyone blames the government for the loss of tree cover. Rup Lal Khati, an older man of the carpenter caste, reflective and intelligent, attributes the major share of blame to the community. He described the situation for us in terms of a classic commons tragedy: under conditions of increasing scarcity old rules of communal self-restraint are jettisoned, resulting in a free-for-all:

> **Rup Lal:** Before people needed firewood and today they need firewood, but when they saw that the wood was being used up, everyone thought, "I need some for myself," and they cut it even faster. They stored in advance.[21]
>
> And if at that time people had only taken what they needed, then the jungle wouldn't have been finished and everyone, and the cows, goats and buffaloes, all could have lived at ease.

The destruction of trees understood as sinful is evidently embedded in other concurrent degenerations both ecological and moral. Haidar Ali's portrayal of the forestry agent, and all those who negotiate with him, as engaged in a "sin-game" (*pāp līlā*) effectively expresses this convergence of wanton environmental destruction and lack of moral sensibilities. Rup Lal's account argues further that such selfishness is dangerously, rampantly contagious.

## Why Rain Is Less

In recent years the monsoon rains have often been inadequate. Although terrible famines were known in the past, people say that the good years were better, drought years fewer and further between, and that in general there was more rain. It is beyond this chapter's scope to assess the validity of this conviction—universally held in Ghatiyali to the extent of my knowledge—that there used to be more rain. Here my interest is in theories, not realities, of climate change.[22] Interviews evoked two pervasive explanations of why there is less rain today than there used to be. The most prevalent of these—one we heard from school children as well as nonliterate old men and women—poses a direct causal relationship between deforestation and drought. It asserts graphically that the trees now vanished from the hilltops had formerly "pulled" the rain clouds to the village.

The other theory, less widely held and sometimes offered with less conviction, has to do with the decay of social life, religion, and love among human beings—all of which are understood to displease God. "In the days when God was happy there was rain and the wells were full, but now God is angry." Reasons posited for divine anger include humans' lack of compassion, insolence towards elders and caste superiors, decline of community life involving disrespect for common property (including trees), and increasing indifference toward proper celebration of collective rituals.[23] Obviously, the tree theory and the sin theory are not fully separable for—as the preceding section suggests—the destruction of the trees is part and parcel of current degenerate moralities.

While Ghatiyalians conceive of God or the Lord *(bhagvān)* as meting out punishment in exchange for sin, this conception is very close to Hindu theories of *karma* and its inevitable fruits. It ought not to suggest Judaeo-Christian theories of a vengeful God who does not want His rules crossed. Notably, no one with whom we spoke named the author of divine punishment by any of the scores of names available in village religion, whether pan-Hindu Lord Śiva or Rajasthani Dev Nārāyaṇ. Rather, what we hear is a conviction that wrong actions reap evil rewards, and a tendency to personify the mechanism of punishment as "the Lord."

In a compelling study of explanation for tragic loss of life through a devastating fire in an Uttar Pradesh village, Wadley and Derr describe a very similar phenomenon. Complex understandings of individual sin and its probable fruits merge in villagers' testimonies with a concept of a God who acts to punish sinners, or more globally to punish human sin. Thus there are many small reasons different persons' *karma* might lead to evil fruits. Yet, as Wadley and Derr point out, "the magnitude of the fire demanded an explanation at a higher level." Thus one man concluded, "No one's power can help when Bhagvān wants to destroy something" (Wadley and Derr 1990, 147). While the environmental deterioration experienced by rural Rajasthanis is by no means as sudden, concentrated, or acute a tragedy as the fire discussed by Wadley and Derr, it is certainly a loss of great magnitude. Similar processes of explanation are apparently at work.[24]

While discussing with Ghatiyalians why there is less rain today—a situation about which everyone agrees—we heard causal factors of deforestation and sin articulated independently of one another, as well as complexly interrelated and counterpoised in ways that eloquently express the vision of moral ecology I wish to highlight.

## The Trees Pulled the Rain

I treat the straight "less trees less rain" theory briefly, in the interests of space and to avoid redundancy. We heard this very many times from persons of all ages, all castes, both sexes. It was usually stated in a remarkably similar fashion. I give just two examples from different social positions of the way people formulated this perception.

Pyarelal Mahajan is probably one of Ghatiyali's wealthiest men. He runs a shop selling household and worship staples (oil, sugar, tea, incense, coconuts, and so forth) and also lends cash at profitable interest rates. Pyarelal has only an elementary education, but knows sufficient writing and numbers for his bookkeeping needs. He was not born in Ghatiyali, but moved there in his early youth. He is now in his sixties.

**Pyarelal:** For the last fifteen years there hasn't been so much water.

**Bhoju:** Why has rain become less?

**Pyarelal:** Because of the trees not remaining. This is what I think: there are no trees, therefore there is no rain. When I first came here there were so many trees on Tikhyā ["pointed," the name of one of the hills surrounding the village] that you couldn't see the earth or the rocks. But now you can easily see livestock there.

So, when the clouds come there is nothing to stop them.

Hardev Chamar, a poor and nonliterate leatherworker, probably in his fifties, also speaks of the connection between poor rainfall and fewer trees.

**Hardev:** Rain is less, and population has increased. Forty years ago, when we used to plant in the land near New Well,[25] then from five maunds [of seed grain] we'd get two hundred maunds.[26] The land was so strong, without fertilizer, the strength was in the water.

**Bhoju:** Why is rain less today?

**Hardev:** Because the trees are less. The trees pulled the rain with the wind, and now there are less trees. The wind pulled the rain. It was the effect of the wind. The trees pulled the wind, but now there are no trees.

These and many similar statements offer a climate change theory based on a physical situation. According to this theory, tall trees engender wind and wind brings clouds to the vicinity of the trees. The trees also serve to block or hold clouds in an area, allowing precipitation to take place. Sin is not expressed as a factor in these explanations, but it is implicit in the realities of deforestation. A certain embarrassment was evident when some persons expressed a theory of divine causality to Bhoju as teacher and to me as foreigner. This could well have influenced the preponderance of the "less trees" theory in our interview material.

**God Is Angry**

Only a handful of people made no reference at all to trees when speaking of climate change. These sought direct reasons in God's anger at human beings' declining compassion. Polu Kumhar, a potter by birth, had attained an economic status beyond most of his caste fellows through a riverbed gardening venture. A reflective, articulate, successful man, Polu spoke thoughtfully of the lessening of rain and affection.

> **Polu:** Just as the world's portion has decreased, so God too has become angry.
>
> **Bhoju:** What do you mean?
>
> **Polu:** We used to hug one another in greeting; we were happy. But today when a person comes, we say, "So what, he's come!" In this way, people's affection is reduced, and in the same way God doesn't love people, and so there is less rain.

Polu thus poses parallels between the dwindling of human affection and the dwindling of God's affection for humans—an analogy he is not the only one to articulate.

Rup Lal Khati spoke of how people are today richer in material things but poorer in spirit, as consumerism and the jealousies it provokes enter their lives. He sees this as one reason why God no longer hears human prayers for rain.

> **Bhoju:** People used to have less money, but they still had love. But today . . . ?
>
> **Rup Lal:** Today there is no love at all.
>
> **Bhoju:** Why?
>
> **Rup Lal:** People are envious of one another *(apas mẽ jalan).* Like suppose somebody, like you, earns two cents—whether in sorrow or happiness—and then I see you and I feel envy, and I think, "Why should he earn money? He ought to stay like me." There is no progress, just envy.
>
> Like, we see that he washes with soap, he washes his clothes with soap, and we feel envy, and try to do the same. But you

have money and I don't, so I get even poorer [from spending money on soap].

So for this reason some farmers are in tight circumstances.

**Bhoju:** Before, when it did not rain, people used to worship all the gods, and perform the worship of Indra.[27]

**Rup Lal:** Yes, they used to get the drum and go to worship, and it used to rain even before they got back to the village.

**Bhoju:** But today they don't do it. Why?

**Rup Lal:** Because people's lots have turned bad, and God too has changed toward people (bhagvān bhī logoṇ se badal gayā).

Rup Lal very explicitly identifies envy as the source of reduced love among villagers, leading in turn to divine displeasure. The decline of ritual is embedded in the decline of love and community through a circular causality that cannot be untangled. Ritual action has decreased because rituals do not work anymore. Rituals do not work anymore because God is angry or has turned away from people. God has turned away from people because people no longer worship as they once did.

## Deforestation, Divine Anger, Less Rain Are One Story

Several interviews expressed a completely merged understanding of environmental and moral deterioration. These to me are the most suggestive discussions, posing as they do a tightly knit moral ecology. Ugma Loda, a farmer in his mid-sixties, offered this complex account.

**Bhoju:** Why is there less rain?

**Ugma:** Because of the trees being cut. . . . Nowadays there are no gardens and no forest.

**Bhoju:** Why?

**Ugma:** Literate people say there is no rain because of the trees.[28]

**Bhoju:** But what do farmers think about this?

**Ugma:** We think the same thing as the rest of the world. I think what you think and accept it. What could I say if I didn't?

[He is silent and looks down, and then he looks up again and resumes:]

It is God's manifestation in nature[29] that there is less rain. In the days when God was happy, there was rain and the wells were full, but now God is angry.

**Bhoju:** Why is God angry? With what things is God angry?

**Ugma:** People's behavior has changed. The biggest thing is that there is no longer compassion in any human vessel (kisī ke ghaṭ mẽ koī dayā nahīṅ hai). Before, if someone fell or was hurt, people would come and take care. But nowadays, nothing.

**Bhoju:** Before people worried a lot, were concerned, so what happened?

**Ugma:** Today our neighbor's son falls and is lying on the road and we may be crossing the road, but we are not going to help him.

**Bhoju:** Who is responsible for all these changes?

**Ugma:** There is no responsible authority (*zimmedār*).... People's behavior is less—their feelings, their love. Take my father [for example]: we never sat on a bed in his presence, never spoke before him. If we were playing and he came, we all became quiet. But my grandson, I can call him five times and he comes and says "What is it?" [in the insolent tone of an irritated brat].... Because cooking oil isn't pure, and grain is grown with chemicals, people's tempers have become hot like the food....

It used to be that we had four or five buffalo in my house. So what did we eat? Milk and butter and yogurt. And we went out all day and weren't hungry. And in the afternoon we ate more butter and bread, and we were vigorous, and lived at our ease.

> Today nothing is pure; food and drink are bad, and from this our behavior, compassion, love, have all decreased.

It is evident from Ugma Loda's reflections that he understands many aspects of the changing world in which he lives to be causally interlocked. And this is realistic. As noted in the introductory section, there are less dairy animals today because increased population and increased ambition have motivated farmers to put former grazing lands under cultivation. For the same reasons, dung is scarcer, causing farmers more and more to rely on chemical fertilizers. Ugma further associates children's lack of respect and humans' generally reduced health, stamina, and good tempers with changed diets that directly result from these other transformations.

Damodar Sharma Gujarati, an elderly Brahmin about twenty years Ugma Loda's senior, offered this vivid account of environmental and social history:

> **Damodar:** In 2004 [by the *samvat* dating system; c. 1947 C.E.] all the wells in the *goriyā* [fertile land near the village] were so full that you could bend over and drink out of them with your hands. That's how much rain there was.
>
> **Bhoju:** Why isn't there as much rain now?
>
> **Damodar:** Because the jungle is destroyed. Because rain comes from trees.
>
> There is an area near Bundi . . . where the jungle is so dense that if a man goes in it he will get lost. So even today there are still trees in that place and there is still rain. That's why there is no rain [here, where there are no trees].
>
> **Bhoju:** Why do trees cause rain?
>
> **Damodar:** Scientists know.
>
> **Bhoju:** But why?
>
> **Damodar:** Farmers say that rain comes from the trees, and there used to be much *dharma*. For example, people used to feed Brahmins, and people used to do fire oblations (*havan*) for the goddesses and gods, and spread fodder for the cows.

But now the Degenerate Age [Kali Yuga] has come. The times used to be good. Men used to look on women as their sisters and daughters. But today, I am a Brahmin and my daughter could marry someone of any caste.

**Bhoju:** People don't pay attention to caste *dharma*?

**Damodar:** Now *dharma* is completely suppressed; but if you protect *dharma* then *dharma* will protect you. It is my *dharma* that I won't drink water from anybody's hands.[30] Then he [Dharma, now personified as a divinity] will protect me. But today, the sweepers, the leatherworkers—we have all become one. It used to be that sweepers and leatherworkers could not come near me, but now . . . it is as if God has forgotten us as we have forgotten him.

And today's politics are the worst of all. Today any low-caste person can lie to the police and say, "This person has insulted me." And they do not require a proof, they just come and grab us. For this reason I don't ever sit at the bus stand. Better for me to sit alone in the temple.

**Bhoju:** What change do you see in people's behavior?

**Damodar:** The Kali Yuga has come one hundred percent. People used to be very happy and generous, but now they are misers. It used to be if I had grain and saw a hungry person I would give, and even if only women were home and one had no grain, she could borrow from another and clean it and grind it and make bread so no one could go to bed hungry.

And there was so much power in the grain that when you boiled it, it spit [literally, it kicked] so no one could stand near the pot. But today there is no such spitting, no strength in the grain . . . Just as the strength of grain is finished, so is people's love.

**Bhoju:** OK, people have changed because of selfishness, but there is no selfishness in grain, so what happened?

**Damodar:** It is because we don't use goat dung and cow dung fertilizer any more. From urea [a chemical fertilizer] more heat grows in the grain, and from this people also have greater heat. And that is why people have much more anger and egotism. People today get angry very quickly at everything.

I have quoted Damodar at length, in order to show just how fluidly he moves among changes in the environment, changes in religious behavior, intercaste relationships, sexual morality, agricultural technology, and human character. From his decidedly positioned perspective as a Brahmin, he understandably deplores the reduction of Brahminical ritual status and political clout. Concerning other elements in the situation, his views are identical with farmers' views.

Damodar uses the ancient Hindu cosmological model of a dark and degenerate age to encompass and account for all these changes. Although this was not common, he was not the only one to speak of Kali Yuga. In another conversation with two farmers, Ram Narayan Mali and Shiv Ram Mali, Bhoju and I heard the "no trees therefore no rain" and the "no *dharma* therefore no rain" diagnoses both posed and debated. This conversation also included references to a notion, probably learned from radio or television, that the polar caps might melt and flood the earth. Ram Narayan authoritatively predicted the end of the world on several merged bases. We hear him thoughtfully integrate new information available through modern media with local theories.

**Shiv Ram:** There is less rain and that's why there are no trees and plants.

**Bhoju:** What is the connection between trees and rain?

**Ram Narayan:** The trees pull the clouds, they pull the pressure.

**Shiv Ram:** No, that's not the reason. It is because people have no *dharma*. That's why there is no more rain.

**Bhoju:** You say that where there are trees there will be more clouds and more rain?

**Ram Narayan:** From the influence of the trees, the clouds stay.

**Shiv Ram:** Everything has its ending. For example, once there was the rule of the *rājā mahārājā,* but that is finished.

And there were wild animals, but they are finished. And as for the thick woods, it too came to an end. In the same way, now the end of humankind is coming and everything will be finished.

**Bhoju:** Our end is also coming?

**Shiv Ram:** Yes.

**Bhoju:** Do you know when that time will come?

**Shiv Ram:** We will die after fifty to sixty years, so you don't have to worry.

**Ram Narayan:** That time [the end of the world] is very close.

**Bhoju:** How long?

[Silence, as he thinks.]

**Ram Narayan:** In about three hundred years; it will happen before three hundred years. Within three hundred years this whole place will be an ocean.

[There ensued a discussion between Ram Narayan and Bhoju in which Bhoju shifted his role from inquiring ethnographer to educated source of outside knowledge. Ram Narayan had heard of global warming melting the polar caps, and the two discussed the possible end of the world because of this. Bhoju then returned to his more formal interviewer role.]

**Bhoju:** Is it humankind's *karma* or is it because of nature *(prakṛti)*?

**Ram Narayan:** It is humankind's *karma*, our own *karma*.

**Bhoju:** So the responsibility belongs to humankind's *karma*?

**Ram Narayan:** When human *karma* changes, then God also changes.

Ram Narayan proceeded to sing for us a kind of ballad announcing the advent of the Kali Yuga. Each verse described laxness similar to that noted by Damodar Gujarati: immodest women, no respect of high caste by low, no authority of elders in the household.

## Moral Orders and Magical Landscapes

Scholars of religion have long been interested in the mythic and practical continuities between environment and society. In 1929, British social anthropologist A. R. Radcliffe-Brown wrote:

> For certain purposes this contrast between society and environment, or man and nature, is a useful one, but we must not let it mislead us. From another and very important point of view the natural order enters into and becomes part of the social order. . . . For primitive man the universe as a whole is a moral or social order governed not by what we call natural law but rather by what we must call moral or ritual law. (1965, 130)

Half a century after Radcliffe-Brown's structural-functionalism, Michael Taussig said of pre-capitalist Andean cosmology: "The organization of kith and kin, political organization, use of the ecosphere, healing, the rhythm of production and reproduction—all echo each other within the one living structure that is the language of the magical landscape" (1980, 167). Both these passages represent attempts to envision and convey a profound interweaving of the natural world with human society in religious thought from cultures contrasting with the scholars' own.

Ghatiyali narratives such as those described in this chapter also present a merged vision of human morality with nature's bounty or depletion. Some pose a straightforward description of damage done to nature and the social order when an immoral ruler illegally sells off shade trees. Others evoke more complex, less direct, religious explanations. These imply that non-adherence to *dharma*, lack of compassion, avariciousness, and other moral and social deficiencies have far-reaching geophysical consequences.

In Kali Yuga lore from Sanskrit texts of over a millennium ago, we find remarkably resonant images linking selfish behavior with ecological disaster. The Kali Yuga is said to end in drought, and eventual dissolution (*pralaya*)—a process conveyed in what Kane calls "harrowing descriptions." To cite his digest of *dharmaśāstra*: "There is the absence of rain for a hundred years; the result is that living beings perish and are reduced to earth; the sun's rays become unbearable, and even the ocean is dried up; the earth is burnt by the fierce heat of the sun together with its mountains, forests and continents" (vol. 5, pt. 1:694).

According to the *Viṣṇu Purāṇa* (c. 450 C.E.) a sheerly instrumental and exploitative morality prevails in the Kali Yuga. Much as Ram Narayan Mali and Damodar Gujarati explained it, this text equally sees exploitation and selfishness affecting relations among humans as well as relations between humans and their natural surroundings:

> Then property alone will confer rank; wealth will be the only source of dharma; passion will be the sole bond of union between the sexes; falsehood will be the only means of success in litigation; and women will be objects merely of sensual gratification. Earth will be venerated but for its mineral treasures. (Dayal 1983, 65)

A text from the *Liṅga Purāṇa*, dated several centuries later, tells what sounds much like an ecological parable. In earlier, better eras, this text informs us, magic trees

> brought forth clothing and fruits and jewelry; and on the very same trees there would grow, in bud after bud, honey made by no bees, powerful honey of superb aroma, colour, and taste. People lived on that honey, lived happily all their life long, finding their delight and their nourishment in that perfection, always free from fever.

However, greed and selfishness eventually came to dominate those people, and "They lopped off the limbs of the trees and took by force the honey that no bees had made. As a result of that crime that they committed in their greed, the magic trees, together with their honey, vanished" (O'Flaherty 1988, 69).

The text goes on to describe the Dark Age as one in which:

> There is always carelessness, passion, hunger, and fear; the terrible fear of drought pits one against another. Scripture has no authority, and men take to the violation of dharma; they act without dharma, without morality; they are very angry and not very smart. (O'Flaherty 1988, 71)

In a sense these Kali Yuga texts put the current discourse on environmental and moral degradation in perspective as cultural constructs: the past always paradisiacal, the present shadowed and corrupt. I have more than once encountered skepticism when presenting these interview texts to American audiences. Some suggest that nostalgia or a "good old days" mentality may be at work in Ghatiyalians' memories of verdure and social harmony. However, much that once was—autocracy, forced labor, smallpox, for example—is by no means missed. More importantly, I am convinced that the changes in landscape and in society witnessed by Ghatiyalians (and by much of the subcontinent) over the past fifty years are truly unprecedented. Population increase as well as deforestation are statistically documented.[31] Old people with whom we spoke were well aware of increasing numbers of humanity, to which they attributed constricted space and social graces. As one of them put it succinctly: "Love is less. Why? Because people are more."

I cannot argue that Ghatiyalians' traditional understandings of ecological morality have moved them to work collectively toward ecological recovery. There are many reasons for this. Some we have seen expounded here: changes in polity and environment so rapid and radical that they have left people stunned in some ways, although not into inaction. Rather, most villagers are working as hard as possible—harder than ever before as many assert—to take advantage of new technologies, cash crops, new educational and professional opportunities. Programs to help the lower castes have been effective in certain areas such as housing, and—as expressed in our interview with Damodar Sharma—legal matters. Many villagers at most levels of the social hierarchy appraise their best option to be a ready stride into a future they have not yet distinctly envisioned. But they do distinctly comprehend—as Dayal Gujar and many others told us—that the era of kings and trees and wild animals is finished.

Of course, some farmers stubbornly continue to farm traditionally because, they say, the food tastes better. Some housewives laboriously raise *pīpal* and *nīm* trees because their leaves have ritual and medicinal uses, and because deities both cherish and at times inhabit them. But there is thus far no organized resistance to agro-technology, to reforestation projects that propagate alien and despised tree species, to irrigation schemes that deplete the water table. Indeed, most villagers readily and understandably accept conveniences instituted and funded by outside agencies.

In an essay provocatively titled "No Nature without Social Justice," activist-scholars Smitu Kothari and Pramod Parajuli set forth an eloquent plea for "cultural and ecological pluralism in India." They draw on two important cultural strands: (1) traditional Hinduism's coding of ecological knowledge in its social customs and religious teachings and (2) evidence from grassroots movements where communities have mobilized from within to save local environments from various forms of degradation and to save valued traditions rooted in those threatened landscapes.[32] Kothari and Parajuli thus take their stand on a moral order emerging within given historical contexts and sustaining locally appropriate ecological balances.

The environmentalism Kothari and Parajuli advocate neither grants autonomous value to a privileged nonhuman domain as do some radical ecologies of recent Western origin, nor does it concede mastery to human wisdom or human need.[33] Rather, they argue for equity among humans and between humans and their nonhuman surroundings, and insist that one kind of justice implies the other. Their landscapes are not ultimately magical and their methods must be ultimately political. Nonetheless, they look to mythic and customary interpretations of nature—to sensibilities such as those Ghatiyalians express—for keys to sustainability and justice.

In Ghatiyali, as in most human communities, the landscape and its uses have always been multiply contested. Those in power have had different and often opposing interests from those who labored in the fields; women from men; herders from farmers; landless from landed.[34] In one vivid myth I recorded, a tribal woman wins the boon from Lord Śiva of sending hail to knock the grain from its stalks before harvest: the ultimate disaster for farmers is divine aid to the landless Bhils who laboriously glean food the cultivators consider ruined. Nonetheless, understandings of environmental change such as those I have transcribed in this chapter do posit a more general human morality interdependent with its natural surroundings. And, in spite of sad depletion, the Ghatiyali landscape remains convincingly magical. It is inhabited yet by deities and their stories, and subject to divine as well as human manipulations (Gold and Gujar 1995).

Barring a new cycle of *yugas,* current degradation may be irreversible. But understandings such as Ghatiyalians express—that selfishness causes drought and that the environment inevitably participates in the fruits of human sin—appear to be important sources of practical and ideological strength infusing India's environmental movements. Magical landscapes are not necessarily imaginary ones. Convictions founded in moral ecology pervade Rajasthani villagers' practical interpretations of ongoing social and technological transformation, and of their own active parts in the tides of history. This ethos rooted in religion and experience will surely influence their determinations regarding future sustainable livelihoods.

## Notes

1. My fieldwork in Rajasthan was supported by a senior research Fulbright fellowship administered by CIES in the United States and by USEFI in India. I am very grateful to these institutions. I also thank Daniel Gold and Lance Nelson for much constructive criticism, and Bhoju Ram Gujar for everything. I alone am responsible for errors in fact or judgment.

2. See Comaroff 1985 for symbolism and praxis; for explorations linking environment and production with religious and symbolic configurations in specific cultural and ecological settings, see for example, Brightman 1993, Croll and Parkin 1992, Lansing 1991, Sen 1992.

3. In the case of agricultural rituals, for example, farmers directly attribute the marked decrease in ritual activity to the increasing use of machine power and the consequent detachment of agricultural schedules from priestly astrological knowledge (Gold 1995).

4. See Jodha 1985; 1990.

5. When using my own words, I say "forest" for a wooded area. When translating interviews, I use "forest" if the speaker has said *van* and "jungle" if they have said *jangal.* A certain amount of confusion arises from the different meanings of *jangal* and "jungle" as they have evolved over time in Indian languages and in English. Appadurai notes, "the radical rupture between our modern Western conception of jungle (as a dank, luxuriant, moist place) and the ancient Indian category, which referred to a dry and austere natural setting, which was nevertheless ideal for human subsistence practices" (Appadurai 1988, 206; see also Zimmermann 1987). The

English implications have, however, slipped back into Hindi, I believe. For example, the *Rājasthānī Sabad Kos* (hereafter RSK; Lalas 1967, 2:1,025) offers as definition number one for *jangal: van* and *araṇya*, both terms for "forest." However, definition number three is *registān* or desert. For further elucidation of "jungle" and *jangal* in South Asia, see Dove 1992.

6. For some recent, varied explorations of emotional and poetic ties between persons and the changing, contested landscapes they inhabit see, for example, Cronon 1983, Roseman 1991, Slater 1994, Tsing 1993.

7. Bhoju Ram Gujar was my research assistant for many years, and more recently has been a coauthor. We have worked together since 1979 and it is difficult to disentangle our respective contributions to this research.

8. Age was not the only factor affecting interview situations. Interpersonal relationships, including status and personalities of each person on the scene, significantly shape the verbal texts I present. Most acutely, gender differences altered interview styles and results, so that although I recorded many interviews with women, male voices dominate the oral-historical accounts selected for this chapter. Bhoju Ram Gujar was the lead questioner in interviews with men and I in interviews with women. Because his questioning style is more forceful than mine, this led to differences structured by gender, but not necessarily representing it. Women often deflected questions about general patterns to reflect on personal experiences. Their voices will be fully integrated into the larger project of which this chapter is a part.

9. For brief descriptions of this chronology and of the Kali Yuga, see for example Biardeau 1989, 100–104; Dimmitt and van Buitenen 1978, 19–24, 36–44.

10. For an interesting comparative case, see Ross's "The Drought this Time" (1991, 193–249) on "global warming" as an interpretive narrative similar to those found in other cultural worlds. Ross argues that "ethnometeorology"—of which Ghatiyali discourse on rain would be a good example—is no different from global warming theory except that the latter "is itself an exercise of cultural power" (217). He does not thereby challenge the truth of any weather theories.

11. Sawar was not among the princely states of Rajputana, but was under direct British rule as part of the joined administrative districts "Ajmer-Merwara." See Imperial Gazetteer 1989.

12. Historian Ed Haynes notes that this decade witnessed deforestation throughout the region of former Rajputana: "From 1950 to 1960, the decade

of the abolition of *jagirs*, the rate of decline in *jagirdari* woods increased dramatically as areas which had been previously preserved appear to have been converted to agriculture or simply degraded by public demands for firewood, grazing land, fodder, and other forest products" (1984, 32).

13. Elsewhere I have attempted to set forth and explore some other dimensions of these mutually engendered changes (Gold and Gujar 1994, Gold 1997). See Greenberg 1994 for a fine description of interlocked causalities of environmental deterioration in another region of India.

14. I most often retain the original term, which has an emphatic potency beyond "kings."

15. In the old Indian currency there were sixteen *ānās* in a rupee; today, in spite of the decimal system, people still refer to one-quarter of a rupee as "four *ānās*," and use these fourths of a rupee as common figures of speech for estimated percentages.

16. Kane's *History of Dharmaśāstra* includes the following statements concerning the proper relationship between rulers and trees: "Trees have life since they feel pain and pleasure and grow though cut." "The king should award... [fines] against those who wrongfully cut a tree . . . " (Kane 1974, vol. 2, pt. 2:895). For strong associations between kingship and environmental well-being, see also Ludden 1984. For some Maharashtrian kings' varied and deliberately instrumental manipulations of nature, see Guha 1995.

17. See Smith 1989 for eating, superior power, and violence in ancient Hindu theories of hierarchy.

18. For a broad and deep discussion of theories of common property and collective good, with reference to some South Asian situations, see Herring 1990.

19. Haidar Ali uses Hindu terminology in spite of his Muslim identity. Bhoju interpreted this idiosyncratic usage as meaning: "No one is responsible for anything; you can use money to pay for sin."

20. See the fifteenth-century poet-saint Kabir's *sākhī* 106 in Hess and Singh: "Protect the field with a hedge, the hedge eats up the field. The three worlds whirl in doubt. To whom can I explain?" (1983, 101). For Kabir the protector's inherent unreliability is a sign of cosmic doubt.

21. Bhoju told me, as we translated this interview together, that members of his own household had participated in this wood gathering, stockpiling several years worth of firewood in their cattle shed. Because women used the cattle shed as a place to urinate in the daytime, I had often

contemplated this massive old woodpile, been warned that it might shelter scorpions and, most recently, known it as a hiding place for newborn kittens. But I had never realized it was a sign of the very sources of deforestation I was researching.

22. In future work, I hope to correlate local perceptions with recorded annual rainfall data. See Bharara 1982 for a study of the startlingly accurate memories of some other Rajasthani farmers for good and bad rainy seasons. See also INTACH 1989 for connections between deforestation and "desertification." The monsoon of 1994 brought, according to letters from Bhoju Ram Gujar, the heaviest rains seen in this part of Rajasthan for at least one hundred years. I do not yet have any indication of how this most recent geophysical phenomenon affected the theories reported here.

23. Wadley 1994 reports on similar perceptions from a different North Indian region with a different local history.

24. The formulations of a moral ecology that emerge in rural Rajasthani discourse, and those described by Kelly Alley (this volume) for urban Banaras, have some striking similarities. However, one notable contrast is in the idea of God punishing sin. According to Alley, people in Banaras understand the river goddess Ganges Mother to be eternally and infinitely forgiving. It may be that rural Hindus—as in Ghatiyali and Karimpur—are more inclined to think of *karma* anthropomorphically, while the urbanites of Banaras do not.

25. This land is behind the school, very close to the village dwellings. It belongs to Gujarati Brahmins; Chamars were probably sharecroppers on this land, as they might be for Brahmin landowners today.

26. One maund is forty kilograms.

27. See Gold 1988, 53–58 for a description of a collective ritual performed in Ghatiyali in 1980 to entreat the Vedic rain god, Indra, who has no temple.

28. As the interview with Hardev Chamar cited above indicates, the "no trees no rain" theory is hardly exclusive to literate villagers. I was initially convinced by strikingly widespread and consistent adherence to this theory that it was locally generated. However, one account of a campaign for environmental restoration in another district of Rajasthan suggests that outside activists may consciously and strategically reinforce, if they do not initiate, ideas about the importance of trees for climatic well-being (Saint 1989).

29. This is an awkward but deliberate translation of *bhagvān kī kudarat*; it might be more simply rendered as: "God's nature" or "God's being."

30. Damodar's subcaste, the Gujarati Brahmins, hold themselves to be ritually superior to all other communities, and take no cooked food or water from any other castes.

31. See Richards, Haynes, and Hagen 1985 for a statistical analysis of some dimensions of environmental change in North India during this period.

32. See also Gadgil and Guha 1992.

33. A full discussion of these issues is far beyond my present scope; for one view see Guha 1989.

34. See S. Guha 1995, who writes of the politics of nature in seventeenth–nineteenth century Maharashtra: "a variety of human agencies impacted upon the landscape."

## References

Appadurai, Arjun. 1988. "Comments on 'The Jungle and the Aroma of Meats: An Ecological Theme in Hindu Medicine.'" *Social Science and Medicine* 27(3): 206–207.

Bharara, L. P. 1982. "Notes on the Experience of Drought: Perception, Recollection and Prediction." In *Desertification and Development: Dryland Ecology in Social Perspective*, ed. Brian Spooner and H. S. Mann, 351–361. London: Academic Press.

Biardeau, Madeleine. 1989. *Hinduism: The Anthropology of a Civilization.* Delhi: Oxford University Press.

Brightman, Robert. 1993. *Grateful Prey: Rock Cree Human-Animal Relationships.* Berkeley: University of California Press.

Comaroff, Jean. 1985. *Body of Power, Spirit of Resistance: The Culture and History of a South African People.* Chicago: University of Chicago Press.

Croll, Elisabeth, and David Parkin, eds. 1992. *Bush Base: Forest Farm: Culture, Environment and Development.* London: Routledge.

Cronon, W. 1983. *Changes in the Land: Indians, Colonists, and the Ecology of New England.* New York: Hill and Wang.

Dayal, T. H. 1983. *The Viṣṇu Purāṇa.* Delhi: Sundeep Prakashan.

Dimmitt, Cornelia, and J. A. B. van Buitenen. 1978. *Classical Hindu Mythology: A Reader in the Sanskrit Purāṇas.* Philadelphia: Temple University Press.

Dove, M. R. 1992. "The Dialectical History of 'Jungle' in Pakistan: An Examination of the Relationship between Nature and Culture." *Journal of Anthropological Research* 48: 231–253.

Gadgil, Madhav, and Ramachandra Guha. 1992. *This Fissured Land: An Ecological History of India.* Delhi: Oxford University Press.

Gold, Ann Grodzins. 1988. *Fruitful Journeys: The Ways of Rajasthani Pilgrims*. Berkeley: University of California Press.

———. 1995. "Abandoned Rituals: Knowledge, Time, and Rhetorics of Modernity in Rural India." Paper presented at the Annual Meeting of the American Anthropological Association, Washington, D.C.

———. 1997. "Wild Pigs and Kings: Remembered Landscapes in Rajasthan." *American Anthropologist* 99 (1): 70–84.

Gold, Ann Grodzins, and Bhoju Ram Gujar. 1994. "Drawing Pictures in the Dust: Rajasthani Children's Landscapes." *Childhood* 2: 73–91 (special issue on "Children and Environment: Local Worlds and Global Connections," ed. Sharon Stephens).

———. 1995. "Of Gods, Trees and Boundaries: Divine Conservation in Rajasthan." In *Folk, Faith and Feudalism*, ed. N. K. Singhi and Rajendra Joshi, 33–54. Jaipur: Rawat Publications.

Greenberg, Brian. 1994. "Sustainable Futures and Romantic Pasts: Political Ecology and Environmental History in North India." Unpublished paper presented in SAME Workshop, University of Chicago.

Guha, Ramachandra. 1989. "Radical American Environmentalism and Wilderness Preservation: A Third World Critique." *Environmental Ethics* 2: 71–83.

Guha, Sumit. 1995. "Kings, Commoners and the Commons: People and Environments in Western India, 1600–1900." Paper presented at Cornell University, Ithaca, New York.

Haynes, Edward. 1984. "Land Use and Land-Use Ethic in Rajasthan, 1850–1980." Paper presented at Conference on South Asia, Madison, Wisconsin.

Herring, Ronald J. 1990. "Rethinking the Commons." *Agriculture and Human Values* 7 (2): 88–104.

Hess, Linda, and Shukdev Singh. 1983. *The Bījak of Kabir*. San Francisco: North Point Press.

Imperial Gazetteer of India. 1989. *Rājputāna*. Calcutta: Superintendent of Government Printing, 1908; reprint, New Delhi: Usha Rani Jain (page references are to reprint edition).

INTACH (Indian National Trust for Art and Cultural Heritage), ed. 1989. *Deforestation, Drought and Desertification: Perceptions on a Growing Ecological Crisis*. New Delhi: INTACH.

Jodha, N. S. 1985. "Population Growth and the Decline of Common Property Resources in Rajasthan, India." *Population and Development Review* 11 (2): 247–264.

———. 1990. "Rural Common Property Resources: Contributions and Crisis." *Economic and Political Weekly*, 30 June, A65–A78.

Kane, P. V. 1974. *History of Dharmaśāstra*. 2d ed. 8 vols. Poona: Bhandarkar Oriental Research Institute.

Kothari, Smitu, and Pramod Parajuli. 1993. "No Nature without Social Justice: A Plea for Cultural and Ecological Pluralism in India." In *Global Ecology: A New Arena of Political Conflict*, ed. Wolfgang Sachs, 224–241. London: Zed Books.

Lalas, Sitaram. 1962–1978. *Rājasthānī Sabad Kos*. 9 vols. Jodhpur: Rajasthani Shodh Sansthan.

Lansing, J. S. 1991. *Priests and Programmers: Technologies of Power in the Engineered Landscape of Bali*. Princeton: Princeton University Press.

Ludden, David. 1984. "Productive Power in Agriculture: A Survey of Work on the Local History of British India." In *Agrarian Power and Agricultural Productivity in South Asia*, ed. M. Desai, S. H. Rudolph, and A. Rudra, 51–99. Delhi: Oxford University Press.

Mathur, Jivanlal. 1977. *Bṛj-Bāvanī*. Sawar: Mani Raj Singh.

O'Flaherty, Wendy Doniger. 1988. *Textual Sources for the Study of Hinduism*. Chicago: University of Chicago Press.

Radcliffe–Brown, A. R. 1965. *Structure and Function in Primitive Society*. New York: The Free Press.

Richards, John F., Edward S. Haynes, and James R. Hagen. 1985. "Changes in the Land and Human Productivity in Northern India, 1870–1970." *Agricultural History* 59 (4):523–548.

Roseman, Marina. 1991. *Healing Sounds from the Malaysian Rainforest: Temiar Music and Medicine*. Berkeley: University of California Press.

Ross, Andrew. 1991. *Strange Weather: Culture, Science and Technology in the Age of Limits*. London: Verso.

Saint, Kishore. 1989. "Aravalli Abhiyan—Save Aravalli Campaign." In *Deforestation, Drought and Desertification: Perceptions on a Growing Ecological Crisis*, ed. INTACH, 110–115. New Delhi: INTACH.

Sen, Geeti, ed. 1992. *Indigenous Vision*. New Delhi: Sage Publications.

Slater, Candace. 1994. *Dance of the Dolphin: Transformation and Disenchantment in the Amazonian Imagination*. Chicago: The University of Chicago Press.

Smith, Brian K. 1989. "Classifying the Universe: Ancient Indian Cosmogonies and the Varṇa System." *Contributions to Indian Sociology* 23 (2): 241–260.

Taussig, Michael T. 1980. *The Devil and Commodity Fetishism in South America*. Chapel Hill: University of North Carolina Press.

Tsing, Anna Lowenhaupt. 1993. *In the Realm of the Diamond Queen*. Princeton: Princeton University Press.

Wadley, Susan S. 1994. *Struggling with Destiny in Karimpur, 1925–1984*. Berkeley: University of California Press.

Wadley, Susan S., and Bruce W. Derr. 1990. “Eating Sins in Karimpur.” In *India Through Hindu Categories*, ed. McKim Marriott, 131–148. New Delhi: Sage Publications.

Zimmermann, F. 1987. *The Jungle and the Aroma of Meats: An Ecological Theme in Hindu Medicine*. Berkeley: University of California Press.

Frank J. Korom

# 8

# On the Ethics and Aesthetics of Recycling in India

> In some respects artifacts are like new species that reproduce themselves alongside biological ones. . . . We like to think that because objects are humanmade they must be under our control. However, this is not necessarily the case. An object with a specific form and function inevitably suggests the next incarnation of that object, which then almost certainly will come about.
>
> —Mihaly Csikszentmihaly (1993, 21)

> I must confess that I do not draw a sharp line or any distinction between economics and ethics. Economics that hurt the moral well-being of an individual or a nation are immoral and, therefore, sinful. Thus, the economics that permit one country to prey upon another are immoral.
>
> —Mahatma Gandhi (in Kripalini 1960, 160)

## A Place Upon Which to Dump

This essay has to do with the ethics and aesthetics of a tradition that has been much maligned on socio-religious grounds in many parts of the world but praised by ecological crusaders in Europe and America. I refer to the phenomenon known in Western nations as recycling, something that occurs everywhere where humans have chosen to reuse material objects consciously for new purposes. Recycling refers both to the simple removal and reuse of discarded items and the artistic re-creation of new objects from castaway materials. I will offer a more elaborate definition below, but first let me focus on a specific geographical context.

In South Asia, recycling has developed a unique role due to the caste system. As in some other places in the world where marginalized people take up the trade of making a living from discarded items, in India recyclers are scorned by many of their fellow countrymen. But because of the unique indigenous ideology of the Hindu caste system, the phenomenon of handling garbage, for whatever purposes, has developed in a way that is comparable to, yet different from, other similar systems operating in numerous societies, both simple and complex, throughout the world. It is important to state at the outset that as an outsider I am not in a position to make a moral value judgment about the whys and hows of the recycling phenomenon in South Asia. I do feel, however, that it is still possible to raise issues which may be relevant to any basic philosophical and theological discussion on the moral, ethical, and aesthetic grounds for understanding the practice of recycling in Hindu India. Because the topic is a relatively new one, this paper addresses some, but not all, of the issues involved in creating an aesthetic ethic of recycling. Although I focus on examples drawn from India, I hope that what I propose has broader, cross-cultural relevance.[1]

The negative evaluation of recycling in India is deeply rooted in the ideology of caste, making it both a social and a theological problem simultaneously. In what follows I intend to raise issues for further reflection. I do not claim to speak for recyclers, nor do I claim any role of authority or advocacy for their position in Indian society. I simply wish to suggest some methodological resolutions that may begin to open up a buffer zone for dialogue between philosophers, ecologists, and social scientists who are interested in discussing possible ways to create a cross-cultural aesthetic of recycling.

In a world in which everyone produces trash but only a select, marginalized few wade in and transform it, a dialogue about trash and its concommitant social status is not only timely but absolutely necessary for a balanced ecological perspective on the future of the earth. Recycling in India has an important role to play in a dialogue concerning religion and ecology because the uncollected garbage in the country provides a livelihood for a number of people who would find little work in any other industry due to their low socio-economic status and minimal level of education. Moreover, the country serves as a dumping ground for more economically privileged countries wishing to dispose of their own toxic wastes (*India Currents Magazine* 1995, 13). The latter fact alone is reason enough for concern.

This paper is intended to suggest ways that may increase the conceptual value of what people working in the trash industry do by attempting to come up with a set of ideas that may connect the concerns of certain Indian recyclers with their counterparts in other countries. I refer here to those marginal few who utilize trash for artistic purposes. Since many people who aesthetically reuse garbage are often labelled pejoratively as "naive," "outside," or "visionary" in specific cultural contexts (cf. Hall and Metcalf 1994), the very possibility of creating a cross-cultural aesthetic of recycling is problematic. Nevertheless, it is essential to listen to the voices of recyclers and attempt to come up with theoretical clues for the (e)valuation of their work. Indeed, as Ernst Schumacher, the doyen of ecological crusaders and spokesman for appropriate technology, once suggested, there is a need for underprivileged and privileged nations alike to understand the quintessential importance that homegrown sciences such as recycling have in a world of limited resources (1974, 51). I attempt to open up this seemingly impossible task for further interrogation first by looking at the statistical facts and symbolic dimensions of trash production in India, then by moving on to a consideration of the economic potential of transforming trash into goods of worth. Finally, I tentatively propose some guidelines for creating a positive evaluation of garbage renewal through a consideration of its aesthetic potential.[2]

## The Ins and Outs of Garbage

The amount of garbage generated in India's urban centers in modern times is staggering! Bombay produces more garbage per day than any other Indian city: 5,800 tons. New Delhi is next, generating 3,880 tons. Surprisingly, Calcutta contributes slightly less at 3,500 tons, while Madras, which contributes the least to the waste matter created in India's cities on a daily basis, still produces 2,675 tons.[3] What is even more alarming is the amount of trash that is not cleared and disposed of each day. Consider the following statistics: Although New Delhi produces less garbage each day than Bombay, the leading trash producer, more remains unaccounted for. Of the 3,880 tons produced daily, 1,460 tons remain heaped on the streets of neighborhoods throughout the capital city. Bombay leaves only 800 tons unaccounted for, and Madras runs close behind at 535. Calcutta leaves the least uncollected, but it still amounts to no less than 350 tons daily.[4]

One could, with all justification, wonder why so much trash remains uncollected. Certainly economic, demographic, and political factors play a significant role in the management of waste in India,[5] yet one must also take into account religion as a contributor to India's urban decay. From a theological and philosophical point of view, one would have to reflect upon the pervasive impact that the Hindu caste system has on the dynamics of Indian garbage disposal.[6] I have suggested elsewhere (Korom 1996, 123) that the ideology of purity and pollution has figured implicitly in the overall scenario of garbage dynamics in India, since contact with polluting agents threatens the ritual purity of the twice-born castes (Orenstein 1968, 1965). This ideology is not something simply confined to the ritual realm; rather, it permeates every aspect of domestic and public life. Because the upper castes fear substance pollution, the onerous task of dealing with human-produced garbage falls on the so-called service castes or on the *dalits*, the former untouchables.[7]

The contested issue of relegating the task of cleaning up garbage to the poverty stricken layer of Indian society is precisely what Mahatma Gandhi, himself an avid ecological crusader and practitioner of recycling, rebelled against when he wrote, "I cannot imagine anything nobler or more national than that, for say, one hour in the day, we should all do the labour that the poor must do, and thus identify ourselves with them and through them with all mankind" (Kripalini 1960, 171). Gandhi problematizes the unequal distribution of labor in India by suggesting that the need for all people to take responsibility for their own contributions to "social evils" is something that should be carried out on a global scale, not just on the regional or national level.

Although colonization, urbanization, and poverty are clearly related (Grothues 1984, 103), it would be too easy to explain the phenomena of urban squalor and garbage production in India as only the economic result of colonialist practices, for as Dipesh Chakrabarty has pointed out, the contemporary dilemma of dealing with garbage in India "bears a constant testimony to a gap that persists well into the present day between the modernist desires inherent in imperialist/nationalist projects of social reform . . . and popular practices."[8] This is an issue that I should like to return to, but first it will be necessary to explore the "place" that garbage has been given as a consequence of pollution ideology in India.

The problem here is really one of conceiving and demarcating the spaces reserved for trash in Indian society. To begin, we must take our methodological cue from Mary Douglas (1984), whose work on the symbolic danger of dirt is a watershed in anthropological musings concerning the cross-cultural analysis of pollution taboos. Douglas's major premise is that dirt—and by extension, pollution—is the detritus resulting from the creation of order in spiritual and material culture. Both ideas and things are thus implicated in the process of creating pure and impure realms of existence. Like the cosmogonical act of creating differentiation from a nondifferentiated state in an attempt to bring order out of chaos, the distinction between that which is pure and that which is not is formulated to insure socio-religious divisions of order.[9] The encroachment of elements from one category into the realm of the other induces a threatening state of existence. Garbage, like dirt, threatens clean realms by creating a potential for defilement and pollution in the same way that weeds threaten a garden (cf. Gill 1982, 76).

Chakrabarty (1991) applies Douglas's model to the Indian context by suggesting that the distinction between purity and pollution is based on indigenous conceptions of private and public space respectively. He argues that the problem of trash in India is an indigenously formulated distinction between inside ("home") and outside ("world"). As he writes, "The dirt that goes out of the house marks a boundary between the inside and the outside. . . . For, the outside, in this conception, always carries 'substances' that threaten one's well-being" (Chakrabarty 1991, 20). This is essentially a religious argument based on popular beliefs pertaining to the Hindu householder's auspiciousness, as other social scientists have pointed out.[10] In other words, keeping polluted substances on the inner side of the domestic threshold amounts to increasing the danger of ritual contamination and, thereby, decreasing the auspiciousness of those living within the house.

Beyond the house, too, other borders are demarcated for "protective" purposes. These demarcations spread out in concentric rings from the home. First, we might point out highly localized boundaries within a community such as those around a neighborhood (*mohalla*). Moving outward from such distinct, yet interconnected, areas we find trash moving through bazaars, those communally designated sites of social and economic interaction, to larger arenas determined by regional planners in consort with local politicians. Finally, we reach the border of a town or city; and here it is that we often find trash dumps alongside the makeshift dwellings of the marginalized people who are responsible for removing waste products.[11]

The "life cycle" (Blincow 1986, 96) of garbage quite often follows these same routes of demarcation as refuse moves from within the home to the street, then out of the neighborhood altogether, ultimately along a course that leads to a centralized dumping ground outside a civic community's habitable perimeter (Bhide and Sundaresan 1984, 144–147). But the trail does not end here, for all objects—even trash—have complex "cultural biographies" (Kopytoff 1986). On the contrary, it continues in a number of directions when individuals, forced by their low status and poverty, sort trash by kind either to reuse or sell, leaving for the dump only those items which have no remaining function or culturally-defined, retrievable economic value.[12] This sort of activity might be referred to as "recycling," so long as we are aware of the term's limitations resulting from its specific association with the ecological concerns that emerged from industrial development in the Occident.[13] Malcolm Blincow's characterization of recycling as the "secondhand trade, rummage/garage sales, pawn-shops, and auctions; the 'hidden/informal' economy; and the disposal of waste materials, their recovery and recuperation, and their eventual reuse" (1986, 97) is broad enough to serve as a general and comparative description of the phenomenon I take up below.

## Recycling and the Informal Sector

It is certainly correct to assume that recycling as a reflexive, self-conscious practice to save the environment is associated with the West. It would be blatantly inaccurate, however, to presume that recycling occurs only in the economically privileged nations, for creating secondary products out of discarded materials is something of an everyday occurrence and economic necessity in the rest of the world as well.[14] Indeed, recycling plays a central role in what Gavin Smith (1985) has termed "simple commodity production," and understanding its importance in informal sector economies provides a challenge to social scientists and humanists alike who are interested "in the co-existence and combination of varied forms of production, distribution and exchange" (Long and Richardson 1978, 176) that operate in the poorer sectors of less advantaged countries throughout the world.[15] Moreover, studying recycling allows us to acknowledge the permeability between formal and informal sector boundaries in socio-economic systems that demonstrate and support the interdependence of capitalist and non-capitalist modes of production (Blincow 1986, 98; Breman 1977); that is, because many recyclers depend on middlemen and intermediaries to sell their scrap, their small-scale enterprises tap into larger networks of economic, social, and symbolic exchange.[16] In the Indian context, recycling also allows us to establish a dialogue concerning the nature of social reciprocity as formulated in certain key texts in the Hindu tradition.

The process of recycling, and the related activity of scavenging,[17] is widespread in India, as it is in other parts of South Asia and beyond. Recycling is not only a result of modernity, as some popular notions convey, since we have numerous historical examples of remade and reused things dating well before British colonial expansion in the subcontinent (Korom 1996, 122). Pre-nineteenth century objects such as the Bengali *kā̃thā*, a homemade quilt with embroidery on layers of old sari material, *cūṛīs* (glass bangles) and beads made from remelted glass, and *huqqah*s crafted out of coconut shells are just a few examples of preindustrial recyclia produced in India (Korom, forthcoming).

The ubiquitous nature of recycling becomes increasingly apparent in industrial India, however, as waste items such as metals, rubber, and plastic culled from factory refuse begin to be used more regularly for secondary purposes. Today, it is difficult not to notice recyclia in the urban marketplaces of India. Utilitarian items such as tools made from steel reinforcement rods; domestic appliances consisting of lamps; and furniture, rag rugs, baskets and containers, toys, and even architecture using recycled materials are to be found in abundance throughout South Asia.[18] While some commercial products made from reused materials circulate openly in the bazaars of India for consumption by the middle and higher castes (or anyone who can afford them), the recycling phenomenon in general is a highly localized enterprise, providing low-budget goods for people who cannot afford newly made objects priced beyond their means. This notwithstanding, impoverished recyclers and the consumers of the resultant goods participate in larger market forces, since recycling depots throughout the country that serve as "way stations" for the redistribution of discarded raw materials are most often owned by middle or upper class individuals of twice-born caste status.

Clearly, people from all strata of Indian society benefit from recycling in one way or another, yet the paradoxical fact remains that the work of recyclers is devalued and even despised by many Indian citizens because of the low status, abject poverty, and ritual impurity of most of those engaged in the trash trade. My own research in New Delhi and Calcutta with people employed in the recycling industry has led me to the conclusion that most of these folk do the work because they do not have other alternatives. Although some of the anthropological literature on low caste workers in the garbage industry points out a distinct conception of self-worth (e.g., Searle-Chatterjee 1979), a number with whom I have spoken share an attitude of simple resignation to fate, stating that their own *karma* has determined their economic status and involvement in this marginalized occupation.[19] But it is important to note that there are always exceptions to every rule. Not all recyclers are victims of an inescapable cycle of poverty, though most are bound up by it. As Blincow (1986, 98) reminds us, recyclers operate in numerous socio-economic environments and are not "invariably destitute or even poor." Some have even exploited the recycling phenomenon for economic gain. Nevertheless, except for a few very rare cases that I shall explore below, capitalizing on recycling is often done at the expense of social prestige.

Even in the few situations where scavengers and recyclers come from higher castes, their mode of subsistence is not given any greater credibility. In an earlier article (cf. Korom 1996, 123–128), I demonstrated this point by exploring the world of Vinod Kumar Sharma, a Brahmin recycler living on the outskirts of New Delhi who claims to make three thousand different objects from rubbish. Although he is not totally impoverished and considers himself an artisan (*śilpakār*), performing work distinct from that of garbage pickers and sorters, his hand-crafted objects have not received the aesthetic appreciation that he would like. In fact, his chosen trade has hindered any significant recognition of his creations by art collectors, even though he has demonstrated his techniques at a well-known museum in the city. To be sure, the exposure he has received aids him economically, but his involvement with the garbage industry has led to what I have called a "downward spiral of status" (Korom 1996, 124). I assumed that his case was an unusual or idiosyncratic occurrence until I began to search for other accounts.

In a series of life histories, Kalpagam (1985) has pointed out that "polluted" high caste garbage pickers in Madras are subject to a similar disdain. Two of his interviewees, Lakshmi and Gopal, were born into the Naicker caste, a group whose status is fairly high because of their reputed descent from local leaders or village headmen. Kalpagam writes:

> It is Lakshmi's disappointment that despite being of Naicker caste they are engaged in this occupation of garbage picking, a demeaning job that respectable people do not take up. None of Lakshmi's relations including her own father like to maintain contacts with them.[20] Gopal's brother and family are unaware of it. The[ir] three older children know this and told me that if their uncle's family came to know of the work they are doing, they would be ostracized. (1985, 4)

The irony of this confession is that the couple earns more income picking, sorting, and reselling garbage than they would as domestic servants. The implication in the two cases cited above is that it is not the level of income but the type of services they perform that forces such people to the periphery of Indian society. In addition to economic position, symbolic meaning and ideologically determined power relationships must thus be accounted for when attempting to explain the marginalization of the people plying this trade.

The paradox that recyclers in India and elsewhere in South Asia face today is that their work is a fundamental part of the reciprocal interaction needed to bridge different levels of economic reality, yet essential as it is, their occupation is still perceived to be repugnant by a great majority of the population. In this regard, one could look for textual precedents in Hindu literature to legitimate the interaction that takes place between castes and people of different socio-economic orders. From another point of view the reciprocity adumbrated in Sanskrit texts on social order and hierarchy can also be understood as a subtle mechanism for justifying the marginalization of the lowest *varṇa*. The *Puruṣa Sūkta* (*Ṛg Veda* 10.90), for example, makes this point clearer than any other texts in the Hindu canon. In it, the four *varṇa*s are described as emerging from four distinct anatomical sections of *puruṣa*, the Cosmic Person: the mouth, arms, thighs, and feet. In a utopian world in which texts reflected reality rather than Weberian ideal types, the metaphor of "human body as social organism" and Émile Durkheim's reversal of it could certainly have served as a working model for economic and ritual reciprocity. However, the fact that the lowest group in the Hindu social order is presented as one born of the Cosmic Person's feet sets up a symbolic hierarchy difficult to transcend even in modern times, since the feet are intimately associated with dirt, impurity, and pollution in Hindu thought. Moreover, it was precisely the rigidness of the social system that devotional poets—many of them low caste members themselves—rebelled against in their attempts to create a cultural environment supportive of spiritual and social equity, regardless of occupation or economic class.

It is not my task to assess or evaluate the relative success or failure of the endeavors of medieval poets as social reformers, but it is important to keep in mind that numerous voices of dissent have emerged over time to question the normative dimension of the kinds of textual pronouncements found in Brahminical literature.[21] Mahatma Gandhi's voice, echoed at the outset, adumbrates such dissension when he ethically bridges religious morality and economics by claiming immoral labor practices as sins. Is the devaluation of any work done within the overall framework of the caste system moral? Ideally it is not. But this does not change the fact that recyclers still retain the stigma of marginality because of their occupation.

While there is no easy answer to the problem of increasing the cultural value of recycling, one could begin a fruitful dialogue in search of a solution by proposing a methodology that acknowledges the social worth of such practices which, in turn, would lead to a greater sense of empowerment among people who perform the polluting tasks discussed above. One way might be to reexamine the ideological bases of negative evaluations pertaining to recycling by creating an aesthetic niche for the phenomenon in India. Recognizing the artistic worth of remade objects would allow recyclia to enter into the process of commercialization and become what Pierre Bourdieu (1984) has called "cultural capital," thereby increasing its socio-economic status. In essence, a transformation of "rags to riches" (Yoshida and Williams 1994) could take place if public consensus were to be conditioned to see recycled products in a different way, namely, as objects of "dirty beauty." Raising the status of the object, in turn, would enhance the social position of the makers of those items. To do this would require a distinct form of mediation or cultural brokerage by someone external to the community in question.

These are issues I contextualize in the final section of my chapter. In an attempt to embed the socialization of recycling in a broader discourse on the production of aesthetic and monetary value and the transactional nature of art in the global arena, I hope to suggest some possible strategies to increase awareness about the phenomenon under consideration.[22]

## The Aesthetics of Recycling

Economic and political theorists, as well as anthropologists, have been analyzing the dialectics of value construction since the time of Marx, albeit for different purposes.[23] But one thing that most analysts have agreed upon is that "intrinsic" value is extremely difficult, if not impossible, to determine. Folk wisdom found in sayings such as "one man's wine is another man's poison" or "beauty is in the eye of the beholder" point out the cultural relativity of taste formulation, while other genres of folklore clearly demonstrate the ethnic and class-based determinism of value construction. Michael Thompson (1979, 1), for example, cites a British riddle to point out the relativity and class consciousness involved in determining a commodity's value: "What is it that a rich man puts in his pocket that the poor man throws away? Snot."[24] Thompson goes on to explain: "A poor man, since he has few possessions, can afford to discard very little; a rich man will be able to discard much more. . . . People in different cultures may value different things, and they may value the same things differently, but all cultures insist upon some distinction between the valued and the valueless" (1979, 2). Where aesthetics is concerned, the relativity of value must then be linked with culturally specific definitions of art, as Crowley (1958) had already brought to our attention nearly four decades ago.[25]

While aesthetic judgements are locally bound, they address larger, comparative issues that can affect global thinking and policy-making when a particular sensibility is wrenched from one specific context and juxtaposed with that of another. This often happens as a result of cross-cultural advocacy, an issue that I will touch upon below. But for the time being let us pursue some possible ideas, themselves "recycled" from a vast pool of writings on art and environment, in an attempt to shift discussions of Indian recycling from the rhetoric of development to the discourse of ecological concern through art, something we might refer to as "ecoart."

The solution to finding value in Indian recycling lies in locating an indigenous conception of beauty that may tie in with universal concerns about ecology and the future of the earth. The theoretical space between aesthetics, city planning, and cultural advocacy is precisely the area within which to frame a discussion of recycling in India so as to devise a sense of beauty that allows sewage systems and garbage collection to be a part of an urban ecosystem joining together ethical, moral, economic, and aesthetic concerns (Berleant 1992, 57–98). Doing this is not an easy task, for only a handful of thinkers have dealt with the problem of urban aesthetics in any significant way. This is not to say that artistic and ecological pursuits have been ignored by humanists in the past; rather, because art has been divorced from the experiences of everyday life, there has been a strong tendency on the part of philosophers and other humanists to view the aesthetic attitude as "contemplative, passive, and disinterested, quite removed from the dynamic physical engagement that characterizes the way we usually react with our surroundings" (Berleant 1992, 59). Social scientists working on artistic systems have provided some correctives to the narrow point of view just presented, by interrogating the basic assumptions underlying the study of aesthetics in the West. This has subsequently led to the deconstruction of the idea that art can be separated from other domains of life, something earlier referred to by John Dewey (1934) as the "integral" quality of aesthetics.

Bennetta Jules-Rosette (1986, 41), for example, building on the pioneering work of d'Azevedo (1973) and other Africanists, has asserted that the concept of aesthetics is a red herring because it is most often equated with technique and adherence to dominant themes of a particular school of art. An anthropologically oriented dissatisfaction with such structurally deterministic tenets grounded in Euro-American philosophy led to the development of the interdisciplinary field of ethnoaesthetics, which sought to question conventional presuppositions concerning art through inquiries into the meanings emerging from the conjunction of the artist's intention and the criticism generated by the audience experiencing the object's form and presence.[26] In his discussion of aesthetics and the traditional arts, Michael Owen Jones makes this quite clear when he states:

> The most common response to art . . . seems to be submission to associations that develop in the individual who is witness to the art, rather than an aloof and "objective" evaluation of formal elements . . . Nor should art . . . be conceived of and evaluated as divorced from daily life and fitness for use, since much art . . . is intended to solve practical problems of communication, environmental control, individual survival and social interaction." (1971, 103)

Jones, like Glassie (1972), makes a fundamental connection between the utilitarian nature of an object and its beauty, but goes one step further by introducing the ecological dimension into the production of everyday objects. I have previously attempted to make this point about South Asian recyclia in particular, since a distinction between purely functional and aesthetic concerns cannot be made in the case of reused things (Korom, forthcoming). The intricately painted rickshaw panels made from recycled tin in urban Bangladesh are a good case in point (Kirkpatrick 1984). The sections of the carriage portion are most often made from sheets of defective aluminum bearing misprinted labels and purchased at low prices in local markets. Rickshaw painters create designs for these sheets, both narrative and symbolic, to paint onto the exterior surfaces. As a result, the rickshaw fulfills a dual, culturally anticipated function by simultaneously pleasing the eye and serving as a mode of conveyance.[27]

Objects of material culture such as the rickshaws made from recycled material have the potential to be considered a genre of art if we first divest ourselves of the false idea that humanmade materials and their eventual reuse are somehow less a part of our ecological environment than natural objects. By doing so, a teleology of recycling could be posited as an alternative. Infusing a sense of agency, aesthetic or functional, into the work of the recycler would allow us to place the activity within an urban framework that does not devalue their products as an unnatural residue or ecological anomaly. Roland Dipert, writing about the ecological/philosophical paradox of dichotomizing natural and artificial things, has suggested that "all material is natural, and at worst *whatever* human beings do on the earth is to rearrange matter and alter some energy states."[28] He goes on to argue that human products must be seen as natural if one of the purposes of nature is its aesthetic usefulness. Thus, he considers, "the possibility that what is 'natural' is not in virtue of what it *is* but in how we think about it" (Dipert 1993, 234). Here the philosophical issue of intentionality overlaps with the anthropological concerns expressed above pertaining to the need to situate aesthetic discourse within a culturally appropriate context. A recycling aesthetic must thus be grounded in the notion of artistic agency.[29]

To illustrate this, let me return to Vinod Kumar Sharma, the recycler from New Delhi whom I briefly mentioned above. Sharma considers himself an artist and craftsman with a mission in life. Through his recycled creations (toys, domestic appliances, ornamental objects, and so forth), made with materials that he seeks out, purchases, and reshapes on a daily basis, he wishes to raise awareness about the state of India's urban environment. Moreover, he feels that it is possible to beautify India's cities by reclaiming the waste produced in them for constructive and creative purposes. His personal mission is thus both ecologically motivated and artistically expressed, while providing a modest and honest livelihood. Although Vinod is serious about his intentions, he has received much opposition from the Indian public because of the negative stereotypes attached to his occupation.

Vinod the craftsman is adamant about his work's beauty and value. He asks, "If one can make useful things from the waste (*jūṭhā)* of others, what harm is there in it?" Like any other craftsperson or artist, Vinod envisions a finished product from raw stuff; he breathes life into objects by giving them form. The qualitative difference, Sharma contends, between conventional artists and himself is to be located in the kinds of material used to create. Sharma, making things from scrap, also realizes that most of what he bends, turns, pounds, and cuts with his hands is despised by many people in his own community. This has not slowed his progress, and he is even beginning to attract a small following through his numerous but tenuous associations with educational programs and museums (cf. Korom 1996, 127).

In a sense, Sharma is crafting his own reputation as an artist through repeatedly "recycling" his identity. This is what I understood him to mean when he stated that he has "changed himself" to keep up with the demands of his clientele. When he wears a shirt woven of plastic cement bag strips, for example, Sharma is creating an image of himself as an eccentric artist, intentionally outside the definitions of good taste and etiquette. However, his tactics at attracting a broad audience for his skills suggest a deeply felt personal longing for public acceptance, even though he still has not managed to place himself squarely in the center of New Delhi's fashionable art circles. Vinod Kumar Sharma's struggle for artistic recognition continues even as he strives to propagate the latent message of recyclia's inherent merit.

Sharma's creations are "artistic" if understood in the sense intended by Lévi-Strauss's (1969) term *bricolage*, a process by which an individual uses whatever means and resources are available to her/him in order to create wrought things. It is thus an artistic process of re-creation out of preexisting materials. Although the famed structuralist had in mind a distinct degree of randomness when he developed the idea (cf. Lévi-Strauss 1969, 17), there is much we can salvage from his groundbreaking concept without sacrificing the intentionality of the recycled object's maker.[30] Commenting on counterparts to Sharma in West Africa, Roberts (1992, 56) focuses on Lévi-Strauss's idea of the *bricoleur* as one who uses "devious means" to create ironic collages which often serve as social commentaries. Roberts correctly interprets "devious" here not as something underhanded, but rather as an acute ability to transgress the normal or expected course of action in order to provide a service, however incongruous, to the community in question. In this way, the purposiveness of the recycler's action is central to the process of creating from scrap. Herein also lies the key to formulating an indigenous recycling aesthetic. By viewing the recycler's work as non-threatening and artistic—as Sharma, for example, does—there is the possibility of positively evaluating the phenomenon and its byproducts. Using the criteria applied by recyclers themselves would allow us to re-evaluate the recycling phenomenon and appreciate the artistic merit of remade objects.[31]

No increase in status for relatively unknown recyclers such as Vinod Kumar Sharma is yet visible in India. But Nek Chand, the visionary artist responsible for the Rock Garden in Chandigarh, Punjab, fully exemplifies the potential of recycling (cf. Schiff 1984). Nek Chand's garden, an evergrowing fantasy land of creatures and landscapes made from broken pots, porcelain and other scraps, has received international recognition some thirty-six years after his project began. But prior to his international success, he suffered much scorn at home.

Originally a menial laborer for the public works department in New Delhi, he went to Chandigarh and was put in charge of a dumpsite. This he gradually transformed into what it is today, a magnificent work of art seen by thousands of locals and tourists each week. But S. S. Bhatti, who devoted his graduate studies to writing about Nek Chand's garden, suggests that people did not take him seriously in India until he received international acclaim and official recognition in India (Schiff 1984, 130–131). As acceptance of his project grew in art circles due to media exposure, so too did his status. Today, Nek Chand's work stands as a monumental testament to the recycling message: garbage can indeed be turned into gold.

It is doubtful whether Nek Chand could have achieved the level of success that he did without the recognition he received first from authorities in the Punjab and later by winning numerous awards abroad. Because of the negative and polluting associations surrounding recycling in India, it is equally difficult for individuals such as Vinod Kumar Sharma to utilize their visionary skills in the pursuit of social, spiritual, and economic equity for recyclers. While common recyclers who collect, sort, and resell junk have some recourse to power through group solidarity, the lone maker of recycled art needs the assistance and patronage of a sympathetic public. In this case, it seems absolutely essential to involve intermediaries, such as "culture brokers" (cf. Steiner 1994), in the process of evaluating Indian recyclia. In her or his role as "someone who demystifies demand for the producer and communicates some form of authenticity or cultural meaning to the consumer" (White 1995, 7), the culture broker is in a position of power to condition the way people perceive things, thereby possibly swaying popular opinion. Culture brokers abound in India, acting as liaisons between numerous social groups and economic communities. Some even act as links with the world outside of India through their advocacy for Indian culture abroad (cf. Kurin 1991).

Museums, being purveyors of popular taste, could provide an institutional setting for raising consciousness about recycling because they speak with a collective voice of authority, with "the aesthetic knowledgeability, experience, and preferences of the entire population" (Harris 1990, 57). In the role of advocate, the museum, by recognizing the ecological soundness, artistic merit, and social value of recycling, can assist in elevating the status of the recycled object as well as its maker. I mentioned above that Sharma had demonstrated his talents at a prominent museum in New Delhi. That brief period of his life led to other opportunities to demonstrate his recycling prowess, educate children in the ingenuity involved in remaking things, and market his wares to a broader audience. This broader audience is now expanding to include international collectors from Europe and North America, some of whom are affiliated with museums and art galleries.[32] Needless to say, the transformation from "quaint" object to museum or gallery piece also increases the monetary value of recycling.[33] Through the aestheticization and institutionalization of his work, Sharma is slowly emerging as spokesperson for the usefulness of recycling in general and the art of recycling specifically. However, his own empowerment has not had any great effect on the hundreds of thousands of other recyclers who walk the streets of India regularly in search of materials to scavenge. Unfortunately, Sharma's is a unique case; it is highly idiosyncratic and does not reflect the general scenario for most workers in the industry to which he claims allegiance.

The problem remains one of ostracism. Quite plainly, recyclers are perceived to be polluted in India. By and large, they have a difficult time pulling themselves towards the center of Indian society from their precarious position on the periphery. Yet the moral and ethical issue one must constantly keep in mind is that everyone produces garbage. So why is it, by and large, the responsibility of outcaste classes to clean up the refuse of other people? I have suggested that this is, to a great extent, due to the pollution ideology associated with handling impure substances in Hindu India. If a dialogue about the positive environmental and artistic benefits of recycling were to continue, it could eventually overshadow or at least balance such negative associations. Although a communal transformation on the individual magnitude experienced by Nek Chand could not possibly occur overnight, the need to continue "talking trash" (Reynolds 1994) in India is everpresent.

I am not suggesting external political advocacy for the overall betterment of Indian recyclers (this is a task to be taken up by Indian citizens themselves); but perhaps through professional exchange, continued discourse, and the advancement of modes of appropriate technology utilizing recycled materials (Bauer 1993, 1994), an applied ethno-philosophy could develop that would be sensitive to local and regional needs and increase awareness about the phenomenon on a national level. Moreover, it could contribute to the enrichment of cross-cultural knowledge about a phenomenon that is practiced worldwide, and that has economic, political, social, and spiritual consequences. In so doing, we might all be in a better position to create a more habitable planet as we continue to adapt to an increasingly urban environment that demands to be understood both ecologically and aesthetically.

## Notes

Earlier versions of this paper were first read at the annual meeting of the *American Folklore Society*, held in Lafayette, Louisiana during October of 1995, and at the *World Art Research Seminar*, University of East Anglia, December 1996. I wish to thank Jürgen Frembgen, Ann Gold, Clare Harris, Lance Nelson, and Chris Steiner for their insightful comments on earlier drafts of this chapter.

1. A note of caution is also advised here, however, since analysts and theorists need to be equally aware of recyclia's cultural specificity prior to making general claims. Moreover, because the category of "recyclia" is a Western concept, we must admit and be aware of its limitations before applying the term for comparative purposes. See Korom 1996, 123; Kratz 1995, 7.

2. Useful in this regard is Brown's discussion of art and impurity (1989, 77–78).

3. *India Today* 1994, 40–41. For supplementary statistical data, see Nath 1984.

4. *India Today* 1994, 40–41. This might be explained by the fact that of all the Indian cities Calcutta has the most complex structure of local government, having 2 municipal corporations, 33 municipal councils, 37 non-municipal urban centers and 544 rural units. See Nath 1984, 48.

5. Ghosh 1993. See also Bauer 1994, 89–120; Bhide and Sundaresan 1984; Nath 1984; Panwalkar 1990; Vogler 1984.

6. I realize that viewing garbage from only a Hindu perspective, without taking into consideration other religious views, provides only a partial picture. Nonetheless, I will limit my comments to Hindu India in this chapter, since I cannot do complete justice to the role that Islam has played in the formulation of Indian conceptions of waste disposal. Recycling has a very different status in South Asian Islam, in which reused objects do not always carry the same Hindu ideological message of impurity discussed below. Basu (1995, 67–68), for example, has shown that discarded things can even be used to make sacred ritual objects in Gujarat. On recycling in Islam more broadly construed, see Grothues 1984, 1988.

7. See, for example, Searle-Chatterjee 1979.

8. 1991, 18. On this, see also the insightful summation of a Wenner-Gren symposium on the historical development of "shantytowns" by Peter

Lloyd (1979, 115), in which he writes that "economic models were seen as often incapable of grappling with all the dimensions of power, and some discussion centered on the symbolic mechanisms through which power is transformed into capital and vice versa."

9. In this regard, we should also remember the connection made by David Knipe (1993, 798–799) between creation and recycling in the Hindu context.

10. For example, Raheja 1988, 43ff. Raheja's argument has to do with transferring inauspiciousness inhering in "gifts" out of the house. While the gifts discussed by Raheja are certainly not trash, they embody a similar quality in the fact that they are threats to auspiciousness.

11. See again, Lloyd 1979.

12. It is not my purpose here to explore the full ramifications of garbage's multiple uses in India. However, a larger project to document the social perceptions and practical uses of garbage in South Asia would be timely and could benefit methodologically from the ethnoarchaeological work done on trash in the United States by Rathje 1978.

13. For a more detailed exploration of the terminological problem, see Korom 1996, 191; Blincow 1986, 97–101; Furedy 1984, 129–30; Sicular 1992, 16–23. Grothues (1984, 105) also calls for the need to make a clear distinction between recycling in the First World and the Third World. See also the reservations expressed by Kratz 1995.

14. For the most recent and detailed case study of recycling in the Third World, see Sicular's 1992 monograph on the practice in Indonesia. For West Africa, see Grendreau 1994; Roberts 1989, 1992, and for North Africa, see Grothues 1988. Bartolomé 1984 deals with Latin America. Bauer 1993, 1994, Kalpagam 1985, and Panwalkar 1990 explore the phenomenon in India, as does Korom 1996, forthcoming. For overviews of recycling in general, see Blincow 1986, Guibbert 1990, Vogler 1984.

15. It further allows us to get at philosophical issues underlying the moral nature of economic activity. On moral economy in South Asia, see Appadurai 1984. Although his concerns in this review article pertain to food production and distribution specifically, the issues he raises are easily applicable to other aspects of economic activity.

16. The idea of Steiner's (1994) "culture broker," a person who mediates between different individuals and levels of society for economic and cultural reasons, figures significantly in the purveyance of aesthetic taste and the construction of value, as I shall suggest below. See also Appadurai 1986.

17. Here I follow the definition put forth by Blincow (1986, 97), where he states that it is an "activity involved in the collection and disposal of

culturally-defined waste materials, whether that activity be done directly for subsistence (food, clothing, and artifacts), for exchange, for sale, or for wages—or, as is sometimes the case, for some combination of these."

18. Herald 1993, 183–89; Korom 1996, 122; Lal 1989; Grothues 1984, 109. Consider the following account by journalist Alexander Frater concerning his serendipitous visit to a slum dweller's home outside of Bombay: "The dappled light had the soft iridescence of a rainbow's interior. It came from a wall made entirely from plastic shopping bags, blue, red, green and yellow, which also laid a ghostly mosaic across the floor. Some bore commercial logos; one said Thai Royal Orchid Service; others Rajaram Quality Wines and Peter Stuyvesant" (Frater 1991, 138). Not only does this pedestrian account suggest the international flow of goods that get recycled but it also hints at the aesthetic dimension of recycling, an issue that I will discuss below.

19. The role of *karma* in recyclers' self-perceived destiny has not been discussed to any great extent in the literature on poverty and development in India, but it begs for further inquiry because of its obvious implications in determining the socially constructed devaluation of recycling.

20. Sharma, the Brahmin recycler referred to above, made a similar complaint. Although his father resides with Sharma's nuclear family, he constantly complains about the nature of his son's work.

21. I do not wish to suggest that texts such as the *Puruṣa Sūkta* serve as blueprints for Hindu society. But I would contend that the ideology found in Brahminical literature on caste is deeply embedded in the Hindu psyche.

22. For an earlier dicussion of market forces' influence on taste and value, see Fabian and Szombati-Fabian 1980. They have discussed the economic role of art in terms of the "logic of the market." Although their argument is compelling, it is more deterministic than I would like to conceive it, since other factors beyond economic considerations equally contribute to an object's aesthetic appeal. See, for example, Dickie 1964.

23. For the anthropological angle on the social construction of value, see Douglas and Isherwood 1979, Bourdieu 1984. A more recent attempt to summarize the literature on the political economy of capitalism can be found in Appadurai 1984.

24. A narrative version of the above riddle in the Native American tradition, for example, can be found in Jones (1986, 245), attesting to a concern that transcends the local in favor of the transnational.

25. See also Dickie 1964. Geertz (1983, 109) has articulated eloquently this position more recently in his assertion that providing art with cultural

significance is always a local matter of cultivating involvement in social process: "It is out of participation in the general system of symbolic forms we call culture that participation in the particular we call art . . . is possible." Such an approach to embedding art in the everyday experiences that comprise culture might seem commonplace today in anthropological circles, but a philosophical division between life and art still seems very pervasive in much of the literature by historians and critics of art, as in, for example, the works of such doyens as Arthur Danto (1981, 1986). For a cogent reassessment and critique of this position, see Novitz 1992, especially the essay titled "The Integrity of Aesthetics."

26. For an overview of the extensive literature on this subject, see Silver 1979.

27. It is also worth noting that the rickshaw painters, mostly low class citizens, are not considered to be artists by the general public, even though they themselves would like to be thought of as such. See Gallagher 1992, 637–54.

28. 1993, 232. Compare with the statement by Csikszentmihaly quoted at the beginning of this chapter, in which he argues that the evolution of objects parallels the evolution of species. From this point of view, objects and their reuse, must be seen as part of a wholistic continuum within the "natural" order of things.

29. For the epistemological issue of agency's role in Indological studies in general, see Inden 1990, as well as Ahmad 1991.

30. Berlo (1991, 459) urges us to go "beyond bricolage," for haphazard ingenuity is only one facet of the bricoleur's work. Instead, she suggests that we view the work of such artisans as a "deliberately multivocal aesthetic. . . . Not merely constructed of the cultural flotsam and jetsam of the West overlaid on native ground, these works are purposeful collages."

31. Not much attention has been paid to recycling in the world of Indian art, although the Crafts Museum in New Delhi has displayed recycled objects in the past (cf. Lal 1989). Recycled art from Africa, however, has received considerably more attention. See Grendreau 1994.

32. It is thus no coincidence that I worked with Sharma to acquire pieces of his own making for a museum exhibition on recycling. For a more detailed exploration of Sharma and my involvement with him, see Korom 1996, 123–28.

33. As in the case of three-piece metal suitcases fashioned out of recycled tins in India which sell for well over $100 in museum gift shops in

New York City, while they are produced for under $10 in India (see also, for example, *The Natural Choice Catalogue* 1995: 47). We must ask ourselves who profits the most from these transactions. Certainly not the recycler! Sharma himself briefly worked for a commercial firm in Ahmadabad, Gujarat, to design and create usable things from recycled materials to be marketed abroad, but abandoned his post and returned to New Delhi, complaining that his salary was inadequate (personal communication 1995). The head of the firm (whose identity shall remain anonymous) insists, however, that all of his employees are dealt with "under fair labor conditions" (personal communication 1995).

## References

Ahmad, Aijaz. 1991. "Between Orientalism and Historicism: Anthropological Knowledge of India." *Studies in History* 7 (1): 135–63.

Appadurai, Arjun. 1984. "How Moral is South Asia's Economy?—A Review Article." *Journal of Asian Studies* 43 (3): 481–97.

———. 1986. "Introduction: Commodities and the Politics of Value." In *The Social Life of Things: Commodities in Cultural Perspective*, ed. Arjun Appadurai, 3–63. Cambridge: Cambridge University Press.

Bartolomé, Leopoldo J. 1984. "Forced Resettlement and the Survival Systems of the Urban Poor." *Ethnology* 23 (3): 177–92.

Basu, Helene. 1995. *Habshi-Sklaven, Sidi-Fakire: Muslimische Heiligenverehrung im westlichen Indien*. Berlin: Das Arabische Buch Verlag.

Bauer, Stefan. 1993. "Bambus: Angepasste Anwendungen in der Architektur tropischer und subtropischer Länder." *Archiv für Völkerkunde* 47: 161–89.

———. 1994. *Angepasste Technologie: Ausgewählte ethnologische Fallbeispiele aus Indien unter besonderer Berücksichtigung der Abfallverwertung*. Magistergrades der Philosophie: Universität Wien.

Berleant, Arnold. 1992. *The Aesthetics of Environment*. Philadelphia: Temple University Press.

Berlo, Janet Catherine. 1991. "Beyond *Bricolage*: Women and Aesthetic Strategies in Latin American Textiles." In *Textile Traditions of Mesoamerica and the Andes: An Anthology*, ed. Margot B. Schevill, J. C. Berlo, and E. B. Dwyer, 437–82. New York: Garland Press.

Bhide, A. D., and B. B. Sundaresan. 1984. "Street Cleansing and Waste Storage and Collection in India." In *Managing Solid Wastes in Developing Countries*, ed. John R. Holmes, 139–49. New York: John Wiley and Sons Ltd.

Blincow, Malcolm. 1986. "Scavengers and Recycling: A Neglected Domain of Production." *Labour, Capital and Society* 19 (1): 94–115.

Bourdieu, Pierre. 1984. *Distinction: A Social Critique of the Judgement of Taste*. Cambridge: Harvard University Press.

Bremen, Jan. 1977. "Labor Relations in the 'Formal' and 'Informal' Sectors: Report of a Case Study in South Gujarat, India." *Journal of Peasant Studies* 4 (3–4): 171–205, 337–59.

Brown, Frank Burch. 1989. *Religious Aesthetics: A Theological Study of Making and Meaning*. Princeton: Princeton University Press.

Chakrabarty, Dipesh. 1991. "Open Space/Public Place: Garbage, Modernity and India." *South Asia* 14 (1): 15–31.

Crowley, Daniel J. 1958. "Aesthetic Judgement and Cultural Relativism." *Journal of Aesthetics and Art Criticism* 17 (2): 187–93.

Csikszentmihaly, Mihaly. 1993. "Why We Need Things." In *History from Things: Essays on Material Culture*, ed. Steven Lubar and W. David Kingery, 20–29. Washington, D.C.: Smithsonian Institution Press.

Danto, Arthur. 1981. *The Transfiguration of the Commonplace: A Philosophy of Art*. Cambridge: Harvard University Press.

———. 1986. *The Philosophical Disenfranchisement of Art*. New York: Columbia University Press.

d'Azevedo, Warren, ed. 1973. *The Traditional Artist in African Societies*. Bloomington: Indiana University Press.

Dewey, John. 1934. *Art as Experience*. New York: Minton, Balch & Company.

Dickey, George. 1964. "The Myth of the Aesthetic Attitude." *American Philosophical Quarterly* 1 (1964): 55–65.

Dipert, Randall R. 1993. *Artifacts, Art Works, and Agency*. Philadelphia: Temple University Press.

Douglas, Mary. 1984. *Purity and Danger: An Analysis of the Concepts of Pollution and Taboo*. London: Routledge, Chapman and Hall.

Douglas, Mary, and Baron Isherwood. 1979. *The World of Goods: Towards an Anthropology of Consumption*. London: Allen Lane.

Fabian, Johannes, and Ilona Szombati-Fabian. 1980. "Folk Art from an Anthropological Perspective." In *Perspectives on American Folk Art*, ed. Ian M. G. Quimby and Scott Swank, 247–92. New York: W. W. Norton.

Frater, Alexander. 1991. *Chasing the Monsoon*. Calcutta: Penguin Books.

Furedy, Christine. 1984. "Survival Strategies of the Urban Poor—Scavenging and Recuperation in Calcutta." *Geo-Journal* 8 (2): 129–36.

Gallagher, Robert. 1992. *The Rickshaws of Bangladesh*. Dhaka: The University Press, Ltd.

Geertz, Clifford. 1983. "Art as a Cultural System." In *Local Knowledge: Further Essays in Interpretive Anthropology*, 94–120. New York: Basic Books.

Ghosh, Arun. 1993. "Ecology and Environment." In *Nature, Man and the Indian Economy*, ed. Tapas Majumdar, 64–80. Delhi: Oxford University Press.

Gill, Sam D. 1982. *Native American Religions: An Introduction*. Belmont: Wadsworth Publishing Company.

Glassie, Henry. 1972. "Folk Art." In *Folklore and Folklife: An Introduction*, ed. Richard M. Dorson, 253–80. Chicago: University of Chicago Press.

Grendreau, Andrée. 1994. *Ingénieuse Afrique: Artisans de la Récupération et du Recyclage*. Montreal: Musée de la Civilisation.

Grothues, Jürgen. 1984. "Recycling als Handwerk." *Archiv für Völkerkunde* 38: 103–31.

———. 1988. *Aladins Neue Lampe: Recycling in der Dritten Welt*. München: Trickster Verlag.

Guibbert, Jean-Jacques. 1990. "Ecologie populaire urbaine et assainissement environnemental dans le Tiers Monde." *Environnement Africain* 8 (1–2): 21–50.

Hall, Michael D., and Eugene W. Metcalf, Jr., eds. 1994. *The Artist Outsider: Creativity and the Boundaries of Culture*. Washington, D.C.: Smithsonian Institution Press.

Harris, Neil. 1990. *Cultural Excursions: Marketing Appetites and Cultural Tastes in Modern America*. Chicago: University of Chicago Press.

Herald, Jacqueline. 1993. *World Crafts: A Celebration of Designs and Skills*. Hong Kong: Lark Books.

Inden, Ronald. 1990. *Imagining India*. London: Basil Blackwell.

*India Currents Magazine*. 1995. "World's Toxic Trash Bin: India Accepting Toxic Products from Industrialized Nations." July, 13.

*India Today*. 1994. "Our Filthy Cities." 31 October, 37–47.

Jones, Michael Owen. 1971. "The Concept of 'Aesthetic' in the Traditional Arts." *Western Folklore* 30 (2): 77–104.

Jones, Suzi. 1986. "Art by Fiat, and Other Dilemmas of Cross-Cultural Collecting." In *Folk Art and Art Worlds*, ed. John Michael Vlach and Simon J. Bronner, 243–66. Ann Arbor: UMI Research Press.

Jules-Rosette, Bennetta. 1986. "Aesthetics and Market Demand: The Structure of the Tourist Art Market in Three African Settings." *African Studies Review* 29 (1): 41–59.

Kalpagam, U. 1985. "Coping with Urban Poverty in India." *Bulletin of Concerned Asian Scholars* 17 (1): 2–18.

Kirkpatrick, Joanna. 1984. "The Painted Rickshaw as Culture Theater." *Studies in Visual Communication* 10 (3): 73–85.

Knipe, David M. 1993. "Hinduism: Experiments with the Sacred." In *Religious Traditions of the World*, ed. H. Byron Earhart, 715–846. San Francisco: Harper San Francisco.

Kopytoff, Igor. 1986. "The Cultural Biography of Things." In *The Social Life of Things: Commodities in Cultural Perspective*, ed. Arjun Appadurai, 64–91. Cambridge: Cambridge University Press.

Korom, Frank J. 1996. "Recycling in India: Status and Economic Realities." In *Recycled, Reseen: Folk Art from the Global Scrap Heap*, ed. Charlene Cerny and Suzanne Seriff, 118–29, 190–92. New York: Harry Abrams, Inc.

———. Forthcoming. "Recycling." In *South Asian Folklore: An Encyclopedia*, ed. Margaret Mills and Peter J. Claus. New York: Garland Press.

Kratz, Corinne A. 1995. "Rethinking Recyclia." *African Arts* 28 (3): 1, 7–12.

Kripalini, Krishna. 1960. *All Men are Brothers: Life and Thoughts of Mahatma Gandhi as Told in His own Words*. Ahmadabad, India: Navajivan Publishing House.

Kurin, Richard. 1991. "Cultural Conservation through Representation: Festival of India Folklife Exhibitions at the Smithsonian Institution." In *Exhibiting Cultures: The Poetics and Politics of Museum Display*, ed. Ivan Karp and Steven D. Levine, 315–43. Washington, DC: Smithsonian Institution Press.

Lal, Anupa. 1989. "Toys from Cowdung, Glass and Sawdust." *Indian Express* 15 April, 3.

Lévi-Strauss, Claude. 1969. *The Savage Mind*. Chicago: University of Chicago Press.

Lloyd, Peter. 1979. "Shantytowns in Developing Nations." *Current Anthropology* 20 (1): 114–17.

Long, Norman, and Paul Richardson. 1978. "Informal Sector, Petty Commodity Production, and the Social Relations of Small-Scale Enterprise." In *The New Economic Anthropology*, ed. John Clammer, 176–209. New York: St. Martin's Press.

Nath, K. J. 1984. "Metropolitan Solid Waste Management in India." In *Managing Solid Wastes in Developing Countries*, ed. John R. Holmes, 47–69. New York: John Wiley and Sons Ltd.

Novitz, David. 1992. *The Boundaries of Art*. Philadelphia: Temple University Press.

Orenstein, Henry. 1968. "Toward a Grammar of Defilement in Hindu Sacred Law." In *Structure and Change in Indian Society*, ed. Milton Singer and Bernard S. Cohn, 115–31. New York: Wenner-Gren Foundation for Anthropological Research, Inc.

———. 1965. "The Structure of Hindu Caste Values: A Preliminary Study of Hierarchy and Ritual Defilement." *Ethnology* 4 (1): 1–15.

Panwalkar, Pratima. 1990. "Processus de Recyclage du Plastique à Bombay." *Environnement Africain* 8 (1–2): 153–57.

Raheja, Gloria Goodwin. 1988. *The Poison in the Gift: Ritual, Prestation and the Dominant Caste in a North Indian Village*. Chicago: University of Chicago Press.

Rathje, William L. 1978. "Archaeological Ethnography . . . Because Sometimes It Is Better to Give than to Receive." In *Explorations in Ethnoarchaeology*, ed. Richard A. Gould, 49–75. Albuquerque: University of New Mexico Press.

Reynolds, Michael. 1994. "Talking Trash." *Vogue* 5: 320.

Roberts, Allen F. 1992. "Chance Encounters, Ironic Collage." *African Arts* 25 (2): 54–98.

———. 1989. "Some Ironies of African Innovation: The Arts of Recycling and Recuperation." In *Redefining the 'Artisan': Traditional Technicians in Changing Societies*, ed. Paul Greenough, 189–204. Iowa City: Center for International and Comparative Studies, University of Iowa.

Schiff, Bennett. 1984. "A Fantasy Garden by Nek Chand Flourishes in India." *Smithsonian* 15 (3): 126–36.

Schumacher, Ernst Friedrich. 1974. *Es Geht auch Anders: Jenseits des Wachstums, Technik und Wirtschaft nach Menschenmass.* München: Desch.

Searle-Chatterjee, Mary. 1979. "The Polluted Identity of Work." In *Social Anthropology at Work*, ed. Sandra Wallman, 269–86. London: Academic Press.

Sicular, Daniel T. 1992. *Scavengers, Recyclers, and Solutions for Solid Waste Management in Indonesia*. Berkeley: Center for Southeast Asia Studies, University of California.

Silver, Harry R. 1979. "Ethnoart." *Annual Review of Anthropology* 8: 267–307.

Smith, Gavin. 1985. "Reflections on the Social Relations of Simple Commodity Production." *Journal of Peasant Studies* 13 (1): 99–108.

Steiner, Christopher. 1994. *African Art in Transit*. Cambridge: Cambridge University Press.

Thompson, Michael. 1979. *Rubbish Theory: The Creation and Destruction of Value*. Oxford: Oxford University Press.

Vogler, J. A. 1984. "Waste Recycling in Developing Countries: A Review of the Social, Technological, and Market Forces." In *Managing Solid Wastes in Developing Countries*, ed. John R. Holmes, 241–66. New York: John Wiley and Sons Ltd.

White, Robert W. 1995. "Culture as Commodity: Transaction and Meaning in Congo-Zaire Dance Music." Paper presented at the annual meeting of the Society for Economic Anthropology, Santa Fe.

Yoshida, Shin-Ichiro, and Dai Williams. 1994. *Riches from Rags: Saki-Ori and Other Recycling Traditions in Japanese Rural Clothing*. San Francisco: Craft & Folk Art Museum.

David Kinsley

# 9

# Learning the Story of the Land: Reflections on the Liberating Power of Geography and Pilgrimage in the Hindu Tradition

> Landscape is first of all an effort of the imagination—a construed way of seeing the world which is distinctive to a people, their culture, and even their anticipated means of encountering the holy. (Lane 1988, 103)

## Introduction

In this chapter I will propose a model for understanding aspects of pilgrimage in Hindu India based on the phenomenon of the "walkabout" in Australian Aboriginal religion. In the process, I will reflect on the ecological implications of both religious practices. I begin with a discussion of certain parallels between Australian spiritual geography and the Hindu understanding of sacred land.

### Australian Aboriginal "Songlines"

In Australian Aboriginal religion, the land came to take on its particular form in the Dreamtime, when totemic ancestors first lived on the land. As they traveled the land, they shaped it with their actions and songs. They left behind their footsteps, which form trails, or "songlines," that cover the entire Australian continent. In the imagery of Bruce Chatwin, "One should perhaps visualize the Songlines as a spaghetti of Iliads and Odysseys [in the Hindu context, *Mahābhāratas* and *Rāmāyaṇas* would be more apt], writhing this way and that, in which every 'episode' was readable in terms of geology" (Chatwin 1987, 13). The songlines connect special places, often referred to simply as Dreamings, where mythical ancestors rested, ate meals, or otherwise stopped their wanderings. These sacred places are often associated with a dramatic geographical feature of the land and contain sacred objects (*churingas*) or paintings on rocks and cliff faces. As Mircea Eliade put it, in Australian Aboriginal religion, "the sacred stories are imprinted in the landscape."[1] The Dreamtime stories, the songlines, situate Australian geography in a narrative context. The story lends the landscape an underlying, implicit structure that makes the landscape "speak" to those who are initiated into its story. Those who are initiated, furthermore, realize that they are part of that story. They learn that their entire culture was formed by the Dreamtime ancestors and that this distinctive culture is wedded to the landscape that contains it. The landscape and Aboriginal culture are intimately related to and reinforce each other.

To grow up in traditional Aboriginal culture, to become fully human, to become oriented requires learning the story of the land, learning how to read the landscape. Although many Aboriginal peoples are nomadic or seminomadic, they are always at home in the sense of knowing the songlines, which they recite or sing as they pass through it; they always "know the score," as it were.[2] Aboriginal religion is strongly marked by what one might call "geographical spirituality," a sensitivity to the story of how the land came to be and where human beings fit into that story. For Aborigines, the landscape is a sacred "text." In this sense, their religion is marked by what one might term an implicit ecological spirituality, a sensitivity to the fact that human beings are primarily and essentially an intricate part of the landscape from which they have emerged and in which they live.

In Aboriginal religion, geographical spirituality is often heightened or intensified while traveling. As nomads, or seminomads (by which I mean people who routinely move within a certain geographical boundary), the Aborigines find their way and always remain oriented while on the move by identifying geographical features with stories of the Dreaming. The Aborigines "map" their terrain with Dreamtime narratives. Like other travelers who use maps primarily while on the move, the Aborigines, while on "walkabout," recite stories from the Dreaming as the landscape unfolds. The maplike nature of the songlines is suggested in this exchange between Bruce Chatwin and Arkady, an Aborigine:

> Certain phrases, certain combinations of musical notes, are thought to describe the action of the Ancestor's *feet*. One phrase would say, "Salt-pan"; another "Creek-bed," "Spinifex," "Sandhill," "Mulga-scrub," "Rock-face" and so forth. An expert songman, by listening to their order of succession, would count how many times his hero crossed a river, or scaled a ridge—and be able to calculate where, and how far along, a Songline he was.
>
> "He'd be able," said Arkady, "to hear a few bars and say, 'This is Middle Bore' or 'That is Oodnadatta'—where the Ancestor did X or Y or Z."
>
> "So a musical phrase," I said, "is a map reference?"
>
> "Music," said Arkady, "is a memory bank for finding one's way about the world." (Chatwin 1987, 108)

In short, Aboriginal religion is characterized by a geographical spirituality that is heightened or intensified when Aborigines are in a nomadic mode, on walkabout. For traditional Aborigines, one's identity is largely constructed and maintained with reference to local geography. This is confirmed every time one moves through the landscape. Aborigines discover their spiritual identity primarily in reference to the landscape, by discerning its implicit structure, which is revealed in Dreamtime tales.

## Hindu Ecological Spirituality

In thinking about the place of geography in the Hindu tradition, especially as it relates to pilgrimage, I have found the Australian materials suggestive. Like the Australian traditions, Hinduism knows a Dreamtime—earlier *yugas*, periods when divine or heroic figures roamed the land and marked it in special ways, lending the geography its characteristic features. Mountain ranges (such as the Vindhyas) and rivers (such as the Ganges) acquired their present forms as the result of events featuring gods, *ṛṣis* (visionaries), or heroes in the mythical or legendary past.

Like the Australian traditions, most Hindu pilgrimage sites (*tīrthas, pīṭhas*) have stories connected with them (*sthala-purāṇas*), which pilgrims learn and sometimes recite while on pilgrimage. As in the Australian traditions, becoming spiritually awakened or mature in Hinduism may require learning the story of the land. Like Australian Aboriginal spirituality, Hindu spirituality is strongly geographical and involves learning how to read the landscape. While on pilgrimage, furthermore, in what we might term their "nomadic mode," Hindus are often preoccupied with learning the story of the land. Hindu pilgrimage often involves a self-conscious attempt to cultivate a rapport with Indian geography that establishes, reaffirms, or transforms one's religious identity. As in Australian Aboriginal tradition, the divine and heroic narratives that are basic to the Hindu textual and oral traditions are stamped in the landscape. The landscape is numinous with transformative, redemptive tales that can be read and appreciated by those intitiated into its secrets.

## The Implicit Structure of the Land

In Australian Aboriginal tradition, the landscape has an implicit structure. In essence, the land as it now exists is the residue (the traces or tracks) of Dreamtime ancestors or sacred beings. It is infused with sacred nodes, special places where physical objects represent the remains, or the continued presence, of Dreamtime heroes. Those sacred shrines, often identified with or located at striking geographical features of the land, are all "notes" in the songlines that follow the wanderings of the Dreamtime figures. These spiritual ancestors, furthermore, may be reincarnated in living Aborigines.

In central Australia, for example, in the region of the Arunta tribe, natives identify a gap in the mountains as a place where their ancestors were created from Dreamtime beings. The place is full of small, round stones said to be the eggs that the Dreamtime beings left behind. Natives carry these stones with them and believe they represent the embryonic forms of future generations. Trees, shrubs, and other features of this area are identified with specific Dreamtime ancestors, who in turn are often identified with living people in whom the ancestor has been reincarnated.

> For example, a gaunt old gum tree, with a large projecting bole about the middle of the trunk, indicates the exact spot where an Alcheringa man [a Dreamtime ancestor], who was very full of eggs, arose when he was transformed out of a witchetty grub. When he died his spirit part remained behind along with his Churinga, and used to especially frequent this tree, and . . . went inside a woman of the local group and was reincarnated in the form of a man who died a few years ago . . . An insignificant looking splinter of black, gneissic rock, projecting from the ground at another spot, indicates the exact place at which a woman of the Alcheringa arose whose living reincarnation—an old woman—is now seen at Alice Springs. (Spencer and Gillen 1899, 424)

We might picture the implicit structure of the land in Aboriginal thought as an immense web with many nodes all tied together by lines representing the original or primordial walkabouts of the ancient heroes; or it might be thought of as a score sung by those who travel the land; or it might be imagined as a text containing a detailed narrative incorporating every feature of the land into a numinous drama. I refer to this structure as implicit, because it is only known, understood, and appreciated by Aboriginals who are initiated into the mysteries of the land. This structure, for the most part, is neither apparent nor comprehensible to non-Aboriginals. To a great extent, it defines the Aborigine, suggesting her/his essential identity as a creature embedded in the land.

## Hindu Spiritual Geography

### The Indian Subcontinent as a Goddess

In Hinduism, too, the landscape has an implicit structure. The land is not what it seems to an outsider. At the most general level in Hindu tradition, the earth (or the Indian subcontinent) is said to be a goddess (Pṛthivī, Bhū Devī, or Bhārat Mā). In the *Devībhāgavata Purāṇa* it is said that the oceans are the Devī's bowels, the mountains are her bones, the rivers are her veins, and the trees are her body hair. The sun and moon are her eyes, and the nether worlds are her hips, legs, and feet (*Devībhāgavata Purāṇa* 7.33.21–41). Somadeva's *Yaśastilaka* says that the goddess Aparājitā has the stars for pearls in her hair, the sun and moon for eyes, the heavenly rivers as her girdle, and Mount Meru as her body (Mishra 1973, 25). A Gupta inscription says that Kumāragupta rules over the whole earth, whose "marriage-string is the verge of the four oceans; whose large breasts are [the mountains] Sumeru and Kailāsa; [and] whose laughter is the full-blown flowers showered forth from the borders of the woods" (Fleet 1970, 86).

A particularly striking example of the Hindu intuition that the Indian subcontinent is a goddess is seen in the Bhārat Mā temple in Varanasi. Instead of an anthropomorphic or symbolic form of the deity, the temple contains a large relief map of India. The goddess of this temple is the Indian subcontinent itself.

Another vivid expression of this Hindu belief is the cult of the *śākta-pīṭhas*, holy places associated with the goddess Satī. According to this tradition, the body of Satī was dismembered and its many pieces distributed throughout the world (that is, the Indian subcontinent). In the myth, Śiva, Satī's aggrieved husband, carried her body throughout the world, reluctant to let her go. Viṣṇu gradually cut her body apart with his discus, "seeding" the earth, as it were, with pieces of her corpse. Wherever a piece of Satī's body fell, a sacred shrine was established. In effect, India became her burial ground and was thus sacralized. The myth also stresses that the numerous and varied *pīṭhas* and the goddesses worshipped at them are a part of a larger, unified whole. Each *pīṭha* represents a part of Satī's body or one of her ornaments. Taken together, the *pīṭhas* constitute or point toward a transcendent (or, perhaps better, a universally immanent) goddess whose being encompasses, underlies, infuses, and unifies the Indian subcontinent as a whole. In short, the Indian subcontinent is the goddess Satī. As Bhattacharyya observes:

> In this vast country, holy resorts of the goddess are innumerable and the popularity of her cult is proved even in the place-

names of India. Referring to the Panjab region Prof. Niharranjan Ray observed: "Very few people pause to consider this social phenomenon, or to consider the significance of such toponymns in these regions as, for instance, Ambala, which is derived from Amba, one of the many names of Durgā, Chandigarh which is named after Caṇḍī, . . . Kalka which is a vulgarisation of Kālikā, Simla which is Śyāmalā Devī in its anglicised version. A careful and close look at the postal directories of the Panjab, Hariyana and Himachal would yield a long list of such toponyms from which one may draw one's own conclusion. Besides, throughout these regions one still finds a countless number of small, lowly shrines with all but shapeless or crude forms placed on their altars, which worshippers, lowly village folks, describe as Manasā, Caṇḍī, Kālī, Naynā, Durgā, etc. (Bhattacharyya 1974, 139–40)

**Sacred Rivers**

Another vivid example of the implicit structure of the landscape that renders it numinous or sacred is the Hindu reverence for rivers. Most important rivers in India, from the Hindu perspective, are goddesses. In some cases, there are well-known myths concerning the origin of these rivers, which are said to have their sources in heaven and to have been brought to earth to bless humankind in some way.

Hindu reverence for rivers is particularly intense in the case of the Ganges. Several myths tell of her descent to earth. The best-known story concerns the restoration of the sixty thousand sons of King Sagara. In this myth, Sagara's sons were dull-witted and impetuous; while searching the world for their father's sacrificial horse, they insulted and disturbed the tranquility of the sage Kapila. In anger, Kapila burned them all to ashes with the fire of his ascetic rage. Sagara's descendents, despite their piety and ascetic efforts, were unable to restore their incinerated forefathers until the saintly and mighty Bhagīratha, the great-great-great-great-grandson of Sagara, undertook the task. He gave up his kingdom and went to the Himalayas to undertake heroic austerities. After he had mortified himself for centuries, the Ganges appeared to him in bodily form and granted his wish: she would descend to earth, provided someone could be found to break her mighty fall, which otherwise would destroy the earth. Śiva volunteered to have the Ganges fall on his head, and so the great river descended to earth, her fall softened by Śiva's massive locks. His hair divided her into many streams, each of which flowed to a different region of the earth and sanctified that area. Her principal artery that emerged from Śiva's hair came to India, and under Bhagīratha's guidance, it cut a channel to where the ashes of Sagara's sons were piled. Moistened by her waters, the souls of the sixty thousand sons were purified and freed to undertake their journey to the land of the fathers, where they could be duly worshipped by their descendents.[3]

Other accounts of the descent of the Ganges feature Viṣṇu and sometimes Kṛṣṇa. After assuming his dwarf *avatāra* to trick the demon Bali, Viṣṇu strode across the cosmos to appropriate the vault of heaven and broke it. The Ganges poured through the hole and eventually found her way to earth. Falling on Mount Meru, the cosmic axis, the Ganges divided into four parts, and as she flowed onto the four continents, she purified the world in every direction.[4] In some versions of the myth, the god Brahmā, who is said to hold the heavenly Ganges in his water pot, poured the Ganges on Viṣṇu's foot when it stretched into the heavenly sphere.[5] In still other versions of the myth, Viṣṇu became liquified when he heard a particularly sublime song sung in his praise, and in this form he entered Brahmā's water pot, containing the Ganges, and sacralized her.[6]

In one way or another, these myths about the descent of the Ganges to earth stress the river's heavenly origin, her essentially divine nature, and her association with the great male gods Brahmā, Viṣṇu, and Śiva. Spilling out of heaven from Viṣṇu's foot, containing Viṣṇu's liquified essence according to some myths, and falling onto Śiva's head, where she meandered through his tangled locks, the Ganges appeared in this world after having been made more sacred by direct contact with these gods. The river then spread the divine potency of these gods into the world when she flowed onto the earthly plane. A dip in her sacred waters purifies devotees of sin and physically connects them with a transcendent, heavenly sphere. In the case of the ashes and bones of the dead, which are often consigned to the Ganges by their descendents (especially at Varanasi), the Ganges transports them to the land of the ancestors, as it did in the case of the sons of Sagara. Her waters are cleansing (both physically and morally) and transformative.

### Lotus, *Maṇḍala,* and *Liṅga*

At what we might think of as the macrolevel, the earth or cosmos is thought of in Hinduism as a lotus, *maṇḍala*, *yantra*, egg, or *liṅga*. As a lotus, the cosmos is viewed as essentially organic, emerging and "blossoming" at the beginning of each cosmic *yuga*. As a *liṅga*, another organic symbol, the earth is viewed as a vibrant extension of the god Śiva; the world is understood to be infused with his great, fecund power. As a *maṇḍala* or *yantra*, the world is perceived to be a coherent, patterned, unified structure containing powerful nodes and connecting lines that lend the world a weblike, interconnected aspect. Each of these symbols suggests in a different way that the cosmos has an essential "deep structure," a mystical quality that lends it a numinous nature. This nature can be transformative to those who learn to discern it and establish a rapport with it.

The general point I have tried to make is this: implicit in the geography of India from the Hindu point of view is a spiritual structure that lends the land both coherence and power. To know that structure (the "story" of the land in a general sense) is to become oriented and empowered.

## Learning/Knowing the Story of the Land as Transformative

### The Ban Yātrā of Braj

> The whole of India's sacred geography, with its many *tīrthas*—those inherent in its natural landscape and those sanctified by the deeds of gods and the footsteps of heroes—is a living geography. As such it has been central in the shaping of an Indian sense of regional and national unity. The recognition of India as sacred landscape, woven together north and south, east and west, by the paths of pilgrims, has created a powerful sense of India as Bhārat Mātā—Mother India. (Eck 1981, 336)

In Australian Aboriginal religion, the sacrality of the geography is asserted and reiterated whenever people move across the land, for when they travel the land the Aborigines recite or sing the story of the particular landscape through which they are traveling. In a sense, we could think of the Australian walkabout as a kind of permanent or persistent form of pilgrimage. Similarly in Hinduism, pilgrimage is often the process of affirming, or learning, the story of the land. The major and minor pilgrimage routes, some of which have existed for thousands of years, represent "lines" that correspond to the inherent, implicit spiritual structures of the land. If we imagine a map of the Indian subcontinent tracing the routes of pilgrims, we would have something similar in appearance to what Chatwin refers to as the "spaghetti" of lines forming the Australian songlines. And, while the centrality of narrative is probably stronger in the Australian materials, Hindu pilgrims, like Australian Aboriginals, often relate the landscape through which they travel to sacred narratives.

The underlying or unifying narrative that is imprinted on the land in India is often related to the two Hindu epics, the *Mahābhārata* and *Rāmāyaṇa*. Diana Eck says:

> The stories of India's *tīrthas* are told in the popular praise literature, the *māhātmyas*, sometimes called *sthala purāṇas*, the "ancient stories of the place." This literature contains a thousand variations of the themes of divine hierophany. Considering this vast corpus of Indian mythology, which recounts the deeds of the gods and heroes, it is not difficult to imagine that the whole of India's geography is engraved with traces of mythic events. . . . [T]housands of places claim to have been visited by Rāma, Sītā, and Lakshmana in their journey described in the *Rāmāyaṇa*, or by the Pāṇḍava brothers in their forest exile recounted in the *Mahābhārata*. (Eck 1982, 35–36)

In my own travels around India I have been told many times that the location of a temple or shrine is related to an event from the epics, that Rāma performed a ritual or killed a demon at this place, or that Sītā cooked at this very spot, or that the Pāṇḍava brothers visited this area during their forest sojourn. In Maharashtra, places where the Pāṇḍava brothers defeated demons have marked the landscape. A ravine in the neighborhood of Wāī, for example, was made by the toe of Kīcak, a monster slain by Bhīma (Feldhaus 1995, 100). In many cases in Maharashtra, rivers and pools are said to have been made when the epic heroes needed water for certain purposes. Rāma and Lakṣmana created pools and rivers by digging with the ends of their bows or shooting arrows into the ground (Feldhaus 1995, 101). In such cases, the rivers are held to have their sources in the underworld. The Golā River, for example, was created when Rāma shot an arrow into the ground and brought water up "through the underworld from the back of the [cosmic] tortoise" (Feldhaus 1995, 101). In Rajasthan, near Ajmer, a series of temples marks the places where the body of Jaipalji, the legendary founding king of Ajmer, who battled the demon Rāvaṇa, the villain of the *Rāmāyaṇa*, became deposited (Gold 1988, 44–45).

In Hinduism, pilgrimage is often the process of learning to see the underlying or implicit spiritual structure of the land; this often involves a change in perspective, a change that is religiously transformative. Pilgrimage is the process whereby pilgrims open themselves to the sacred power, the numinous quality, of the landscape, whereby they establish a rapport with the land that is spiritually empowering. An underlying assumption of pilgrimage seems to be that the land cannot be intensely known and experienced from a distance; it can be fully known, its story deeply appreciated, only by traveling the land itself. The physical immediacy of pilgrimage, the actual contact with the land, intensifies the experience of appropriating the story of the land, learning to see its underlying, implicit structure, sensing its spiritually enlivening power. The experience can be lasting, transforming one's perspective permanently.

The Ban Yātrā (forest journey) of Braj, an arduous pilgrimage that takes three to five weeks and covers about two hundred miles, illustrates these themes well. This pilgrimage has been described in wonderfully sensitive detail by David Haberman in his book *Journey through the Twelve Forests* (1994). Haberman's account, based on his own participation in this sacred journey around and through Braj, vividly describes how the landscape (uninteresting to those not initiated into the mysteries of Kṛṣṇa devotion) comes alive to the pilgrims for whom the landscape becomes a sacred "text."

The Braj Ban Yātrā is undertaken every year by thousands of pilgrims near the end of the rainy season (early September through early October). Braj is the region in western Uttar Pradesh and eastern Rajasthan that is associated with the early life of Kṛṣṇa. This area is referred to by his devotees as his *dhām*, his "dwelling place."

It is important to begin the journey on Kṛṣṇa's birthday, Janmāṣṭami (the eighth of Bhādoṃ, which is usually early September or late August). It is often the case that pilgrimage to (or in) particular sites is made only (or primarily) at certain times (certain days of the lunar month, certain days during the year, and the like). In the case of the Ban Yātrā, the auspicious time to undertake the pilgrimage is linked directly to the story of Kṛṣṇa. In undertaking a tour of his "home," one begins on his birthday. On this day, many pilgrims actually go to the town of Mathura (within the Braj *maṇḍala*), where Kṛṣṇa is said to have been born. The pilgrimage route is said to traverse twelve forests, which are depicted on maps as the petals of a lotus. Here is the *maṇḍala* theme, the idea that within the geography of the place is an implicit, spiritual structure. Kṛṣṇa's *dhām* is perceived by his devotees as an immense lotus with forests forming each of the twelve petals.

## The World as Kṛṣṇa's Body

At the most general level, the Ban Yātrā teaches pilgrims that the whole area they traverse is Kṛṣṇa's body (by extension, they also learn that the whole world is Kṛṣṇa's body). The pilgrims learn that the underlying, implicit structure of the land is God's body, the divine made present in geographical form. Nārāyaṇa Bhaṭṭa was a central figure in establishing Braj as a pilgrimage center in the sixteenth century. In a late-seventeenth-century biography, the *Nārāyaṇa Bhaṭṭa Caritāmṛta* of Jānakī Prasād Bhaṭṭ, Kṛṣṇa says to Nārāyaṇa in a vision:

> You have seen all of Braj. You have seen Mathura and Vrindaban. You have seen the Yamuna, the best of rivers, and Govardhan, the best of mountains; you have seen the hills marked with my footprints and all my groves and forests. There is no pilgrimage

> site on earth known to surpass Braj, *the highest form of my own body*, which steals the mind of the devotee. I dwell here eternally, never leaving Braj. (Haberman 1994, 56)

In his *Vrajabhaktivilāsa*, Nārāyaṇa Bhaṭṭa says: "The Braj Mandal is an essential form of the Lord consisting of organs and limbs," and he proceeds to identify particular geographical features of the area with specific body parts: "Mathura is his heart; Madhuban is his navel; Kamudban and Talban are his breasts; Vrindaban is his brow; Bahulaban and Hamaban are his two arms; Bhandiraban and Kokilaban are his two legs; Khadiraban and Bhadrikaban are his two shoulders; Chatraban and Lohaban are his two eyes; Belban and Bhadraban are his two ears; Kamaban is his chin; Triveni and Sakhikubaban are his two lips," and so on (Haberman 1994, 126). The point is clear: the natural world of Braj is divine. "Krishna is Braj, and Braj is Krishna" (Haberman 1994, 127). For the pilgrim, the aim is to be able to perceive the landscape in this special way.

## Stories and Places: The Imprint of Kṛṣṇa on the Land

At a less general level, many specific geographical features (often marked by temples, shrines, or tanks) are identified with Kṛṣṇa's *līlās* (literally, "sports"; Kṛṣṇa's activities are referred to as "play" or "sport").[7] Ban Yātrā pilgrims visit hundreds of these places in the course of their two-hundred-mile journey. A few examples will make clear how the geography is identified with the story of Kṛṣṇa.

Midway through their journey, pilgrims visit a pond named Vimala (pure) near Kāmaban (the forest of desire). The area is presided over by Vimala Devī, the goddess of this place. The story of the pond is this:

> There was once a king from the northwestern region of Sindh named Vimala. King Vimala had a problem: he had no children. One day the king met the sage Yajnavalkya in a forest and, in the course of conversation, revealed his problem. Yajnavalkya took pity on him and blessed him, foretelling that he would not have a son but would have many daughters, all

> destined to surrender to Krishna. The six thousand wives of the king soon gave birth to twelve thousand daughters. When these had grown into beautiful women, a messenger was sent to find suitable husbands. The messenger arrived in Braj and found Krishna, who was quickly judged to be man enough for all. The king's daughters were soon sent to Braj to join Krishna. In the forest of Kamaban, Krishna met and began dancing with them all in a circular love dance in which he multiplied himself to equal the number of women. As Krishna made love to each of them, tears of joy flowed profusely from their eyes. The pond of Vimala Kund was formed from these tears. (Haberman 1994, 168)

Not far from this pond, on top of a small hill called Charan Pahari, there is an indentation in the rock in the shape of a foot. The story is that once Kṛṣṇa came to this place and played his flute. While listening to the gorgeous notes of the Lord's flute, the rock softened, thereby capturing Kṛṣṇa's footprint forever (Haberman 1994, 168). At another place, an indentation in a rocky surface is known as Eating Dish. This is where Kṛṣṇa made a dish out of rock when he and his companions had nothing on which to eat their food (Haberman 1994, 171).

In the forest called Barṣaṇa is a hill that is said to have been created by the four-headed god Brahmā. He created the hill to sit upon, the better to view Kṛṣṇa's dalliance with his female companions. The hill today is said to have the four faces of Brahmā (Haberman 1994, 173). The pond called Prema Sarovar (pond of love) was created when Radhā, in Kṛṣṇa's presence, was overcome with a mood of love in separation, because she anticipated having to leave him. Kṛṣṇa in turn was overcome by emotion at her deep feelings, and together they wept, forming the pond (Haberman 1994, 180). A sharp bend in the river Yamuna, which meanders through Braj, is said to have been formed when Balarāma, Kṛṣṇa's brother, got drunk on wine and love of the *gopīs* (cowherd women), and dragged his plow about in a drunken manner (Haberman 1994, 198).

Veṇukūp, "flute well," is so named because it arose when Kṛṣṇa and his playmates were very thirsty and Kṛṣṇa stuck his flute in the ground and produced cool, fresh water there (Haberman 1994, 204). Another pond is called Mānsarovar, the Lake of Sulking.

Once, Rādhā was waiting for Kṛṣṇa, who was late, and she suspected that he had been making love to other women. When he finally arrived, his body bore the marks of lovemaking and, overcome with jealousy, she fled from him and ran into the forest. The place where she stopped and shed a torrent of tears is this very same Mānsarovar Lake (Haberman 1994, 208). At another place, the pilgrims view a shallow ravine said to have been made by the demoness Pūtanā. Pūtanā tried to kill the infant Kṛṣṇa by poisoning her nipples and then offering to suckle him. Kṛṣṇa, unaffected by the poison, instead sucked the life from her. The ravine was formed by the writhing of her body in her death throes (Haberman 1994, 217).

A final example will suffice to suggest the extent to which the geography of Braj is suffused with the story of Kṛṣṇa. The Yamuna River itself is said to have been formed by the "drops of perspiration that fell from Krishna's body during lovemaking. It therefore is typically thought to consist of waves of bliss. In a popular poster sold in the bazaars of Braj, Yamuna is pictured as a female form of Krishna" (Haberman 1994, 192–93).

## Transformation of Perspective

Learning the story of the land can be transformative for the Ban Yātrā pilgrim. In the process of the pilgrimage, the pilgrim comes to view Braj geography in a special way. Where we might see simply rivers, hills, ponds, and forests, the pilgrim sees a landscape charged with divinity, a land that was actually shaped by mythic events.

Transformed perspective as both a precondition and result of the Ban Yātrā is suggested at one of the first stops the pilgrims make on their long journey. In Vrindavan (or Vrindaban), pilgrims visit a Śiva temple named Gopīśvar (lord of the *gopīs*). Like all Śiva temples, the central icon is a *liṅga*. In this particular temple, however, the worship of the *liṅga* is distinctive. Each evening the priests of the temple dress the *liṅga* in a sari, then add female adornments, put the mask of a beautiful woman on the *liṅga*, mark the eyes with eyeliner, put a jeweled nose ring on the mask, apply bright lipstick, and finally place a silver crown on the top of the *liṅga*. The image is then revered by regular sixteen-part *pūjā* (Haberman 1994, 20–22).

The story of this temple (the *sthala-purāṇa*) is this: Once upon a time, Kṛṣṇa played his flute to summon the *gopīs* to make love in the forests of Vrindavan. Śiva, the great ascetic, was sitting in meditation in the Himalayas and heard the sweet music. He felt a strong urge to take part in the love dance of Kṛṣṇa and, abandoning his ascetic resolve, left his mountain home and rushed off to Vrindavan. When he got there, though, he could not cross the Yamuna River. The river appeared to him in goddess form and said that he could not enter Vrindavan and take part in the Lord's love games while he was in the form of a male ascetic. She advised him to bathe in her waters; when he did, he emerged as a stunningly attractive woman. As Śiva had never applied makeup before, knowing only how to smear ashes on his body, the goddess Yamunā helped him apply his makeup. Transformed into a *gopī*, fittingly beautified with makeup and ornaments, Śiva entered Vrindavan and joined the circle of Kṛṣṇa's love play. Kṛṣṇa was so pleased with Śiva's ability to dance (Śiva is Lord of the Dance) that he allowed him to dwell permanently in Vrindavan in the form of Gopīśvar (Haberman 1994, 23–27).

The role of Śiva is taken to be exemplary for pilgrims. That is, they too seek to adopt the attitude, perspective, and identity of a *gopī*, a true lover of the Lord, in order to see and experience the evidence of Kṛṣṇa's *līlā* in the twelve forests. One guidebook says: "In this pilgrimage all devotees should maintain the emotional state of a female companion of Shri Radha and Krishna; they should not think of themselves as a male" (Haberman 1994, 156).

Pilgrims often say that they have no practical goal in undertaking the Ban Yātrā. They say they want to experience bliss. One way they accomplish this is by means of a shift in perspective that allows them to discern the underlying, implicit sacrality of the landscape. Through this transformation of perspective, pilgrims, like the *gopīs*, see nothing but Kṛṣṇa everywhere and thereby know bliss.

## The Walkabout as a Model for Hindu Pilgrimage

Pilgrimage is so central and diverse in the Hindu tradition that it is unlikely that any one model of pilgrimage would be satisfactory to describe all examples. What I would like to term the walkabout model (from Australian Aboriginal materials) seems helpful in explaining a strong geographical aspect of Hindu pilgrimage that is lacking in Victor Turner's model of pilgrimage. Turner (1979) sees pilgrimage as consisting of three phases: preliminal (leaving a familiar place), liminal (entering a period that is betwixt and between familiar boundaries, the period of travel or journey), and postliminal (in which the pilgrim appropriates the sacred power or meaning of the "new center out there" and is thereby transformed). Turner's structure undoubtedly helps us understand much about Hindu pilgrimage. However, there is a nonlinear, continuous, repetitive, aimless aspect to much Hindu pilgrimage that seems to escape, or only loosely fit, Turner's model.

In many cases, such as the Braj Ban Yātrā, it is not so much the specific sacred places that are the focus of the pilgrims as it is the journey itself. And on the journey, it is not so much concrete goals that are pursued as it is an appreciation for the story of the land, which can only be experienced while traveling, while in a nomadic mode. Whether actually at a sacred center or traveling between centers, the pilgrims are more or less continuously attentive to the story of the land. They wander in order to learn the story, or to enjoy the story in its immediate setting. Like the Australian Aboriginal walkabout, there is no beginning or end. For the Aborigines, the aim is to get or stay oriented in the land by learning and singing its songs, to live life with a perspective that is sensitive to what the land has to say.

It has been said of the pilgrims who undertake the Ban Yātrā that "pilgrimage is an exercise in seeing the world correctly as god's *līlā* and experiencing it emotionally as his eternal bliss" (Lynch 1988, 180). In this sense, the aim is never to stop, to keep going, to remain "on the road," where this perspective is heightened and reinforced.

## Ecological Implications

The question arises: What are the ecological implications of Hindu geographical spirituality? It would be comforting to suppose that the Hindu emphasis on a spirituality rooted in the land has primarily, or exclusively, positive ecological repercussions. However, this is not the case. This is made apparent by the range and seriousness of ecological problems in India today—desertification, dwindling forests, polluted rivers, widespread air pollution. Although it is likely that Hindu geographical spirituality has positive ecological effects, certain aspects of Hindu reverence for the land might be understood to have negative effects.

The Hindu tendency to sacralize certain natural phenomena, such as the Ganges River and the area around Braj, has a counterpoint: other places are, relatively speaking, profane. Although there is a tradition in Hinduism of revering the earth as a whole (or the Indian subcontinent as a whole) as a goddess, and of revering certain natural phenomena such as fire and wind as sacred, the tendency toward selectivity in focusing on particular sacred places emphasizes a dichotomy between sacred and profane space. The possible negative ecological implications of this are suggested in rules governing the behavior of pilgrims in the annual pilgrimage around the city of Varanasi. Pilgrims circumambulate the city in the standard clockwise direction, always keeping the sacred Varanasi *maṇḍala* to their right. They are instructed never to defecate or urinate on the right side of the pilgrimage path, as this would pollute the sacred city. To defecate or urinate on the left side of the path, on profane ground, however, is perfectly acceptable.

The Hindu emphasis on long and often arduous pilgrimages also implies that the terrain pilgrims travel through, or their own locales, are, relatively speaking, profane. Crowded train and bus stations, heavily trafficked, dusty roads, noisy, dirty accommodations, and other rigors of the journey reinforce the idea that nature is indeed sacred and worthy of reverence in some places but not in others and that the boon of making a pilgrimage is to escape from areas where the natural world is profaned. Traveling from one's own home in quest of the sacred as manifest in some natural phenomenon far away might imply to pilgrims that their own homes, villages, or regions are correspondingly less sacred and less in need of reverence.

It can also be argued that the Hindu tendency to affirm an implicit structure in the natural environment has the effect of so obscuring nature that harmful ecological effects are not even discerned. Many pious Hindus are distracted from fully appreciating the extent to which the Ganges River and the city of Varanasi are suffering from pollution in their reverence for the city as a sacred center and the river as a goddess (see Alley, this volume). Similarly, Vrindavan, while acknowledged to be Kṛṣṇa's dwelling place, suffers from serious pollution problems, many associated with pilgrims (see Sullivan, this volume). Pious Hindus, it might be argued, are encouraged by their tradition to discern the mystical dimensions of the landscape, but this may obscure their perception of its physical, natural features.

The negative ecological effect of revering certain natural phenomena as sacred was brought home to me in Varanasi by Hindus who told me that the inherent purity of the Ganges made it impossible for her to become seriously polluted. The Ganges in particular in Hindu tradition is believed to have unlimited purifying powers. The story of her descent to earth is predicated precisely on this point: the goddess in riverine form descends to earth to purify the ashes of the sixty-thousand sons of Sagara so they will be fit for heaven. Examples abound in Hindu scriptures concerning the miraculous effects of Ganges water. The most sinful individuals are completely purified and rendered fit for heaven, or made impervious to appropriate karmic consequences, when they come in contact with a drop of Ganges water, or even when they merely come in contact with a being who has been blessed by Ganges water. In the *Bṛhaddharma Purāṇa*, for example, a sinful king is said to have been spared untimely death because he lived for a while with a merchant who used to bathe in the Ganges (*madhyakhaṇḍa* 26). The *Mahābhāgavata Purāṇa* tells of a robber who, though sent to hell after death, was subsequently sent to heaven because his flesh was eaten by a jackal who had drunk Ganges water (74). How is it possible, some pious Hindus ask, to harm such a goddess with pollution?

## Conclusion

In Australian Aboriginal religion, we have a particularly vivid example of a topographically based religion. Human beings are essentially defined by the land from which they have emerged and in which they live. The mythic universe in which they live and which orients their lives is imprinted on the landscape. The landscape is dense with meaning and numinous in nature.

There is a similar topographical spirituality in Hinduism, which is particularly strong in the context of certain pilgrimages. In what we might term their nomadic mode, millions of Hindus at any given time are on pilgrimage, traversing the Indian subcontinent by rail, bus, bullock cart, bicycle, and foot. In many cases, the sacred sites they visit are themselves distinctive geographical features: sacred rivers (often river confluences, sources, and mouths), lakes, mountains, hills, caves, trees, groves, seashores, and dramatic ice formations (ice *liṅgas*). These topographical sites are often related to an underlying spiritual structure, or a sacred narrative, that enriches and intensifies their numinous quality. This structure or story reveals the true nature of the landscape, providing a context in which the pilgrim can relate directly to the land. Hindu pilgrimage, like the Australian walkabout, is much more than an appreciative tour of the landscape: it is an experience in learning the implicit spiritual meaning or story of the land, by means of which the pilgrim is able to discern the imprint of the gods and heroes on the land and thereby appropriate spiritual rootedness.

## Notes

1. Mircea Eliade 1973, 57. On the centrality of the land being imprinted by Dreamtime ancestors, see Rose 1992, Steele 1983, and Strehlow 1947.

2. I use the present tense despite the fact that many, probably most, Aboriginals no longer live in traditional circumstances.

3. *Mahābhārata, vanaparva* 104–08; *Rāmāyaṇa* 1.38–44; *Bhāgavata Purāṇa* 9.8–9; *Brahmavaivarta Purāṇa, prakṛtikhaṇḍa* 10; *Devībhāgavata Purāṇa* 9.11.

4. *Kūrma Purāṇa* 1.44; *Brahmavaivarta Purāṇa, kṛṣṇajanmakhaṇḍa* 34; *Bhāgavata Purāṇa* 5.17; *Devībhāgavata Purāṇa* 8.7; *Viṣṇu Purāṇa* 2.2.8.

5. *Mahābhāgavata Purāṇa* 65; *Bṛhaddharma Purāṇa, madhya-khaṇḍa* 17.

6. *Bṛhaddharma Purāṇa, madhya-khaṇḍa* 14.

7. Some other examples of the identification of geographical or topographical features of the land with mythic events or legends are the pilgrimage to the temple of Vaiṣṇo Devī (Erndl 1993, 60, 64), the pilgrimage of Nandā Devī (Sax 1991, 52, 95–96, 133–35), the topography surrounding the city of Madurai (Harman 1989, 35, 38), and "localizations" of the *Rāmāyaṇa* in folk cults in Maharashtra (Sontheimer 1991, 115–37).

## References

Bhattacharyya, Narendra Nath. 1974. *History of the Śākta Religion*. New Delhi: Munshiram Manoharlal Publishers.

Chatwin, Bruce. 1987. *The Songlines*. New York: Penguin Books.

Eck, Diana L. 1981. "India's *Tīrthas*: 'Crossings' in Sacred Geography." *History of Religions* 20 (4): 323–44.

———. 1982. *Banaras: City of Light*. Princeton: Princeton University Press.

Eliade, Mircea. 1973. *Australian Religions: An Introduction*. Ithaca: Cornell University Press.

Erndl, Kathleen M. 1993. *Victory to the Mother: The Hindu Goddess of Northwest India in Myth, Ritual, and Symbol*. New York: Oxford University Press.

Feldhaus, Anne. 1995. *Water and Womanhood: Religious Meanings of Rivers in Maharashtra*. New York: Oxford University Press.

Fleet, John F. 1970. *Inscriptions of the Early Gupta Kings and their Successors*. Varanasi: Indological Book House.

Gold, Ann Grodzins. 1988. *Fruitful Journeys: The Way of Rajasthani Pilgrims*. Berkeley: University of California Press.

Haberman, David. 1994. *Journey through the Twelve Forests: An Encounter with Krishna*. New York: Oxford University Press.

Harman, William P. 1989. *The Sacred Marriage of a Hindu Goddess*. Bloomington: Indiana University Press.

Lane, Belden C. 1988. *Landscapes of the Sacred: Geography and Narrative in American Spirituality*. New York: Paulist Press.

Lynch, Owen. 1988. "Pilgrimage with Krishna, Sovereign of Emotions." *Contributions to Indian Sociology* 22 (2): 171–94.

Mishra, Vibhuti Bhushan. 1973. *Religious Beliefs and Practices of North India during the Early Medieval Period*. Leiden: E. J. Brill.

Rose, Deborah Bird. 1992. *Dingo Makes Us Human: Life and Land in an Aboriginal Australian Culture*. Cambridge: Cambridge University Press.

Sax, William S. 1991. *Mountain Goddess: Gender and Politics in a Himalayan Pilgrimage*. New York: Oxford University Press.

Sontheimer, Gunther-Dietz. 1991. "The *Rāmāyaṇa* in Contemporary Folk Traditions of Maharashtra." In *Rāmāyaṇa and Rāmāyaṇas*, ed. Monika Thiel-Horstmann. Wiesbaden: Otto Harassowitz.

Spencer, Baldwin, and F. J. Gillen. 1968. *The Native Tribes of Central Australia*. New York: Dover Publications.

Steele, John G. 1983. *Aboriginal Pathways in Southeast Queensland and the Richmond River*. St. Lucia: University of Queensland Press.

Strehlow, T. G. H. 1947. *Aranda Traditions*. Melbourne: Melbourne University Press.

Turner, Victor. 1979. *Process, Performance, and Pilgrimage: A Study in Comparative Symbology*. New Delhi: Concept Publishing Company.

Bruce M. Sullivan

# 10

# Theology and Ecology at the Birthplace of Kṛṣṇa

## Introduction

The religions of the West have often been criticized for their theologies in which humanity is given "dominion" over nature, but they also include the conception of humanity's "stewardship" of nature, which may be more conducive to an ecological ethic. Indic religious traditions are often cited as possibly providing a corrective to the widely perceived lack of regard for nature in Western religions.[1] But Christianity and Hinduism are both extremely diverse traditions, in each of which a variety of views may be found. Theists may tend to value the world because it is the work of the divine Creator, seeing in nature a reflection of God. On the other hand, world-renouncing ascetics may regard the natural world very differently, seeing it as a source of temptations and distractions, their priorities lying elsewhere.

Hindus of theistic traditions in which Kṛṣṇa is the object of worship have recently initiated a program of reforestation and ecological activity with international support. The program is centered in the town of Vrindavan (Vṛndāvana in Sanskrit) in the state of Uttar Pradesh in north-central India, regarded as sacred because it is the site of Kṛṣṇa's early life. Devotees have begun an ecological movement in the region of Kṛṣṇa's birth—known as Braj in the vernacular Hindi, Vraja in Sanskrit—motivated largely by religious concerns and ideals.

## Historical and Theological Background

A brief passage from the *Bhāgavata Purāṇa* will highlight themes to be encountered throughout this chapter.

> The glorious Lord [Kṛṣṇa], the son of Devakī, accompanied by Balarāma and surrounded by cowherds, went a distance from Vṛndāvana, grazing the cattle.
>
> Observing that the trees served as parasols by spreading their shade in the scorching heat of the sun, Kṛṣṇa addressed his cowherd friends, the residents of Vraja:
>
> "Look at these great blessed souls, who live only for the welfare of others, suffering stormy winds, heavy rains, heat and frost, sparing us.
>
> "The birth of trees is truly the most blessed in the world, for they contribute to the well-being of all creatures. Just as no one needy returns disappointed from generous persons, so too one who approaches trees for shelter.
>
> "They meet the needs of others with their leaves, flowers, fruits, shade, roots, bark, wood, fragrance, sap, ashes, and charcoal.
>
> "Offering life, wealth, intellect and speech to benefit others is the height of service of embodied beings for fellow creatures."
>
> Praising the trees in this way, the Lord proceeded to the Yamunā, passing between rows of trees whose branches were bent low with clusters of sprouts, foliage, bunches of fruits, and flowers.
>
> Having made their cattle drink of the sweet, cool, healthy water of the Yamunā, the cowherds themselves drank that sweet water to their hearts' content.[2]

So ends a chapter of the *Bhāgavata Purāṇa* describing the environment around Vrindavan, Kṛṣṇa's home.

Vrindavan is important in the worship of Kṛṣṇa, and has been for centuries, precisely because Kṛṣṇa lived there. Bengali (or Gauḍīya) Vaiṣṇavism has been very prominent and influential in Vrindavan as well as Bengal for five centuries now.[3] The importance attached to Vrindavan by this tradition is indicated by the fact that Caitanya, reviver of Vaiṣṇavism in Bengal in the sixteenth century, sent several of his most trusted disciples there to establish a presence in the area, and himself made the long pilgrimage west some eight hundred miles to see the sites associated with Kṛṣṇa's youth. Similarly, in the twentieth century Swami Bhaktivedanta Prabhupada, the founder of the International Society for Krishna Consciousness (ISKCON, also popularly known as the "Hare Krishnas"), lived for a decade in Vrindavan before coming to America in 1966; he returned periodically until his death there in 1977, and his tomb is on the grounds of the large ISKCON temple he founded in Vrindavan (Brooks 1989a, 95). As will be shown below, the town itself, as a sacred center regarded as spiritually efficacious, plays a crucial role in the religious thought of devotees of Kṛṣṇa.

In the distinctive theology of this variety of Vaiṣṇavism, systematized in Vrindavan after the death of Caitanya by six scholarly theologians known collectively as the Gosvāmins, Kṛṣṇa is the object of worship and is regarded as the true form of Ultimate Reality. He is not an *avatāra*, or divine manifestation, of Viṣṇu, not a portion of God on earth, but Ultimate Reality embodied. One of the most important ideas in this tradition is its emphasis on the eternal *līlā* (play, sport) of Kṛṣṇa in Vrindavan;[4] the tradition's most distinctive practice is the visualization of oneself as a participant in that divine play.

The Gosvāmin theologians drew upon the aesthetic theory of *rasa* to articulate their devotional system. In the *rasa* theory, a dramatic or poetic work of art is a precondition, presentation of which allows the audience member to experience, not merely a personal emotional state (*bhāva*) tied to specific personal experiences, but a generalized state of emotional consciousness (*rasa*) that is joyful aesthetic appreciation. Eight or nine *rasas* can be experienced, though aesthetic theorists had long regarded *śṛṅgāra* (love) as the most effective primary *rasa* for a work of art.[5] The Gosvāmins utilized the terminology of this aesthetic theory, but in important ways changed its purpose. For them, Kṛṣṇa became the only hero (*nāyaka*), and his life story the only play; moreover, the spectator was transformed from a passive observer relishing the state of consciousness evoked to an active participant in the drama itself. And while the aesthetic theorist Abhinavagupta had written that the *rasa* experience was analogous to the attainment of *mokṣa* but only temporary, lasting as long as the drama that was its catalyst, Rūpa Gosvāmin wrote that the attainment of *rasa* through Kṛṣṇa *bhakti* (devotion) was equivalent to *mokṣa* (Gerow 1981, 239–43; Larson 1976; Wulff 1986, 679–81). Associates of Kṛṣṇa depicted in the scriptures are taken as the models for loving relationships to him, and one is to identify oneself with one of these associates. Four positive relationships with Kṛṣṇa are enumerated: (1) servant (*dāsa*), (2) parent (*vatsālya*), (3) friend (*sākhya*), and (4) lover (*madhurya*).[6] All four relationships are regarded as varieties of love; indeed, the objective is to develop loving devotion to Kṛṣṇa in one or another of these ways.

The milkmaids (*gopīs*) of Braj embody the ideal of selfless devotion to the beloved, and are regarded as the model devotees. Chief among them is Rādhā, who, although not specifically named in the *Bhāgavata Purāṇa*, is celebrated as Kṛṣṇa's beloved some two hundred years later in a Sanskrit poem from Bengal, the *Gītagovinda*. She is sometimes regarded as the symbolic representation of the human soul, displaying in her relationship to Kṛṣṇa the devotional ideal; and she is sometimes regarded as the divine feminine principle, inseparable from Kṛṣṇa, the two together constituting Ultimate Reality.[7] The highest religious goal is the perfection of selfless devotion to and love for God, and the afterlife is conceived as a continuation of that *līlā* in Kṛṣṇa's paradise, known variously as Vaikuṇṭha ("free from misery," though the name is often used for the paradise of Viṣṇu) or Goloka ("realm of cows") or Vṛndāvana or Vraja (De 1961, 333–39). As Kinsley (1979, 113) observes, Kṛṣṇa's heaven "is nothing else but the idyllic forest town of Vṛndāvana [Vrindavan] unabashedly magnified," and "Kṛṣṇa's heavenly sporting ground is identical with the scene of his earthly life as a youth." The heavenly paradise and the earthly town of the texts are often not distinguished, as they are regarded as identical; the earthly town of Vrindavan today is regarded by devotees as the site of Kṛṣṇa's eternal *līlā*. In short, one is to visualize oneself in Vrindavan during this lifetime imitating the paradigmatic actions of devotees of Kṛṣṇa, attaining liberation from rebirth through pure loving devotion so that one's service and devotion to Kṛṣṇa may continue eternally in the celestial Vrindavan.

The worshippers of Kṛṣṇa particularly revere the tenth book of the *Bhāgavata Purāṇa* for what it reveals about Kṛṣṇa's human life, especially his youth in and around Vrindavan. This *Purāṇa* was so important for the Gosvāmin theologians of Gauḍīya Vaiṣṇavism that they rejected all other sources of knowledge (*pramāṇa*) except for divine revelation (*śabda*), and regarded this work as the quintessential revelation and the ideal text for this era.[8] The *Bhāgavata Purāṇa*, other texts, and devotional songs make references to deeds of Kṛṣṇa in specific places in the vicinity of Vrindavan: Mount Govardhana, the Yamuna River, and others. Devotees are strongly encouraged to go to such places where they can feel a special closeness to Kṛṣṇa and Rādhā because of their actions there, and many will imitate certain of their actions at particular sites. The texts also refer to the beauty of Vrindavan and the surrounding land of Braj (as in the *Bhāgavata Purāṇa* passage above), with cattle grazing contentedly among flowering trees and clear waters—a land made perpetually lovely by Kṛṣṇa. The region of Braj is even said to be identical with the body of Kṛṣṇa himself, a topographic form of God, a physical manifestation of the love of Rādhā and Kṛṣṇa (Haberman 1994, 125–27; see Kinsley, this volume). Specific sites are identified with specific body parts of Kṛṣṇa, such that Mathura is his heart, Vrindavan his brow, and so on. Hence, pilgrims may regard the very dirt of the area as sacred for having been walked on by God, even non-different from God, and will rub handfuls on their heads and ingest some, taking it as *prasāda* (Brooks 1989a, 6), an edible substance infused with God's grace. As Brooks (1989b, 185; cf. 1989a, 56) has observed, "every place in the town has some sacred significance," and "it cannot be said that there is a secular part and a sacred part." Specificity adds value, however, and while every molecule of dust may be sanctified, certain sites are regarded by devotees as more sacred than others because of particular deeds of Kṛṣṇa and Rādhā there.

Numerous Vaiṣṇava texts extoll the beauties of Braj, where leaves and fruits are envisioned as gleaming like jewels; indeed, the loveliness of nature has been seen as evidence that this spot was blessed with a divine presence (Kinsley 1979, 117–19). The *Gītagovinda* is a particularly vivid example of a Vaiṣṇava poet employing all his eloquence to describe the beauty of nature in the land of Rādhā and Kṛṣṇa. Other texts also present the region as inspiringly beautiful. For example, the *Harivaṃśa*, an appendix (*khila*) to the *Mahābhārata*, perhaps composed about five centuries before the *Gītagovinda* in the fifth century C.E., refers to the beauty of the forests of Braj as the reason the cowherds had chosen to live there.[9] The theme of the beauty of Braj is a constant in the literature devoted to the life of Kṛṣṇa. This paradise on earth was the scene of Kṛṣṇa's *līlā*, and is regarded as identical with his celestial paradise, where the *līlā* is eternal.

## The Ecological Program

But there is trouble in paradise today, on earth if not in heaven. The town of Vrindavan has become badly deforested, and the area is rapidly turning into a desert such as is found just to the west in Rajasthan. Studies are said to indicate that the water table is falling by as much as five feet a year, and the quality of the available water is deteriorating (Dasa 1992, 27). The Yamuna River is also heavily polluted by industrial runoff from factories upriver and from sewage, some of which comes from Vrindavan itself. Raw sewage flows over the *parikrama* pilgrimage path and discharges directly into the Yamuna in many places. The problem is so serious that the Government of India has declared the Yamuna unfit for drinking or bathing.[10] One might think that such a pronouncement would affect the activities of devotees and pilgrims, but apparently it has not so far. A large oil refinery in Mathura, only about seven miles downriver, pollutes the air throughout the region. Sadly, ecological damage is not unique to this area. Large tracts of India have been deforested due to the need for housing, farmland, and firewood by a rapidly increasing population. And sewage treatment is a widespread problem as well; it is estimated that only 10 percent of India's cities have sewage systems that could be described as "adequate."[11] The highly publicized deaths by plague in 1994, while not numerous, emphasize the point. But Vrindavan is unusual, and faces special ecological problems, because it receives over two million pilgrims per year. Modern transportation and the big business of guiding pilgrims to the sacred sites have increased traffic greatly, straining the capacity of municipal services such as water and sewage treatment.

The environment in and around Vrindavan has also suffered from an influx of people coming to live there. Relatively well-to-do Vaiṣṇavas want to retire to the scene of Kṛṣṇa's earthly activities, there to live out their days in the setting most conducive to worship and the liberation from rebirth that is its reward. Some of Delhi's wealthy devotees maintain second homes here. For them to live in Kṛṣṇa's land requires the building of new houses and flats in large number; the sign of one real estate developer in Vrindavan read:

> Welcome to this holy land of Lord Krishna. Holy forest plots for sale. Freehold residential complex in very peaceful and tranquility [*sic*] atmosphere.[12]

Ironically, the atmosphere of tranquility and peace that is advertized so persuasively will be destroyed with the bulldozing of the "holy forest" at the site. When sacredness is a marketable commodity, can any other outcome be expected? Perceiving this entrepreneurial activity as a problem, the devotees of ISKCON have raised money to purchase a forested plot called Ramaṇa Retī, famed as a place where Kṛṣṇa and his brother Balarāma played in their youth, and recently the target of real estate developers.[13] Thus one grove has been saved, but in a large region—all of which devotees regard as sacred—not all the forests of Kṛṣṇa are being saved. Many once forested areas are already treeless, or are being covered with buildings and roads as the town grows.

Obviously the degradation of the environment is an ecological problem for the Vrindavan area, and a problem for the quality of life, but it is also a specifically religious problem for the devotee of Kṛṣṇa. Pilgrims come to Vrindavan with the hope of seeing Kṛṣṇa's land, that is, having *darśana* of God in the form of his ponds and forests. Devotees want to bathe in the Yamuna to gain merit, but as already noted, to do so could now be dangerous to one's health;

observers have commented that parasites and illnesses are often the result of prolonged exposure to the Yamuna, and skin rashes from even brief exposure (Prime, 108). Deforestation and desertification are also a religious problem because one is to visualize oneself as a participant in Kṛṣṇa's *līlā* in the beautiful setting he creates for devotees eternally, but the earthly manifestation of Kṛṣṇa's *līlā* is not as inspirational or conducive to a sense of wonder as could be desired. Devotees have cited the appearance of the region as causing despair (Dasa 1992; WWF 1993; WWF 1995), so that a pilgrimage now might occasion loss of faith instead of deepening it. The conflict between descriptions in ancient devotional texts and the reality of Vrindavan today is stark.

The response to the ecocide in Vrindavan has been led by devotees of Kṛṣṇa, both Western converts and Indians. The general approach could be described by the following slogan, used to generate support: "one who cares for Kṛṣṇa cares for His land" (Dasa 1992, 30). Indeed, as noted above, for many worshippers of Kṛṣṇa, the region of Braj with Vrindavan at its center is seen as identical with Kṛṣṇa, the land being his physical manifestation. One well-known Indian devotee instrumental in the effort is Shrivatsa Goswami, who points to Kṛṣṇa as the paradigm of reverence for nature; not only did he defeat the river-polluting demon Kāliya, but the only two occasions on which Kṛṣṇa worshipped were when he led the cowherds in worshipping Mount Govardhana and when he worshipped the Sun God to cure his son of leprosy (Prime 1992, 54–56). In short, Goswami maintains that Kṛṣṇa worshipped nature.

A major effort to reforest the area began as follows. Ranchor Prime, an English member of ISKCON, who is known also as Ranchor Dasa and is familiar with the situation in Vrindavan, conceived a plan with Sewak Sharan, longtime resident of the area, to plant trees along the eleven-kilometer *parikrama* path that encircles the town. The importance of the pilgrimage path in Vrindavan is indicated by the fact that, upon his death on November 14, 1977, the body of Swami Bhaktivedanta Prabhupada of ISKCON was taken on a final *parikrama* around the town, allowing fellow Vaiṣṇavas to honor him (Brooks 1989a, 95). Its importance is indicated, too, by the fact that it is traveled by over two million pilgrims per year.[14] But the path is no longer the sylvan and pastoral setting for envisioning Kṛṣṇa's *līlā* which it once apparently was. Now the path is highly urbanized and suffers from the problems of deforestation and pollution already mentioned. Ranchor Prime prepared a report to the World Wide Fund for Nature (WWF) in Geneva, an international ecological agency that gives grants for environmental projects. WWF especially wants to highlight the ecological values of the cultures and religious traditions where projects are funded, and this seemed to them an opportunity to do so. Funding was granted for three years, to run from mid-1991 through mid-1994, some $40,000 per year. ISKCON donated use of one and a half acres beside the pilgrimage path for a nursery to raise some 10,000 trees of local origin to be planted in succeeding months (WWF 1993; Prime 1992, 104–18).

Ranchor Prime (or Dasa) was a consultant and a major influence from the outset in the Vrindavan Forest Revival Project. The project was formally initiated on November 21, 1991, the festival day of Vṛndā Devī, the goddess regarded as representing the local flora. All present took the following pledge:

> The forest of Vrindavan is the sacred playground of Rādhā and Kṛṣṇa. However, we, the people of this region, have cut its trees, polluted its Yamunā River, and spoilt its sacred dust with our rubbish and sewage. I pledge that from now on I will do all within my power to protect Vrindavan from further destruction and to restore it to its original beauty.[15]

Stage One of the project was to encourage community involvement so that the trees planted would be protected and would survive. Planting began with some two thousand trees and shrubs along a two-kilometer segment of the path. Stage Two has included further planting along the entire pathway, and continued outreach efforts to involve the populace. Assorted eyesores and environmental problems have been dealt with along the way also.

A more serious problem, and one that is even more difficult to solve, is presented by the sewage system of Vrindavan. Prior to 1970 the traditional latrine method was employed, waste being recycled into fields as fertilizer. At that time work began on a modern system that was designed to treat sewage so that it could be safely dumped into the Yamuna. Some underground pipes were laid and toilets were connected all over town, but the main line was never completed! Blockages and breaks in the lines occurred almost immediately and have never been fixed. Worse still, the treatment plant was never built! Now sewage that does not overflow into the streets and gather in low spots, polluting the groundwater supply, is simply dumped untreated into the river, and most of the municipal water supply is drawn from that same river. Ranchor Prime argues that the traditional method worked and should be implemented again, abandoning the inadequate and inappropriate sewage system. In making his case, he marshals religious arguments, citing the ancient Sanskrit religio-legal text *Manu Smṛti* as follows:

> One should not cause urine, stool, or mucus to enter water. Anything mixed with these unholy substances, or with blood or poison, should never be thrown into water. (4.56)

Ranchor Prime accuses Indians of becoming enamored of new Western technology and of applying the technology inappropriately, in the process forgetting their own ancient and time-tested technology which is appropriate to the situation, and ignoring the venerable injunctions such as those found in *Manu Smṛti*. He offers the view that the Western lifestyle is overly materialistic, consumption oriented, not ecological, and therefore must be abandoned both by Indians who have adopted it and by Westerners themselves. He also cites the words of Mahatma Gandhi, warning Indians against mechanization and technology and advocating a simple lifestyle.[16]

Ranchor Prime (1992, 112) points to underlying causes of the widespread abandonment of traditional Hindu values and technology, citing centuries of Muslim and British rule as detrimental to traditional Hindu culture and practices:

> For 800 years Muslims ruled from Delhi. The whole surrounding region, including Vrindavan, bears the deep impression of this rule, which did nothing to foster Hindu culture, and at times bitterly suppressed it. Then the British, with their more subtle form of tyranny, made Hindus second-class citizens in their own land. The effect of this subjugation has been to drain the enterprising spirit, the self-determination and inner resourcefulness from a people who had their affairs run for

> them by outsiders for longer than most nations or cultures have endured. This is why Gandhi stressed that India would not be able to have true independence until her people discovered *swaraj*—the power of self-rule—within themselves. This day has not yet come.

He concludes his discussion of the water pollution problems of the area by referring—like Shrivatsa Goswami above—to the myth of Kṛṣṇa overcoming the demon Kāliya, who was poisoning the Yamuna, with the result that trees and animals were dying. Finally the cowherds themselves drank the water and fell ill. Kṛṣṇa wrestled with the demon and subdued it, saving the region from the effects of poisoned water; for this, he is seen by an activist-devotee as "Kṛṣṇa the environmentalist" (Dasa 1992, 31). For many devotees of Kṛṣṇa, Vrindavan's problems are linked with a worldwide environmental crisis, the solution to which lies in the adoption of traditional Hindu values and practices. Clearly, the deforestation and water pollution in the Vrindavan region are not being caused by the widespread raising of cattle for slaughter, for their meat, as is the case in other parts of the world such as Brazil or the United States, where similar ecological problems abound. Indeed, in Vrindavan, because of the importance of vegetarianism to the Hare Krishna movement and to other Vaiṣṇavas, it is almost impossible to find meat or even eggs for sale, a rare situation even in India. For the same reason, devotees are writing works in which meat-eating is identified as a serious, worldwide ecological problem (Prime 1992; Cremo and Goswami 1995). They state that a meat-based diet causes tremendous petroleum usage, and creates many polluting waste products. The *Manu Smṛti* (5.51) is cited as prohibiting the eating of meat, saying that the butcher, vendor, cook and consumer all are murderers and reap bad karmic consequences.[17] Nonviolence (*ahiṃsā*) is cited as a traditional Hindu value, adherence to which is conducive to the well-being of the individual and the world as a whole. In this way, Vaiṣṇavas are advocating a lifestyle based on traditional Hindu religious ideals of *ahiṃsā* and vegetarianism as a solution to modern environmental crises.

Those who worship Kṛṣṇa see his divine example, recounted in ancient myths, as still relevant today, and as the paradigm for human action that is desperately needed. As Sewak Sharan observed,

"Krishna didn't kill the *nāga* [Kāliya]—if he had he would have eliminated pollution forever. No, he just banished the pollution dragon. All we can do is try to manage the dirt better" (Sochaczewski 1994). Swami Raman Das, a forest-dwelling ascetic, similarly sees God's actions on earth as indicative of humanity's task: "Krishna shows that a two-armed, flesh-and-blood mortal, when energized by the spirit of the highest god Vishnu, can stand up to myriads of multi-armed demons. Every human being can perform miracles" (Sochaczewski 1994). These leaders hope that Kṛṣṇa will be the inspiration for this environmental program.

Hindu religious ideas, values, and practices are being marshalled to support a program, funded both by the Government of India and internationally, to restore the natural beauty of a Hindu pilgrimage site. The effort to save Vrindavan from ecocide by deforestation and polluted water, an undertaking that is essentially religious in inspiration and intent, is based on the hope that people will love the Earth just as they love Kṛṣṇa.

## Conclusions

For devotees of Kṛṣṇa, the earthly Vrindavan is identical with Kṛṣṇa's heavenly paradise. To those who are truly devoted, everything is beautiful because it is God's creation, and they may have developed an interior life in which participation in the divine sport is continuous; for them, one might think that the visible world in which we live is irrelevant. However, it seems that precisely those who are most devoted are taking the lead in the environmental cleanup of Braj. And for those who have not yet matured in their devotion, the beautification of the environment may be an aid to devotional practice. Certainly it can be regarded as service of Kṛṣṇa and an appropriate way of caring for Kṛṣṇa's creation.

The World Wide Fund for Nature (WWF) is hopeful that a successful project in Vrindavan will encourage others throughout India to examine their environment and find ways of improving the situation. Indeed, it has already had an effect internationally; residents of the English city of Leicester, with a large community of South Asian heritage, by July 1993 had donated some £8000 to the project in Vrindavan, and residents have been motivated to plant over 22,000 trees in Leicester (Friends of Vrindavan 1993). The project in Vrindavan has completed the three years of its original funding period and has been renewed by WWF for an additional three years, though there have been many changes in the project's leadership. Ranchor Prime, the ISKCON devotee who wrote the original grant proposal to WWF and was a major figure in the project's leadership from the outset, is no longer affiliated with this program; in fact, ISKCON itself, so instrumental in the early stages of the effort, is not now involved with it.[18] Leadership has passed to other devotees of Kṛṣṇa, Indians who are not members of ISKCON, while ISKCON concentrates its efforts on other sacred sites in the region of Braj outside of town, such as near Mount Govardhana. It remains to be seen whether this one project will have an effect throughout India, helping to create a view of the world as sacred and to be protected from pollution. But Hindus do not view all places with the same reverence as they do Vrindavan. And even in Vrindavan itself not everyone is a devotee of Kṛṣṇa who for that reason can be convinced to love the land; some of the trees so recently planted have already been bulldozed for a new road.[19] While the Vrindavan region would benefit from solving its sewage problem and planting trees, can the nation as a whole be said to have benefitted if pollution is simply shifted to other regions that are not viewed with the same degree of reverence?

WWF wants this project to serve as a means to increase awareness throughout India of the importance of protecting the natural world. The main purpose of the program according to WWF India has been "to promote an awareness and understanding of environmental values contained in the [Hindu] community's religious tradition, and to actively have them care for their environment" (WWF 1994, 1). WWF India reports that from mid-1993 through mid-1994, "cultural activities by children were an important instrument for influencing parents and the community," including the staging of four folk dramas on Kṛṣṇa and Rādhā's love for the environment (WWF 1994, 6; cf. WWF 1995, with picture). The report goes on to state that at the end of three years of work the program has successfully "evoked the people's collective religious conscience; previously they had no answer to the drastic decline in their environment, and the quiet abandonment of religious conservation practice is now being slowly reversed" (WWF 1994, 7). One practical outcome is that traditional religious views of nature are to be included in the official curriculum of Uttar Pradesh state: "This is partly due to WWF's helping to increase visibility about the importance of nature," according to Dr. Vinod Banerjee, spokesperson for the state teachers association (WWF 1995). Reports from Vrindavan on All-India Radio and the national television network Doordarshan have enabled WWF to take to the entire nation its message on the vital need for ecological action.

Other environmental movements exist in South Asia: the Chipko movement in the Himalayas, where people are protecting trees from clear-cutting by loggers (Gruzalski 1993; Shiva and Bandyopadhyay 1988), and the Trees for Life organization, which has given out over a million saplings for planting all over India (Prime 1992, 80–89). Sunderlal Bahuguna of Chipko tells stories of the life of Kṛṣṇa in his ceaseless efforts to better the environment: "There are people in India who are very devoted to religion and that is the secret of success of the Chipko movement" (Prime 1992, 96). Bahuguna himself has fasted repeatedly to combat deforestation, a technique of nonviolent non-cooperation he learned as a young follower of Mahatma Gandhi (Gruzalski 1993, 104–19; Shiva and Bandyopadhyay 1988, 231–34), and a tactic with a religious heritage in the idea of *ahiṃsā* and ascetic practices. Balbir Mathur of Trees for Life has his fruit tree saplings blessed by someone popularly regarded as possessing spiritual power, then gives the saplings as *prasāda* from a temple (Prime 1992, 85–87). Both these movements draw upon traditional Hindu religious ideas, values, and practices, to which they owe a considerable proportion of their popularity and success. And although none of these sources cites this example, there is a long tradition in India of state-sponsored protection of trees in public areas such as parks, sacred places, and along boundaries and highways (*Arthaśāstra* 3.19.28–30); one can only wonder whether respect for nature, fear of the king, or the perception of the practical value of trees played the greatest role in such a policy.

The World Wide Fund for Nature has established an office called the Conservation and Beliefs Network to coordinate their programs with the teachings of ecological significance in the religions of the world. WWF has also sponsored publication of a World Religions and Ecology series, of which Prime's book is one. A new international organization called the Alliance of Religions and Conservation (ARC) has been established with WWF sponsorship to fund ecological projects based on religious ideals.[20] Emphasizing the religious significance of nature in India seems an especially effective approach to encourage ecological activity. As the case of the Ganges indicates, many Hindus are skeptical of scientific justifications for ecological programs and might be more receptive to programs that have religiously sensitive approaches and religiously significant outcomes (see Alley, this volume). Hence, a government pronouncement that the water of the Yamuna or Ganges River is not sanitary for bathing does not deter a pilgrim who places greater value on its salvific power than its cleansing ability.

Nonetheless, it is also apparent that an ecological program based on traditional religious values can be successful only to the extent that people adhere to and continue to honor those traditional values. Many in India have expressed the view that their traditional values are being abandoned, and that the younger generation is being inculcated with Western culture, particularly through communications media, a potential problem for ecology programs based on traditional religious values. And it must be noted that ascetic and monistic traditions, which are very strong in India, tend to see the natural world as a realm of suffering from which to escape, not as an environment to be cared for in the way Vrindavan's Kṛṣṇa worshippers do; such ascetic worldviews may undercut ecological efforts (see Nelson, this volume). Even within movements as thoroughly theistic as ISKCON or others devoted to Kṛṣṇa such as those that derive from Nimbārka or Vallabha, there are elements that may vitiate ecological action. After all, if one successfully visualizes an alternative reality (or as devotees would have it, true reality), and experiences oneself as dwelling within it blissfully serving God, mundane reality with its shortcomings, environmental or otherwise, might seem irrelevant or merely a distraction.

In India, where numerous religious traditions coexist, both Hindu and non-Hindu, finding the most ecologically useful of many available traditional value systems will be a challenge for those who want to preserve or restore the natural world.

## Notes

1. The classic source on the anti-ecological worldview of Western religions, particularly Christianity, is White 1967. Leaders of Jainism, Sikhism, Buddhism and Hinduism at a conference in England in April, 1995, are quoted by Mathur 1995 to the effect that Western religions, especially Christianity, do not value nature; cf. Benthall 1995, 18. Rolston (1987, 172–74) makes a similar observation; however, his discussion (175–76) of the Hindu and Buddhist conception of *karma* is one with which I take issue. Hindus do not value animals "as once-upon-a-time moral agents" embodying "unsolved moral problems from human life," that is, as beings who in previous lives were human, "someone's grandmother" in Rolston's sarcastic terms. Rather, for the sake of his/her own *karma* and future rebirths, a Hindu seeks to behave morally toward animals, minimizing their suffering and acting to preserve their lives. Hindus and Jains would regard behaving in this way toward their fellow creatures as in accord with the religious ideal of *ahiṃsā*, often translated as nonviolence or not harming.

2. *Bhāgavata Purāṇa* 10.22.29–37, my translation from the Gita Press edition; the text is a Sanskrit devotional work composed about the tenth century C.E. The Sanskrit passage is as follows:

> atha gopaiḥ parivṛto bhagavān devakīsutaḥ /
> vṛndāvanād gato dūraṃ cārayan gāḥ sahāgrajaḥ // 29
> nidāghārkātape tigme chāyābhiḥ svābhirātmanaḥ /
> ātapatrāyitān vīkṣya drumānāha vrajaukasaḥ // 30
> he stokakṛṣṇa he aṃśo śrīdāman subalārjuna /
> viśālarṣabha tejasvin devaprastha varūthapa // 31
> paśyataitān mahābhāgān parārthaikāntajīvitān /
> vātavarṣātapahimān sahanto vārayanti naḥ // 32
> aho eṣāṃ varaṃ janma sarvaprāṇyupajīvanam /
> sujanasyeva yeṣāṃ vai vimukhā yānti nārthinaḥ // 33
> patrapuṣpaphalacchāyāmūlavalkaladārubhiḥ /
> gandhaniryāsabhasmāsthitokmāiḥ kāmān vitanvate // 34
> etāvajjanmasāphalyaṃ dehināmiha dehiṣu /
> prāṇairarthairdhayā vācā śreya evācaret sadā // 35
> iti pravālastabakaphalapuṣpadalotkaraiḥ /
> tarūṇāṃ namraśākhānāṃ madhyena yamunāṃ gataḥ // 36
> tatra gāḥ pāyayitvāpaḥ sumṛṣṭāḥ śītalāḥ śivāḥ /
> tato nṛpa svayaṃ gopāḥ kāmaṃ svādu papurjalam // 37

3. On the representation of Vrindavan in the religious literature of those devoted to Kṛṣṇa, see Corcoran 1995. The Sanskrit names Vṛndāvana and Vraja appear, with variations, in the vernacular Hindi as Vṛndāvan,

Vṛndāban, or Bṛndāban (typically written Vrindavan, Vrindaban, and Brindaban), and Braj. There are in the Vrindavan region other sects or schools of Kṛṣṇa-worshipping Vaiṣṇavism in addition to the Bengali, notably those of Vallabha and Nimbārka. Some understand Kṛṣṇa as an *avatāra* of Viṣṇu, the supreme deity; others regard Kṛṣṇa as supreme. Note that they refer to themselves as Vaiṣṇavas despite the fact that for some Kṛṣṇa and not Viṣṇu as such is the focus of devotional activity. De 1961 and Dimock 1963 provide excellent treatments of the theological aspects of the Bengali movement.

4. For a variety of views of the important concept *līlā*, see Sax 1995, especially the essays of Norvin Hein, "*Līlā*," Donna Wulff, "The Play of Emotion: *Līlākīrtan* in Bengal," and John Stratton Hawley, "Every Play a Play Within a Play." See also Hospital 1980 for a study most relevant to the theology of devotion underlying this ecological movement.

5. See Gerow 1981 for an excellent discussion of the *rasa* theory in literary criticism and its devotional application by the Gosvāmins.

6. De (1961, 176–97) gives the most detailed discussion of the relationships; for Rūpa Gosvāmin's treatment of the relationship as lover in his *Ujjvala-nīlamaṇi*, see 203–20. See also Dimock 1963, 116–18. Another possible relationship to God (called *śānta-bhāva*) is one in which the devotee regards Kṛṣṇa with awe and humility as Ultimate Reality, but not all authorities accept this *bhāva* as valid in the devotional context since one cannot know and love Ultimate Reality. One might also have a negative, hateful relationship with Kṛṣṇa, as for example Kaṃsa did, and have thoughts of him so fill one's mind as to be salvific, but such an attitude toward God is not advocated. Haberman 1988 is a detailed presentation of the devotional practice of "imitation" of, or identification of oneself with, Kṛṣṇa's companions and lovers.

7. On Rādhā, see Hawley and Wulff 1982; for the purposes of this chapter, see especially the essays of Charlotte Vaudeville, "Krishna Gopāla, Rādhā, and The Great Goddess," Barbara Stoler Miller, "The Divine Duality of Rādhā and Krishna," Donna Marie Wulff, "A Sanskrit Portrait: Rādhā in the Plays of Rūpa Goswāmī," C. Mackenzie Brown, "The Theology of Rādhā in the Purāṇas," and Shrivatsa Goswami, "Rādhā: The Play and Perfection of *Rasa*."

8. Dimock 1963, 108; De 1961, 169; both citing Jīva Gosvāmin's *Tattva-saṃdarbha*. For Jīva, the *Purāṇas* supersede the *Vedas* as revelation and are the texts to be used in the present era of Kali Yuga. The *Bhāgavata Purāṇa* is the greatest of them all for the Gosvāmins; they see it as Vyāsa's commentary on his own *Brahma-sūtras*.

In the Vedānta school generally six *pramāṇas* are accepted: *pratyakṣa* (sense perceptions), *anumāna* (inference), *upamāna* (analogy), *śabda* (revelation), *abhāva-pratyakṣa* (negative proof), and *arthāpatti* (inference from circumstances). The Nyāya school allows only four, excluding the last two listed above. Other schools allow fewer or even more *pramāṇas*.

9. For example, *Harivaṃśa* 53.30ab: *tad vrajasthānam adhikaṃ cakāśe kānanāvṛtam* (That place Vraja, surrounded by forests, looked even more beautiful).

10. Prime 1992, 108 citing the government report *The State of India's Environment* (New Delhi: Centre for Science and the Environment, 1982). Yet the Yamuna is still pure and purifying to devotees. This difference of views is comparable to the differing views of the purity/impurity of the Ganges, as discussed in Kelly D. Alley's chapter in this volume.

11. News broadcast on National Public Radio (U.S.A.), October 5, 1994.

12. Dasa 1992, 27, and pictured in WWF 1993.

13. Dasa 1992, 24–27, including a picture.

14. Prime 1992, 105 gives a figure of two million pilgrims per year; Sochaczewski 1994 says two and a half million; Friends of Vrindavan (1993, 4) says three million. In addition to these estimates, Brooks (1989a, 108–11) gives figures for the distribution of pilgrims per month during 1982–1983, with an annual total of 2.325 million, and notes that this is approximately triple the state government's survey figures of only a decade earlier! It may safely be assumed that the number of pilgrims is even higher now than in the survey by Brooks.

15. Quoted in WWF 1993 in both English and Hindi.

16. Prime 1992, 109–12; see also Cremo and Goswami, *passim*. Judah 1974 reveals a strong tendency among Hare Krishna members to criticize Western materialism and advocate a simple lifestyle based on self-sufficiency. My own M.A. thesis (Sullivan 1975) produced similar findings from interviews of Hare Krishnas in Texas. The theme has been a constant for the Hare Krishna movement in the West.

17. Prime 1992, 102; see also Cremo and Goswami, especially chapters 2 and 6. It may be noted that *Manu Smṛti* 5.27–44 discusses occasions on which eating meat may be acceptable (e.g., when the meat is consecrated by sprinkling water on it for Vedic sacrifice, or when one's life is in danger), but Manu then goes on to discuss (5.45–56) the karmic benefits of vegetarianism.

18. Letter from Ranchor Prime, April 17, 1995.

19. Conversation with David Haberman, November 20, 1994.

20. Letter from Ranchor Prime, April 17, 1995; Benthall 1995, 18. The Pilkington Foundation and MOA International, a Japanese cultural and religious organization, are co-sponsors of ARC.

## References

### Sanskrit Texts Cited

*Bhāgavata Purāṇa*. 2 vols. Gorakhpur: Gita Press, 1971.

*Harivaṃśa*. 2 vols. Edited by P. L. Vaidya. Poona: Bhandarkar Oriental Research Institute, 1969–71.

*Kauṭilīya Arthaśāstra*. 3 vols. 2d ed. Edited and translated by R. P. Kangle. Bombay: University of Bombay, 1969–72.

### Secondary Works Cited

Benthall, Jonathan. 1995. "The Greening of the Purple." *Anthropology Today* 11 (June): 18–20.

Brooks, Charles R. 1989a. *The Hare Krishnas in India*. Princeton: Princeton University Press.

———. 1989b. "A Unique Conjuncture: The Incorporation of ISKCON in Vrindaban." In *Krishna Consciousness in the West*, ed. David G. Bromley and Larry D. Shinn, 165–87. Lewisburg, Penn.: Bucknell University Press.

Corcoran, Maura. 1995. *Vṛndāvana in Vaiṣṇava Literature: History, Mythology, Symbolism*. New Delhi and Vrindaban: D. K. Printworld and Vrindaban Research Institute.

Cremo, Michael A., and Mukunda Goswami. 1995. *Divine Nature: A Spiritual Perspective on the Environmental Crisis*. Los Angeles: Bhaktivedānta Institute.

Dasa, Ranchor. [Ranchor Prime]. 1992. "Reviving the Forests of Vṛndāvana." *Back to Godhead: The Magazine of the Hare Krishna Movement* 26 (September–October): 24–39.

De, Sushil Kumar. 1961. *The Early History of the Vaisnava Faith and Movement in Bengal*. 2d ed. Calcutta: Firma K. L. Mukhopadhyay.

Dimock, Edward C., Jr. 1963. "Doctrine and Practice Among the Vaiṣṇavas of Bengal." *History of Religions* 3 (Summer): 106–27. Reprinted in *Krishna: Myths, Rites and Attitudes*, ed. Milton Singer, 41–63. Chicago: University of Chicago Press, 1966.

Friends of Vrindavan. 1993. "Protecting Sacred Forests: Linking Leicester's Community with the Sacred Forests of India."

Gerow, Edwin. 1981. "*Rasa* as a Category of Literary Criticism." In *Sanskrit Drama in Performance*, ed. Rachel Van M. Baumer and James R. Brandon, 226–57. Honolulu: University Press of Hawaii.

Gruzalski, Bart. 1993. "The Chipko Movement: A Gandhian Approach to Ecological Sustainability and Liberation from Economic Colonization." In *Ethical and Political Dilemmas of Modern India*, ed. Ninian Smart and Shivesh Thakur, 100–25. New York: St. Martin's Press.

Haberman, David L. 1988. *Acting as a Way of Salvation: A Study of Rāgānugā Bhakti Sādhana*. New York: Oxford University Press.

———. 1994. *Journey Through the Twelve Forests: An Encounter with Krishna*. New York: Oxford University Press.

Hawley, John Stratton, and Donna M. Wulff, eds. 1982. *The Divine Consort: Rādhā and the Goddesses of India*. Berkeley and Delhi: Graduate Theological Union and Motilal Banarsidass; reprint ed., Boston: Beacon Press, 1986.

Hospital, Clifford G. 1980. "Līlā in the *Bhāgavata Purāṇa*." *Purāṇa* 22: 4–22.

Judah, J. Stillson. 1974. *Hare Krishna and the Counterculture*. New York: John Wiley & Sons.

Kinsley, David R. 1979. *The Divine Player: A Study of Kṛṣṇa Līlā*. Delhi: Motilal Banarsidass.

Larson, Gerald J. 1976. "The Aesthetic (*rasāsvāda*) and the Religious (*brahmāsvāda*) in Abhinavagupta's Kashmir Śaivism." *Philosophy East and West* 26: 371–87.

Mathur, Sri Rakesh. 1995. "Can India's Timeworn Dharma Help Renew a Careworn World?" *Hinduism Today* 17 (July): 1, 9.

Prime, Ranchor. [Ranchor Dasa]. 1992. *Hinduism and Ecology: Seeds of Truth*. London: Cassell.

Rolston, Holmes, III. 1987. "Can the East Help the West to Value Nature?" *Philosophy East and West* 37 (April): 172–90.

Sax, William S., ed. 1995. *The Gods At Play: Līlā in South Asia*. New York: Oxford University Press.

Shiva, Vandana, and J. Bandyopadhyay. 1988. "The Chipko Movement." In *Deforestation: Social Dynamics in Watersheds and Mountain Ecosystems*, ed. J. Ives and D. Pitt, 224–41. London: Routledge.

Sochaczewski, Paul Spencer. 1994. "The Saga of Krishna's Gardens: Can Love and Faith Heal Environmental Sacrilege?" *International Herald Tribune*, 18 October.

Sullivan, Bruce M. 1975. "The Place of the Spiritual Master: A Study of The International Society for Krishna Consciousness." Unpublished M.A. thesis, Trinity University.

White, Lynn. 1967. "The Religious Roots of our Ecological Crisis." *Science*, 10 March, 1203–07.

World Wide Fund for Nature (WWF). 1993. "Vrindavan Forest Revival Project." WWF India brochure.

———. 1994. "Reviving the Sacred Forests of Vrindavana. WWF India Technical Report, July 1993 to June 1994."

———. 1995. "Vrindavan Conservation Project." WWF India brochure.

Wulff, Donna M. 1986. "Religion in a New Mode: The Convergence of the Aesthetic and the Religious in Medieval India." *Journal of the American Academy of Religion* 54: 673–88.

WWF. See World Wide Fund for Nature.

**Vijaya Rettakudi Nagarajan**

# 11

# The Earth as Goddess Bhū Devī: Toward a Theory of "Embedded Ecologies" in Folk Hinduism

> What we separate as art, economics, and religion appear intermeshed as aspects of the same performance. The aesthetics, ethos, and worldview of a person are shaped in childhood and throughout early life, and reinforced later, by these verbal and nonverbal environments.
>
> —A. K. Ramanujan (1993, iv)

## Introduction

I sat with Jaya Mami in the cool and open rectangular inner courtyard (*muṟṟam*) in the center of her house, the sun streaming in through the red-tiled roof which outlined the cloudless sky.[1] Even in December in Tamil Nadu, the southeastern coastal state in India, it was hot in the noonday sun, hot enough so that people needed umbrellas to shield themselves against the searing heat and light. As usual, I arrived in India during the inauspicious month of Mārgaḷi, which falls between mid-December to mid-January.[2] Mārgaḷi drew me there as the most important ritual month for the religious practice of the *kōlam*.[3]

In creating the *kōlam*, the first ritual act of the early morning, Tamil women say they become aware of Bhū Devī, the earth goddess:

> We draw the *kōlam* as our first ritual act in the morning to remember Bhū Devī. We walk on her. We spit on her; we poke her; we burden her. We expect her to bear us and all the activities we do on her with endless patience. So, we do the *kōlam*. (Jaya Mami, Thiruvaiyāru village, Thanjāvūr District)

This chapter is a theoretical exploration of what I call "embedded" notions of ecology, where cultural, aesthetic, and religious conceptions orient perceptions of natural spaces. I present the presence of Bhū Devī in the *kōlam* discourses as a rich example of an "embedded ecology" in folk Hinduism. The concept of embedded ecologies is partly derived from Karl Polanyi and partly my own coinage.[4] Looking at embedded ecologies in Hinduism, I ask the questions: How has Hinduism been understood and interpreted as "ecological"? How has the notion of sacred landscapes been understood to be "ecological," especially by Indian environmentalists such as Vandana Shiva? How can we be more precise in illuminating the contradictions between an imagined ideal behavior and what actually happens in everyday life? I introduce the concept of intermittent sacrality to resolve, at least in part, apparent tensions within environmental understandings in folk Hinduism.

## The *Kōlam*

The *kōlam* is a women's ritual art tradition performed throughout Tamil Nadu (see frontispiece).[5] The *kōlam* is drawn by millions of women in the misty light of pre-dawn; it is created on the threshold space in front of the house, at the feet of divine images in the main domestic shrine, and on temple grounds. Before the *kōlam* is made, a mixture of cowdung and water is ritually splashed on the floor or soil, creating a darkened, wet canvas. The *kōlam* can be simple or elaborate, made from wet or dry rice flour or, more recently, from ground stone powder and bright bazaar-bought colors. A sign of the social circulation of women's energies, it is located at the edge of the woman's spatial world, the threshold between home and street, between the inside and outside of the household.[6] It is an identity marker of gender, bearing the traces of a woman's presence in the vicinity.[7] The *kōlam* also plays an important role during festival days for women and various goddesses. Drawn most elaborately to mark a woman's marriage and the occasion of childbirth, and significantly absent during menstruation and mourning times, the *kōlam* visually celebrates states of transition in time and space.[8] It is often the first step toward creating a sense of sacred space in household or public rituals. Thought to be a seat for welcoming the goddesses Lakṣmī and Māriyamman, it deflects the ill effects of the evil eye. Attracting auspiciousness and well-being, the *kōlam* is associated with bringing prosperity and good health into the household.

Four goddesses constantly circulate in the women's *kōlam* discourses: Bhū Devī (or Bhūmi Devī), the earth goddess; Lakṣmī, the goddess of wealth, good fortune, prosperity, and rice; Mū Devī, the goddess of laziness, sleepiness, and poverty; and Tulasī Devī, the goddess of the Indian basil. Mū Devī and Lakṣmī are a pair of natural opposites; laziness and sleepiness are opposed to activeness and diligence (*curucuruppu*), poverty to wealth, ill-luck to good fortune, an empty bowl of rice to an overflowing bowl. The two opposing goddesses are constantly at war with each other and they cannot be found in the same room.[9] Wherever Mū Devī is found, Lakṣmī will not come.[10] Tulasī Devī, like Lakṣmī, is another wife of Viṣṇu and also brings good fortune and protection from evil. Bhū Devī is the mythic, iconic, and metonymic personification of the earth in Hinduism.[11] She is also another wife of Viṣṇu, flanking him along with Lakṣmī in iconographic representations.

## The *Kōlam* and Bhū Devī

In Hindu mythology, Bhū Devī's call for help initiates many of Viṣṇu's incarnations. For example, in the story of Viṣṇu's Boar *avatār*, Bhū Devī is carried off by *asuras* (demons) and submerged in the ocean. When she cries for help to Viṣṇu, the Lord comes in the form of Varāha, the Boar, and rescues her. One of the most common iconographic representations of Bhū Devī shows Varāha carrying her aloft on his tusks. The image of Bhū Devī is small, fragile, and feminine, in contrast to Varāha, who is portrayed as large, virile, and masculine. In this image, it is generally understood that an underlying concern for the earth as vulnerable is expressed. The effect of her weakening is perceived as disastrous. The earth, the soil, is fragile, just as the earth goddess is fragile. Both need protection. This linking of the soil and Bhū Devī is common in women's everyday language.[12] In the village Enangudi near Thanjāvūr, a middle-aged woman, Sarada, told me:

> Bhūmi Devī puts in a complaint (*muṛaiyiṭu*) to Viṣṇu, "I cannot stand all this meanness. The wickedness (*aṭṭūḷiyam*) of humans to the earth. You must do something, find some way to alleviate my pain." She is upset and keeps complaining of the weight (*pāram*) on her. The weight of human actions on her. That is why the *avatārs* come down to earth, because of Bhūmi Devī's complaints and pleas for help.

An explicit language of protection and vulnerability runs alongside the mythologization of the earth as goddess.

How is the appearance of Bhū Devī in the *kōlam* discourses and the myth of Varāha and Bhū Devī related to women's ritual practices and their perception of the natural world? At first glance, the *kōlam* appears to be a simple and beautiful ritual performed by women that has little consequence for understanding Tamil culture. However, the *kōlam* is packed, dense with knowledge, both implicit and explicit, embodied and aesthetic. The irony is that the *kōlam* itself is very light, ephemeral, almost weightless; it appears as shadowy bodily gestures and handstrokes in the early morning light. Located physically on the spatial periphery of the threshold of the household, the *kōlam* quickly disappears under people's feet and into the soil.

I propose to name such implicit and embodied ways of seeing and relating to the natural world "embedded ecologies." The invocation of Bhū Devī is one of the key subtexts of the *kōlam* discourses, the stories and common understandings that circulate around the making of the *kōlam* within women's everyday lives. Bhū Devī acts as a reminder of the fragility of the soils and the earth; she is a mnemonic device serving to shape the conceptualization of the natural world. The making of the *kōlam* is then clearly a way of culturally remembering the natural world. To better understand these perceptions of the natural world, I have chosen to observe conversations where the natural world is described in particular cultural frameworks, where the natural world circles around and through the cultural world, and is in turn shaped by it.

One of the reasons for doing the *kōlam* first thing in the morning is to exercise the memory of the debt felt to the earth goddess, who bears all human and nonhuman actions on her surface. In my conversations with Tamil women, Bhū Devī was referenced both as the physical earth, a large living being with a soul, and as the particular soil at a woman's feet in a particular village, town, or city. Bhū Devī is imagined to be simultaneously both cosmic and local.

I believe that every woman who makes a *kōlam* makes a conscious effort to think of Bhū Devī. As Chittra from the town of Thanjāvūr commented, "Bhū Devī must be one of our first thoughts in the morning." A woman in her fifties, a grandmother from the village of Thilaikkudi which lies along the Kāverī River in Thanjāvūr District, explained Bhūmi Devī in this way:

> Bhūmi Devī is our mother. She is everyone's source of existence. Nothing would exist without her. The entire world depends on her for sustenance and life. So, we draw the *kōlam* first to remind ourselves of her. All day we walk on Bhū Devī. All night we sleep on her. We spit on her. We poke her. We burden her. We do *everything* on her. We expect her to bear us and all the activities we do on her with endless patience. That is why we do the *kōlam*.

These words echo those of Jaya Mami and many others. The articulation of the earth goddess's plight, and the daily offering of the *kōlam* as a way of paying attention to the ground that we walk on daily, bring to a more conscious level our connectedness and dependence on the earth. A subtext within the *kōlam* discourses, then, is the identification of the material earth as the goddess Bhū Devī. She is perceived as the support on which we stand, sleep, and step in our daily activities. What does this embedded subtext, not only recognizing the earth as goddess Bhū Devī, but also acknowledging the burden we humans cause by "poking her" and "spitting on her," mean ecologically? It seems that this ritual, like other rituals to Bhū Devī, is—while deeply symbolic—a gesture the influence of which evaporates all too rapidly. Acknowledging her contribution through a ritual does not imply that the actions carried out during the rest of the day must incorporate the notion of the earth's divinity. Thus, the notion that the earth needs to be "conserved" in the sense that we understand the word in the environmental movement should not be expected in the everyday context of South India. The *kōlam* may be in a class of *compensatory* rituals that do not imply a change of behavior in non-ritual time and space.[13] Bhū Devī's patience, her willingness to bear the world, is constantly invoked in the *kōlam* discourses; the making of the *kōlam* is a set of gestures with a function that is directly compensatory. It is a way of "thanking Bhū Devī for bearing us."[14] A comparable compensatory gestural movement is the first ritual prayer a Bharata Nāṭyam dancer makes before she begins her performance; the dancer asks Bhū Devī to forgive her for stamping on her. Yet, the dance performance itself continues.

## Contradictions

The threshold where a *kōlam* is drawn, dividing the familial from the community space, becomes the invisible line beyond which familial and individual responsibility is different from what it is within the household. Throwing garbage just beyond the boundary of the family property is a common daily practice (see Korom, this volume). Sometimes, the compostable garbage is eaten by a cow or dog sauntering by, or a crow. I remember one day at my maternal grandparent's house in Kunnam village, when I was nineteen, I was told to throw my menstrual pads in the direction of a common place, away from our own backyard. People visiting India have often remarked on the fact that spaces exterior to the household are cared for differently than those interior to the household. In the past, when household waste was organic material, this was perhaps not too serious a threat to the environment. However, now waste often is not organic, but rather consists of non-biodegradable plastics, rubber, pesticides, and other modern sundries, and the soils, waters, and the forests are thereby polluted with toxic chemicals. People are aware that plastics and similar household products do not disintegrate like bamboo and other natural materials. This change has even affected the practice of the *kōlam*, in which nowadays ground stone powder and plastic (stick-on) decals are often substituted for ground rice flour. Janaki, an elderly woman in her early sixties, bemoaned the change:

> We do not know why we do the *kōlam* anymore. We have forgotten. If we had not, we would not make the *kōlam* out of plastic or white stone powder. Now, everything is modern, modern, modern (*nākarīkam*)![15] Before we would make it with rice. One reason we made the *kōlam* is to feed a thousand souls. According to our way, households are supposed to feed a thousand souls every day. And who can feed so many people-souls? Only kings and very wealthy people can fulfill this obligation. We do the *kōlam* to feed a thousand souls. You see, ants, birds and other small worms, insects, and maggots (*kirimigal*) are invited to eat the *kōlam*. The knowledge of the *kōlam* has been lost. Otherwise, why would we try to feed a thousand souls with plastic or stone? The idea of giving to others is being slowly forgotten. How ungenerous we are becoming!

Janaki's sadness in the loss of meaning surrounding the *kōlam* practice was echoed in many other women's response to the coming of modernity.[16] Individual women's—and by extension, their households'—generosity of spirit towards human and nonhuman souls is highly valued and is made visible publicly through the *kōlam*. However, the throwing of garbage on Bhū Devī and the effect of the plastic stick-on decal were rarely if ever mentioned as inimical to Bhū Devī. I was puzzled by the contradiction between women's reverence for Bhū Devī and their seeming disrespect to her throughout the day, as they threw trash and garbage on the earth, the very same place that they considered to be sacred. Was it my own "ecological" hope that a mythological link to the earth would lead to a greater reverence to the soil in everyday life? Yet, something about this paradox seemed oddly familiar. I was reminded of an experience that had happened some years earlier.

Early one morning I sat on the shore of the Kāverī River's Grand Anicut Canal, which skirts the medieval moat in the town of Thanjāvūr in central Tamil Nadu, watching one of my favorite sights, a temple elephant frolicking in the widest part of the channeled river. You could feel the pleasure of the young elephant bathing in the gently flowing waters of the Kāverī, an embodiment of a river goddess similar to the goddess Gaṅgā in North India. This morning three friends from the United States were with me. I turned to my companions to see if they were feeling the same pleasure watching the elephant's joyfulness in the water. To my surprise, a distinct awkwardness had arisen in their bodies and a look of horror had spread on all three faces. I looked again, puzzled over what was disturbing them. It was light now. People were lined up along the *ghāṭs*, the stone steps on the river's edge. Women in underskirts were taking their baths, laughing together, and just a few yards away, an old man standing, knee-deep in the water, was brushing his teeth with a neem stick.

All of a sudden, I saw what my American friends saw. The elephant had paused momentarily, and a few minutes later three or four huge droppings floated downstream, a few yards from the old man brushing his teeth. I recoiled from the sight, then realized with a shock that this scene must have happened with some regularity during my earlier visits when I had come alone, but I could not see it then. It was only after I saw through my friends' eyes that I could read the consequences of a few fresh elephant droppings floating by.

Educated mostly in America, I was well-versed in basic environmental concerns and public hygiene. Yet, I also felt at home in India, and part of that feeling came from getting into a state of mind where I could slip out of my Western education and norms with the ease of slipping into a sari. Now as I watched the elephant dung floating towards a denser crowd of people bathing further down the river, I realized that the locals did not see the elephant droppings as "dangerous" or "polluting." Only a moment before I had seen the way they did.

Reflecting on the elephant's dung in the Kāverī River and the garbage on Bhū Devī, another memory comes back to me. When I had worked in 1985–1986 as an environmental researcher for Swatcha Ganga Campaign–Friends of the Ganges, a community activist group based in Banaras (with a branch in San Francisco), one of the key obstacles in the way of the group's campaign to clean the Ganges was the mythology of the river as the goddess Gaṅgā.[17] Hindus living and bathing along the river viewed the Ganges as sacred and worshipped her. At the same time, the lack of care and protectiveness towards the Ganges was also abundantly clear. People using the river tended to trust the sanctity of the river and dismissed the allegations of pollution and their health effects. The goddess was pure and clean; the river cleaned both sin and pollutants precisely because she was sacred. The goddess protected the human, not the other way around (see Alley, this volume).

The puzzling paradox became a familiar pattern: garbage on Bhū Devī, elephant dung in the Kāverī River, human and industrial pollutants in the Ganges—soil goddess and river goddess. Waste, sin, and pollution collapse into a category that is seen to be absorbable by both Bhū Devī and Gaṅgā Devī; the goddesses are so large and indeterminant that the waste of humanity is seen as just a speck in the vast expanse of sky, earth, and water. The natural world is a divine being and therefore capable of cleaning herself. The very nature of the goddess implies her ability to automatically clean the river of pollution. The goddess transforms dirt, pollution, and sin into pure, clean, and fresh natural substances.[18] Human scale is seen as so small in the cosmological map that the effect of human actions on the natural landscape is negligible. The human is insignificant when compared to the divinity of the natural world. In fact, it would be considered arrogance and folly to assert that human effort could impinge on the infinite divine, much less hurt the divine. As I reflected on these notions, I began to see the complexity of the dense layers of meaning that flow between a culture and its landscape.

## Intermittent Sacrality

For a long time I puzzled over the contradictions between religious ideology and religious practice. If the perception of natural objects were steeped in sacrality, why did that not lead naturally to a consummate sense of care and protection of that natural object? In conversations, when I pointed out what seemed to me to be a contradiction between belief and action, both women and men would laugh and repeatedly tell me,

> Oh, what we believe does not have to rule at all times and at all places. Just because one place is made sacred at one particular time does not necessarily mean that it remains special throughout the day. You have misunderstood. How could we live on this earth otherwise? We could not do anything, now, could we? There are so many rules and rituals that we have to follow. It is understood that we are human and that we need to live too. So, there is no expectation that we need to care for everything that is sacred all the time. We could not do it. We could not live. We have human needs and we must fulfill them.[19]

In short, natural objects are shot through with sticky notions of sacrality embedded within and through them. From the point of view of women I spoke with, sacrality is both a force and a substance. It moves around; it has volition; it is characterized by ritual hospitality. Sometimes the object, whether natural or human, previously not acknowledged as sacred, becomes actively sacred during a specific time period. But sacrality lapses. Intermittent sacrality occurs as a particular divinity is invited at a specific moment to come and be in a particular place, a site, or substance, and then at a later moment, is asked courteously to leave. Many rituals host and dehost the divine as guest; the departure of the divine is essential to the structure of the ritual. Hospitality is not expected to last forever, for the divine or for the human beings. However, it should be noted that despite the existence of this intermittent sacrality, some objects and places are considered permanently sacred or occupied by the gods, for example, temples, household shrines (semi-permanently), and large natural places such as mountains, rivers, and the earth itself. In these cases, although the sacrality of the natural object does not expire, the active human relationship acknowledging sacrality to that natural place is temporary. That *relationship* is, therefore, also intermittent.[20] What is important to note is that the belief in the intermittent manifestation of—or conscious human relationship with—the divine has an impact on everyday attitudes toward natural places.[21]

The *kōlam*, a "painted prayer" for women to acknowledge the goddess Bhū Devī, participates in this hosting and dehosting of the divine (see Nagarajan 1993 and Huyler 1994). As a result, the sacrality that is attached to the locus of the *kōlam* is temporary, not permanent. Therefore, there seems to be no apparent contradiction, at least in the minds of the villagers, between the sacrality (ritually created or not) attached to a particular site at one moment in time and the act of casting waste on the same site later. The *kōlam* is a call to Bhū Devī to forgive humankind's intransigent neglect of her well-being. The expression most often used by women is *manippu kekarathu*, or "asking for forgiveness." This expression implies care of that space for that period of time, but it does not imply subsequent conservation and protection. Soon after the *kōlam* is made—that is, soon after Bhū Devī is recognized, decorated, and hosted into being—Bhū Devī is dehosted from that space by the gradual dispersal of the rice flour patterns. The idea of intermittent sacrality then explains what on the surface seems a contradiction: the pollution of the goddess Earth despite acknowledgement of her sacrality.

In a now classic essay, A. K. Ramanujan writes about context-sensitive thinking. He says,

> I think cultures (may be said to) have overall tendencies (for whatever complex reasons)—tendencies to *idealize*, and think in terms of, either the context-free or the context-sensitive kind of rules. Actual behavior may be more complex, though the rules . . . are a crucial factor in guiding the behavior. In cultures like India's, the context-sensitive kind of rule is the preferred formulation.[22]

Context-sensitive thinking is another way of understanding the seeming contradiction between a belief and the way it is applied in everyday life. The context determines the regime of a belief, a rule, or a ritual. Context-sensitive thinking is an important element of the embedded ecologies I am describing for Hindu India. It should not surprise us if Hindu beliefs about the sacrality of the natural environment do not always lead to a more conservation-oriented practice, because the context changes from one moment to another. One context may require asking for forgiveness, another may involve human needs of the moment, like removing garbage to an unseen place.[23]

## Embedded Ecologies

In speaking of "embedded ecologies," I want to open up a theoretical and ethnographic space for reflection on the cultural construction of nature in India. Karl Polanyi, the economic anthropologist, formulated the notion of embeddedness in his attempts to understand non-Western economies. Polanyi asserts, "The prime reason for the absence of any concept of the economy [in more traditional cultures] is the difficulty of identifying the economic process under conditions where it is embedded in noneconomic institutions" (1957, 71). For example, the economy is embedded in ritual practices and organizational strategies at the kinship and clan level, both orienting cultural production and consumption. The notion of the "economic" is itself subsumed under other cultural categories. Polanyi also contends that attempts to separate the economy as a category from the rest of life is an artificial construct based on Western categories.

I propose to extend Polanyi's understanding of embedded economies to that of embedded ecologies. Thus, echoing Polanyi, we might say of India: The prime reason for the absence of any concept of *ecology* is the difficulty of identifying *ecological* processes under conditions where they are embedded in *nonecological* institutions.[24] Ecological notions, beliefs, and practices are embedded in cultural forms, particularly in religious and aesthetic practices and institutions. With Polanyi, I would argue that in South Asia and elsewhere ecological practices and beliefs are situated in a matrix of larger cultural ideas and practices and therefore require a much more nuanced deconstruction than has been previously attempted. The difficulty in identifying ecological processes when they are bound together within nonecological institutions and understandings has been emphasized for the West by the cultural historian Simon Schama in his book, *Landscape and Memory* (1995). He writes, "Instead of assuming the mutually exclusive character of Western culture and nature, I want to suggest the strength of the links that have bound them together."[25]

The words ecology, conservation, and preservation are modern words and have been deployed historically in different guises in the U.S. and Western Europe (see Chapple, this volume, and Deval and Sessions 1985). Today, the word *ecological* has a particular sense, implying a conservationist attitude. When we say, for example, that the practice of recycling is "ecological," we mean that it is a reflection of the inherent limits on our using the environment beyond its capacity to renew itself.

Eco-thinkers, myself included, have tended to assume that a mythological link between the natural and cultural worlds leads to a more conservation-oriented practice. As we have seen in the three examples, however, these implicit attitudes or embedded ecologies are not necessarily linked to a more "ecological" way of life, in the sense that we understand it in the West. That does not mean that they are necessarily unecological. The notion of being "ecological" itself must be deconstructed historically and culturally. Cultural variations of ecological beliefs and practices must be explored within their own frames of reference.

The concept of embedded ecologies does not refer to an idealized or romanticized notion of the past in India, where people are depicted as living in a relatively benign, balanced, and ever-harmonious relationship with the natural world. It does not depend on a dehistoricized, decontextualized, and oversimplified assertion that "everything is related to everything else." In fact, the notion of embedded ecologies that I propose is contested, historicized, and culturally specific. Within the Hindu tradition, too, there are contesting, coexisting, and multiple points of view. Depending on caste, class, religion, community, and bio-region, different people arrange natural substances according to a diverse range of values. For example, the hierarchical importance of the position of a cow in one's everyday life would be very differently constituted for a cobbler, a priest, or a merchant. A key area for future exploration of embedded ecologies is sacred geographies, where particular rivers, soils, groves, and mountains are imbued with sacrality. In such cases, geography describes a religious landscape.[26]

The phrase "embedded ecologies," moreover, does not refer to an embedded world that is automatically enrolled in a project of ecology or environmentalism in the sense that we understand these concepts in Euro-American conservation discourse. This, I believe, is the prime reason for the confusion of our reading contemporary ecological notions about conservation into religious and gendered ideological frameworks. In other words, a subtext underlying our discourse on religion and environment is the proposition that sacrality, when attached to a natural object, makes that object revered and therefore automatically more protected. The sacrality of a natural object is thought to inspire people to be more careful and "ecologically" sensitive to the consequences of using that natural resource. An embedded ecological belief however could at one moment refer to a practice that is at one moment "ecological" and the next moment "unecological," that is, non-conservation oriented. A belief or practice that is labeled or believed to be ecological will have to be scrutinized much more carefully to see if it fits a conservation-based framework.

## Sacred Landscape as Ecological?

Over the past few years, there has been an increased desire to understand the ecological beliefs of non-Westerners, especially more recently with increasing environmental pollution and the breakdown of community-based structures of moral order and restraint throughout the world (see Nelson 1983, Sachs 1993, Shiva 1989, and Zimmerman 1987).[27] Attention has focused on religious conceptions of nature in relation to landscapes, rivers, mountains, forests, and even the earth itself. An excellent example of this is the work of the environmental and feminist activist Vandana Shiva, who was trained as a physicist in the 1970s in Canada and subsequently returned to India. Shiva's effectiveness in generating environmental thought and action in India and abroad is laudable. Her remarkable work on understanding the Chipko women's movement and her current work on recovering native seed varieties in India is a courageous voice of resistance to the "monoculturalization" of the mind. Her most popular book, *Staying Alive: Women, Ecology and Development*, has been translated into several languages and has widely influenced Western perceptions of the Indian sacred landscape.

Much of this text is devoted to arguing against the ideology of Western development and its concomitant grid of dams, mechanized agriculture, pesticides, and misguided commercial forestry schemes. Yet, the subtle assumption that Hindu women have been and continue to be naturally and "culturally" ecological pervades the text. One example she uses is the ritual worship of the *tulasī* plant—the sacred basil—that is regarded as a goddess. She argues,

> Tulsi is a little herb planted in every home, and worshipped daily. . . . The tulsi is sacred not merely as a plant with beneficial properties but as Brindāvan, the symbol of the cosmos. In their daily watering and worship women renew the relationship of the home with the cosmos and with the world process. . . . Ontologically there is no divide between man and nature. (1989, 39–40)

Vandana Shiva contrasts the Cartesian mechanistic view of the universe, characteristic of the post-Enlightenment period in the West, and the lack of division between humanity and nature in India. In Hinduism, she argues, everything is pervaded by the sacred. Shiva interprets the Hindu perception of the sacred in nature as intrinsically conducive to ecological protection.

I want to point out here the false leap or slurring that we sometimes allow within environmental discourse between identifying a belief or a way of life as ecological because a natural object is imbued with sacrality and the belief that it is thus necessarily conservation-oriented. Shiva assumes that if a natural object is labeled as sacred, then it will call forth a cultural lifestyle that is conserving of the environment, creating less waste and pollution, and which therefore can be termed ecological. She uses the image of the traditional Hindu woman who performs her *tulasī* rites in her household to epitomize a vision of conservation and environmental ethics that *seems* to derive as much from Hinduism as from Western notions of ecology and environmental care.[28] In fact, the *tulasī* plant may be the *only* plant that is conserved in the vicinity of the household, and the practice of worshipping it does not necessarily reflect on the conservation of the natural world outside the household. Therefore, the assumption of Shiva and others (including myself at an earlier date) that worshipping the *tulasī* plant leads to a concomitant and parallel preservation of both the *tulasī* plant and the rest of the natural world is unfounded. This correspondence between ritual care, acknowledgement, and offerings to a place and the concomitant protection of a place may be highly accurate in some instances, but not necessarily so in all instances. I would argue that the assumption that attribution of sacrality to nature leads to "ecological" behavior is highly problematic. The perception of the natural world as sacred does not necessarily lead to more environmental or ecological attitudes or behavior toward nature. Having a religious attitude toward a plant such as *tulasī* may indeed be taken as a kind of embedded ecology, but it does not necessarily imply concerns similar to those that emerged in the history of Western conservation movements. Embedded ecologies are not intrinsically conservation-oriented.

More broadly, one could say that, although non-Western religions may have a reverence towards landscapes and therefore may contain innumerable embedded ecologies, these beliefs do not necessarily lead to ecological practices that resemble conservationism in the sense that the West has come to know it. While it is true, to a certain extent, that the infusion of the natural world with notions of sacrality does affect the behavior of people towards the natural world, I have misgivings about the implications that Indian culture, because of its notions of sacredness, has intrinsic checks and balances to restrain the rapaciousness of human greed.[29] I am uneasy with Shiva's subtext, which claims a general ecological virtue that follows from Indian women's daily watering of *tulasī* plants, although not long ago, I too thought this way. The cosmological reference of the *tulasī* plant may indeed be there, but whether or not it will support a conservation-oriented Hinduism remains to be seen. Although Shiva roots her argument in Hindu mythology and Hindu notions of sacrality, her judgment of the effect of these rituals, myths, and notions is too broad and generalized. Shiva implies that women intuitively and articulately understand the limits of the natural world's capacity to provide an endless supply of resources. I am now unconvinced that a Hindu woman who, as part of her daily religious practice, waters her *tulasī* plant or creates a *kōlam* in worship of Bhū Devī is automatically enrolled in a general ecological project of conservation and protection of natural resources.

In the case of the *tulasī* plant—as in those of Bhū Devī, Kāverī, and Gaṅgā—nature is coded as divine and feminine, and is personified as a goddess. These goddesses, as we have seen, are expected to transform ritual as well as natural pollution into purity and cleanliness (see also Douglas 1984). At the community, village, and neighborhood scale, this transformation of pollution into purity may indeed have been true ecologically for two reasons. Because of the ability of the soil and river ecosystem to transform the pollution by decomposition, an ecosystemic equilibrium could have been achieved.[30] And because the scale of the action was within the responsiblity of the community, village, or neighborhood, there were customary rules of behavior towards natural places that perhaps did stem some of the excesses of pollution. The notion of sacrality could have acted as a brake to individual desires, ambitions, and greed. But once the horizon of everyday life changes from a community to a mass-oriented scale, it becomes difficult to imagine a religiously or community derived set of customary limits on using the environment holding firm.[31] Furthermore, such traditional parameters themselves may not necessarily continue to limit. They could just as well act as licenses to pollute.

## Conclusion

The appearance of Bhū Devī in the *kōlam* ritual is an example of an embedded ecology. Similarly, cultural practices such as basket weaving, pottery, and textiles, among others, evoke certain attitudes to the natural world.[32] Whether sacredness is imputed to earth, basil, or water by these or related activities, I have argued that Hindu religious belief is not sufficient to create an environmental attitude.

According to the worldview of the Tamil women I spoke with, the *tulasī* plant is connected to the larger cosmological self. Like Bhū Devī, the *tulasī* plant holds intrinsically the powers of purification, regardless of human actions towards her. The earth goddess Bhū Devī, and the river goddesses Kāverī and Gaṅgā, have the power to absorb, purify, and cleanse pollutants, regardless of size and scale. They possess the powers of purification, not just as a symbolic means, but as connected to the vast, broader powers of purification that are coded as feminine.

It is this very quality of sacrality that may make people believe they cannot destroy the soils or the waters. Paradoxically it could be the very belief in their sacredness that prevents traditional Hindus from seeing Tulasī, Gaṅgā, or Bhū Devī as needing protection from human beings. In other words, we must ask if it is the very act of sacralization that obscures the necessity of conservation, in the Western sense.

Scholars and activists who study Hindu ecological beliefs and practices will need some understanding of how ecology has come to be formed as a concept and practice in the modern West, as well as a certain self-reflexive attitude towards that understanding.[33] The discipline of ecology has emerged in the context of the modern history of Western science. It would be misleading to take that intellectual development as normative when interpreting Hindu traditions. Hindu traditions concerning the natural world are deeply embedded in particular cultural matrices, as Vandana Shiva rightly points out, but not necessarily with the same consequences as Western notions of ecology and conservation. Indeed Western notions of ecology are equally embedded (see Schama 1995). In both cases institutional structures frame ecological beliefs and are themselves embedded in a complex of assumptions, histories, and contestations. Implicit in the use of such a term as "ecology" is the understanding that each culture and each community within a culture has its own myths, memories, associations, and to use Schama's word, cultural "obsessions" about the natural world.[34]

To understand the complexity of "ecological" readings in texts, and aesthetic and religious beliefs, I have articulated the beginnings of a theory of embedded ecologies, that is, culturally or religiously framed ecological conceptions. I call for a reexamination of religious beliefs for a more careful understanding of embedded ecological knowledge. We must not only listen to what men and women say about what they do, but observe what people choose to do in their everyday life.[35] We need to re-understand, re-invent, and re-imagine the specific ways cultural notions of conservation, preservation, and ecology are constituted and framed within everyday discourse. The tragedy of the commons that we witness everyday in the Indian landscape—with its polluted rivers, mountains, and soils—is not necessarily mitigated by the landscape's sacrality. Once we clearly see that sacrality of natural spaces is not traditionally connected with environmental protection or conservation, we can begin to see the need for a more honest awareness of a difficult and profound question: What *does* motivate people to protect and preserve their natural environments? I hope I have contributed here to an understanding of the complexity inherent in the discussion of this question.[36]

## Notes

1. This chapter is based on my doctoral dissertation, entitled: "Hosting the Divine: The *Kōlam* as Embedded Ritual, Aesthetics and Ecology in Tamil Nadu" at the University of California, Berkeley. A Fulbright-Hays Doctoral Dissertation Grant, from the United States Department of Education, and a UC Berkeley Chancellor's Writing Fellowship provided the funding to enable the research and writing of this dissertation. Earlier research journeys conducted in Tamil Nadu during four consecutive winter seasons from 1987–1991, supported by grants from the Institute for the Study of Natural and Cultural Resources and the Tides Foundation, shaped this work. I am grateful to all these agencies for their support. I would like to also thank Swatcha Ganga Campaign–Friends of the Ganges and, especially, that organization's founder, V. B. Mishra, known affectionately as Mahentji. For their helpful comments and discussions on earlier drafts of this chapter, I am grateful to Jennifer Beckman, Aditya Behl, Elizabeth Collins, Elizabeth Crane, Ann Gold, George Hart, Linda Hess, Eugene Irschick, Malcolm Margolin, Rettakudi Nagarajan, Lee Swenson, and Kristi Wiley.

2. I spent the seven winters from 1987–1993 in India. When I would ask why was the month so inauspicious, people would often reply, "The month of Mārgaḷi is inauspicious for humans, but very auspicious for the divine. The doorway between the human and divine world is the most wide open during this month and this is why we think of Svāmī [God] during this time. We go on pilgrimages and chant special saints' songs like Āṇṭāḷ's 'Tiruppāvai' and Mānikkavācagar's 'Tiruvempāvai.' "

3. The *kōlam* has been a constant physical presence throughout my life. My mother drew the *kōlam* on our threshold every day, whether we were in Rettakudi, our ancestral village, Motibagh, in New Delhi, or in the Washington D.C. area. See Nagarajan 1993 for a brief introduction to the *kōlam* in women's everyday lives. As a subject of study, the *kōlam* was first introduced to me in the fall of 1984 by a teacher and friend, Ivan Illich. I remember the moment clearly. At the edges of a conference in Claremont, we discussed one early morning a footnote on Indian floor paintings for his then working manuscript, *$H_2O$ and The Waters of Forgetfulness*. Indian floor paintings are referred to from within the context of the relationship between ritual construction of space and the creation of the doorway, the asymmetric separation between inside and outside (see Illich 1985, 14–5). After our discussion, I was staggered by the number of questions that emerged from the *kōlam*. Illich's piece (1985) is an excellent essay on the historical and social construction of water and waste in the West, from Roman times to

contemporary sites in the U.S. He delineates the dense and intimate relationship between the perceptions of the human and social bodies.

4. It is important to be clear about the words *ecology, ecological,* and *ecologies*. *Ecological* does not necessarily imply the potential of positive change for the environment, even though that is how we use it colloquially. It is a reference to relationships, which could be neutral, positive, or negative. The denotations of the word *ecology* are (1) "the branch of biology that deals with the relation between living organisms and their environment" and (2) "the study of the relationship of adjustment of human groups to their geographical environment," a more sociological conception (see Guralnik 1980). To avoid confusion of the different senses, however, I will use the word "ecological" in a more ordinary sense to denote a positive relationship between a living organism and its environment (with the understanding that what is "positive" is culturally constituted and sometimes can be "negative" or "neutral" in different cultures, which is precisely what I am trying to point out in this paper) and the word *ecology* to denote the sociological "relationship of adjustment of human groups to their geographical environment."

The narrow scientific sense, the first definition above, which is a common definition of the word *ecology,* is no longer satisfying to me. I think it is important to recall and highlight the secondary meaning of the word, the sociological orientation, evoking the "relationships of adjustment" between human groups and their environment. These relationships are differently constituted, shaped by culture, religion, and politics. Hence there is a plurality of different "adjustments." I think it is useful therefore to extend the word *ecology* to "ecologies" in a plural sense to signify the various culturally distinctive, embedded ways of seeing and relating to the natural world. I remember first thinking of this term during my talk, "Hosting the Divine: Ganges, Cowdung and Other Everyday Ecolog(ies) of the Imagination," at UC Berkeley on May 10, 1995, as part of a series on *The Himalayan Experience* organized by Meenu Singh.

5. Although little has been written in English on the *kōlam* ritual, a few scattered references exist. In English, see Miller 1983, 105–7; Schulman 1985; Trawick 1990; Daniel 1986; Layard 1937, 1952–53; Nagarajan 1993. In Tamil, see Saroja 1992. There are however numerous bazaar chapbooks on the *kōlam*; most of them have bright, colorful covers and are books of sample designs, for example, Saraswathi 1991 and Parisura 1980.

6. See Ardener 1993 and Skar 1993.

7. Although I have concentrated on the particular women's ritual art called the *kōlam* in Tamil Nadu, the form itself is by no means unique to

that region of India. Similar ritual arts are performed by women and men throughout India. For example, the parallel form is called *muggū* in Andhra Pradesh (see Kilambi 1986), *rangōli* or *rangāvalli* in much of northern India, *māndanā* in Rajasthan (see Saksena 1985), and *alpanā* in Bengal (see Das Gupta 1960).

8. The *kōlam* is primarily made by body movements and gestures, almost resembling a dance. In a sense, it is a performed cultural "text" and practice in a landscape of oral recirculation of common knowledge. The knowledge of the *kōlam* is rooted in this genre, which is considered to be common knowledge. According to the *Tamil Lexicon*, the primary meanings of *kōlam* are beauty, gracefulness, color, form, and external appearance. Secondary meanings include nature, costume, ornament, adornment, and embellishment, especially in relation to the floor drawings.

9. *Cōmbērithannam*, the quality of sluggishness and idleness, is opposed to *curucuruppu*, alertness and activity. "Don't just sit there staring looking like Mū Devī, get up and move," is an admonishment often used to get young girls up and about in household and school work. Bhū Devī is also constantly used in everyday discourse to describe a woman's behavior: "She has the patience of Bhū Devī" or "she has Bhū Devī's ability to bear such burdens of life."

10. See Leslie 1992 and Narayan 1989, 221–24 for brief but interesting descriptions and narrations of the tense relationship between Lakṣmī and Mū Devī.

11. For a broad introduction to the incarnation of Viṣṇu as Varāha, see Nagar 1993. See also Mumme, this volume.

12. I am looking at this phenomenologically and also at how this belief operates ecologically. As far as the feminist issues this gendered image of earth brings up, those are another matter and cannot be discussed adequately in this short paper.

13. I am grateful to Bob Goldman for this insight.

14. It is interesting to note here a comparison between hunting cultures and the prayers that hunters make before and after the hunt, in a spirit of both thankfulness and forgiveness. This highlights the question: what do we mean by the very notion of "ecological," the idea of a balanced population, and so forth. See the fascinating Nelson 1973.

15. *Nākarīkam* is a very interesting term. It has a sense of "something new" or "something curious."

16. See the classical proverbs collection *The Kural* by Tiruvalluvar 1989 for an entire section on hospitality. *Kural* 86 says: "Who is host to the passing guests and waits for more will be hosted by the gods."

17. See Eck 1982a, 1982b and Darian 1978. For an excellent understanding of the religious meanings of rivers in Maharashtra, and especially their feminine qualities, see the excellent Feldhaus 1995.

18. For an excellent examination of anthropological theories of pollution, see the classics Buckley 1988 and Douglas 1984 (1966).

19. For a fascinating exploration of ritual, see Humphrey 1994, vii where she begins with a description of a seemingly ambiguous stance towards ritual, "We grew increasingly puzzled: what were these 'meanings' which seemed so weighty in import, and yet so lightly and variously applied?" Humphrey delves into a theory of ritual action that captures its nondogmatic and playful side. See also Bell 1992 for an excellent overview of the ritual literature.

20. See Stanley 1977 for another kind of intermittent sacrality, here defined by both time and space.

21. One of the most fascinating areas of inquiry is pilgrimage to natural places. See Eck 1982a and Haberman 1994.

22. Ramanujan 1989, 47.

23. See Douglas 1984 (1966) and Ortner 1974, 72 for important theoretical discussions of pollution and taboo and the feminization of the nature and culture distinction. According to Ortner,

> The categories of "nature" and "culture" are of course conceptual categories—one can find no boundary out in the actual world between the two states or realms of being. And there is no question that some cultures articulate a much stronger opposition between the two categories than others—it has even been argued that primitive peoples (some or all) do not see or intuit any distinction between the human cultural state and the state of nature at all. Yet I would maintain that the universality of ritual betokens an assertion in all human cultures of the specifically human ability to act upon and regulate, rather than passively move with and be moved by, the givens of natural existence. In ritual, the purposive manipulation of given forms toward regulating and sustaining order, every culture asserts that proper relations between human existence and natural forces depend upon culture's employing its special powers to regulate the overall processes of the world and life.

24. Italicized words are my substitutions of *ecology* for *economy*, and so on. For other elaborations of this theme in terms of economics, see Polanyi 1957.

25. See Schama 1995, 13–14. Italics added.

26. A longer version of this paper will explore the details of this religious construction of landscape. For religious constitution of rivers, see especially Eck 1982 on the Ganges as a goddess and Feldhaus 1995 on an ethnographic and textual exploration of rivers as women in Maharashtra. See also chapters by Sherma, Kinsley, and Alley in this volume.

27. For a general overview of ecology and religion, see Kinsey 1995. For particular ethnographies of religion and environment in specific places, see for Northern California, Margolin 1978; for Alaska, Nelson 1983; for South Asia, Zimmerman 1987.

28. Schama recognizes the historicity of the perception of the environment in the American environmental movement. He refers to the American environmentalists' desire to have the landscape be emptied of humans, to be pure and preserved, in order to save the environment. In the late nineteenth century, this movement was able to save Yosemite in California, but only at the cost of removing indigenous peoples already living there. Early environmentalists did not see the removal of indigenous peoples as inimical to the environmental movement. The sacred *tulasī* plant represents, similarly for Shiva, a way of seeing the world that is automatically believed to be conservation-oriented. Here, too, the complexity of the assumptions tied to this belief is not made clear.

29. Furthermore, in this text Shiva fails to draw sufficient distinctions between Hinduism and other religious communities within India. India is made equivalent to Hinduism and vice versa. Certain aspects of isolated pieces of classical Hindu myths are, moreover, essentialized to represent all of Hinduism.

30. In the specific example of the Ganges watershed, two large dams were built by the British colonialists in the 1860s, which significantly altered the quality and quantity of water flowing downstream. The population explosion is another factor contributing to the change in scale of pollution and its effects.

31. Although I point to Vandana Shiva's work as an example, I want to make it clear that it was only throughout the course of my past fifteen years of work in India, both as an ethnographic researcher and as an

associate of several non-governmental associations, that I came slowly to realize that there was as much disjunction as correlation between the perception of the natural world as "sacred" and the consequent "ecological" and "non-ecological" actions that result from this perception. Most of us working as environmentalists have made assumptions similar to Shiva's.

32. The complexity of ecological themes embedded within cultural traditions is hinted at in the following works: For South Asia, Zimmerman 1987 is an excellent exposition of the notion of "jungle," both in the Indian landscape as well in Indian medicine. His comparison and analysis of categories that flow back and forth between the body and the landscape remains one of the key contributions to the conceptualization of "embedded ecologies." Reichel-Dolmatoff 1996 is a remarkable testimonial to a carefully researched and lived understanding of the Amazon Tukano people. He is concerned with "meaning, with the ways in which the Indians interpret their lives and their environments. . . . Meaning can be found in attitudes and daily conversations, in myths and spells, in the manner in which people describe events and emotions, or in the words they use to explain rules of behavior, the do's and don'ts of everyday existence"(7). See Guss 1989 for a story that begins with basketry and ends with cosmology among the Yekuana in Venezuela. Jackson 1995 is a meditation on the understanding of home and the world within the landscape of Australian Aboriginals. Lansing 1991 and Evers 1987 provide other examples, of water tanks in Bali and deer songs among the Yaqui in the southwestern United States.

33. See Worster 1977, Devall and Session 1985, Chapple 1993, and Schama 1995 for an introduction to this field. See also Arnold and Guha 1995 for an extended introduction into the environmental history of South Asia. For important insights into the relationship between knowledge and environmental destruction, see Banuri 1993.

34. For a brilliant description and poetic analysis of Tamil notions of landscape, see Ramanujan 1994; 1985, 229–317. See also Kellert 1993.

35. For a fascinating pamphlet on the complex relationship between "faith" and "reason" in the recent Indian context, see Bharucha 1993.

36. Several major movements come to mind: in Vrindavan, the reforestation campaign (see Sullivan, this volume); in Banaras, the Swatcha Ganga Campaign to clean the river Ganges (see Alley, this volume); and in the foothills of the Himalayas, the Chipko Movement to plant trees and prevent deforestation.

## References


Ardener, Shirley, ed. 1993. *Women and Space: Ground Rules and Social Maps.* Oxford: Berg Publishers.

Arnold, David, and Ramchandra Guha, eds. 1995. *Nature, Culture, Imperialism: Essays on the Environmental History of South Asia.* Oxford: Oxford University Press.

Banuri, Tariq, and Frederick Apffel Marglin, eds. 1993. *Who Will Save the Forests? Knowledge, Power and Environmental Destruction.* London: Zed Books.

Bell, Catherine. 1992. *Ritual Theory, Ritual Practice.* Oxford: Oxford University Press.

Bharucha, Rustom. 1993. *The Question of Faith.* Madras: Orient Longman.

Buckley, Thomas, and Alma Gottlieb, eds. 1988. *Blood Magic: The Anthropology of Menstruation.* Berkeley: University of California Press.

Chapple, Christopher Key. 1993. *Nonviolence to Animals, Earth, and Self in Asian Traditions.* Albany, N.Y.: State University of New York Press.

Daniel, Valentine E. 1986. "Kolam." Paper presented at the South Asia Conference, University of Wisconsin, Madison, Wisconsin.

Darian, Steven G. 1978. *The Ganges in Myth and History.* Honolulu: University Press of Hawaii.

Das Gupta, S. 1960. *Alpana.* Delhi: Ministry of Information.

Devall, Bill, and George Sessions. 1985. *Deep Ecology: Living as if Nature Mattered.* Salt Lake City: Peregrine Smith Books.

Douglas, Mary. 1984 (1966). *Purity and Danger: An Analysis of the Concepts of Pollution and Taboo.* London: Ark Paperbacks.

Eck, Diana. 1982a. *Banaras: City of Light.* New York: Knopf, Inc.

———. 1982b. "Ganga: The Goddess in Hindu Sacred Geography." In *The Divine Consort: Radha and the Goddesses of India,* ed. John Stratton Hawley and Donna Marie Wulff, 166–83. Boston: Beacon Press.

Evers, Larry, and Felipe S. Molina. 1987. *Yaqui Deer Songs: Maso Bwikam, A Native American Poetry.* Tucson: Sun Tracks and University of Arizona Press.

Feldhaus, Anne. 1995. *Water and Womanhood: Religious Meanings of Rivers in Maharashtra.* Oxford: Oxford University Press.

Guralnik, David B., ed. 1980. *Webster's New World Dictionary of the American Language.* Cleveland: Collins Publishers, Inc.

Guss, David M. 1989. *To Weave and Sing: Art, Symbol and Narrative in the South American Rain Forest.* Berkeley: University of California Press.

Haberman, David. 1994. *Journey through Twelve Forests.* Oxford: Oxford University Press.

Humphrey, Caroline, and James Laidlaw. 1994. *The Archetypal Actions of Ritual: A Theory of Ritual Illustrated by the Jain Rite of Worship.* Oxford: Clarendon Press.

Illich, Ivan. 1985. *$H_2O$ and the Waters of Forgetfulness: Reflections on the Historicity of "Stuff."* Dallas: Dallas Institute of Humanities and Culture.

Jackson, Michael. 1995. *At Home in the World.* Durham and London: Duke University Press.

Kellert, Stephen R., and Edward O. Wilson. 1993. *The Biophilia Hypothesis.* Washington D.C.: Island Press.

Kilambi, Jyotsna. 1986. "Muggu: Threshold Art in South India." *Res: The Journal of Aesthetics and Anthropology* 10: 71–102.

Kinsley, David. 1995. *Ecology and Religion: Ecological Spirituality in Cross-Cultural Perspective.* Englewood Cliffs, N.J.: Prentice-Hall.

Lansing, J. Stephen. 1991. *Priests and Programmers: Technologies of Power in the Engineered Landscape of Bali.* Princeton: Princeton University Press.

Layard, John. 1937. "Labyrinth Ritual in South India: Threshold and Tattoo Designs." *Folklore* 48: 115–82.

Leslie, Julie, ed. 1992. *Sri and Jyestha: Ambivalent Role Models for Women.* New Delhi: Motilal Banarsidass.

Margolin, Malcolm. 1978. *The Ohlone Way: Indian Life in the San Francisco–Monterey Bay Area.* Berkeley: Heyday Books.

Miller, Barbara Stoler, ed. 1983. *Exploring India's Sacred Art: Selected Writings of Stella Kramrisch.* Philadelphia: University of Pennsylvania Press.

Nagar, Shanti Lal. 1993. *Varaha in Indian Art, Culture and Literature.* New Delhi: Aryan Books International.

Nagarajan, Vijaya. 1993. "Hosting the Divine: The Kolam in Tamil Nadu." In *Mud, Mirror and Thread: Folk Traditions of Rural India,* ed. Nora Fisher. Albuquerque: Museum of New Mexico Press.

Narayan, Kirin. 1989. *Storytellers, Saints, and Scoundrels: Folk Narrative in Hindu Religious Teaching.* Philadelphia: University of Pennsylvania Press.

Nelson, Richard K. 1973. *Hunters of the Northern Forest: Designs for Survival among the Alaskan Kutchin.* Chicago: University of Chicago Press.

———. 1983. *Make Prayers to the Raven.* Chicago: University of Chicago Press.

Ortner, Sherry. 1974. "Is Female to Male as Nature is to Culture?" In *Woman, Culture, and Society,* ed. Michelle Zimbalist Rosaldo and Louise Lamphere. Stanford: Stanford University Press.

Parisura, Manimekalai. 1980. *Vagai Vagaiyāna Kōlangal.* Madras: Manimekalai Pirusuram.

Polanyi, Karl. 1957. *Trade and Market in Early Empires: Economies in History and Theory.* Chicago: Gateway Edition.

Ramanujan, A. K. 1985. *Poems of Love and War.* Oxford: Oxford University Press.

———. 1990. "Is There an Indian Way of Thinking? An Informal Essay." In *India through Hindu Categories,* ed. Mckim Marriott, 41–58. New Delhi: Sage Publications.

———. 1993. *Folktales from India: A Selection of Oral Tales from Twenty-two Languages.* New Delhi: Viking.

———. 1994 (1966). *The Interior Landscape: Love Poems from a Classical Tamil Anthology.* Oxford: Oxford University Press.

Reichel-Dolmatoff, Gerardo. 1996. *The Forest Within: The World-View of the Tukano Amazonian Indians.* Devon: Themis Books.

Sachs, Wolfgang. 1993. *Global Ecology: A New Arena of Political Conflict.* London: Zed Books.

Saksena, Jogendra. 1985. *Mandana: A Folk Art of Rajasthan.* New Delhi: Crafts Museum.

Saraswathi R., and L. Vijayalakshmi. 1991. *Kōthaiyār idum kōlangal.* Madras: Lakkumi Nilayam.

Saroja, V. 1992. *Mannin manam.* Madurai: Vanjiko Pathipaham.

Schama, Simon. 1995. *Landscape and Memory.* New York: Knopf.

Schulman, David. 1985. *The King and the Clown in South Indian Myth and Poetry.* Princeton: Princeton University Press.

Shiva, Vandana. 1989. *Staying Alive: Women, Ecology and Development.* London: Zed Books.

Skar, Sarah L. 1993. "Andean Women and the Concept of Space/Time." In *Women and Space: Ground Rules and Social Maps,* ed. Shirley Ardener, 31–45. Oxford: Berg Publishers.

Stanley, John. 1977. "Special Time, Special Power: The Fluidity of Power in a Popular Hindu Festival." *Journal of Asian Studies* 37 (1): 27–43.

Thiruvalluvar. 1989. *The Kural.* Translated by P. Sunderam. New Delhi: Penguin Books.

Trawick, Margaret. 1990. *Notes on Love in a Tamil Family.* Berkeley: University of California Press.

University of Madras. 1982. *Tamil Lexicon.* Vol. 1–6, plus Supplement. Madras: University of Madras.

Worster, Donald. 1977. *Nature's Economy: A History of Ecological Ideas.* Cambridge: Cambridge University Press.

Zimmerman, Francis. 1987. *The Jungle and the Aroma of Meats.* Berkeley: University of California Press.

Kelly D. Alley

# 12

# Idioms of Degeneracy: Assessing Gaṅgā's Purity and Pollution

## Introduction: Assessments and Worldviews

Scientists, government workers, and religious leaders in India hold differing conceptions of the purity and pollution of the natural world. Their conflicting assessments reflect a larger debate between worldviews and the divergent ways worldviews define the sacred and the profane. Especially in discussions about the river Gaṅgā (or Ganges), the sacred river that flows across northern India, we find marked disagreement between arguments defending the Gaṅgā's sacred purity and warnings about river pollution. These arguments point to a conflict of worldviews holding different assumptions about human existence. The various assessments of the river draw logical and moral or ethical legitimacy from theology, scientific discourse, and the secular policies of the state and, therefore, are windows into the ways Indian citizens use wider networks of knowledge. In this paper, I examine the most recent assessments of the condition of this river and demonstrate how specific groups of Indian citizens and state officials use these assessments to articulate their worldview differences in public debates.

Theological discourses, more than scientific and secular ones, establish various connections between moral and ecological values through sacred texts, drama, and iconography (see, for example,

Hargrove 1986, Spring and Spring 1974, Suzuki and Knudtson 1992). Several contemporary social scientists have attempted to find common threads in these diverse renderings of the universe, seeking the means to create a universally plausible environmental ethic.[1] But this goal assumes far too much. The ways that people define nature cannot be idealized solely in terms of ethical and rational notions of sustainable, equitable resource use. Portrayals of Banaras in the Hindu sacred texts (*śāstras*), for example, depict this famous pilgrimage place on the bank of the sacred river Gaṅgā as a conch shell, or the trident of Lord Śiva. These religious images have no parallel in materialist interpretations of space and create symbolic dissonance with spatial meanings constructed by scientific and official governmental worldviews. Hindu representations such as these underscore, as Singh (1993b, 113) has noted, a vision that integrates matter, mind, and spirit. Symbolic representations of space in Hindu sacred texts and the ancient concepts associated with them call for an approach to ecological understanding that moves beyond secular notions of "environment." To understand this we need to examine, in a particular locale such as Banaras, the cognitive categories and symbolic processes giving religious meaning to "natural resources" such as the Gaṅgā. This will allow us to analyze how residents respond to or resist the environmental ideologies more familiar to secular thinking.

Banaras is an important pilgrimage place and urban center bordering the sacred river. Residents and pilgrims regard Banaras as the center of Śiva's universe, as well as the beginning and end point of human civilization. Eck (1982, 23) notes that local residents claim that Kāśī, the ancient name for Banaras, contains the whole world and everything on earth that is powerful and auspicious. The Mahāśmāśāna, the great cremation ground of Banaras, survives the cyclic dissolution of the cosmos brought about by Śiva's ascetic power (see Parry 1980, 89; 1981, 339). On a more secular note, Banaras is the site of the largest combined pilgrim/tourist trade in India today. It is therefore an important locale for witnessing transformations taking place in the politics of pilgrimage.

Not sharing the ideology of the typical Hindu world-renouncer (*saṃnyāsin*), pilgrims who visit Banaras and residents who live in neighborhoods along the riverbank do not denigrate or seek detachment from the physical or natural world. Rather, pilgrims and residents alike believe that rivers and mountains are sacred and powerful. This is why many sacred places in India are located aside rivers or on top of mountains (see Feldhaus 1995). The river Gaṅgā, in the Hindu religious vision, takes the form of a goddess who possesses the power to purify all sorts of human and worldly impurities. Hindu residents and pilgrims invoke the purifying power of "Mā Gaṅgā" (Mother Gaṅgā) through ritual ablution, meditation, and worship (*snān*, *dhyān,* and *pūjā*). Even as officials in state and central government offices espouse scientific theories of river pollution to undermine what they dub a "traditional" religious relationship with the river, devout Hindus of Banaras reject these alienating claims. This is because, as we shall see, many residents of this pilgrimage place see science and the state as powers which bring on ecological degeneracy in the name of preventing it.

In what follows, I explore assessments of the state of the river Gaṅgā and the larger worldview issues that contextualize them by presenting the perspectives of three groups of people. These are: (1) *paṇḍās* or pilgrim priests working on southern Daśāśvamedha in Banaras, (2) members of the Clean Ganga Campaign or CGC (Swatcha Ganga Abhiyan), who also live in Banaras, and (3) officials working in projects under the Ganga Project Directorate or GPD. Some government officials in the third group are Banaras residents while others reside in Delhi and other major Indian cities. Despite their varied orientations toward the sacred and secular, members of these groups have one thing in common: they consider the present period a degenerate one. The ways that each group locates spheres of degeneracy are connected to their assessments of the river's condition.

Scientific assessments made by government officials and members of the Clean Ganga Campaign locate degeneracy in ecological systems. From their point of view, human processes of population growth, urbanization, and industrial and technological development have brought on the decline in ecological balance. In contrast, residents of southern Daśāśvamedha, a neighborhood of the city which flanks the river, envision themselves at the end of a cosmic cycle. In this context, they interpret immoral behavior and abuses of the Gaṅgā as signs of diminished virtue and moral degeneracy. Scientific theories use terms such as Biological Oxygen Demand (BOD) and Fecal Coliform Count (FCC) to indicate a decline in the quality of river water. Residents of Daśāśvamedha explain that marketplace competition, cheating, and corruption are signs of the moral degeneracy of the current age. These factors, they believe, create an atmosphere in which people disrespect Gaṅgā. The former group measures how polluted the Gaṅgā has become, while the latter ponders how Gaṅgā herself might help reset the degenerate moral and cosmic order.

### The Gaṅgā at Daśāśvamedha

The pilgrim priests residing and working on the southern half of Daśāśvamedha express a theory of degeneracy based on their understanding of the immediate surroundings. They link degeneracy to the religious significance of their neighborhood and the Gaṅgā at that spot. Daśāśvamedha is a sacred place (*tīrth*) as well as a residential neighborhood. Its border with the river is fortified by a series of stone steps called *ghāṭs* which give pilgrims access to the Gaṅgā. The *ghāṭ* at Daśāśvamedha is a meritorious site for ritual ablution and is ranked in sacred importance with the other important *ghāṭs* of Asi, Varaṇā, Maṇikarṇikā, Kedār, and Pañcagaṅgā.[2] The *ghāṭ* marks the place where Lord Brahmā performed a ten horse sacrifice (*daśa-aśva-medha*) to gain power over the reigning King Divodāsa. Pilgrims visit the temples of Śulataṅkeśvara, Brahmeśvara, Vārāheśvara, Abhaya Vināyaka, Gaṅgā Devī, and Bandī Devī on this *ghāṭ* (Singh 1993a, 82).

The physical features of the *ghāṭ* tell another story. In its present form, the *ghāṭ* is divided into southern and northern sections (the Gaṅgā flows northward at Banaras). The sections were once divided by the Godāvarī, a tributary that drained into the Gaṅgā. In 1740, the southern section of the *ghāṭ* was fortified by Bajirao Pesava I. Ahilyabhai Holkar of Indore then extended the *ghāṭ* in 1775 (Singh 1993a, 82). At the turn of the twentieth century, Havell (1905, 106) wrote that Daśāśvamedha was the *ghāṭ* toward which the principal roads of the city converged. It was also an important point for boats bringing stone from the Chunar quarries upstream. In 1904, Maharani Puthia of the former state of Digpatia in North Bengal constructed another *ghāṭ*. She laid the foundation on the island created where the Godāvarī separated into a fork before reaching the Gaṅgā. This became Prayāg Ghāṭ. Urban construction eventually covered over the Godāvarī and residents changed the name of the area to Godaulia (Singh 1993a, 39, 84). The area lying between Prayāg Ghāṭ and Rājendra Prasād Ghāṭ (formerly Ghoḍā Ghāṭ) is the northern part of ancient Daśāśvamedha. On the southern section, we find the Śītalā Temple, which still contains the ancient *liṅga* of Daśāśvamedheśvara Mahādev, Śiva as Lord of Daśāśvamedha (see also Vidyarthi et al., 29). Behind this temple, the shrine of Prayāgeśvara lies buried beneath the house of a powerful pilgrim priest (*paṇḍā*). The *Kāśī Khaṇḍa (KKh),* a sacred text describing Banaras from the eighth to thirteenth century, refers to this *liṅga* and shrine (see Havell 1905, 110; *KKh* 44.16–47, *KKh* 61.36–38; Singh 1993a, 48, 82–85). On a more profane note, the *ghāṭ* at Daśāśvamedha is also known for its "mafia-like" businesses fed by the reverence of pilgrims (see also Parry 1994, van der Veer 1988).

Most residents of Banaras, whether they work in government service or private business, emphasize the sacred purity of the Gaṅgā. They do this by calling upon her divine power in worship rituals (*pūjā*). They understand Gaṅgā's deep symbolic history and cite eulogies to her developed in the sacred texts. In the *Rāmāyaṇa*, *Mahābhārata*, the *purāṇas*, and the *māhātmyas*—and in temple sculpture and art—she is worshiped as a purifier, mother, sustainer, and daughter or co-wife of Śiva.[3] A popular narrative, drawn from a chapter of the *Rāmāyaṇa*, describes how she descended from heaven onto the locks of Lord Śiva (see Vatsyayan 1992). Her motherly character is praised in the *Mahābhārata,* and the *purāṇas* extoll her powers to purify. Several places of healing and sacred power for Hindus are located along her 2,525 kilometer traverse across northern India (Vidyarthi et al. 1979). In these sacred complexes, pilgrims and residents perform ablutions and undertake the ritual of *āratī* to revere her. Devotees perform *āratī* by waving an oil lamp in front of Gaṅgā while standing on the riverbank. The sounds of bells, gongs, drums, and conch shells play a prominent role in the ritual. The festivals of Gaṅgā Daśaharā and Gaṅgā Saptamī celebrate her purifying power. But while they can please Gaṅgā, these rituals and festivals cannot purify her. Purity is part of a more holistic process of cosmic order and balance, within which humans should strive to live harmoniously (see also Fuller 1979, 460; 1992, 76). Still, when Gaṅgā is pleased she blesses the faithful and purifies their minds and souls. She may also grant a devotee's wishes if they are requested through worship with pure faith.

When asked how the sacred texts (*śāstras)* guide their relationships with Gaṅgā, many residents of Daśāśvamedha point to rituals of *snān* and *pūjā* and the importance of *gaṅgā jal* (sacred Gaṅgā water) in Hindu life. When pilgrims perform *snān* or ritual ablution, Gaṅgā absolves religious impurities and, with her flow, carries away physical uncleanness. This creates, at one level, an interlocking relationship between ritual, spiritual purity, and physical cleanness. As one merchant on Daśāśvamedha put it, "People who bathe and do meditation and ritual worship of gods and goddesses understand that this is our history (*itihās*) and knowledge (*jñān*)." Dumont and Pocock (1959, 30) point out that one must be spiritually pure to approach gods and goddesses. Even though humans may not reach the purity of the divine, there is some expectation that purity is a condition for contact with deities to be beneficial.

There are two views in current popular discourse at Daśāśvamedha about whether Gaṅgā can purify an impure person. In one view, an impure person cannot become pure simply by bathing in a sacred place. Rather, one must engage in the more holistic process of committing one's soul to Śiva. The other, more lenient view holds that one who merely recites the name of Gaṅgā gains mastery over "sin" (*pāp*). One who takes auspicious sight (*darśan*) of her achieves well-being (*kalyāṇ)*, and one who performs *snān* purifies seventy generations.[4] The *Gaṅgā Stuti,* a hymn to Gaṅgā sung in Hindi by a *paṇḍā* of Daśāśvamedha, carries this theme. One *paṇḍā* sings this eulogy in Hindi during Ganga *āratī*:

> From the place where the lotus foot of the Lord,
> where Bhagīrath did great *tapasyā* (ritual austerities),
> Gaṅgā flowed out from Brahmā's jug into the locks of Śiv-Śaṅkar.
> She then descended to earth on a mountain of countless sins.
> Tulsī Dās says, Open your two eyes and see how naturally she flows as a stream of nectar.
> Those who take her name in memory will get *mukti* (liberation);
> Those who do *praṇām* (salutation) will arrive at God's place.

Those who come to the banks of Gaṅgā will find heaven;
Those who see the waves of emotion will get *mokṣa* (liberation).
O Taraṅginī [Gaṅgā], this is the nature God has given to you.
O Bhāgīrathī [Gaṅgā], though I am full of sin and dirtiness,
I believe you will give me *mukti* and a place at your feet.[5]

## Idioms of Degeneracy: *Gandagī* and Dirty Business

Pilgrims who visit Daśāśvamedha relate moral values to the Gaṅgā through rituals of ablution and worship. Therefore, ritual specialists become important players in the relationships pilgrims forge with the Gaṅgā. This makes the perspective of pilgrim priests especially significant and central to the exchanges conducted on an everyday basis with the river. Much of the scholarly literature on Hinduism has treated pilgrim priests as if they were members of a common caste (*jāti*) association. But *paṇḍās* explain that the *paṇḍā* profession (*paṇḍāgīrī*) is not a *jāt* (caste group) but a *peśā* (occupation).[6] This *peśā* is concerned with serving specific groups of pilgrims. *Paṇḍās* in this occupation establish hereditary title to identified groups of pilgrims and then defend their hereditary rights to serve those pilgrims against shifting claims made by individuals with "man and money power."

A pilgrim priest maintains his position and gains power vis-à-vis other priests by controlling access to clients. Rights to act as head priest for specified groups of pilgrims may pass through male and female lines. Affinal bequests, however, are less prestigious, so *paṇḍās* often disguise them as gifts from the patrilineage. As local accounts go, many priests are unable to keep these rights within the family without struggle. As one informant explained it, inserting an English phrase into his Hindi dialogue, members of the community with more "man and money power" wrestle away these titles from those who inherited them. Curiously enough, this informant chose to use the English phrase "man and money power" whenever referring to this form of influence.

*Paṇḍās* say that a good moral order exists when hereditary titles are honored. This allows the occupation to retain the family pride and honor that has surrounded it for generations. A corrupt (*gandā*) moral order, on the other hand, emerges when this family honor is threatened by members representing other family lines or outsiders with "man and money power." Outsiders use "man and money power" to usurp hereditary rights. By "man and money power," *paṇḍās* mean power exercised by physical coercion and violence. Individuals using this power manipulate others by controlling their labor and selling them protection. A powerful individual of this nature has many men to do his work for him (to divert pilgrims to the location he controls and to perform the rituals they request) and the coercive might to make sure that at the end of the day these men turn over part of their earnings to him. When this kind of power succeeds in Banaras, the *paṇḍās* of Daśāśvamedha say, cheating and corruption rear their ugly heads and create a dirty social condition.

These Banaras residents, like many others, express degeneracy through the notion of *gandagī*. *Gandagī* is the Hindi term for filth and dirtiness. It refers to material waste and some forms of human excretion. In the Hindu worldview expressed by Banaras residents, *gandagī* is also a metaphor for corrupt religious, social, and political relations and, generally, for the undesirable conditions of existence. To focus the discussion on how *gandagī* impacts the river Gaṅgā, we must understand the concept in relation to the more complicated term *purity* and its opposite *impurity*, and the related but not synonymous term *pollution*.

Mary Douglas (1966) explained the concept of pollution as referring to that which is not included in the conceptual category of purity and is therefore powerful by virtue of its marginality. Dumont, in *Homo Hierarchicus* (1970), saw impurity as the conceptual opposite of purity, and argued that the two were inextricably bound up with social status (see also Dumont and Pocock 1959). After that, studies of Hindu caste and ritual began to use the English terms impurity and pollution interchangeably to code status and variables such as sin and evil, other aspects of morality, and the relations between gods and human beings (Das 1977; Fuller 1977, 473; O'Flaherty 1976). Later studies highlighting the centrality of the concepts of auspiciousness and inauspiciousness in Hindu ritual and caste relations expanded the understanding of the Hindu worldview.[7] But the term pollution remained confused in these accounts, clouding the Hindu distinction between ritual impurity and material dirtiness. Use of the word pollution becomes even more problematic when attempting to differentiate the meanings of environmental pollution and ritual impurity when they occur in the same context.

The notion of environmental pollution is an important term in the modern scientific worldview, crucial to a vision that seeks to expand human control of natural processes and forces. Residents of Daśāśvamedha, however, give little credence to the notion espoused in scientific and official circles. To understand how they think about physical dirtiness, it would be helpful to abandon use of the term *pollution* in its religious sense of ritual pollution. Instead I will use the term *ritual impurity* when speaking of the conceptual opposite of ritual purity. This way we will avoid any confusion between ritual impurity and the very different notion of environmental pollution.

In this chapter, the term *pollution* will denote the form of environmental degeneracy that is the subject of scientific and official government worldviews. The terms *purity* and *impurity*, on the other hand, will stand for the moral, bodily, and cosmic states proper to the religious concerns of Banaras residents. This attempt at conceptual clarification is not, however, intended to obscure the fact that Hindus recognize material waste. The notion of waste or dirtiness is an important part of the Hindu view as well. But the local understanding of material waste, encompassed by the term *gandagī,* must be understood in its own terms, as something somewhat different from the scientific/official notion of environmental pollution.

This allows us to move into a discussion of the distinction between physical cleanness and religious purity (and their antonyms) as they are elaborated in the Hindi language. As the discussion will show, at times the distinction appears blurred. But it becomes strikingly clear when *paṇḍās* explain the impact of waste on the Gaṅgā. The Clean Ganga Campaign also relies upon this distinction to articulate its focus. Understanding how residents articulate these concepts is a difficult task because the sets of terms I will describe are sometimes used interchangeably. Nevertheless, the distinction remains an important element of the Hindu worldview and Hindu assessments of the Gaṅgā.

The social scientific literature has had little to say about this distinction. The few exceptions are found in references made by Srinivas in 1952 and, more recently, by Alter in his account of the wrestling ground. Srinivas (1952, 105) argued that ritual purity cannot be simply associated with cleanliness. This is because one may find a ritually pure robe that is very dirty or snow-white clothes that are ritually impure. In his discussion of the Mīnākṣī Temple in Madurai, Fuller (1979, 473) hinted that these categories function independently in this way. He pointed out that the physical cleanness of the temple is a precondition for its spiritual purity. Alter (1990) has contributed the most thus far in his elaboration of the spatial dimensions that mark off the pure from the unclean at the *akhāṛā* grounds in Bananas. I will return to Alter's account in a moment.

The ways that *paṇḍās* of Daśāśvamedha distinguish between physical cleanness and ritual purity are central to how they define *gandagī* and assess its impact on the river. Again, their concept of *gandagī* is altogether different, conceptually, from the notion of environmental pollution espoused by science and government. *Paṇḍās* use eight Hindi terms to explain the impact of *gandagī*. Operating as four sets of binary oppositions, they are: *sāf* and *gandā*, *svaccha* and *asvaccha*, *śuddha* and *aśuddha*, and *pavitra* and *apavitra*. The first two pairs—*sāf/gandā* and *svaccha/asvaccha*—refer to material or external cleanness and uncleanness. The other two—*śuddha/aśuddha* and *pavitra/apavitra*—refer to purity and impurity of cosmos, soul, and heart. Although residents treat them as sets of binary oppositions, they do not necessarily exclude one set when using the other to signify an event or condition. This is because residents demonstrate considerable flexibility when using these terms to define their world. For example, a Banaras resident might say that Gaṅgā water is *śuddha* as if he or she means both good to drink in the sense of cleanness and good to worship in the sense of possessing eternal power. This means that *sāf/svaccha* and *śuddha/pavitra* can signify similar conditions. In many ritual contexts, cleanness and purity are closely linked. Likewise, terms designating physical uncleanness and ritual impurity may signify the same condition. *But this is not always the case.* This interchangeability demonstrates how the use of these terms is complicated. But when we focus on discussions of the river Gaṅgā, the importance of these terminological distinctions becomes more apparent.

Most informants on Daśāśvamedha define the following elements that enter the Gaṅgā as materially unclean (*gandā* or *asvaccha*): dirty water from drains (*nālās*), industrial waste, household trash, soap from bathing and washing clothes, human excrement from "doing latrine" on the riverbank, and betelnut (*pān*) spit. Many believe that material dirtiness and bodily wastes have a similar impact on Gaṅgā. Residents do not say that such *gandagī* is dangerous for the Gaṅgā, but they do value the rule for keeping dirtiness away from Gaṅgā and other places of worship. Sacred texts and popular manuals on pilgrimage, spiritual life, and good conduct communicate ideas about distancing unclean bodily functions from bodies of pure water. The *Śiva Purāṇa* (*ŚP*), for example, makes numerous references to proper conduct near bodies of water, and particularly next to rivers and tanks. About morning defecation and other routine activities, it teaches as follows:

> [For defecation,] he must never sit in front of water, fire, a brahmin or the idol of any god. He must screen the penis with the left hand and the mouth with the right. After evacuating the bowels, the feces should not be looked at. Water drawn out in a vessel should not be used for cleaning (i.e. no one should sit inside the tank or river-water for cleaning purposes). No one shall enter the holy tanks and rivers dedicated to deities, manes, etc. and frequented by the sages. The rectum must be cleaned with mud seven, five or three times. . . .
>
> For gargling, the water can be taken in any vessel or a wooden cup; but water shall be spit outside (not in the river or tank). Washing of the teeth with any leaf or twig must be without using the index finger and outside the water. . . . In all sacred rites the upper cloth should also be used while taking bath in the holy river or tank; the cloth worn shall not be rinsed or beaten. The sensible man shall take it to a separate tank or well or to the house itself and beat it on a rock or on a plank to the gratification of the manes, O brahmins. (*ŚP* 13.10–13, 15–18)

These passages direct people to distance some everyday human processes such as defecation, brushing teeth, spitting, and washing clothes from the riverbank. This principle of distancing, also mentioned in a favorite text of one *paṇḍā*, the *Paramśānti Kā Mārg* ("Path to Great Peace"), appears to serve as a well-understood spatial benchmark for keeping uncleanness away from the Gaṅgā.

Alter's description of the *akhāṛā* (wrestling) ground reflects this spatial ordering. He outlines (1990, 33) how Banaras residents distance uncleanness and human dirtiness from the center of the *akhāṛā* ground. In the center lies a deep well of pure water which draws its strength from the soil of the *akhāṛā* (considered a tonic of sorts), the trees, and its proximity to the Gaṅgā. Swampy ponds encircle the clean area of the compound. Wrestlers use these ponds for cleaning after defecation. The swampy area is the unclean periphery, where the dirtiness accrued to the body through everyday life is washed away. Alter finds that a system of hydraulic classification structures *akhāṛā* space and the residents' movement through it. Wrestlers distinguish between swampy water used to clean one's anus, water from a peripheral well used to dampen the ground, water from another tank used to wash one's self and one's clothes, and water from the well in the center of the *akhāṛā*, which is for drinking. In this case, the pure well lies closest to the *akhāṛā* ground, and both together constitute the center of the arena. This hydraulic classification shows that physical cleanness and ritual purity alike are distanced from physical and bodily uncleanness.

On Daśāśvamedha, this rule is recognized as the ideal, even when it is breached. Unfortunately, residents claim, this spatial order is exactly what cannot be enforced on the *ghāṭ*. For many, the rule of distancing seems impossibly difficult to follow. On Daśāśvamedha *ghāṭ*, while pilgrims perform ablutions, others wash clothes with soap, a *paṇḍā* spits, an old woman "does latrine" on a corner of the *ghāṭ* (for lack of public facilities), and urban sewage flows into the river under the *ghāṭ* floor. *Gandagī* surrounds the people seeking purification.

The collapse of the spatial ideal of separating what is unclean from what is pure disturbs most residents. However, they claim they cannot do much to change the situation. In fact, apathy about control of public behavior runs high on Daśāśvamedha. Most argue that the public nature of the *ghāṭ* at this spot makes regulation virtually impossible. Banaras, some point out, does not have a strong centralized religious authority, like that in the city of Hardwar, to enforce rules strictly.

Many residents point out the rise in dead bodies immersed in wholly uncremated form in the Gaṅgā. Local residents complain that the police are often responsible for the problem because they dispose of unclaimed dead bodies in the river to avoid the costs of electric cremation, which their department has to bear. Along with unclaimed bodies, corpses are brought to the river by families who are unable to afford proper cremation. According to Hindu ritual, corpses are carriers of ritual impurity. The Hindu practice of cremation along the banks of the river, at the two auspicious *ghāṭs* of Maṇikarṇikā and Harīścandra, aims to reduce the corpse into the five basic elements of existence: fire, air, water, ether, and earth. Hindus use the words *aśuddha* or *apavitra* to describe the ritual impurity of the corpse as well as the ritual impurity of the surviving family members in charge of performing the cremation rituals. After cremation, the ashes and any remaining bones are immersed in the Gaṅgā and purified by her. The impurity associated with the surviving family members is absolved after they perform rituals of *śrāddha* (rites in honor of the spirits of the deceased) over a prescribed period of time. According to the sacred texts, some individuals are not allowed to be cremated, namely holy men (*sādhus*), children, lepers, and smallpox victims (see Das 1982, 123; Parry 1994, 184–5). In the religious view, therefore, dead bodies, per se, are not problematic for Gaṅgā, because she can ritually purify them. However, cremation does constitute a good sacrificial death for corpses (other than those specified above) and absolves the impurity of the physical body. The *paṇḍās* of Daśāśvamedha point out that most of the fully uncremated corpses found floating down the Gaṅgā should have been cremated according to rules set out in the *śāstras* (because they were neither *sādhus*, children, lepers, nor smallpox victims). To the priests, this indicates a lapse in the public respect for ritual order. The practice of partially cremating corpses in the wood or electric crematorium, and then dumping the partially burned remains in the Gaṅgā, is more excusable because the ritual procedure, although short circuited due to financial constraints, has been respected.

The *paṇḍās'* views about corpses, however, are more complicated because, when they make references to fully uncremated dead bodies in the Gaṅgā, they sometimes conflate notions of ritual impurity and physical uncleanness. That is, they also refer to these corpses as signs of *gandagī*. The fact that residents of Daśāśvamedha refer to dead bodies as *gandagī* is the result of more than a decade of media reports on river pollution, which have defined corpses as secular bodies.

Since the 1980s, media and official reports have claimed that the number of dead bodies immersed in the Gaṅgā in uncremated or partially cremated form has visibly increased. Officials have attributed this to the rising cost of cremation, which is making it difficult for some families to cremate their deceased kin. Media reports began to publicize this phenomenon toward the end of the decade. From 1985 through 1990, reporters from Delhi and abroad published descriptions and photos of floating corpses in reports of "Ganga pollution."[8]

Although they were meant to shock the citizenry into a concern for ecological degeneracy, these media reports did little to convince Daśāśvamedha residents of Gaṅgā's impending demise. On the contrary, residents continue to believe that Gaṅgā purifies the ashes of cremated individuals and, if need be, carries away the partially cremated—or even fully uncremated—bodies without being adversely affected. What residents of Daśāśvamedha argue is that fully uncremated bodies in the Gaṅgā are less dangerous than the social conditions they reflect. These bodies represent, to them, a decline in the practice of cremation and therefore mark the moral degeneracy of contemporary society.

*Paṇḍās* tend to refer to corpses as *gandagī* when speaking with others who appear to embrace a scientific or ecological view of the river. Although, in these discussions, they tend to consider corpses in a secular sense, they also mock the very argument put forth by media and official reports that dead bodies, as *gandagī*, are harmful for the river. They often pointed out dead bodies to me in phrases such as, "Look Madam, dead body!" and then laughed at my disgust. Such mocking exclamations made me realize that they were not as alarmed about the uncleanness of Gaṅgā caused by corpses as scientists and officials claimed to be. In fact, they generally tended to steer the discussion about fully uncremated dead bodies back to the societal ills that the bodies reflected, which they believed were far more disturbing to their values and occupational existence.

Some residents blame pollution prevention projects for the rise in cases of partially cremated and fully uncremated corpses. Under the Ganga Action Plan, the government constructed an electric crematorium on Harīścandra Ghāṭ to ease the pollution load on the river. In addition, this was to provide a viable solution to the increasing cost of wood for cremation. When it began, pilgrim priests involved with cremation rituals opposed the project because it threatened to disturb traditional Hindu practices of wood cremation (see Parry 1994, 67–68). Today, the increasing use of the electric crematorium still disturbs them, especially those priests whose services are tied up with wood cremation. The fully uncremated dead bodies floating down the Gaṅgā today do not come from the electric crematorium. Still, in the minds of the *paṇḍās*, the facility is implicated. They are a result, the *paṇḍās* say, of the further decline in respect for traditional practices set in motion when the government established an alternate form of cremation.

Residents often complain that government projects rarely serve the best interests of the public. In 1987, Ganga Action Plan authorities created a turtle breeding farm to raise and release turtles into the river to eat the flesh of floating corpses. Most residents consider this project a complete failure because they never see the turtles consuming corpses. A bicycle rickshaw pedaler I have used for many years often finds the turtles swimming up the Varaṇā river. They tend to make life difficult for residents taking their morning bath in that tributary. The turtle breeding farm at Sarnath outside the city limits of Banaras showed signs of downsizing in 1993. By 1995, the project had been eliminated from Phase II of the Ganga Action Plan.

As indicated above, *paṇḍās* firmly believe that partially cremated or fully uncremated dead bodies dumped in the river do not threaten Gaṅgā's spiritual integrity. But they seem to fear that industrial waste, or more generally "dirty water" from drains, may have a harmful impact over time, by making the Gaṅgā *asvaccha* or physically unclean. Still residents insist that *gandagī* cannot alter Gaṅgā's power to give liberation (*mukti* or *mokṣa*) and purify the ashes of the deceased. This power is eternal and not subject to fluctuations in material reality. They add that as long as humans demonstrate their reverence through ritual ablution, *āratī*, and other forms of worship, Gaṅgā will remain happy. As long as she is happy, she will purify the cosmos, soul, body, and heart. But even if, in theory, Gaṅgā's purificatory power remains infinite, residents do express concern about their personal health and appear disturbed by *gandagī*. Two of the three dominant *paṇḍās* of Daśāśvamedha rarely bathe at their *ghāṭ*. They recommend cleaner locations! The most powerful boatman in the area complains that his doctor suggested he also avoid bathing at Daśāśvamedha—to prevent skin disease.

In *Water and Womanhood*, Feldhaus (1995) describes how residents of Maharashtra associate the river with feminine imagery. She argues that they stress a river's female attributes over its purificatory power. Banaras residents also conceive of the river in feminine terms, but they link femininity with motherliness, housekeeping and clean-up, and forgiveness. Many Daśāśvamedha residents and pilgrims remark that Gaṅgā, like a good mother, cleans up the messes her children make and forgives them lovingly. In this way, she cleans up other kinds of dirtiness people bring to her and excuses dirty behavior with maternal kindness.[9] Gaṅgā is forgiving rather than angry about human dirtiness.

Residents of Banaras, therefore, differ quite markedly from residents of the village of Ghatiyali in Rajasthan described by Gold (this volume). Residents of Ghatiyali claim that God is angered by deforestation and, in retaliation, withholds rain. The forgiving nature of Gaṅgā that Banaras residents describe is problematic for the environmental activists in the Clean Ganga Campaign, who hope to raise awareness about pollution prevention. Environmental activists in Banaras argue that this view of sacred purity and loving tolerance leads to a passive acceptance of polluting behavior. However, these very activists understand that revising this deep religious association between water and long-suffering womanhood, so as to include human responsibility for Gaṅgā's well-being, will be difficult indeed. The villagers Gold describes may be in a better position to accept the message of environmental activism because they understand that the environment participates in the fruits of human sin. Residents of Daśāśvamedha, on the other hand, link morality to *gandagī* but do not find that the Gaṅgā participates in the sin-game (*pāp-līlā*) of humans. This means that she is, by extension, unaffected by the sins of humans and not motivated toward retaliation. She did, after all, descend to earth to wash away those very misdeeds.

Environmental activists are frustrated by the fact that residents of Daśāśvamedha passively accept the conditions of *gandagī* by pointing to Gaṅgā's own power to solve the problem. To understand the broader context of this apparent complacency, however, we must trace how pilgrim priests connect Gaṅgā's purity (and purificatory power) to their own occupational interests. *Paṇḍās* consistently defend their conviction that human-created *gandagī* does not alter Gaṅgā's purity. But they do not deny the presence of *gandagī* in the river. This position is most noticeable when they argue that Gaṅgā may be materially unclean (*gandā* or *asvaccha*)—that is, affected by *gandagī*—but not impure (*aśuddha* or *apavitra*). In their discussions about how waste impacts the Gaṅgā, the distinction between physical cleanness and sacred purity is most salient. Their comments allow us to see that the blurring of the distinction in the spatial dimensions of the *akhāṛā* does not mean that, because purity and cleanness are closely connected, they mean the same thing all the time. Impurity and uncleanness are also intimately linked in references to the fully uncremated dead bodies floating in the Gaṅgā. But when residents attempt to logically explain how uncleanness and sacred purity coexist in the Gaṅgā, they allow the conceptual categories to work independently. Gaṅgā, while she can be dirty, cannot be impure. Therefore, like the robe Srinivas found, she is both dirty and pure. However, if she is dirty (*gandā/asvaccha*), it is because people have made her that way (see Alley 1994, 130).

The idea that Gaṅgā's purity overrides human *gandagī* is a self-serving one for *paṇḍās*. Pilgrim service is lucrative and *paṇḍās* want it to remain that way. As one *paṇḍā* put it, "From sunrise to sunset, it is just earning, earning, earning." Many scholarly accounts have estimated that over the past four decades the number of pilgrims visiting Banaras daily to see the divine (take *darśan*) has steadily increased (see Fuller 1992, 205; Parry 1994, 108; Veer 1994, 122). Local gossip puts the *paṇḍās'* earnings at well above average for Banaras. *Paṇḍās* do in fact own substantial homes on southern Daśāśvamedha. In them sacred icons are enshrined. One mansion towers above the Rām temple on Prayāg Ghāṭ. Another home contains the Prayāgeśvara shrine, and a third shelters a goddess, reputedly made of gold. From look-out points on their property, these *paṇḍās* watch over the activities on the *ghāṭ* and oversee the exchanges that the lower-ranked pilgrim priests, *tīrth purohits* and *ghāṭiyas*, undertake with pilgrims. For over three generations, the *paṇḍās* of southern Daśāśvamedha have retained their rights to serve pilgrims coming from the former princely states of Palamu, Singrauli, and Sonbhadhra. Even as the district names have changed over time, many pilgrims continue to identify—when looking for the Banaras priest who serves clients from their region—with the former princely states within whose old borders they still live.

These princely states were located in regions which now extend across the north Indian states of Uttar Pradesh and Bihar. They mark the historical homelands of several tribal groups in India. These tribal groups now comprise the agricultural or small landholding class in these states. Pilgrims pay fees (*dakṣiṇā*) and offer donations (*dān*) to *paṇḍās* in exchange for shelter, offerings blessed by deities (*prasād*), and ritual services. *Paṇḍās* also receive commissions from the income of the other priests who rent spaces on the *ghāṭ* from them. On their wooden platforms, the lower-ranked priests preside over pilgrims' offerings throughout the morning, assisting them also by watching over their personal possessions.

Like the villagers of Ghatiyali described by Gold (this volume), *paṇḍās* feel caught up in a moral and cosmic degeneracy which sets the context for their social concerns. In their account of the present degenerate state of the world, *paṇḍās* deflect blame from human agency by pointing toward a cosmic design in which truth turns against humankind. The cosmos passes through many aeons in its cyclical passage; the Kali Yuga is the last of four declining ages that form one such aeon. The Kali Yuga, or "Dark Age," began on February 18, 3102 B.C.E. and will continue for another 426,904 years (Fuller 1992, 266). This time spells diminished virtue, moral degeneracy, and sin for all living souls. As Madan (1987, 128) put it, in this age people do not engage in severe penance to gain the favor of gods and goddesses, and therefore very few individuals receive divine blessing. The *Śiva Purāṇa* describes the Kali Age as follows:

> At the advent of the terrible age of *Kali* men have become devoid of merits. They are engaged in evil ways of life. They have turned their faces from truthful avocations. They are engaged in calumniating others. They covet other men's wealth. Their attention is diverted to other men's wives. Injuring others has become their chief aim. (*ŚP* 1.12–13)

For *paṇḍās*, the Kali Yuga forms the cosmic backdrop to their current predicament. *Paṇḍās* argue that "man and money power" has succeeded in dominating the pilgrim services and businesses in Banaras. Because of this, the *paṇḍā* profession has been dirtied. In discussions of power, *paṇḍās* extend the metaphor of *gandagī* to signify immoral and ritually imbalanced social conditions. *Paṇḍās* argue that because they are forced to defend their hereditary right rather than remain divinely entitled to it, their moral authority wanes. This instability contributes to the lax ritual atmosphere in which respect for Gaṅgā is diminishing. But the degenerate pull of the Kali Yuga does not overpower her. She staves off the collapse, retains her purity, and continues to wash away human dirtiness. The *Bhāgavata Purāṇa* powerfully expresses this theme in the myth of Gaṅgā's descent from heaven. Gaṅgā flowed over the foot of Viṣṇu into Brahmā's water jug *(kamaṇḍal)* and "washed away the dirt, in the form of the sins of the whole of the world, by her touch, and yet, remained pure" (*BhP* 5.17.1).

Given Gaṅgā's transcendent power, people can aim to please her and thereby assist in partially rejuvenating the moral order. *Paṇḍās* believe that pilgrims can please Gaṅgā by worshiping her, even if they cannot purify her. Purificatory power can be achieved only by the few. The rare individuals who have purified themselves through *yoga* and become saints, channels of divine blessing, do have powers to repurify Gaṅgā. As Vatsyayan (1993, 167) writes, the respect paid to Gaṅgā by saints is especially important, as the transfer of their ascetic power (*tapas*) to Gaṅgā can re-purify the cosmos. But ordinary pilgrims and residents cannot emulate saints. *Paṇḍās* know their spiritual power is limited, because they have not renounced the material world and live amidst human *gandagī*. Nevertheless, they know they can at least please Gaṅgā by performing *āratī* on auspicious occasions.

At the time of my field study, I suggested to the *paṇḍās* that they make speeches in their forthcoming *āratī* celebration to raise awareness about the problems *gandagī* creates for Gaṅgā. This was not an entirely unusual proposition. In February of 1994, they performed their first big *āratī* (*mahāratī*) on the auspicious occasion of Māgha Pūrṇimā. Māgha Pūrṇimā is the full moon day in Māgh (January–February), a day when Gaṅgā *snān* is especially meritorious. The group claimed a concern for cleanness then, and media reports praised them for their efforts to clean the *ghāṭs* before the worship ceremony. They performed their second public *āratī* alongside a music festival organized by the Clean Ganga Campaign on Tulsī Ghāṭ. The third performance fell on Kārtik Pūrṇimā, the full moon day in the auspicious month of Kārtik.

While *āratī* evokes public praise for Gaṅgā and affirms her purifying power, *paṇḍās* also expect the ceremony to generate donations. They often complained to me that *āratī* was expensive for them. They had imported the silver lamps and whisks (*cavār*) from Bengal and had the "gents and ladies" costumes made with fine cloth. *Paṇḍās* claim that it is difficult to bear the cost of *āratī* on a monthly basis. They continue to conclude, however, that *āratī* is the only method they can use to encourage reverence for Gaṅgā.[10] The relationship that people establish with Ganga through *āratī* is meant to be morally uplifting. Proper morality is reflected in the respect worshipers give to powerful cosmic forces (such as Gaṅgā's purificatory power). Efforts to please the gods and goddesses that control these forces are meritorious moral acts that can help to bring the population out of the current state of degeneracy.

This assessment, that Gaṅgā's purity is the primary force staving off moral and cosmic degeneracy as well as physical pollution, puts the *paṇḍās* outside policy discourses on pollution prevention carried out by government agencies and non-governmental citizen-action groups. The *paṇḍās* do not act as city advisors or assume positions in organizations such as the Rotary Club, the Lions Club, or the Clean Ganga Campaign. Their own organization is called the Ganga Seva Sangh, which means "Association for [Religious] Service to Gaṅgā." It is focused exclusively on the religious concerns of Hindu pilgrims.

## Degeneracy and the Genealogy of Environmental Pollution

Government officials and scientists articulate idioms of degeneracy markedly different from those expressed by the *paṇḍās* of southern Daśāśvamedha. Unlike the *paṇḍās*, they locate degeneracy in the physical river Gaṅgā and in the ecological system within which the river is an integral water supplier. Ecological degeneracy is, for them, a consequence of human activities associated with industrialization, urban growth, and the overpopulation of the river basin.

Discussions of ecological degeneracy go back no more than fifteen years in Indian scientific and secular discourses. Three professors who teach engineering at Banaras Hindu University were the first to focus public attention on problems of river pollution. In 1982, they formed an organization called the Clean Ganga Campaign (Swatcha Ganga Abhiyan) and listed it under a religious institution run by one of its principal members. They find that the distinction between physical cleanness and sacred purity is crucial to their environmental message, and they evoke it as a way to form a syncretism of Hinduism and science. The importance of this distinction is at first evident in their organization's name. They use the word *svaccha* (which they spell *swatcha)* to show that they are an organization concerned with physical cleanness rather than sacred purity. But CGC members are not removed from religious concerns. The leading member of the group is also the head priest of a religious institution, the Sankat Mochan Foundation. This organization manages the Saṅkaṭ Mocan Temple, an important Hindu temple where the saint-poet Tulsī Dās received his vision of Hanumān, the monkey-god of the *Rāmāyaṇa*. The leaders explain that their concern is with the impact of waste on the physical Gaṅgā. They do not contest or seek to denigrate her eternal sacred purity.[11] While they revere Gaṅgā through worship rituals in their private lives, they do not claim to promote a revitalization of such rituals through their own organization work.

The Clean Ganga Campaign's agitation in the early 1980s focused Indira Gandhi's attention on issues of river pollution. They asked her to consider establishing sewage management programs in cities bordering the river. After Mrs. Gandhi's death and the passage of power to her son Rajiv, the first official policies addressing sewage management and pollution prevention were drawn up. In 1986, Rajiv Gandhi established an agency called the Ganga Project Directorate to oversee the Ganga Action Plan. The Ganga Action Plan or GAP was set up to create pollution prevention programs and sewage treatment infrastructure in five Class I cities (those with populations over 100,000) bordering the Gaṅgā. Well before sufficient data had been collected to understand the waste complex, decisions were made on sewage treatment and management. The many contracts for treatment plants, funded by foreign lenders, were modeled on energy-intensive methods more suitable for climates in Western countries. In Kanpur and Mirzapur, for example, the Indo-Dutch Cooperation Programme established treatment plants according to the process called the Upflow Anaerobic Sludge Blanket (UASB). Using a different method in Banaras, the government built one activated sludge treatment plant to treat eighty million liters of urban sewage per day (mld). They made other renovations to sewage lines and pumping stations under the first phase of the Plan. In June of 1993, the Ministry of Environment and Forests announced that under Phase I of the Ganga Action Plan they had commissioned fifteen treatment plants. All the plants combined are able to treat 300 million liters of sewage per day.[12]

In official and scientific reports, the parameters of Biological Oxygen Demand (BOD) and Fecal Coliform Count (FCC) have been used to measure levels of river pollution. Under the first phase of the Plan, several universities in the Gangetic plain received grants to establish water monitoring programs in four cities—Hardwar, Allahabad, Banaras, and Patna (Murti et al. 1991). Until 1992, data were forwarded to the Ganga Project Directorate, which then published results selectively. Since that time, however, the CGC members have considered the data passed to the Directorate by academic departments and government water monitoring agencies invalid (see Sankat Mochan Foundation 1990, 1992, 1994). The CGC has, in fact, used the issue of validity to challenge government monitoring programs in a more comprehensive way. To do this, in 1992 they established their own water monitoring laboratory with domestic and foreign financial assistance. But their aim was not simply to generate alternate data. They pressed the GPD to expand its own monitoring program. While official monitoring used the parameter of BOD—along with others such as dissolved oxygen, conductivity, pH and temperature—it did not include the parameter of fecal coliform count (FCC) (see Alley 1994, 134–36). Clean Ganga Campaign members argued that fecal coliform, an important indicator of human sewage levels, ought to be a required component of monitoring. Furthermore, the FCC data could be used to evaluate the effectiveness of the sewage management system. After the CGC made this argument in many meetings, the government agreed to include this parameter and began testing for it in 1994. The Clean Ganga Campaign, on the other hand, began monitoring water quality with the FCC parameter in 1992.

In their June 1993 report, the GPD announced that pollution levels in the Gaṅgā were declining because of infrastructural improvements in sewage management and treatment. They reported a decline in BOD levels in Banaras from ten mg/liter in 1986 to between one and two mg/liter in 1992 (Ministry of Environment and Forests 1993). Members of the Clean Ganga Campaign charged that these declines were exaggerated. According to CGC reports published in 1994, BOD levels just downstream from Daśāśvamedha Ghāṭ were much more variable. In May, BOD varied from 1.11 mg/liter to 26.50, depending on the time of day monitoring occurred. Higher figures tended to reflect times when the sewage lines leading to the Gaṅgā under the *ghāṭs* were open (see Sankat Mochan Foundation 1994). FCC levels were as high as 440,000 colonies per 100 ml in March and exceeded 320,000 in April of 1994.[13]

### Assessing Pollution in Order to Treat It

After the treatment plant in Banaras was completed in the spring of 1993, the Clean Ganga Campaign began to notice various operational problems. For example, the plant's collection chamber proved too small to hold incoming discharge from the city during the monsoon. Consequently, the sewage backed up through the main trunk line after heavy rains. During previous monsoons, officials had diverted the city's discharge into the Gaṅgā through the outlet point lying downstream from Rāj Ghāṭ (see Alley 1992, 126–27; Alley 1994, 132–34). In early 1994, the Clean Ganga Campaign members demanded that government officials close the outlet drain to the Gaṅgā. They asked them to comply with the stated objectives of the project and divert all sewage to the plant. Consequently, the sewage backed up, creating what they called a "surcharge" in the main trunk line. The CGC pointed to this as proof of the inappropriate design of the collection chamber. After many requests from the CGC, the Ganga Project Directorate convened a meeting of technical experts in the field of sewage treatment to discuss the problems at the Banaras plant. This occurred in August of 1994. The CGC was invited to attend, and I followed along as a foreign member. At the forum, CGC members charged that monitoring officials had not conducted a thorough study of city waste discharge before designing the plant. Consequently, they constructed the collection chamber improperly. They added that discharge rates put out by the Ganga Project Directorate in 1994 were also dubious. Pointing out that the data from their research contradicted official reports, they demanded a role as an outside witness in future discharge measurement and monitoring.

Additionally, the Clean Ganga Campaign members presented a proposal for oxidation ponds as an alternate method of sewage treatment. This proposal had the support of their cadre of foreign experts, which included researchers at the University of California at Berkeley and the University of Stockholm. More suited to India's hot climate, it uses only a fraction of the energy consumed by the activated sludge process. This alternative, they submitted, would avoid the high energy costs incurred by the activated sludge plant. This is crucial because the electric board of the state of Uttar Pradesh has not consistently supplied the required energy to the plant since its commissioning.

Alongside its role as a watchdog of official policy, the Clean Ganga Campaign also considers itself the local vanguard for raising awareness about pollution prevention. Since 1982, it has organized many educational programs to bring this issue to public attention. In late 1994, they hosted a "Public Forum" with Dr. Karan Singh, the chairman of the People's Commission on Environment and Development and former Indian Ambassador to the United States. They organized this event to hear residents' opinions on waste problems affecting their sacred river. During my fieldwork, I passed on to the *paṇḍās* of Daśāśvamedha invitations to the event. They attended under the banner of their organization, the Ganga Seva Sangh, and had their first formal meeting with Clean Ganga Campaign members.

The CGC maintains respect for religious notions of Gaṅgā's purificatory power, while pleading for measures to reduce the material waste load on the river. They do not state that Gaṅgā is impure in a sacred sense, for they do not believe this and science provides no proof for it. Instead, they maintain the distinction between physical cleanness and purity to argue that despite her purificatory power, she is becoming *asvaccha* and needs to be *svaccha*. At the same time, in official circles using scientific language, they publish their water quality data to argue for accountability in sewage management and treatment. The individuals who debate about measurement and data, however, constitute a small circle. This circle does not include any residents of Daśāśvamedha. While discourse on water quality data does not alienate other Banaras residents, it has not achieved the effect of increasing local membership in environmental groups such as the CGC. This is precisely because residents do not understand the scientific ideas within their assessments.

There are no other organized groups which challenge government projects in Banaras. There are a few smaller clubs which claim concern for the environment and several professors, journalists, and playwrights who are, in passing, critical of current sewage management. But they do not regularly contest the official view. Therefore, the gradual increase in government attention to waste management projects has not coincided with the emergence of an environmental movement. Terms such as BOD and FCC mean nothing to most residents of Banaras. Moreover, citizens interpret the tendencies of officials to package their environmental goals with instrumental-scientific rationality as attempts to forward the material interests of the elite. For them, this means that everything, in the final analysis, is reduced to money. Both governmental and nongovernmental organizations tend to talk in a scientific language that assumes a position of superiority. At the same time, the government's assessments imply the inferiority of religious modes of discourse. Defensively, the *paṇḍās* of Daśāśvamedha argue that their knowledge, informed by sacred texts, is more authoritative. *Paṇḍās* admit, however, that sacred (*śāstrik*) knowledge is weak in material power and explanation, and therefore threatened in the Kali Yuga by science and the "man and money power" behind it. Thus, according to *paṇḍās*, not only does science negate divine power, but it is associated, through money, with the moral degeneracy of the Kali Yuga.

## In the Name of Gaṅgā

While there is no sociologically recognizable environmental movement in Banaras today (see, for example, Buttel 1987, 1992; Buttel and Taylor 1992), residents engage in constant verbal resistance to the government's ineffectual campaign to combat pollution. The CGC does engage in direct confrontation with government officials in the Ganga Project Directorate, but their activities involve only a small minority of the local population. The GPD, the CGC, and residents of Daśāśvamedha are for the most part aware of each other's claims about sacred purity and environmental pollution. However, while all claim to be acting out of genuine concern for her welfare, each group is skeptical of the others' desire to respect the Gaṅgā's purity or prevent her being polluted. In other words, each group accuses the other of acting "in the name of Gaṅgā" (*gaṅgā ke nām par*), not in true service to her. There is a sense on all sides that concern for the Gaṅgā is more often than not rhetorically staged to obfuscate other, more self-interested motives. *Paṇḍās* see sewage treatment plants and projects as vehicles for state moneymaking. Quite often, they complain that pollution prevention work is merely "on paper" and does not produce any productive results. Many residents of Daśāśvamedha insist that officials have not adequately capped the drains feeding dirty water (*gandā pānī*) into the Gaṅgā. *Paṇḍās* are also suspicious about the activities of the Clean Ganga Campaign, since they remain outside that circle as well. They charge that most of the CGC's work includes foreigners, who are contributing money and material supplies. Moreover, *paṇḍās* argue that all the money allocated for sewage management has been "eaten." They often express this with the phrase, "They've eaten it all up" (*sab khā liyā*). The efforts of both are vitiated, in the *paṇḍās'* eyes, by the money-grabbing ethos of the Kali Yuga.

The CGC agrees that the Government of India has not used public funds properly to build effective sewage treatment plants and to renovate existing infrastructure. In response, the Ganga Project Directorate charges that the CGC is offering exaggerated criticisms and fanciful proposals for alternatives. Government officials also blame pilgrims and residents of Banaras for their adherence to a tradition that encourages an intensive use of the river for religious purposes. Furthermore, government officials point out that *paṇḍās* uphold the ideology of purity to support their own economic interests. Finally, all groups are suspicious that the anthropologist, with her curious concern for Gaṅgā, is studying pollution also to make money.

## Conclusions

Both *paṇḍās* and the scientific-official camp agree that degeneracy exists, but they locate its core in different spheres. For *paṇḍās*, marketplace competition, cheating, and corruption are signs of moral degeneracy and reflect a cosmic cycle. Although to some extent, they believe they are caught in this cosmic cycle, *paṇḍās* suggest that the moral order can be reset by Gaṅgā's power to purify. A conviction among people to follow principles in sacred texts through adherence to ritual, they maintain, could also bring back a popular respect for Hindu beliefs. Religious beliefs do not provide a disincentive for cleaning the river, per se, because they affirm a high value for Gaṅgā and are based upon a deep spiritual understanding of the river. However, that ablution *(snān)* and worship *(pūjā)* continue to occur, even in a context of *gandagī*, reassures Hindu believers that the integrity of Gaṅgā's sacred purity is protected. Moreover, *paṇḍās* make sacred purity a much more complicated issue because they use this conviction to support their occupational activities. The belief in sacred purity in this case makes acceptance of immoral or corrupt behavior possible even when that very behavior is denounced.

I have shown that residents of Daśāśvamedha and the sacred texts they read advocate the distancing principle to deal with the problems of human uncleanness and *gandagī*. Religious attitudes would not, therefore, necessarily bode ill for the ecological future of the river if residents and pilgrims could enforce the distancing principle while worshiping Gaṅgā's sacred purity. The urban predicament, however, is complicated, and even *paṇḍās* know that waste drainage and treatment systems are essential to keeping Daśāśvamedha livable. Residents seem to want better enforcement of both religious and secular laws to regulate public behavior on the *ghāṭs*. Unfortunately, current scientific-official projects do not, in many residents' eyes, meet this need. *Āratī* may please Gaṅgā and help to rejuvenate the moral order, but *paṇḍās* know the ceremony alone cannot enforce the ancient ideal of distancing uncleanness from the river bank.

Academics and officials, even while respecting religious ideas about Gaṅgā's power to provide for human well-being, locate degeneracy in the ecological balance of the river. There is no common agreement between academics, officials, and residents of Daśāśvamedha about how to approach the problem of *gandagī* and its impact on the Gaṅgā. *Paṇḍās* and Clean Ganga Campaign members evoke the distinction between physical cleanness and sacred purity and therefore share some common ground in their assessments. However, the scientific knowledge of the latter group is meaningless to the former. All players do acknowledge that sewage treatment and public activity on the riverbank fall well short of keeping human uncleanness away from the river. But when residents face what they consider are the vacant meanings of scientific concepts and witness the blunders in official cleaning and sewage treatment projects, the divide between the concerned parties is heightened and communication is blocked.

A local journalist recently remarked that I would not find the seeds for a mass revolution (against *gandagī* and dirty business) on Daśāśvamedha. On the other hand, efforts to clean up pollution are tied to infrastructural and monetary assistance at the national and global levels. Therefore, we can expect to find more pollution prevention schemes developed by officials and scientists in the coming years. Indeed, *gandagī* is everywhere, and to everyone a burden. Whatever environmental activists and government officials may think, they need to be aware that the worldview of the local people must be an important factor in any solution. Since environmental activists find that the belief in sacred purity ultimately allows residents to reject or opt out of projects to tackle the problems of *gandagī*, they should try to interact with local religious leaders to sort out how occupational interests linked to ritual purity can become more connected with the need for physical cleanness. Greater communication between environmental activists and residents of Daśāśvamedha and other neighborhoods could also heighten the public awareness needed to force government agencies to be accountable for the municipal cleaning and waste management projects they undertake.

On one occasion, when I pleaded that *paṇḍās* take a greater interest in cleaning their *ghāṭ* and enforcing rules of distancing uncleanness from Gaṅgā, one *paṇḍā* insisted that it was the government's duty to clean the area, through the local municipality. If they do not do their work, he argued, then our only alternative is to turn to Gaṅgā. Reminding me about a passage from the *Gaṅgā Stuti,* he then began to sing, "O Bhāgīrathī [Gaṅgā], though we are full of sin, give us a place at your feet, give us *mukti*."

## Notes

1. See, for example, Callicott 1994, Capra 1991, Fox 1990, India International Centre 1993, Lovelock 1988 and Singh 1993b.

2. See Eck 1993, 13–14; 1982; Havell 1990 (1905), 109–10; Motichandra 1985; Singh 1993a; *KKh* 52.1–10; and Vidyarthi et al. 1979 for discussions of the sacred importance of Daśāśvamedha.

3. See Alley 1994, 130–31 for other references to Gaṅgā's forms and meanings.

4. This account comes from a *paṇḍā*'s favorite text: *PM*, p. 39. In Hindi, the passage is as follows: Gaṅgā apnā nām uccāraṇ karnewāle ke papo kā nāś karti hai, darśan karnewāle kā kalyāṇ karti hai, aur snān-pān karnewāle kī sat pīṛiyo tak ko pavitra karti hai.

5. This *stuti* was written by Kavi Kesav. One *paṇḍā* had the *stuti* hand-written on a single sheet of paper and helped me in translating it. It is sung in their *āratī* ceremonies.

6. See Veer 1988 and Parry 1980, 1981, 1994 for other characterizations of this occupational group. The term *paṇḍā*, however, is a designation that these pilgrim priests do not particularly like, though they use it to refer to each other in local discourse. When I informed them that I use this term in my description of their occupation, they requested that I use a more respectable term to describe their work. They suggested that I use the title *rāj purohit* (the king's priest) or *paṇḍit* (learned Brahmin). These are terms which in their mind do not carry a negative connotation. This discontent with the title *paṇḍā* reflects their feeling that outsiders and brokers have spoiled the image of the *paṇḍāgīrī* by cheating pilgrims and corrupting the service occupation.

7. See Carman and Marglin 1985; Gold 1988; Madan 1985, 1987; and Raheja 1988.

8. English-medium newspapers in India and other countries have tended to sensationalize the issue of dead bodies in the Gaṅgā more than the Indian papers written in the Hindi medium have. An article from the *Washington Post* entitled "Devout Hindus Resist Efforts to Clean Up the Sacred Ganges" (Claiborne 1983) and a report in the *Patriot Magazine* entitled "Save the Ganga" (Singh 1984) are the earliest media reports to highlight dead bodies as signs of Gaṅgā pollution. They predate the formation of GAP. The *Patriot Magazine* opens its article with the following description:

> At the edge of the steps on the Dashasmedh [*sic*] *ghat* a bare bodied man sits cross legged getting ready for his "aachman." A few feet to his right bobs the decayed carcass of a cow in the river, a crow hovering over it. I turn away in disgust, but a more grisly sight awaits me: two dead bodies floating near the edge of a *ghat* and a group of pilgrims having bath completely oblivious to them.

Along with this, the caption for a photograph of a corpse washed up on the riverbank reads: "A *Ghat*: As mysterious as the dead bodies floating." Later reports in the *Star Tribune* (Tempest 1987) and the *Smithsonian* (Ward 1985), among others, also consider dead bodies an environmental problem. The Hindi newspapers have been less inclined to highlight dead bodies, and have tended to focus more on the activities of the Clean Ganga Campaign and on reports of water quality. One of only a few exceptions to this is found in an article in *India Today* entitled "No Bhagirath Came" (Sharma 1987). The article opens with the following passage: "Ganga—one clean [*svaccha*], pure [*śuddha*] and benign [*mṛdu*] Ganga. But there is one dream that burdens the Hindu heart. In Varanasi today half-burnt corpses are seen swimming in this river." In most Hindi reports published from 1987 through 1994, the term *svaccha* is frequently used in calls for a clean Gaṅgā. In a few reports, the word *śuddha* is used interchangeably with *svaccha*. These Hindi reports also use the terms pollution (*pradūṣaṇ*) and polluted (*pradūṣit* or *dūṣit*) when describing the condition of the river. Many reports refer to cleaning projects as methods that will "free Gaṅgā of pollution" (*gaṅgā pradūṣaṇ se mukt hogī*).

9. Curiously, unlike other gods or goddesses who may become angry if defiled by humans (see the chapters by Gold, Sherma, and Nagarajan, this volume; also Dumont and Pocock 1959, 31; Fuller 1979, 469; 1992, 76; Harper 1964, 183–86; Sharma 1970, 1819; Srinivas 1952, 41–42, 78), Gaṅgā does not lash back at this human abuse and defilement.

10. This reminded me of a story that a devotee of Anandamayi Ma, a highly regarded female saint, told me in 1994:

> Śiva and Pārvatī were talking, and Pārvatī asked him a question. She said, "If so many people are taking bath (*snān*) and absolving their sins, why does the same kind of life persist?" Śiva took Pārvatī to the riverbank to demonstrate his response. Śiva disguised himself as an old man with leprosy and stood near the bathing area. As people were leaving, he asked them, "Whoever has been purified and is now without sin, bless me with Gaṅgā water (*gaṅgā jal*) so I may be saved." Despite his requests, no one stopped for him. Finally, one man agreed to bless him because he said he had just performed ablutions. He purified the old man and walked on. Then Śiva said, as he turned to Pārvatī, "Because not enough people have faith, they carry their sin and do ablutions as a mere routine. You cannot simply do it," he concluded, "you must believe it."

11. See Alley 1994, 135 for one leader's formula for reconciling the contradictions between scientific and Hindu worldviews.

12. See Ministry of Environment and Forests pamphlet entitled "Ganga Action Plan Achievements" issued by Project Director, Central Ganga Authority, Ministry of Environment and Forests, 5 June, 1993.

13. Biological Oxygen Demand (BOD) indicates whether there is enough oxygen in the water to sustain aquatic life. Acceptable BOD levels for bathing are set at 1–3 mg/liter and for drinking, at less than 1 mg/liter. Fecal Coliform Count (FCC) is the most probable number of bacterial colonies in a water sample. Acceptable levels for bathing are less than 500 per 100 ml.

## References

### Primary Sources, with Abbreviations

*BhP* *Bhāgavata Purāṇa*. Translated and annotated by G. V. Tagare. Part 2 (*Skandhas* 4–6). Delhi: Motilal Banarsidass, 1976.

*KKh* *Kāśī Khaṇḍa*. Edited by A. S. K. Tripathi. 2 parts. Varanasi: Sampurnanand Sanskrit University, 1991. (All translations cited are from Singh 1993a.)

*PM* *Paramśānti Kā Mārg*. Shri Jaidayaal Goyandka. Varanasi, n.d. (All translations are my own.)

*ŚP* *Śiva Purāṇa*. Translated by a board of scholars and edited by J. L. Shastri. Vol. 1. Delhi: Motilal Banarsidass, 1990.

### Secondary Sources

Alley, Kelly D. 1992. "On the Banks of the Ganga." *Annals of Tourism Research* 19 (Winter): 125–27.

———. 1994. "Ganga and *Gandagi*: Interpretations of Pollution and Waste in Benaras." *Ethnology* 33 (Spring): 127–45.

Buttel, Frederick H. 1987. "New Directions in Environmental Sociology." *Annual Review of Sociology* 13: 465–88.

———. 1992. "Environmentalization: Origins, Processes, and Implications for Rural Social Change." *Rural Sociology* 57 (Spring): 1–27.

Buttel, Frederick, and Peter Taylor. 1992. "Environmental Sociology and Global Environmental Change: A Critical Assessment." *Society and Natural Resources* 5 (July–September): 211–30.

Callicott, J. Baird. 1994. *Earth's Insights: A Survey of Ecological Ethics from the Mediterranean Basin to the Australian Outback*. Berkeley: University of California Press.

Capra, F. 1991. *Belonging to the Universe: Explorations on the Frontiers of Science and Spirituality*. San Francisco: Harper San Francisco.

Carman, J. B., and F. A. Marglin. 1985. *Purity and Auspiciousness in Indian Society*. Leiden: E. J. Brill.

Claiborne, William. 1983. "Devout Hindus Resist Efforts to Clean Up the Sacred Ganges." *The Washington Post,* 8 May, 18–19 (A).

Das, Veena. 1982. *Structure and Cognition: Aspects of Hindu Caste and Ritual*. 2d ed. Delhi: Oxford University Press.

Dimmit, C., and J. A. B. van Buitenen. 1978. *Classical Hindu Mythology*. Philadelphia: University of Pennsylvania Press.

Dumont, L. 1970. *Homo Hierarchicus*. Chicago: University of Chicago Press.

Dumont, L., and D. F. Pocock. 1959. "Pure and Impure." *Contributions to Indian Sociology* 3: 9–34.

Eck, D. 1982. *Banaras: City of Light*. New York: Alfred Knopf.

———. 1993. "A Survey of Sanskrit Sources for the Study of Varanasi." In *Banaras (Varanasi): Cosmic Order, Sacred City, Hindu Traditions,* ed. R. P. B. Singh, 9–19. Varanasi: Tara Book Agency.

Feldhaus, Anne. 1995. *Water and Womanhood: Religious Meanings of Rivers In Maharashtra*. New York: Oxford University Press.

Fuller, C. J. 1979. "Gods, Priests and Purity: On the Relation Between Hinduism and the Caste System." *Man (N.S.)* 14 (September): 459–76.

———. 1992. *The Camphor Flame*. Princeton: Princeton University Press.

Gold, Ann. 1988. *Fruitful Journeys: The Ways of Rajasthani Pilgrims*. Berkeley: University of California Press.

Hargrove, Eugene. 1986. *Religion and Environmental Crisis*. Athens: University of Georgia Press.

Havell, E. B. 1990 (1905). *Benares: The Sacred City*. Varanasi: Vishwavidyalaya Prakashan.

India International Centre. 1993. *Indigenous Vision: Peoples of India, Attitudes to the Environment*. India International Centre Quarterly. Delhi: India International Centre.

Kane, P. V. 1973. *History of Dharmasastra*. 2d ed. 4 vols. Government Oriental Series Class B, No. 6. Poona: Bhandarkar Oriental Research Institute.

Kinsley, D. 1987. *Hindu Goddesses: Visions of the Divine Feminine in the Hindu Religious Tradition*. Delhi: Motilal Banarsidass.

Lovelock, J. 1988. *The Ages of Gaia: A Biography of our Living Earth*. New York: Norton.

Madan, T. N. 1985. "Concerning the Categories Subha and Suddha in Hindu Culture: An Exploratory Essay." In *Purity and Auspiciousness in*

*Indian Society,* ed. J. B. Carman and F. A. Marglin, 11–29. Leiden: E. J. Brill.

———. 1987. *Non-Renunciation: Themes and Interpretations of Hindu Culture.* Delhi: Oxford University Press.

Moti Chandra, D. 1985. *Kashi Ka Itihas* 2d ed. Varanasi: Vishwavidyalaya Prakashan.

Murti, C. R. K., K. S. Bilgrami, T. M. Das, and R. P. Mathur, eds. 1991. *The Ganga: A Scientific Study.* New Delhi: Ganga Project Directorate.

O'Flaherty, W. D. 1976. *The Origins of Evil in Hindu Mythology.* Berkeley: University of California Press.

———. 1981. *The Rig Veda: An Anthology.* London: Penguin Press.

Parry, J. 1980. "Ghosts, Greed and Sin: the Occupational Identity of the Benaras Funeral Priests." *Man (N.S.)* 15 (March): 88–111.

———. 1994. *Death in Banaras.* Cambridge: Cambridge University Press.

Raheja, G. 1988. *The Poison in the Gift: Ritual, Prestation and the Dominant Caste in a North Indian Village.* Chicago: University of Chicago Press.

Sankat Mochan Foundation. 1990. *Swatcha Ganga Campaign Annual Report 1988–1990.* Varanasi: Swatcha Ganga Campaign.

———. 1992. *A Seminar on Pollution Control of River Cities in India: A Case Study of Varanasi.* Varanasi: Swatcha Ganga Campaign.

———. 1994. *Proposal for GAP Phase II at Varanasi.* Varanasi: Swatcha Ganga Campaign.

Sharma, B. K. 1987. "No Bhagirath Came" (*Koī Bhagīrath Nahī Āyā*). *India Today,* 15 July, 80.

Singh, B. R. S. 1984. "Save the Ganga." *Patriot Magazine,* 5 August, 1.

Singh, R. P. B., ed. 1993a. *Banaras (Varanasi): Cosmic Order, Sacred City, Hindu Traditions.* Varanasi: Tara Book Agency.

———. 1993b. *Environmental Ethics.* Varanasi: National Geographic Society.

Sivaramamurti, C. 1976. *Ganga.* Delhi: Orient Longman.

Spring, David, and Eileen Spring, eds. 1974. *Ecology and Religion in History.* New York: Harper and Row.

Srinivas, M. N. 1952. *Religion and Society Among the Coorgs of South India.* Bombay: Asia.

Suzuki, David, and Peter Knudtson. 1992. *Wisdom of the Elders.* New York: Bantam Books.

Tempest, Rone. 1987. "Holy River." *Star Tribune,* 25 October, 25–26 (A).

van Buitenen, J. A. B. 1973. *The Mahabharata.* Chicago: University of Chicago Press.

Vatsyayan, Kapila. 1993. "Ecology and Indian Myth." In *Indigenous Vision: Peoples of India, Attitudes to the Environment,* ed. India International Centre, 157–80. Delhi: India International Centre.

Veer, P. van der. 1988. *Gods on Earth: The Management of Religious Experience and Identity in a North Indian Pilgrimage Center*. London: Athlone Press.

Vidyarthi, L. P. , M. Jha, and B. N. Saraswati. 1979. *The Sacred Complex of Kashi: A Microcosm of Indian Civilization*. Delhi: Concept Publishing.

Ward, Geoffrey. 1985. "Benares, India's Most Holy City, Faces an Unholy Problem." *Smithsonian* 16 (September): 83–85.

**Lance E. Nelson**

# Conclusion

> The wise make skillful use of human effort.
>
> —*Mahābhārata* 10.2.8[1]

This conclusion will summarize the various studies that have preceded and draw together some of their implications. Looking back over the contributions, I am pleased that, among other things, the volume seems to have succeeded in being as multivocal as intended, at least insofar as we have addressed a number of Hindu traditions from a number of scholarly perspectives. This means, however, that it will not be entirely possible to weave into a single, regularly patterned cloth the various strands that the contributors have spun. Nevertheless, certain themes have emerged and can be identified. I will attempt to highlight some of them briefly here. Naturally, the perspective from which this exercise emerges is my own.

The one compelling, overarching fact that seems to bring together all the traditions examined in this volume is the still powerful reality of the mythic cosmography within the horizons of which Hindu India dwells. We come again and again to the realization that thinking and action in this sphere are inevitably colored by, and carried on in the context of, a living (although in some respects seriously threatened) mythic vision of things, one that categorizes and sacralizes the world of nature in distinctive, if not always unique, ways. Here metaphor and reality merge, and nature is not merely nature. All kinds of sacred dimensionalities prevail. Many of the contributors have noted a kind of bilevel or even multilevel cognition, under which things like rivers and mountains, as also the earth in front of one's own home, are perceived in different ways—sacred and mundane, pure and impure—successively or even simultaneously, without dissonance.[2] The religious cosmography, which is assumed when one is looking at things from the inside, is complex and shifting. No doubt we could even identify a number of Hindu worlds, evoking variations on central motifs, prized by the diversity of Hindu theological and ritual traditions. It must surely be true, then, that anyone wishing to understand the relation between religion and ecology in India, or to think or act ecologically in an authentically Hindu context, must come to grips with the mythic and sacral dimensions within which Hindus function—and the ecological implications thereof.

Many elements of this complex mythic cosmography are germane to ecology and ecological consciousness, and indeed several may be identified as important themes linking the various chapters in this volume. I think of three as particularly significant.

The first of these is the pervasiveness of hierarchy. Distinctions of higher and lower, pure and impure, auspicious and inauspicious, are fundamental assumptions within the Hindu universe. The factor of hierarchy informs, in distinctive ways, perceptions of caste, sacred geography, and the final meaning of nature, among other things.

The tension between the world-negating and world-sacralizing movements in the Hindu cosmos, and the problematics associated with both, may be identified as a second theme. Differentiations involved in the forming of hierarchies may involve devaluation of the world, sacralization, or both. In cases where the natural world is consigned to a lower level in the hierarchy, we encounter world-negation. This factor is always present as a background possibility or final option, even in the midst of the more general Hindu tendency toward world-sacralization. The latter, occurring where elements of the natural world are assigned a higher place in the scheme of things, also emerges as an important consideration. World-sacralization, in fact, is typically celebrated by those trying to think ecologically, whereas world-negation is almost universally deplored. Our contributors have warned us, however, that it is not quite that simple. Sacralization may itself serve as a disincentive to environmental activism, as several contributors have suggested might be occurring in the case of the Gaṅgā.

Related in different ways in different contexts to both world-denial and world-sacralization is a third theme, that of moral interconnectedness. Formulated most expansively as *dharma*—cosmic order, moral law, social-religious duty—it manifests with particularity in concerns about *ahiṃsā*, *karma* and karmic retribution, divine displeasure, and so on. I would include under this moral dimension, though it is expressed partly in cosmological terms, the perception of moral decline through successive world ages. Several of the contributors noted awareness of participation in the Kali Yuga or "Dark Age," a cosmic epoch of Hindu myth in which moral decay is coupled with natural disaster, as a factor influencing ecological attitudes and behavior in the traditions they worked with.

An important sub-theme, directly related to the moral, is the place of human effort (*puruṣakāra*) and purposiveness in the Hindu scheme of things. It lies in the wings as we engage in research and reflection, but will emerge more insistently, especially for activists, when an overall assessment of the situation, in view of the pressing ecological need in India and the world, is sought. The question of whether or not any religion or culture provides symbols and structures that can promote the kind of action needed to address the present environmental situation is of course important globally. Certainly the issue must be addressed in reference to the Hindu mythic cosmos, within the structures of which there remain potentialities for other-worldliness and resignation, even fatalism.[3] Given the urgency of the present ecological situation, this question is not one that can be avoided or postponed, and the conventional answers (of either the Hindu tradition's critics or its apologists, both of which have tended to privilege Western values) may no longer be enough. Of course, it must be recognized that the religious, cultural, and technological developments that set the stage for and precipitated this now worldwide ecological crisis originated mostly outside the Hindu mythic canopy.

## Review of Chapters

Christopher Key Chapple began our discussion in chapter 1 with reflections on the problem of developing an authentically indigenous environmentalism in India. His exposition of the differences between environmental movements in the United States and India was a valuable starting point. Among other things, we were given an initial reminder (if we needed it) that pragmatic concerns such as poverty and population density impact ecological thought and action at least as much as religion and culture. Chapple's classification of existing and potential models of ecological thought in India introduced us into its distinctive religious cosmos, as it relates to ecology. His survey highlighted a number of significant attempts to find ecologically supportive ideas, images, and practices therein (and there is indeed much to be found). As he focused in on the environmental potential of renouncer or *śramaṇa* models, we encountered for the first time the ascetic ethic of "letting all things be" that is informed by the movement toward world-negation uniquely structured in this mythic universe. This encounter surely implied a question, one that recurs in the volume: Can a predominantly otherworldly spirituality be successfully reoriented so as to become an element in an ecologically supportive ethos? This is a difficult question, one that, in the end, will be up to India to answer. Chapple showed that efforts to answer it positively are being made from within the several traditions considered. He is by no means naive enough to suggest that an ethic of asceticism will be quickly and enthusiastically embraced by either the economically deprived masses or the emerging consumerist middle classes of India. Still, he believes that the renouncer traditions will be an essential voice in the emerging ecological discussion, particularly in view of their ethics of minimal consumption and non-injury (*ahiṃsā*) toward all beings. He is surely correct in this.

In chapter 2, Harold Coward examined the doctrine of *karma* with a view to its potential contribution to ecological thinking in India. Here the Hindu cosmos was again probed for its environmental implications at the delicate point of world-denial, for *karma* was, of course, classically formulated in terms of bondage to *saṃsāra* and the possibility of liberation therefrom. Coward, like Chapple, focused on the renouncer traditions, Yoga in particular. Because, however, the *karma* doctrine is shared by all Indic religious traditions, the idea has universal importance as a pervasive background concept in the Hindu universe and India in general. It is therefore of utmost importance to contemplate the possibility, suggested by Coward, that Hindus, Jains, and others will able to re-vision the *karma* doctrine in an ecologically supportive direction. *Karma* is one way, Coward argued, that Indic traditions express their intuition that humanity is an "intimately interconnected part of nature," as well as their concern for an ethic of *ahiṃsā* that extends beyond the human sphere to embrace all life. Patañjali's *Yoga Sūtras*, Coward believes, offer an interpretation of *karma* that suggests a strong element of moral responsibility, which could be given an ecological interpretation. A contemporary application of *karma* theory, he argued, could sensitize Hindus to the fact that each action has vast ecological ramifications. It would be hard to conceive of an ecologically supportive Hindu outlook that did not include some such re-visioning, so that *karma* could come to suggest positive interconnection with the natural world (as it does, perhaps, to a greater extent in Buddhist discourse) instead of an undesirable state of bondage thereto.

Chapter 3 by Arvind Sharma began a series of four essays focusing on Hindu theological traditions. Sharma examined two of the earliest Upaniṣads, the *Bṛhadāraṇyaka* and the *Chāndogya*, where he found passages (often neglected) that suggest a profound human appreciation of, and identification with, the natural world. We encountered here for the first time and began to explore the world-sacralizing movement within the Hindu mythic cosmos. Sharma invoked a series of striking images: all beings in the universe manifesting from the one Divinity, the earth itself as a "shining, immortal person" absorbed in meditation, and so on. We heard also of extensions of such thinking in the later tradition through celebration of the goddess Earth (an image expanded by Mumme and Nagarajan in their chapters), injunctions in the *Manu Smṛti* against injuring animals, descriptions of tree festivals, and the like. But even here the world-negating element could not be completely put aside, for—as Sharma reminded us—the later Vedānta traditions extrapolate a more ambivalent view of nature from adjacent passages in the same Upaniṣadic texts. Despite such potentially countervailing tendencies, Sharma believes that the world-sacralizing "frame of mind" embodied in the early Upaniṣads could serve to catalyze the contemporary quest for ecological solutions. One must be hopeful that contemporary Hindus can succeed in recovering and nourishing it.

In chapter 4, Lance Nelson sought to show how an important segment of the theological tradition that bases itself on the

Upaniṣads has lost sight of the world-affirming vision described by Sharma. He thus deliberately and explicitly, if less hopefully, broached the issue of the world-negating dimensions of the Hindu cosmos. Taking the ecofeminist critique of dualism as his starting point, Nelson examined the Advaita Vedānta of Śaṅkara and his followers, in which many writers on religion and ecology have found a "unitive vision" that encourages reverence for the natural world. Nelson's reading of the texts of the tradition showed that, on the contrary, classical Advaita never overcomes the dualistic spirit-matter dichotomy that it inherits from archaic Sāṃkhya thought. It achieves its "nonduality" in the end only by excluding the world from the realm of the real. Advaita, Nelson believes, hardly represents the kind of embodied, world-affirming nondualism that ecofeminists and other eco-thinkers are looking for. Of course, Nelson did point out that Advaita's world-negation represents an elite phenomenon: a final, soteriologically oriented critique of more widely held, world-sacralizing visions. It is also true that Advaita in practice has for centuries been influenced by tantric conceptions, and as well that the modern, so-called "Neo-Vedānta" formulation of Advaita takes a significantly more positive view of the world and engagement therewith than the classical tradition Nelson described. Still, Advaita's world-negation, as well as its historic and continuing prestige as embodying the pinnacle of Hindu spirituality, remain issues that eco-thinkers in India will have to confront more directly.

In chapter 5, Rita DasGupta Sherma provided an extension and a counterpoint to Nelson's critique of Advaita. Moving us back in the direction of world sacralization, Sherma explored the perhaps more authentically nondualistic vision of Hindu Tantra and the Goddess traditions, in which she found images and ways of thinking more clearly supportive of ecological consciousness. At the same time, however, Sherma problematized the discussion by pointing out that, like world-denial, world-sacralization itself—or at least certain strategies therefore—can also create problems for ecological awareness. Here we encountered for the first time in this volume what might be termed (given its recurrence here and notoriety elsewhere) the "Ganges syndrome," wherein sacralization has a tendency to obscure the need for ecological action. Conventional Hindu thinking incorporates the same self-other, spirit-matter distinction found in other patriarchal traditions, and like them associates the feminine with materiality, most typically devaluing both. In being sacralized, Sherma argued, the holy places and landmarks of India are often at the same time feminized, and thus associated with self-sacrificing, all-forgiving motherhood. Conventional Hindu conceptions of purity likewise have a shadow side: they result in a dichotomized approach to the natural world that associates nature, the body, women, and lower-caste persons and occupations with impurity and, hence, otherness. Sherma agrees with Nelson, furthermore, that Hindu philosophies of transcendence lead to a similarly ambivalent attitude toward nature.

This critique of conventional Hindu categories paved the way for Sherma's overview of Tantra. In Śākta thought, the world, the feminine, and embodiment are expressions of *śakti*, divine energy. The latter is identified with the Goddess and given the highest possible ontological valuation. Tantra re-visions traditional Hindu conceptions of purity and impurity, Sherma argued, in an outlook that approaches a thoroughgoing nondualistic appreciation of all of nature. Ethical questions emerged here—first negatively, then positively. Tantra has an antinomian streak that could conceivably undermine environmental activism, Sherma allowed. But the Tantras do denounce destructive, self-centered, "sinful" behavior, and the Goddess is known to manifest herself repeatedly in heroic form to fight the forces of darkness. The image here of the Deity purposively and vigorously mobilized to thwart evil, which we again encountered in Mumme's discussion of the *avatāras* of Viṣṇu (chap. 6), introduced a model of activism that may well be important to the ecological movement in India. Sherma concluded that Tantra—in addition to offering an antidote to a number of Hindu attitudes that are environmentally dubious—provides, from a source indigenous to India, support for ecological values that comport well with the vision of ecofeminism. There can be no doubt that the *śakti*-doctrine, especially if it can be so nuanced as to avoid the problems associated with other efforts at sacralization, will emerge as an important element in Hindu eco-thinking.

Patricia Mumme's essay in chapter 6 concluded our survey of Hindu theological traditions with a search for ecologically helpful material in Śrīvaiṣṇavism. We encountered the theme of world sacralization again as Mumme evoked the powerful Śrīvaiṣṇava image of the universe as the body of God. As the body of God, who is its soul, the world exists to manifest the divine nature and contribute "special excellences" to the Lord. If this kind of world-sacralization can avoid universalizing the Ganges syndrome identified above (Does God need human help to purify his own body?), it might well be a valuable resource. Surely it is significant that ethics also figured prominently in Mumme's discussion, and this time unambiguously. Śrīvaiṣṇavism takes quite seriously the demands of *dharma,* the cosmic order and the moral law that upholds it. Viṣṇu in myth is preeminently the Preserver. As such, he is the establisher and maintainer of *dharma*, valuing and enforcing the ethical and ritual laws expressed in the *smṛtis* and *purāṇas*, among which are many ecologically valuable precepts. Notions of divine displeasure and karmic retribution come into play here, as they do for the Rajasthani villagers discussed by Gold (chap. 7).

Mumme suggested that the Śrīvaiṣṇava concept of *līlā*, which envisions the universe as God's free sport or play, could contribute to an ecologically sensitive Śrīvaiṣṇava theology of nature. There is a final purposelessness implied here, Mumme allowed, but it has the virtue of lifting the vast cosmic drama beyond the limitations of mere anthropocentric values, and it is, moreover, balanced by the divine intentionality toward keeping the drama going. The doctrine of the *avatāra* or divine incarnation, once factored in, provides the *līlā* doctrine with further ethical valence, if not a cosmic teleology. The Lord's descent to earth when evil threatens to prevail vividly demonstrates his "commitment to the preservation of the game and its players." While the *līlā* doctrine does envision God's play as encompassing spiritual realms that are inherently more desirable that the natural world (hierarchy again), it forefronts Viṣṇu as the paradigm (historically prior to representations of the Goddess in this role) of the Deity who incarnates purposively for battling evil. The balance of the cosmos is worth preserving. Significantly from an ecological point of view, the *avatāra* doctrine is concretized mythically in the story of Varāha, the Boar incarnation, who descends to the depths of the ocean to rescue Bhū Devī, the goddess Earth, from an evil demon. Mumme suggested that the popularity of this story could make it a valuable instrument for directing the religious devotion of Śrīvaiṣṇavas, and other Hindus, in an environmentally constructive direction. Certainly the notion of purposive activity on behalf of the earth here finds considerable mythic support.

Ann Grodzins Gold's study in chapter 7 brought us from the realm of texts back to earth, to the village of Ghatiyali in Rajasthan, North India. The ecosystem in Rajasthan has declined seriously in recent decades, and Gold found that the villagers linked changes in landscape and weather with changes in forestry practices, agricultural methods, and politics—and also with human sinfulness—all in complex webs of causal interconnections. The moral dimension of the Hindu cosmos was thus again highlighted: villagers expressed a deeply felt conviction that they were experiencing a moral as well as an ecological degradation, understood as symptomatic of decline in *dharma* and the world's progressively deeper immersion in the Kali Yuga. Awareness of divine displeasure and acceptance of punishment for evil *karma* is combined—at least for some—with anticipation of an imminent apocalyptic end. Whether or not this kind of moral thinking inspires action for ecological betterment (or whether or not, even if inspired, such action would be restricted by circumstantial necessities), it seems certain that those wishing to understand the current ecological situation in village India, and activists wishing to change it, will need to take into account the multidimensional "moral ecology" that Gold has documented.

In chapter 8, Frank Korom took us from village to city, reporting on his studies of recycling and recyclers, largely in Delhi. Among the factors that make the Indian experience of recycling unique, Korom identified as most significant the negative symbolism associated with trash and trash-handling deriving from Hindu conceptions of ritual pollution and associated caste prejudice. Here the theme of hierarchy returned. Addressing an issue also raised by Sherma, Korom argued that urban squalor is not simply a product of colonialist exploitation but has indigenous roots as well: "The negative evaluation of recycling in India is deeply rooted in the ideology of caste, making it both a social and a theological problem." Korom reminded us that the dichotomizing tendencies of Hindu thought (mentioned by Sherma) work themselves out—as well as in the division between upper-caste trash creators and lower-caste trash removers—in the important distinction between private, "inside" space and public, "outside" space. The latter results (as in other cultures) in the progressive removal of trash to the borders and margins—humanly, spatially, and symbolically. For these and other reasons, Korom believes that a South Asian "dialogue about trash and its concomitant social status is . . . absolutely necessary." Based on his study of the travails of artists in India who work with recycled materials, he suggested that part of the solution may lie in an aesthetic revaluation of recycling, a possibility that may well emerge as indigenous values intersect with international cultural and intellectual forces.

In his essay in chapter 9, David Kinsley juxtaposed Hindu conceptions of sacred land and pilgrimage with Australian Aboriginal traditions, suggesting the primordial roots of much of Hindu mythic sensibility and ritual practice (a factor which, in contemporary ecological circles, would be counted a plus). World-sacralization is, of course, the dominant note. In both Aboriginal and Hindu traditions, there is a spirituality of the land involving places and routes of travel that are charged with sacred associations. The landscape thus assumes a sacred structure and becomes numinous for the people who live the stories that render that structure palpable. Aborigines and devout Hindu pilgrims become, in terms of their religious self-identity, embedded in the land. Kinsley sees ecological potential in this, but he also warned of a potential downside. Like Sherma and Korom, Kinsley recognized that sacralization may be a two-edged sword: the recognition of a sacred place is simultaneously the creation of a profane place; the necessity of journey to a sacred place can place undue emphasis on the secular nature of one's point of departure. Moreover, the reverencing of a sacred space itself can, ironically, exact a heavy toll on the land in terms of pilgrimage traffic and other factors. Finally, with other contributors, Kinsley cautioned that Hindu notions of sacred landscape can easily lend themselves to the cause of obscuring the present realities of nature in favor of an idealized, mythologized vision.

Bruce Sullivan's essay in chapter 10 continued the theme of Kṛṣṇaite pilgrimage. Unlike the other contributors, however, Sullivan described a movement that is deliberately attempting to harness imagery derived from the Hindu sacred cosmos, and sentiments connected therewith, to a contemporary eco-activist agenda. Sullivan noted the contrast between the idyllic portrayals in Hindu scripture of the Kṛṣṇaite holy town of Vrindavan, on the one hand, and the dismal present-day ecological situation in that locality, on the other. He went on to describe efforts of various individuals and organizations to dramatize that contrast and evoke a moral response that would inspire ecological activism. Sullivan argued that the success of these efforts will depend upon the extent to which the mythic world and its values remain compelling for the population, which is increasingly exposed to Western and secular influences. Even in relation to those who do remain immersed in the religious universe, however, Sullivan raised a question. Might not aspects of the traditional value system—even some elements that activists now seek to redirect in service of the environment—"vitiate ecological action" by shifting attention from problems of nature towards a supramundane goal? Again we realize that sacralization of land and other natural phenomena may not, in this context or elsewhere, be an ecological panacea. In Hindu India, sacralization moves in a complex, dialectical relationship with the world-negating tendency within the religious cosmos.

Further complexities in Hindu attitudes toward sacrality, as well as outsiders' perceptions thereof, were outlined in chapter 11 by Vijaya Nagarajan. She began with an exploration of the ecological significance of the *kōlam*, a ritual honoring the goddess Earth that is part of the daily routine of village women in South India. It would seem that a ritual honoring the earth as goddess might have tremendous ecological potential, but Nagarajan warned us that "ecologies," systems of human interaction with nature, are embedded in complex cultural webs. The import of ritual practices, as perceived by the outsider, might not be the same for one standing within the tradition. Nagarajan introduced the notion of "intermittent sacrality" to explain how South Indian villagers can have no qualms in dumping garbage on the earth that they have not long before ritually honored as a goddess. In her quest for clues as to the ways in which attitudes toward nature become culturally embedded, Nagarajan—like Alley especially (chap. 12), and also Sherma, Kinsley, and Nelson—reflected on what I have called the "Ganges syndrome." She noted that, like Gaṅgā Devī in the eyes of her devotees, the earth as goddess Bhū Devī is regarded by her informants as incapable of being polluted. "The goddesses," she reported, "are so large and indeterminate that the waste of humanity is seen as just a speck in the vast expanse of sky, earth, and water." With other contributors, Nagarajan is concerned that the very act of sacralizing something can itself obscure the fact that it needs protection from human laziness and greed. But sacrality—like, perhaps, the moral urgency experienced by Gold's villagers—may sometimes in India have to compete as a motivator of action with the pressing needs of daily life.

Kelly Alley's essay in chapter 12 took us through further (and final, as far as this volume is concerned) levels of complexity in the Hindu experience of world-sacralization and at the same time extended Nagarajan's focus on divergent perceptions, from inside and outside the mythic canopy, of environmental issues. Her field work on the banks of the Gaṅgā in Banaras involved attending to the conflicting language and models of reality used by Hindu religious leaders, environmental activists, and government workers as they evaluated the purity and pollution of the river. Like that of the villagers of Ghatiyali, the discourse of the *paṇḍās* of Banaras links concern for the well-being of the natural world with perceptions drawn from Hindu sacred traditions. Here we found particularly vivid examples of the multileveled cognition remarked upon earlier. The *paṇḍās'* understanding combines ordinary notions of physical uncleanness in complex, sometimes shifting patterns of interaction with ritual notions of pollution and moral notions of degeneracy. As noted in several other chapters but most clearly documented here, Hindus' perception of the problem of the river's physical contamination is shaped by their participation in a mythic universe in which Gaṅgā, as goddess, possesses the power to purify all forms of pollution. Alley's analysis of the views of Banaras residents confirmed the suspicion voiced by Sherma and Nagarajan that Hindus link the sacred feminine with "motherliness, housekeeping and cleanup, and forgiveness." It also supports Gold's thesis that traditional Hindus link ecological decline with ideas about moral decay in the Kali Yuga. If ever one were to need a warning against simplistic thinking when it comes to the implications of religion for ecology, this should surely suffice.

## Final Thoughts

The ecological crisis is forcing us to ask fundamental questions about all religious traditions. Just as feminism is pressing us to undertake a thorough reexamination of religious symbols and practice with a view to their assumptions about women, so we are confronted by the necessity to look at our religious traditions anew in light of our present critical situation vis-à-vis the environment. Could it be that a compelling new revelation, inescapable in import, is emerging (or—in Thomas Berry's language—a new story) by which that which has gone before must now be evaluated, perhaps even judged? "By their ecological fruits, sweet and bitter, we shall know them," at the same time remembering that certain traditions bear major responsibility for creating the culture that unleashed the present ecological devastation, while others are merely trying to respond in order to cope. Be that as it may, no religious tradition, including the Hindu, can now rest content with merely examining its inventory of myths, symbols, and ritual practices for "eco-friendly" elements, particularly if there is some notion that such elements could be borrowed by those in other culture zones as correctives to their particular problems, or even promoted universally by advocates as catalysts for global solutions. Profound and thorough reexamination of deep structures of the various religious worldviews with a view to their environmental implications is called for. Hasty or superficial answers, going no further than romanticism, politically correct ideology, or defensive reactions, will not do.

For the Hindu tradition, this effort is just beginning. It is hoped that this volume will make some contribution to the process. Additional study of some of the material here considered, as well as Hindu literature, art, and ethics—not to mention folk and popular culture—will of course be needed. Surely, the Hindu tradition will not be able work out its own private solutions in isolation, even if this were to be desired. Dialogue with global trends of thought is inevitable in the world as constituted today. Surely also, Hindu solutions will be inspired in part by motivations that are not local but universal in nature, such as abhorrence of environmental degradation and fear of impending disaster. But just as surely, Hindu solutions must finally be anchored in the mythic cosmography that structures the Hindu world, combining the need for action to physically purify with respect for the sacrality already present. Indeed, it may be that another instance of the kind of multilevel cognition that several of the contributors have remarked upon is called for. It would be such that Hindus could affirm, on the one hand, that the world is sacred, perhaps even to be reverenced as the body of

God, and on the other, that it is dependent for its purification upon human effort.

## Notes

1. prājñāḥ puruṣakāraṃ tu ghaṭante dākṣyam āsthitāḥ.

2. This formulation arises from conversations with J. G. Arapura and also Shyam Das. Vallabhācārya's theology explicitly recognizes three experiential levels: *adhibhautika* (material), *adhyātmika* (formless spirit), and *adhidaivika* (personal deity).

3. For an interesting study of the latter problem, describing the never-resolved tension between fate (*daiva*) and human effort (*puruṣa-kāra*) in the Hindu tradition, see Sukumari Bhattacharji, *Fatalism in Ancient India* (Calcutta: Baulmon Prakashan, 1995).

# Contributors

KELLY D. ALLEY (Ph.D., University of Wisconsin) is Associate Professor in the Department of Sociology, Anthropology, and Social Work, Auburn University, Auburn, Alabama. Her publications cover topics in the anthropology of South Asia and issues in environmental movements in India and Alabama. Her work has appeared in such scholarly journals as *Ethnology, Modern Asian Studies, Urban Anthropology, Human Organization,* and *Practicing Anthropology,* and as chapters in edited volumes.

CHRISTOPHER KEY CHAPPLE (Ph.D., Fordham University) is Professor of Theological Studies at Loyola Marymount University, Los Angeles. He regularly publishes articles in scholarly journals and is the author of several books, including *Nonviolence to Animals, Earth, and Self in Asian Traditions* (1993) and *Karma and Creativity* (1986). He is the co-translator of the *Yoga Sutras of Patanjali* (with Yogi Anand Viraj, 1990) and the editor of *Ecological Prospects: Scientific, Religious, and Aesthetic Perspectives* (1994) and *The Jesuit Tradition in Education and Missions* (1993).

HAROLD COWARD (Ph.D., McMaster University) is Director of the Center for Studies in Religion and Society and Professor of History at the University of Victoria, British Columbia. His areas of research include Indian philosophy, especially the Grammarian School, Hinduism, religious pluralism, medical ethics, and environmental ethics. His major books include *Mantra: Hearing the*

*Divine in India* (1991), *The Philosophy of the Grammarians* (with K. Kunjunni Raja, 1990), *Derrida and Indian Philosophy* (1990), *Pluralism: Challenge to World Religions* (1995), and *The Sphoṭa Theory of Language* (1980).

ANN GRODZINS GOLD (Ph.D., University of Chicago) is Professor of Religion at Syracuse University. Gold's research has included studies of pilgrimage, gender relations, epic tales of world-renunciation, and cultural constructions of the environment. Her current project on ecological transformations in a North Indian kingdom is being supported during 1997–98 by a University Teachers Fellowship from the National Endowment for the Humanities. Her publications include articles on sacred groves, children's environmental perceptions, moral interpretations of climate change, and three books: *Listen to the Heron's Words: Reimagining Gender and Kinship in North India* (co-authored with Gloria Raheja, 1994), *A Carnival of Parting: The Tales of King Bharthari and King Gopi Chand* (1992), and *Fruitful Journeys: The Ways of Rajasthani Pilgrims* (1988).

DAVID KINSLEY (Ph.D., University of Chicago) is Professor in the Department of Religious Studies, McMaster University, Hamilton, Ontario. A specialist in the religious history of South Asia, his books include *Health, Healing, and Religion: A Cross-Cultural Perspective* (1996), *Ecology and Religion: Ecological Spirituality in Cross-Cultural Perspective* (1995), *The Goddesses' Mirror: Visions of the Divine from East and West* (1989), *Hindu Goddesses: Visions of the Divine Feminine in the Hindu Religious Tradition* (1986), and *The Sword and the Flute: Kali and Kṛṣṇa, Dark Visions of the Terrible and the Sublime in Hindu Mythology* (1975).

FRANK J. KOROM (Ph.D., University of Pennsylvania) is Assistant Professor of Religion and Anthropology, Boston University, formerly Curator of Asian and Middle Eastern Collections at the Museum of International Folk Art, Santa Fe, New Mexico. A specialist in Hindu, Buddhist, and Muslim ritual, myth, folklore, and diaspora cultures, Korom is the author of articles in scholarly journals such as *Asian Folklore Studies, Diaspora,* and the *Journal of South Asian Literature,* as well as in edited volumes and encyclopedias. He has edited *Constructing Tibetan Culture: Contemporary Perspectives* (1997), *Tibetan Culture in the Diaspora* (1997), and *Gender, Genre, and Power in South Asian Expressive Traditions* (with A. Appadurai and M. Mills, 1991). His books include *Folkloristics and Indian Folklore* (co-authored with P. J. Claus, 1991) and *Pakistani Folk Culture: A Select Annotated Bibliography* (1988).

PATRICIA Y. MUMME (Ph.D., University of Pennsylvania) is Assistant Professor of Religion at Capital University, Columbus, Ohio. She has published several books and articles on the Śrīvaiṣṇava tradition, including *The Śrīvaiṣṇava Theological Dispute: Maṇavāḷamāmuni and Vedānta Deśika* (1988). Her most recent work is *Living Liberation in Hindu Thought* (co-edited with Andrew O. Fort, 1996).

VIJAYA RETTAKUDI NAGARAJAN (Ph.D., University of California, Berkeley) is Assistant Professor of Theology and Religious Studies at the University of San Francisco. Her research interests include the fields of cultural studies and ecology, Hinduism, folklore, gender, art history, and South Asian literature. Her essay "Hosting the Divine: The *Kolam* in Tamil Nadu" appeared in *Mud, Mirror and Thread: Folk Traditions of Rural India* (ed. Nora Fisher, 1993). The founder and co-director of The Institute for the Study of Cultural and Natural Resources, she has also consulted with various environmental NGOs including Friends of the Earth, Friends of the Ganges–Swatcha Ganga Campaign, and Recovery of the Commons Project.

LANCE E. NELSON (Ph.D., McMaster University) is Assistant Professor of Theological and Religious Studies at the University of San Diego. His writings on Advaita Vedānta and other aspects of South Asian religion have appeared in books and scholarly journals in the United States and India. His most recent related publication is "Living Liberation in Śaṅkara and Classical Advaita: Sharing the Holy Waiting of God," in Fort and Mumme (eds.), *Living Liberation in Hindu Thought* (1996).

ARVIND SHARMA (Ph.D., Harvard University) is Birks Professor of Comparative Religion in the Faculty of Religious Studies, McGill

University, Montreal. Sharma has published widely in the areas of South Asian studies, philosophy of religion, comparative philosophy and ethics, gender and religion, and religious pluralism. His books include *Hinduism for Our Times* (1996), *The Philosophy of Religion and Advaita Vedanta: A Comparative Study in Religion and Reason* (1995), *A Hindu Perspective on the Philosophy of Religion* (1991), and *The Hindu Gita: Ancient and Classical Interpretations of the Bhagavadgita* (1986), as well as several volumes of which he was the editor. Sharma is currently co-editor of *The Journal of Religious Pluralism.*

RITA DASGUPTA SHERMA (M.A., Claremont Graduate School) is a doctoral student in Theology, Ethics, and Culture at Claremont Graduate School. A multi-media artist and art teacher living in California, she has served as president of the Himalayan Arts Council and has lectured widely on Himalayan art and iconography.

BRUCE M. SULLIVAN (Ph.D., University of Chicago) is Professor of Religious Studies and Coordinator of Asian Studies at Northern Arizona University. His research specialization is in Sanskrit religious literature and drama, especially the *Mahābhārata* and dramas based on it. His publications include *The Sun God's Daughter and King Saṃvaraṇa: "Tapatī-Saṃvaraṇam" and the Kūṭiyāṭṭam Drama Tradition* (with N. P. Unni, 1995) and *Kṛṣṇa Dvaipāyana Vyāsa and the Mahābhārata: A New Interpretation* (1990). He has published a chapter in *This Sacred Earth: Religion, Nature, Environment* (ed. R. S. Gottleib, 1996) and articles in the *Journal of the American Academy of Religion, Asian Theater Journal,* the *Journal of Vaiṣṇava Studies,* and the *International Journal of Hindu Studies.*

# Index